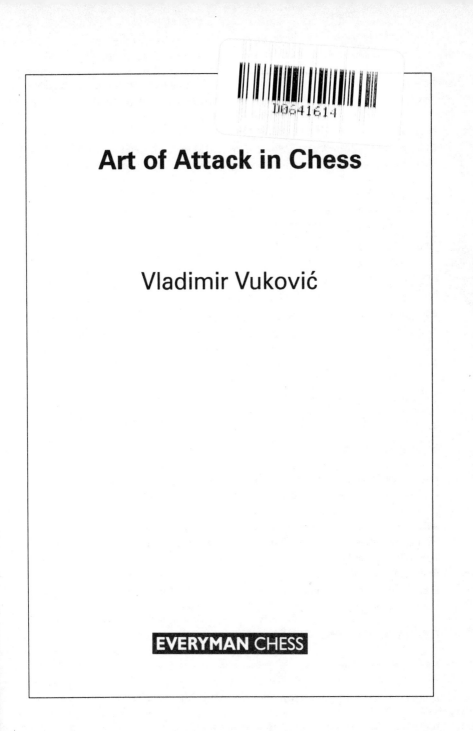

Art of Attack in Chess

Vladimir Vuković

EVERYMAN CHESS

First published in 1998 by Cadogan Books plc, now Everyman Publishers plc
Gloucester Mansions, 4th Floor. 140A Shaftesbury Avenue, London WC2H 8HD

First edition 1965
Reprinted 1968, 1974, 1979, 1982, 1985, 1988, 1991, 1994
First Cadogan Books Edition 1993
Reprinted 1995
First algebraic edition 1998
Reprinted 1999, 2000, 2001,
Reprinted 2002 (twice)

British Library Cataloguing in Publication Data
A CIP catalogue record for this book is available from the British Library.

ISBN 1-85744-400-0

Distributed in North America by The Globe Pequot Press,
P.O. Box 480, 246 Goose Lane, Guildford, CT 06437-0480

All other sales enquiries should be directed to Everyman Chess
Gloucester Mansions, 140A Shaftesbury Avenue, London WC2H 8HD
Tel: 020 7539 7600
Fax: 020 7379 4060
Email: dan@everyman.com
website: www.everyman.uk.com

EVERYMAN CHESS SERIES

Chief Advisor: Garry Kasparov

Edited and typeset by John Nunn for Gambit Publications Ltd.

Printed in Great Britain by The Bath Press, Bath

Contents

Symbols

+	check
#	checkmate
x	capture
!!	brilliant move
!	good move
!?	interesting move
?!	dubious move
?	bad move
??	blunder
Ch	championship
Ct	candidates event
OL	olympiad
1-0	the game ends in a win for White
½-½	the game ends in a draw
0-1	the game ends in a win for Black
(n)	nth match game
(D)	see next diagram

Preface by John Nunn

Attacking the enemy king is one of the most exciting parts of chess, but it is also one of the hardest to play accurately. Every chess player has had the experience of seeing a promising-looking attack crumble into dust, whereupon the enemy counter-attack sweeps aside everything in its path. Vuković's excellent book *The Art of Attack in Chess* is a thought-provoking attempt to explain why some attacks succeed while other fail to reach their goal. The author himself points out that not everything in chess can be reduced to a set of rules, but the general principles he establishes in this book provide excellent guidance on when to launch an attack and how to ensure that it has the maximum chance of success.

As usual with classic books I have edited, I will take a little time to explain exactly how I have prepared this new edition. First and foremost is the conversion to algebraic notation. In addition to this, I have added 128 extra diagrams and in some cases, where it seemed appropriate, I have added further moves from the quoted games (for example, by giving the actual finish instead of 'and White won in another ten moves'). I have lightly edited the rather ponderous English of the original translation, and brought the method of displaying variations into line with current practice. The index of the original book included only complete games, but I have also indexed the game excerpts. In two of the complete games, Alekhine-Asztalos and Alekhine-Kmoch, I have brought the moves of the game into line with the move-order given in the original tournament books.

There are also a fair number of analytical footnotes (readers should note that where there is no room for a footnote on a particular page, the footnote appears on the following page). I hope readers will not form the opinion that Vuković's analysis was especially unsound – this is certainly not the case. The fact is that most authors are prepared to quote the annotations of famous players uncritically, but Vuković brought his own talents to bear and subjected all the positions to careful analysis. Quite often the results were startling; in the well-known game Alekhine-Botvinnik, Nottingham 1936 he found a flaw which had eluded the many annotators who simply accepted the version of events Alekhine gave in the tournament book. Inevitably, the high percentage of original analysis implies a greater risk of the occasional slip, but personally I far prefer original comment to a bland recital of the 'party line'. In any case, it is Vuković's general principles which will prove of most value to the practical player, and here there can be no argument about the enduring quality of his work.

Introduction

Action is the essential basis on which the game of chess is founded and any action which contains a threat – i.e. attack in its widest sense – stands out as a prominent feature of the game. To the outside observer, a chess game is dominated by the conflict between the two players. The ultimate aim of each player is, as a rule, the mating of the opponent's king, and an action with this aim, whether it is direct or indirect, is called an attack (in a narrower sense of the word) or a mating attack; that is the subject of this book.

Being the most important action in chess and the central element of the game in ancient times, attack appears at all stages of the game's development and in various forms of perfection. Moreover, it can be said that the reforms which have been made in the rules of chess have always been in the direction of increasing and stimulating the opportunities for attack.

The great reform of c.1485, which created modern European chess, was particularly responsible for opening up new opportunities for attack and ushered in a period of rich development in chess technique. For three centuries of chess history, attack predominated over defence in the practice of the great players, and mastery at that time meant skill in conducting an attack. Only with Philidor did the first positional ideas appear, and with them more mature defensive strategies; these were to find in Steinitz a century later a legislator of genius.

During the classic era of chess from Morphy to Steinitz and on to Lasker the value placed on attack gradually decreased, for with greater positional understanding the foundations were also provided for the perfection of defensive technique. This, however, was followed by a new period in which Capablanca, and particularly Alekhine, perfected the technique of attack, above all that of the attack on the castled position, founded on exact positional play. With Alekhine the aggressive and dynamic style of play reached a zenith; in the period which followed the tide again turned away gradually from the risks of the direct attack in search of new paths. The main reason for this is not to be found in any weakness inherent in the attacking style, but in the simple fact that, given the conditions of present-day tournaments, it is more profitable and advantageous to make a study of openings. Now, it must be understood that the present theory of openings represents a detailed development of Nimzowitsch's ideas concerning the central squares. There are still many gaps to be filled and there is a wealth of opportunity for innovation; as a result, great masters are inclined to concern themselves intensively with openings and to opt for a 'safety-first' style. When this source of opening innovations begins to dry up, the problem of attack will present itself once more. The time may even come when the principles on which Alekhine built up his attacks will be completely understood, and those ideas which in the case of Alekhine had the appearance of a spark of genius will take on the more approachable aspect of attacking technique. It will be more convenient to discuss these questions at the end of the book. At this point it should be enough to point out that there exists an extremely large group of chess players, who are no longer beginners nor, on the other hand, masters or point-hunters, but players who aim primarily at deriving an aesthetic satisfaction from the game. For such players an attacking game is more attractive than positional technique and they will continue to attack regardless of risk, for their stormy contests are not going to be noted down in theoretical textbooks. So why should such players not become acquainted with the general principles of attack and why should they not perfect themselves in that style of chess with which they are most at home?

Various kinds of attack

We have said that we shall deal with attack in its narrower, or proper, sense, where it involves a direct or indirect threat to the opponent's king. Attacks of this kind can be distinguished according to the following categories.

1) *The main action is not in fact an attack on the king, but there is the possibility of such an attack latent in the position;* some threat or other is being nurtured, or else the attack is concealed in at least one variation.

Let us take the following position as an example *(D)*:

Here White makes the normal positional move **1 d4**, which obviously does not represent an attack against the black king; but in one variation it contains the elements of mate. That is, if Black is careless, and plays for example **1...♗b7?**, there then follows **2 dxc5**, and Black has lost a pawn, since **2...♘xc5?** is answered by **3 ♕d4**, attacking the knight and also threatening mate on g7.

2) *A player's action really does contain a direct threat to his opponent's king, but his opponent can stave off this threat at a certain price, e.g. by giving up material or spoiling his position.*

The vast majority of attacks in fact fall into this very wide category. A simple example is given by this position:

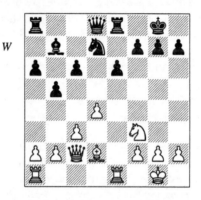

W

White plays **1 ♘g5**, carrying out an attack on h7. Black has three practical alternatives 1...g6, 1...♘f6, and 1...♘f8. If **1...g6**, then **2 ♘e4** with the threat of ♘d6, which gains a tempo; however, White's main plan will be a further attack based on the weaknesses on the dark squares in the region of the king arising from the move ...g6.

If **1...♘f6**, White will no doubt again continue his attacking play, e.g. with **2 ♗f4**, preparing for ♗e5. However, on **1...♘f8**, attacking play does not promise success, and White will be content with a positional alternative, playing **2 ♘e4**. Then Black cannot really prevent **3 ♘c5**, after which the knight will have a strong position on c5 and the black bishop will be poorly placed on b7.

3) *The attacker carries out an uncompromising mating attack, in which he can invest even a considerable amount of material, as long as he is certain of mating in the end.*

This is the third and highest degree of attack.

We can categorize attack in another way if we take castling into account. Thus we have:

1) *Attack before castling,* i.e. against a king which has not yet castled, and
2) *Attack against the castled king.*

Attack can also be divided on the basis of so-called mating patterns; of focal-points; of basic formations of pieces, files, ranks, and diagonals; of basic sacrifices; as well as by the stage which the attack has reached. These divisions according to the spatial, material, and temporal aspects of an attack will help us arrange the material so as to reveal the part played by each factor.

The basic pattern of mate

For mate to be obtained, the king must be deprived of nine squares if it is in the middle of the board, six squares if it is on the edge, or four if it is in the corner. Some of these squares may be blocked by the king's own supporting pieces, but the rest must be taken by the attacker through the agency of his own pieces or pawns. If all the squares surrounding the king are taken from it – some through being blocked, others by being 'in check' – and if the square on which the king stands is also in check and without means of defence, then the king is checkmated. This is well known, and it seems rather banal to start out from this *basic pattern* or *anatomy of mate;* but in fact certain elementary rules can be formulated only on this basis.

In the next position Black, to move, is unable to avoid mate in 4 different variations.

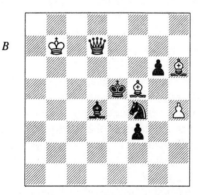

He is threatened by **2 ♗g7#** (first mating pattern). If he plays **1...♔f6**, there follows **2 ♗g7#** (second mating pattern); moving the knight leads to **2 ♕e6#** (third mating pattern); while if **1...gxf5**, we get **2 ♗g7+ ♔e4 3 ♕xd4#** (fourth mating pattern).

The final or mating position is called the *mating pattern,* and this term is espe-cially useful when such a pattern is worth remembering. A mating pattern can be typical (i.e. one which frequently occurs) or *atypical.* We call a mate (or mating pattern) *pure* if none of the squares concerned is covered by two or more attack-ing units. Thus 1...♘e2 2 ♕e6 is a pure mate, whereas 1...♔f6 2 ♗g7 is not, though it would be if we were to remove the bishop on f5. Pure mates are valued in chess problems, but in practical play they are unimportant.

In the mating patterns which we have seen, some of the black king's flight squares have been blocked by its own pieces, while the rest have been covered by the opponent's forces. The sum of these combined factors is known as a *mating net.*

Mating square and focal-point

The mating square is that on which the king stands when it is mated, and the *mat-ing focal-point* is that from which an opponent's piece (other than a king, knight or pawn) mates the king at close quarters. Thus in the above diagram, after 1...♘e2 the focal-point is e6, since it is from there that the queen mates at close quarters. Similarly, after 1...gxf5 2 ♗g7+ ♔e4 the queen mates at close quarters from d4, and that square is then the focal-point. However, if Black plays, for in-stance, 1...♗c3 and is answered by 2 ♗g7#, then we are dealing with a bishop at-tacking at a distance, and here the term 'focal-point' is not used.

To carry out a mating attack successfully it is always useful to survey the pos-sible mating patterns, to prepare a mating net accordingly, and to concentrate on the focal-point. In this connection it is in many cases important to *clear the fo-cal-point,* that is to deprive any opposing pieces of their control over a square which would be convenient as a focal-point.

The following diagram shows us an example of this *(D):*

White, to move, observes correctly that the square d4 is a potential focal-point and that his queen could mate from there, if it were not for its being controlled by Black's knight and bishop. So he clears the focal-point d4 as follows:

1 ♖xe2 (eliminating the knight) **1...dxe2** (if 1...♔d5, then 2 f4#; if 1...♕c1 then 2 ♕d4#, or if 1...f4, then 2 ♕d4+ ♔f5 3 ♕f6#) **2 f4+** (forcing the bishop away from d4) **2...♗xf4 3 ♕d4#.**

Many readers will object that the patterns of mating attack shown here are so obvious, indeed banal, that they need not even have been mentioned. However, I think it is useful to strengthen just this simple kind of knowledge, since in fact there are many mistakes made precisely in this field. Here are a few instances of mistakes concerning mating patterns.

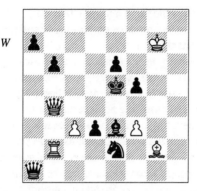

- The attacker fails to perceive that he can neither stop his opponent from moving his king nor drive him into a mating net, but still plays for mate. Such a course of action is naturally futile, and though it may possibly produce perpetual check, it cannot produce mate.
- The attacker plays on the basis of typical mating patterns, overlooking the possibility of an 'atypical' one in a particular continuation.
- The player sees all the possible mating patterns based on one focal-point, but fails to realize that all this is cancelled out when the king moves, and that what matters then are new mating patterns, for which he has not made preparations.
- The player decides on a course of action based on a certain focal-point, without realizing that he cannot provide cover for it or even clear it of the influence of his opponent's pieces. Mistakes made in the selection of a focal-point will be found even in the games of the masters.

So it is useful to get to know the general pattern and structure of mating; less experienced players are especially recommended to study games to see whether a player has made a mistake with regard to the pattern and, if so, where he has made it.

The art of the mating attack

We must now make some finer distinctions, and put a series of questions which arise out of the basic conceptions of a mating attack, and which at the same time also touch on the most difficult departments of the art of chess today.

How does a mating attack relate to the other operations which take place in a game of chess?

How much is a mating attack conditioned by the actual position on the chessboard, and how much by the skill of the attacker?

Where does the risk attached to a mating attack lie?

About which points are the minds of players today still unclear with respect to carrying out a mating attack?

The relationship between these questions can be easily perceived, although they are posed separately. A separate reply, however, cannot be given to each, and an attempt must be made to answer them collectively.

Mate is the final aim and crowning achievement of the contest and the mating attack is the *ultimate* operation in relation to all the rest, which are only *contributory*. Consequently, the mating attack demands more preconditions than other operations. There exist a number of definite preconditions for a mating attack, and these combine to require a considerable degree of superiority on the part of the attacker. In the case where he has abundant superiority, great knowledge and ability on the part of the attacker are not necessary, but if his superiority just borders on what would justify a correct attack, then the *maximum skill* is also required in carrying out the attack. The Romantics knew little, but they had great confidence in themselves; the first small increase in knowledge diverted their style from its course. The new formula, still accepted today, is: carry out a series of preliminary operations, which require only a smaller degree of advantage, and then you will attain the abundant superiority which facilitates a mating attack. However the consequence of this is that there has been a failure to exploit the art of attack to the full and masters have been over-inclined to see a risk in an attack. It is still not clear what the minimum preconditions are, or what *kind of advantage* is necessary, for a mating attack. It may be a question, for example, of a single moment in a game which never returns. Another still unresolved question is that of a player's skill in *weighing up the obligations* which he has undertaken when preparing for an attack. The order of his preparatory moves is extraordinarily important. The only really simple thing is the principle itself – that moves entailing fewer obligations should be carried out before those which are more strongly binding. Putting this principle into practice, however, demands great skill of a kind which is very rare – it was fully possessed by Capablanca and Alekhine, but by few others.

A few more words should be said about the kind of superiority which is necessary before a mating attack can be undertaken. We are interested in the case where the advantage is not one of material but of position and time. The attacker is, as a rule, stronger in the area where the attack takes place by virtue of his material preponderance there, but his superiority in this respect must be considerable. Even a simple pattern with the queen mating from the focal-point needs at least one other piece to cover the focal-point, which already means an advantage of two pieces against a lone king. For such pieces to be brought into the attack, together with any further attacking pieces which may be necessary, one must also have *a temporal advantage,* that is, the ability to carry out a series of attacking moves without one's opponent being able to organize either a direct defence or a sufficiently strong counterattack. A temporal advantage of this kind is usually based on the attacker's positional advantage, i.e. by the comparative lack of mobility of his opponent's pieces for defensive purposes. The attacker often does not possess such outstanding overall superiority at the commencement of his attack, but it may manifest itself later as a consequence of the immobility of some of the defending pieces or through a particular attacking combination. The skill of perceiving the right moment to launch one's attack in fact consists of making a correct assessment of possibilities such as these.

All these points go to show that *the correct launching of an attack* is the crucial difficulty which has caused so many masters to turn away from the attacking style. They would rather try to obtain something through positional technique, where the downside is nothing worse than a draw; all too often this is exactly what they do achieve. Still, if advancement in the art of attack is neglected, if opportunities for a perfectly feasible attack are passed by, how are games going to be won when technique comes up against technique? Without exploring the art of attack more deeply, there can be no further advance in chess. Attack is an essential component of the game of chess; it is a spark which smoulders in every corner and only the player who knows how to keep it alive and make it burst into flame at the right moment has reached the heights of true mastery. Lasker once acutely observed that if there is ever any possibility of an attack one *must* carry it out, since otherwise one's advantage will evaporate.

1 The attack against the uncastled king

Making a mating attack on a king which had not yet castled was one of the joys of chess players in the past. These days the victim of such an attack is usually someone playing a master in a simultaneous display who has failed to castle at the right time.

The initial position of the king before it castles contains two main weaknesses. One is that it is exposed if the e-file is opened up; the second is that the square f7 in Black's position (f2 is the corresponding weak point for White) is vulnerable, since it is covered by the king alone. It is therefore natural that the vast majority of attacks on an uncastled king exploit one of these weaknesses.

The attack along the e-file

The first and most fundamental condition for an attack along the e-file is that the opponent's king should be on that file, and that for some reason it is impossible or difficult for it to move away. If all the adjacent squares are occupied by the king's own pieces or controlled by the opponent's, its escape is absolutely impossible. However, if the player is simply being prevented from castling, but other squares are not covered, the movement of the king is only relatively restricted; in other words, it can move at the cost of losing the right to castle. Castling can also be thwarted indirectly: for instance, if the king has to guard one of the pieces which is protecting it (e.g. on e7 in Black's case).

The second condition for an attack of this kind depends on the attacker's own circumstances. First of all, the e-file should be open, or it should at any rate be in the attacker's power to open it; the attacker should also either have a piece which can control a file (a rook or queen) on the file or be able quickly to post one on it. Besides this, he usually needs to strengthen his pressure on the e-file, for instance by doubling rooks or by attacking one of his opponent's pieces which is on the file and protecting the king.

From these necessary conditions it transpires that in an attack along the e-file there tends to be a chain of defence, and the attack is carried out against the central unit of the chain, that is, the piece protecting the king. If this piece is on the square directly in front of the king (e7 or e2), the attacker may be able to mate by capturing it with his queen (or rook), i.e. by making the square into the *focal-point*.

An attack on the e-file tends to occur most frequently at an early stage of the game. The following miniature is an example of how rapidly this kind of attack may develop after an opening mistake:

Meesen – H. Müller
Correspondence Game, 1928/9
English Opening

1 c4 e5 2 ♘c3 ♘f6 3 ♘f3 ♘c6 4 d4 exd4 5 ♘xd4 ♗b4 6 ♘xc6 bxc6 7 g3? ♕e7

A good move, which counters White's plan (♗g2 and 0-0) by attacking along the e-file. If White were now to play 8 e3, such an attack would admittedly not follow, but he would still be weakening his position.

8 ♗g2 ♗a6 9 ♕d3 d5 10 b3 d4! *(D)*

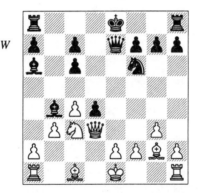

An interesting move; Black abandons his attack on the e-file for the time being, transferring his pressure to the weakened diagonal a5-e1. If White now takes the c6-pawn and then the a8-rook, Black can win a piece by ...♗xc3+ and ...♗xa1.

11 ♕xd4 ♖d8

Forcing the queen to give up the defence of the knight.

12 ♗xc6+ ♔f8 13 ♗d5 ♖xd5! 0-1

White resigns, since 14 cxd5 is followed by 14...♕xe2#. Play returns to the e-file at the final point of victory.

With an attack along the e-file, the main difficulty can often be the actual opening up of the file, especially if everything else has already been achieved, as, for example, in the following game:

Chigorin – Burn
Ostend, 1906
King's Gambit Declined

1 e4 e5 2 f4 &c5 3 &f3 d6 4 &c4 &f6 5 c3 0-0 6 d3 &c6 7 &e2 &e8 8 f5 d5 9 &b3 *(D)*

This position contains the three elements already referred to (king on e1, queen on e2 and the black rook on e8), and it is only a question of opening up the e-file. This aim can be promoted by the sacrifice of Black's bishop on f5:

9...&xf5!

After 10 exf5 e4, the important point is that White cannot avoid opening up the e-file since removing his knight would be followed by 11...exd3. But if Black had played more weakly with 9...dxe4? 10 dxe4 &xf5 11 exf5 e4, he would have lost the chance of playing ...exd3, and White could have moved his knight and avoided opening up the file.

The play after 10...e4 is no longer of interest; White could still try 11 &d1 exf3 12 &xf3, after which 12...&e5 followed by 13...&g4 or 13...d4 would lead to a great advantage for Black.

In the game itself, White declined the sacrifice by **10 &g5**, but lost quickly:
10...dxe4 11 dxe4 &xe4 12 &c4 &d5 13 &b5 &f2+ 0-1

If the e-file is already open and the last defender is a piece on e2 (or e7 for Black) then the operation often takes the form of a systematic attempt to undermine the defence of the critical square, thus making e2 into a *focal-point*. The following diagram gives an example of this kind of operation:

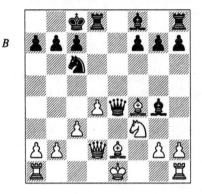

This position is from the game Hansen-Lundin, Oslo 1928.
1...♖xd4! 2 ♘xd4 ♘xd4 3 cxd4
Alternatives were 3 0-0-0 ♘xe2+ and 3 ♖d1 ♕xe2+, etc.
3...♗b4
To avoid mate White now had to consent to the loss of his queen by **4 ♔f2**, but he resigned after **4...♗xd2 5 ♗xg4+ f5 6 ♗xd2 fxg4 7 ♖he1 ♕xd4+ 8 ♗e3 ♕xb2+ 9 ♔f1 ♖e8 0-1**.

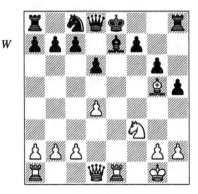

This position supplies a convenient example of the method of play against a piece protecting the king.

White, to move, must discover the correct way to increase his pressure against the bishop on e7. He would not achieve enough by 1 ♕e2 ♔f8 2 ♗xe7+ ♘xe7 3

♘g5 ♘f5, and Black has defended himself successfully. 1 ♖e2 would similarly be useless, while if 1 ♖xe7+ ♘xe7 2 ♗f6 (or 2 ♕e2 f6 and then ...♖f8), Black would still be able to maintain the balance by playing 2...♔d7 (3 ♕e2 c6, etc.). White's only correct move is:

1 ♗f6!

In this way White not only prevents Black from castling but also stops him from countering with ...f6.

1...0-0 would be answered by 2 ♖xe7 ♘xe7 3 ♕e2! ♖e8 4 ♕d2 ♔h7 5 ♘g5+ ♔g8 6 ♘e6! fxe6 7 ♕h6 ♘f5 8 ♕xg6+, and White wins.

1...♖f8 2 ♖xe7+!

A rook sacrifice of this type is often necessary if an attack along the e-file is to be forced home. It is essentially a question of freeing the square e1 for the second rook, while the first, in being sacrificed, eliminates one of the pieces defending e7[1].

2...♘xe7 3 ♕e2 ♕d7

If 3...♔d7, then 4 ♖e1 ♖e8 5 ♕b5+ ♔c8 6 ♕c4 d5 7 ♕e2 ♔d7 8 ♘e5+, and White wins.

4 ♖e1 ♕e6 5 ♕b5+ c6 6 ♕xb7, and White wins.

White's play in the following position (Ravinsky-Panov, Moscow 1943) is an excellent example of a well-conducted attack along the e-file.

W

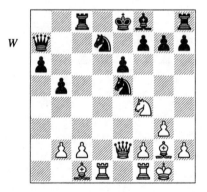

---

1   2 ♕d3! is even more convincing. Black can only prevent the deadly 3 ♖xe7+ ♘xe7 4 ♖e1 by 2...♔d7, but after 3 ♕b5+ his position collapses immediately. In Vuković's main line, 4...0-0-0 5 ♗xe7 ♖de8 would enable Black to fight on.

1 ♖xd7! ♘xd7 2 ♘xe6 fxe6 3 ♕xe6+ ♗e7

If 3...♔d8, then 4 ♗g5+ ♔c7 5 ♕c6+ ♔b8 6 ♗f4+ ♖c7 7 ♗xc7+ ♕xc7 8 ♕a8#.

4 ♖e1 ♕c5 5 b4! ♘f8?

Better would have been 5...♕xb4 6 ♗g5 ♕xe1+ 7 ♕xe1 ♘f6, when Black has excellent drawing chances. After the text move he loses in all variations.

6 ♕g4!

Avoiding exchanges and keeping an eye on c8.

6...♕c3 7 ♖xe7+!

A new and decisive sacrifice.

7...♔xe7 8 ♗g5+ ♔d6 9 ♕d1+ ♔c7 10 ♗f4+ ♔b6 11 ♕d6+ ♔a7 12 ♕e7+ ♖c7 13 ♗xc7

Simpler, of course, would have been 13 ♗e3+ ♔b8 14 ♕d8+ ♖c8 15 ♕b6#.

13...♕a1+ 14 ♗f1 ♘g6 15 ♕c5+ ♔b7 16 ♗a5 ♖f8

Or 16...♖c8 17 ♕b6+ ♔a8 18 ♕xa6+ ♔b8 19 ♗c7+ and 20 ♕xa1.

17 ♕b6+ 1-0

If 17...♔a8, then 18 ♕c6+ ♔b8 19 ♗c7+, mating in a few moves.

The following brilliancy by Steinitz is an example of a game in which White plays consistently to build up pressure on the e-file and finally makes his decisive breakthrough there.

Steinitz – von Bardeleben
Hastings, 1895
Giuoco Piano

1 e4 e5 2 ♘f3 ♘c6 3 ♗c4 ♗c5 4 c3 ♘f6 5 d4 exd4 6 cxd4 ♗b4+ 7 ♘c3 d5

Nowadays one would play 7...♘xe4, which is better.

8 exd5 ♘xd5 9 0-0 ♗e6 10 ♗g5 ♗e7? 11 ♗xd5

White now carries out a series of exchanges to keep up the pressure along the e-file and prevent Black from castling.

11...♗xd5 12 ♘xd5 ♕xd5 13 ♗xe7 ♘xe7 14 ♖e1 f6

Black realizes that he cannot succeed in castling, since if 14...♔d7, White will increase his pressure on e7 by 15 ♕e2. In playing 14...f6, Black aims at 'artificial castling' by means of ...♔f7 followed by ...♖he8 and ...♔g8; the move also limits the activity of White's knight. However, these are all excuses made in a situation which is already unhealthy for Black as a result of his weak 10th move.

15 ♕e2 ♕d7 16 ♖ac1 *(D)*

16...c6?

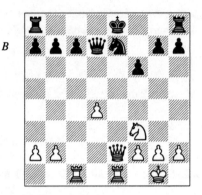

Better would have been 16...♔d8; the text move does not prevent d4-d5, which White now plays with the aim of clearing d4 for his knight[1].

17 d5! cxd5 18 ♘d4 ♔f7 19 ♘e6 ♖hc8 20 ♕g4 g6 21 ♘g5+!

The beginning of a great combination, one of the finest in 19th-century chess. The black king now has to go back on to the dangerous e-file.

21...♔e8 *(D)*

22 ♖xe7+! ♔f8

White's sacrificial assault on e7 crowns his attack on the e-file. As a result of his weakness on that file, Black consented to weaken his position elsewhere, as frequently happens once a basic defect has appeared. If he were to play 22...♔xe7, then 23 ♖e1+ ♔d6 24 ♕b4+ ♔c7 (or 24...♖c5 25 ♖e6+) 25 ♘e6+

---

1   According to contemporary analysis, Black could have equalised by 16...♔f7, but White could have gained the advantage earlier by 16 ♖ad1!.

♔b8 26 ♕f4+ wins, so Black decides to decline the sacrifice, hoping to exploit the fact that he is himself threatening to mate on c1.

23 ♖f7+ ♔g8

23...♕xf7 would, of course, be followed by ♖xc8+.

24 ♖g7+!

Black cannot get rid of this impudent rook, since if 24...♔xg7, then 25 ♕xd7+, or if 24...♕xg7, then 25 ♖xc8+.

24...♔h8 25 ♖xh7+ 1-0

At this point Steinitz's opponent left the tournament hall and never reappeared. By these offensive means he hoped to deprive Steinitz of 'a piece of immortality', but the textbooks have noted White's intentions all the same:

25...♔g8 26 ♖g7+ ♔h8 27 ♕h4+ ♔xg7 28 ♕h7+ ♔f8 29 ♕h8+ ♔e7 30 ♕g7+ ♔e8 31 ♕g8+ ♔e7 32 ♕f7+ ♔d8 33 ♕f8+ ♕e8 34 ♘f7+ ♔d7 35 ♕d6#

The attack on the square f7

Black's weakest square on the board before castling is f7 (f2 for White). Even in the opening stages, threats of a sacrificial assault on f7 (or f2) are common; they are usually connected with an attack on the king or even with the idea of mate, in which case the square becomes the focal-point of a mating attack.

Later on, after castling kingside, the rook protects this vulnerable square and its weakness is greatly diminished, while after castling queenside the weakness of the square has no connection with a mating attack.

The most straightforward examples of assaults on f7 are to be seen at the beginning of certain open games, especially in the Petroff Defence and the Philidor Defence. We shall examine one example of this kind:

1 e4 e5 2 ♘f3 d6 3 ♗c4 ♘e7?

Let us allow Black to play this bad move so as to reach a typical crisis over the square f7 as quickly as possible.

4 ♘g5 d5 5 exd5 ♘xd5 6 ♕f3

6 d4 is also good.

6...♕xg5

After 6...♗e6 7 ♘xe6 fxe6 8 ♕h5+ Black loses a pawn and the right to castle.

7 ♗xd5

and Black loses at least a pawn. If 7...f5, then 8 ♗xb7 e4 9 ♕b3 ♕xg2 10 ♖f1 and White wins.

Naturally, various attacks can be made on the uncastled king other than via the e-file or f7; these are only two of the commonest and most typical methods. The following example shows how a threat along the e-file can be indirectly combined with pre-castling attacks of another kind.

Keres – Kotov
Budapest Ct, 1950
Sicilian Najdorf

1 e4 c5 2 ♘f3 d6 3 d4 cxd4 4 ♘xd4 ♘f6 5 ♘c3 a6 6 ♗e2 ♕c7 7 ♗g5 ♘bd7 8 0-0 e6 9 ♗h5 ♕c4? *(D)*

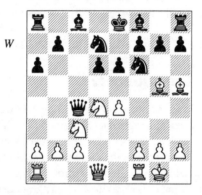

Here White carried out the following Sicilian trick, the kind of thing at which Keres was a master:

10 ♘xe6! ♕xe6 11 ♘d5

Black now went on to parry the threat of ♘c7+ with **11...♔d8?**, and after **12 ♗g4 ♕e5 13 f4 ♕xe4 14 ♗xd7 ♗xd7 15 ♘xf6** he found himself in a hopeless position.

An alternative was to let the e-file be opened up by 11...♘xd5 12 exd5 ♕f5 13 ♖e1+ ♘e5 14 f4, which would perhaps have been less unpleasant for Black, e.g. 14...g6 15 fxe5 (15 g4 is weaker on account of 15...♕xg5 16 fxg5 ♗g7, etc.) 15...dxe5 16 ♕e2 f6, etc[1].

A few further examples will show different aspects of the attack against the square f7:

1　　Indeed, after 16 ♕e2 the reply 16...♕xg5 just leaves Black a piece up. Keres himself gave the continuation 13 ♕e1+ (instead of 13 ♖e1+) 13...♘e5 14 f4 h6 15 fxe5 ♕xg5 16 exd6+ as leading to a winning attack for White.

Keres – Winter
Warsaw OL, 1935
Sicilian, 2...♘f6

1 e4 c5 2 ♘f3 ♘f6 3 e5 ♘d5 4 ♘c3 e6 5 ♘xd5 exd5 6 d4 d6 7 ♗g5 ♕a5+ 8 c3 cxd4 9 ♗d3 dxc3 10 0-0 cxb2 11 ♖b1 dxe5 12 ♘xe5 ♗d6 *(D)*

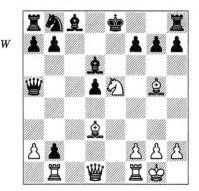

In this position White decided the game by sacrificing his knight on f7:
13 ♘xf7! ♔xf7 14 ♕h5+

A *sacrificial assault* on f7 must as a rule be followed up by aggressive action, so as not to allow Black time to consolidate (e.g. with an artificial castling by means of ...♖f8 and ...♔g8). The advantage of the capture is twofold: the king, in moving to f7, loses the right to castle and is exposed still further; at the same time, a weakness appears on the diagonal h5-e8. Such features should be quickly and energetically exploited, since they are on the whole of a transitory nature.

14...g6

If 14...♔f8, then 15 ♖fe1 ♗d7 16 ♕f3+ ♔g8 17 ♗e7 ♗xe7 18 ♖xe7, etc. Or if 14...♔e6, then 15 ♗f5+! ♔xf5 16 ♗d2+ is strongest.

15 ♗xg6+ hxg6 16 ♕xh8 ♗f5 17 ♖fe1 ♗e4 18 ♖xe4! dxe4 19 ♕f6+ 1-0

Since if 19...♔g8 (or 19...♔e8 20 ♕e6+ ♔f8 21 ♗h6#) then 20 ♕xg6+ ♔f8 21 ♕xd6+, followed by further checks and mate.

The position on the following page is from the game Varein-NN. Here White carried out the following combination:
1 ♗xf7+ ♔xf7 2 ♘d5!

This double attack on Black's b4-bishop and f4-pawn promotes a further attack on the exposed king by means of a rapid deployment of the queen's bishop;

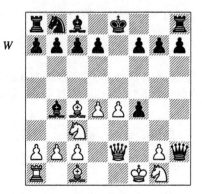

the position of Black's dark-squared bishop and queen helps White to gain some important tempi.

2...♗e7 3 ♗xf4 ♕h4 4 ♘f3 ♕h1+ 5 ♔f2 ♕xa1 6 ♘e5+ ♔e8 7 ♕h5+ g6 8 ♘xc7+ ♔f8 9 ♕h6+ ♔g8 10 ♘e8 ♗f8 11 ♘f6#

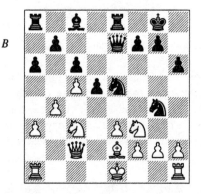

The continuation in this position, which arose in the game Asgeirsson-Raud, Munich OL 1936, is an example of an attack by Black on White's weak square at f2.

1...♘xf2! 2 ♔xf2 ♘g4+ 3 ♔e1

If 3 ♔g3, then Black follows up the attack with 3...♕c7+, and White's king is too exposed.

3...♘xe3 4 ♕d2 d4 5 ♘d1 ♘xg2+ 6 ♔f2 ♘h4 7 ♖f1 ♗h3 8 ♖g1 ♖ad8 9 ♖g3 d3 10 ♗xd3 ♘xf3 11 ♖xf3 ♕h4+ 12 ♖g3 ♖xd3 13 ♕xd3 ♕f4+ 14 ♕f3 ♕d2+ 15 ♔g1 ♖e1+ 0-1

Black mates next move.

A similar assault on f2 by two knights from e5 and g4 earned Black the First Brilliancy Prize in the following game:

Réti – H. Wolf

Teplitz-Schönau, 1922
Queen's Gambit Declined, Orthodox Defence

1 d4 d5 2 c4 e6 3 ♘c3 ♘f6 4 ♗g5 ♗e7 5 e3 0-0 6 ♘f3 ♘bd7 7 ♖c1 c6 8 ♕c2 a6 9 c5?!

Here this method of blocking the position is unsound because of Black's central advance with ...e5. Nowadays one would play 9 a3 or 9 cxd5.

9...e5! 10 dxe5 ♘g4 11 ♗xe7 ♕xe7 12 ♘a4 ♖e8

The pawn on e5 will not escape Black's clutches.

13 ♗d3 h6 14 ♘d4 ♘dxe5 15 ♘b6? *(D)*

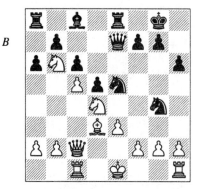

A mistake which allows Black to strike at f2. White should have castled, though even his position would still have been somewhat inferior.

15...♘xf2! 16 ♗h7+

The critical continuation here is 16 ♔xf2 ♘g4+ 17 ♔e1 (17 ♔g3 would allow 17...♕e5+ 18 ♔h4 ♕g5+ etc.) 17...♕xe3+ 18 ♘e2 ♗f5! 19 ♗xf5 ♕f2+ 20 ♔d2 ♖xe2+ 21 ♔c3 ♕xc5+ and Black wins.

16...♔h8 17 0-0

Now 17 ♔xf2 would be even weaker, e.g. 17...♘g4+ 18 ♔e1 ♕xe3+ 19 ♘e2 ♕f2+, etc. White therefore attempts to save himself by castling, reckoning that Black will lose not only his knight but also his rook. However, Black has calculated further:

17...♘fg4 18 ♘xa8 ♘xe3 19 ♕e2

If 19 ♕b1 then 19...♘xf1 20 ♔xf1 (or 20 ♖xf1 ♕xc5) 20...g6 and Black acquires both a material and a positional advantage!

19...♘xf1 20 ♗b1 ♘xh2 21 ♘b6 ♘ef3+! 22 gxf3

If 22 ♔h1 then 22...♘g4! is strongest.

22...♕g5+ 23 ♔xh2 ♖xe2+ 24 ♘xe2 ♕e5+ 25 ♘g3 ♕xb2+ 26 ♖c2 ♕xb1 27 ♖e2 ♗e6 28 f4 g6 29 ♘a8 h5 30 ♘c7 h4 31 ♘h1 ♕d3 32 ♖f2 ♗f5 0-1

To conclude the present chapter, the following game of Rubinstein's will serve to demonstrate a few more features connected with the f7/f2 sacrifice:

Euwe – Rubinstein
The Hague, 1921
Sicilian Defence, 2...♘f6

1 e4 c5 2 ♘f3 ♘f6 3 e5 ♘d5 4 d4

Better is 4 ♘c3.

4...cxd4 5 ♕xd4 e6 6 c4?

A weak move; 6 ♗c4 is correct.

6...♘c6 7 ♕d1 ♘de7! 8 ♗d2 ♘g6 9 ♕e2

After 9 ♗c3 ♕c7 White must also move his queen to e2, thereby blocking his bishop.

9...♕c7 10 ♗c3 b6 *(D)*

By developing his own pieces calmly, Black is making the best possible use of the difficulties experienced by White, who now cannot even fianchetto, e.g. 11 g3? ♗b7 12 ♗g2 ♘cxe5, etc.

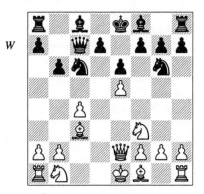

11 h4 d6! 12 exd6 ♗xd6

Black is now both better developed and more powerful in the centre. White's troubles would only be further increased after 13 ♗xg7 ♖g8 14 ♗c3 ♘f4.

13 ♘bd2 ♘f4 14 ♕e3 ♗c5 15 ♕e4 f5 16 ♕c2

The queen's sixth move – not a good augury, as H. Kmoch remarks in his commentary.

16...0-0 17 g3 ♘g6 18 h5

Because of White's weakness in the centre, the pursuit of this knight ends in its centralization.

18...♘ge5 19 ♘xe5 ♘xe5 20 b4 *(D)*

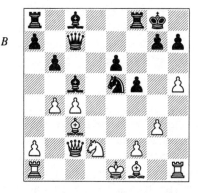

White cannot castle queenside because of the bishop's attack on f2, so he tries to employ power tactics. However, the use of force from a weaker position usually prompts a still more forceful reply from one's opponent. Rubinstein, naturally, does not withdraw his bishop, but captures on f2. In exchange for a piece he gets two pawns and an attack, which is more than sufficient in this position, seeing that he is the better developed and that the extra pawns are in the centre.

20...♗xf2+! 21 ♔xf2 ♘g4+ 22 ♔e2

The king cannot go to e1 or g1 because of 22...♕xg3+, while 22 ♔g2 allows 22...♘e3+.

22...♕xg3 23 ♗d4 ♗b7 24 ♖h3 ♕d6 25 ♕c3 e5

White has averted the direct mating attack, but now Black's centralized pawns come into their own. In such positions they are as valuable as pieces.

26 ♗g1 f4 27 c5 ♕h6 28 ♔e1 e4 29 ♖h4 ♕g5 30 ♕h3 ♘e3! 31 ♗xe3 fxe3 32 ♗c4+ ♔h8 33 ♘f1 ♕f6 0-1

In the tumult of battle it is the point at which the white king's original wound was inflicted, i.e. f2, that is finally decisive.

2 The attack on the king that has lost the right to castle

This situation arises when the king is either no longer able to castle or has been driven by the opponent away from the castling area. In spite of these possible differences of origin, the general picture and the problem involved are identical and ought to be dealt with in one and the same chapter.

First of all, it must be emphasized that the actual fact that a king has lost the right to castle does not necessarily always justify undertaking an attack aimed at mate (as will be shown by the examples of the voluntary loss of castling rights in chapter three). For an attack of this kind to be feasible, the loss of castling rights must at the same time involve the exposure of the king and an increased vulnerability to attack. In the majority of cases the attack is in fact in order, and we shall only consider such positive cases and not the rest. It only remains to be added that the loss of the right to castle can also entail a further weakness besides the danger which faces the king; that is, communication between the rooks is made more difficult. In fact, an attack may logically direct itself against this lack of co-operation between the rooks, e.g. in a struggle for control of an open file.

We shall first examine a few typical examples portraying the drama of the king which has lost the right to castle. Such a drama can be divided up into the following episodes:

1) spoiling the king's castling chances, or drawing it away from the castling position;

2) the pursuit of the king across the board by checking; and

3) the final mating attack in the middle of the board or on the edge.

The following game is an illustration of just such a drama in three acts:

Potemkin – Alekhine
St. Petersburg, 1912
Closed Sicilian

1 e4 c5 2 g3 g6 3 ♗g2 ♗g7 4 ♘e2 ♘c6 5 c3 ♘f6 6 ♘a3? d5 7 exd5 ♘xd5 8 ♘c2 0-0 9 d4 cxd4 10 cxd4 ♗g4 11 f3 ♗f5 12 ♘e3 ♕a5+

The king is forced to move out of position (1st act).

13 ♔f2

Unavoidable, since if 13 ♗d2, then 13...♘xe3 14 ♗xa5 ♘xd1, and Black wins a piece; this also happens after 13 ♕d2 ♘xe3 14 ♕xa5 ♘xg2+, etc.

13...♘db4 14 ♘xf5 ♕xf5 15 g4 ♘d3+

The second act (a short one) starts: the king has to move again. White decides on 16 ♔g3?, a weak move, but even after the stronger 16 ♔f1, Black retains the advantage with 16...♕b5.

16 ♔g3? *(D)*

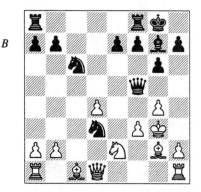

16...♘xd4! 17 gxf5 ♘xf5+ 0-1 as Black mates in 2 moves : 18 ♔g4 h5+ 19 ♔h3 (or 19 ♔g5 ♗h6#) 19...♘f2# (As an old chess player said on a similar occasion, 'He's lucky to be mated, otherwise he would lose his queen...').

We called hunting the king about the board 'the second act of the drama'. However, it must be stressed that it is not the actual fact that the king has to move about that is of prime importance, but the extent to which its position is weakened. Instead of travelling all over the board it may happen that the king merely roams a little and gets itself tied up in a small space of two or three squares, while the opponent harries it with checks and thus manages to bring up his pieces with gain of time. A typical case where checks help to 'nourish the development of the attack' arises in the following short game:

Clemens – Eisenschmidt
St Petersburg, 1890
Evans Gambit

1 e4 e5 2 ♘f3 ♘c6 3 ♗c4 ♗c5 4 b4 ♗xb4 5 c3 ♗c5 6 d4 exd4 7 cxd4 ♗b6 8 0-0 d6 9 ♘c3 ♗d7? 10 e5 dxe5 11 ♖e1 ♘ge7 12 ♘g5 *(D)*

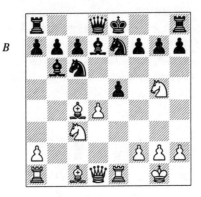

12...♗e6

Black gives up a pawn to get rid of the pressure on f7. Had he castled, then White would have won the exchange and a pawn by 13 ♕h5[1].

13 ♗xe6 fxe6 14 ♘xe6 ♕d6 15 ♘xg7+

Black's king is prevented from castling.

15...♔f8 16 ♕g4 ♗xd4 17 ♘e4 ♕b4 18 ♘e6+ *(D)*

This check is followed by two more, as a result of which White's knights assume increasingly dangerous positions.

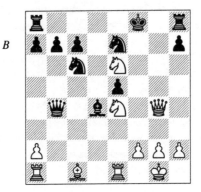

---

1   Not so. After 13 ♕h5 ♗f5 White may have no advantage. 14 ♘xf7 surprisingly fails to 14...♕xd4!, attacking both c4 and f2, when the discovered checks do not help White. Therefore White should try 14 ♗xf7+ ♔h8 15 dxe5, but even here 15...♕d4 16 ♖e3 ♕g4 is unclear.

18...♔e8 19 ♘f6+ ♔f7 20 ♘g5+ ♔f8

If 20...♔xf6, then 21 ♕e6+, followed by mate in a few moves.

21 ♗a3!

Excellent! White has a mating attack ready and needs only to get rid of Black's threat of ...♕xe1#.

21...♕xa3 22 ♕e6 ♘d8 23 ♕f7+! ♘xf7 24 ♘e6#

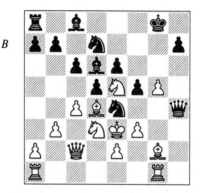

This position is from the game Kotov-Bondarevsky, Leningrad 1936, when these future grandmasters were playing in a first-category tournament. Black, to move, directed the second and third acts of the drama as follows:

1...f4+ 2 ♘xf4 ♕f2+ 3 ♔d3 ♕xd4+ 4 ♔xd4 ♗c5+ 5 ♔d3 ♘xe5#

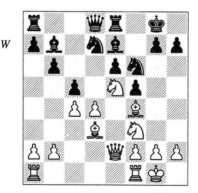

This position is from the game Alekhine-Feldt, blindfold simultaneous display, Tarnopol 1916. White continued:

1 ♘f7! ♔xf7 (otherwise 2 ♕xe6, etc.) **2 ♕xe6+!** (drawing the king out still further; if 2...♔xe6, then 3 ♘g5#) **2...♔g6 3 g4**, with mate next move by 4 ♗xf5# or 4 ♘h4#.

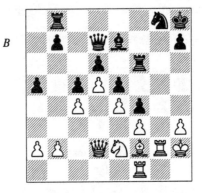

Averbakh-Kotov, Zurich Ct 1953. In order to draw White's king out from the protection of its castled position, Black is prepared to give up his queen:

1...♕xh3+! 2 ♔xh3 ♖h6+ 3 ♔g4 ♘f6+ 4 ♔f5 ♘d7! 5 ♖g5 (the only reply) **5...♖f8+ 6 ♔g4 ♘f6+ 7 ♔f5 ♘g8+ 8 ♔g4 ♘f6+ 9 ♔f5 ♘xd5+ 10 ♔g4 ♘f6+ 11 ♔f5 ♘g8+ 12 ♔g4 ♘f6+ 13 ♔f5 ♘g8+ 14 ♔g4 ♗xg5** (Black repeated moves because he was short of time, but now he proceeds to clear up the position) **15 ♔xg5 ♖f7! 16 ♗h4 ♖g6+ 17 ♔h5 ♖fg7 18 ♗g5 ♖xg5+ 19 ♔h4 ♘f6 20 ♘g3 ♖xg3 21 ♕xd6 ♖3g6 22 ♕b8+ ♖g8 0-1**

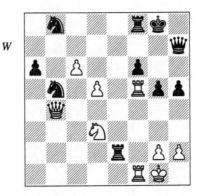

From the game Gligorić-Petrosian, Belgrade 1954. White won as follows:
1 ♖xg5+ ♔f7 2 ♖xf6+ ♔xf6 3 ♕xf8+ ♔xg5 4 h4+ 1-0, since Black is faced with mate.

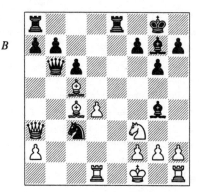

From the game D. Byrne-Fischer, New York Rosenwald 1957. Bobby Fischer, at the time a boy of thirteen, carried out an attack on the white king (which is no longer able to castle) by means of a brilliant queen sacrifice:

1...♗e6! 2 ♗xb6 (if 2 ♕xc3, then 2...♕xc5, while if 2 ♗xe6, then 2...♕b5+) **2...♗xc4+ 3 ♔g1 ♘e2+ 4 ♔f1 ♘xd4+ 5 ♔g1 ♘e2+ 6 ♔f1 ♘c3+ 7 ♔g1 axb6 8 ♕b4 ♖a4 9 ♕xb6 ♘xd1**, and Black won on the basis of his material superiority.

The pursuit of a king that has lost the right to castle is not, however, always such a successful undertaking as in the examples quoted. There have in fact been many occasions when the hunted king has come out the winner by successfully escaping to safety, and when the whole of his flight turns out in the end to be *artificial castling on a large scale!*

A player who is pursuing a king in such circumstances must therefore keep his eyes open to make sure that the prey does not elude him. Two factors are particularly important: the tempo of the attack and slowly but surely building up a mating net from which the king has no escape. As a matter of fact, this net is often of more importance than tempi, and quiet moves which 'spin the threads' often point the correct way, whereas many juicy checks may prove to be mistakes. The position of the king that has lost the right to castle represents, as it were, the attacker's capital, which he has acquired at the price of sacrifices or positional disadvantages. The attacker should retain his hold on this capital without worrying too much about 'short-term gains' in the form of tempting checks; the decisive point in the end is whether the king is going to fall or not.

These remarks are intended to inspire the reader to be cautious in his pursuit of a king that has lost the right to castle. Two maxims here oppose each other: the first instructs one to keep up the tempo of the attack by means of checks in order to give the king no time to recover its breath; the second warns that it is important to finish off the pursuit by cornering the king and forcing it into a mating position. In practice players struggle to find a balance between these two maxims and on their correct choice success itself depends.

Now that the problem is clear, it will be examined in a series of practical examples. Smyslov-Florian and Belavenets-Chistiakov are cases where the building of a mating net takes precedence over the pursuit of the king. In Tartakower-Euwe, however, we shall see the opposite, with Euwe hunting his opponent's king without giving it a moment's respite. In the game Chigorin-Caro we have an illustration of when a king's pursuit should be halted and its retreat cut off, or, conversely, what happens if an opportunity to 'fix' the king is lost and it reaches a position of safety, as in fact occurred in this game.

Smyslov – Florian
Moscow-Budapest Match 1949
Grünfeld Defence

1 d4 ♘f6 2 c4 g6 3 ♘c3 d5 4 ♘f3 ♗g7 5 ♕b3 dxc4 6 ♕xc4 0-0 7 e4 ♘a6 8 ♗e2 c5 9 d5 e6 10 0-0 exd5 11 exd5 ♕a5 12 a3 ♗f5 13 ♕h4 ♖fe8 14 ♗h6 ♘e4 15 ♗xg7 ♔xg7 *(D)*

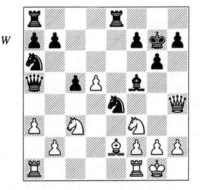

16 ♘g5!
White offers a piece in order to keep up the tempo of the attack. Black should now have played 16...♘xg5, for after 17 ♕xg5 his position would only have been slightly inferior. Instead, he became greedy and replied:
16...♘xc3 17 ♕xh7+ ♔f6 18 bxc3!
White does not hurry with his action against the displaced king, but calmly takes the knight and waits for the mating network to develop of itself.

18...♔xg5? *(D)*

Black loses quickly. The most effective reply would have been 18...♖xe2 19 f4 ♖f8![1].

Other variations, which all lead to the effective construction of a mating net, are:

1) 18...♖xe2 19 f4 ♕c7 20 d6 ♕d7 21 ♖ae1 ♗d3 (if 21...♖ae8 then 22 ♖xe2 ♖xe2 23 ♕h8#) 22 ♖xe2 ♗xe2 23 ♖e1 ♗c4 (otherwise 24 ♖e7) 24 ♘e4+, etc.

2) 18...♖h8 19 ♕xf7+ ♔xg5 20 ♕g7! (depriving the king of the square h6; 20 f4+? ♔h6 is wrong) 20...♔f4 21 ♖ae1[2]. Here again White does not put Black in check but instead prevents the king from using the e-file; if 21...♔e4 White mates with 22 ♗c4+ ♔f4 23 g3+, etc.

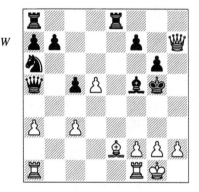

W

19 ♕g7!

A quiet move, cutting off the king's retreat and preparing for mate with 20 f4+, etc.

19...♖e4 20 f4+ ♖xf4 21 ♖xf4 ♔xf4 22 ♖f1+ ♔e3

If 22...♔g5 then 23 h4+ leads to mate, or if 22...♔e4, a mating net is formed by 23 ♗c4.

23 ♕e5+ ♔d2

Well may he run – mate is not far off.

24 ♗c4 ♕xc3 25 ♖f2+ 1-0

It is mate in two more moves.

---

1   Although Smyslov then gives the continuation 20 ♕h6 ♖fe8 21 ♖ae1 ♗d3 22 ♕h4 ♔e7 23 ♘e4+ ♔f8 24 d6 ♔g7 25 f5, with a decisive attack for White.

2   It is even simpler to mate with checks by 21 g3+ ♔e4 22 ♕e7+ ♔xd5 23 c4+ ♔c6 24 ♗f3+, etc.

Belavenets – Chistiakov
Semi-finals, USSR Ch 1938
French Defence, McCutcheon Variation

1 e4 e6 2 d4 d5 3 ♘c3 ♘f6 4 ♗g5 ♗b4

The so-called McCutcheon Variation, which is nowadays regarded as unfavourable for Black.

5 e5 h6 6 ♗d2 ♗xc3 7 bxc3 ♘e4 8 ♕g4 g6 9 ♗d3

9 ♗c1 is also possible, to enable the bishop to exert pressure from a3. In this position it does not matter to White that he loses the right to castle, but he must play sharply and accurately, as otherwise Black's attack along the c-file may prevail.

9...♘xd2 10 ♔xd2 c5 11 ♘f3

Maroczy's move, 11 h4, is an alternative.

11...♘c6 12 ♖hb1?

A poor move. 12 ♖ab1 was preferable[1].

12...♕c7

Note how Black plays from here up to his 15th move. He does not pursue the unfruitful plan of 'looking for checks' with 12...cxd4? 13 cxd4 ♕a5+, but quietly brings his rook on to the c-file; then, and only then, does he strike by means of ...cxd4.

13 ♕h4 ♗d7 14 ♕f6 ♖g8 15 h4 ♖c8 16 h5 gxh5 17 ♕xh6 cxd4 18 cxd4 *(D)*

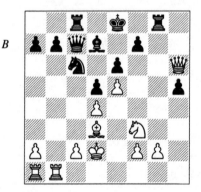

18...♘xd4!

---

1   According to current theory both 12 ♖ab1 and 12 ♕f4 give White a slight advantage.

Now begins a well-prepared attack on the king, which has already been drawn out of position.

19 ♘xd4 ♛c3+ 20 ♔e3 ♖c4 21 ♛f4 ♖g4 22 ♘e2 ♖e4+ 0-1

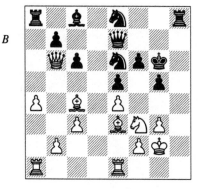

This position arose in the game Tartakower-Euwe, Venice 1948. It is Black's move; first of all, he draws the king out from his castled position by a sacrifice:

1...♘f4+! 2 gxf4 ♗h3+ 3 ♔g3

The king must come out, since 3 ♔g1 would be answered by the still more unpleasant 3...gxf4 4 ♗c5 ♛g7 5 ♔h1 ♗f1+ 6 ♘h2 ♛h7.

3...gxf4+ 4 ♗xf4 ♛d7

At first all is quiet, but then comes the storm.

5 ♘h2 exf4+ 6 ♔xf4 ♖h4+ 7 ♔e3

If 7 ♔f3, then 7...♗g2+!, or if 7 ♔g3, then 7...♖g4+!.

7...♗g2 8 ♘f3 ♖xe4+!

White is not to be allowed a respite! 8...♖h3 9 ♗e2 ♛g4 would have been unclear owing to 10 ♖g1.

9 ♔xe4 ♘d6+

Now Black captures two pieces *en route* by a series of checks.

10 ♔d3 ♛f5+ 11 ♔d4 ♛f4+ 12 ♔d3

If 12 ♔c5, then 12...♛xc4+ 13 ♔xd6 ♛d5+ 14 ♔e7 ♖g8 and mate[1].

12...♛xc4+ 13 ♔c2 ♗xf3 14 b3

White, by allowing himself to be 'bled', has obtained a little breathing space, but not for long.

---

1   Surprisingly, this line is not entirely clear after 15 ♘h4+ ♔h7 16 ♘f5! ♛xf5 17 ♖ad1. The simplest win after 12 ♔c5 is 12...♘xc4 13 ♛xb7 ♛d6+ 14 ♔xc4 ♛d5+ 15 ♔b4 c5+, winning the queen.

14...&e4+ 15 &b2 &d3 16 &g1+ &f7 17 &ac1

Black's king is in a safe enough position after 17 &c7+ &e6.

17...&d2+ 18 &a3 *(D)*

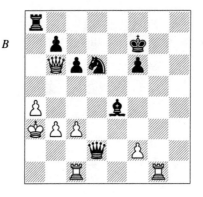

18...&c4+

The storm has regained its force once more; the end is not far off.

19 bxc4 &xa4+ 20 &xa4 &a2+ 21 &b4 &b2+ 0-1

For if 22 &c5, then 22...&xf2+, and White loses his queen; or if 22 &a5, then 22...&a3#.

A fine example of a consistent pursuit of the king.

The following unusual game, which dates from long ago, gave rise to amusement at the tournament itself and only superficial comments in the tournament book. Chess books concerned themselves with the game no further, and in doing so let slip some fine material with which to illustrate the theme of 'the king's wanderings and flight'. Only with the commentary below, containing a discussion of the king's journey and an exposition of the technique of 'net-building', has this game been placed in correct perspective.

Chigorin – Caro
Vienna, 1898
Vienna Game

1 e4 e5 2 &c3 &f6 3 f4 d5 4 d3

Theory discarded this move long ago, since Black, by sacrificing his knight on e4, can obtain at least a draw. Correct is 4 fxe5[1].

4...&b4 5 fxe5 &xe4 6 dxe4 &h4+ 7 &e2

The king, having lost the right to castle, takes the first step on its long journey, which is to end on the square a1!

7...♗xc3 8 bxc3 ♗g4+ 9 ♘f3 dxe4 10 ♕d4 ♗h5! 11 ♔e3 ♗xf3 12 ♗b5+

A risky move, first played by Steinitz against Blackburne in 1876. Correct here is 12 gxf3 on which Black can get a draw with 12...♕e1+ 13 ♔f4 ♕h4+, etc. Chigorin, in playing 12 ♗b5+, avoids this possibility, for a draw was naturally not to his liking.

12...c6 13 gxf3 *(D)*

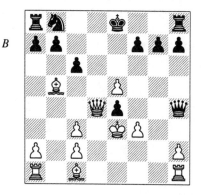

13...♕h6+!

The co-creator of the Caro-Kann Defence departs from the theory of his time and hits on the very best move. The theoreticians of the day rejected it, probably because Caro lost the game, and noted in their books that Black obtains the advantage by continuing 13...cxb5 14 ♕xe4 ♕xe4+ 15 ♔xe4 0-0 16 ♗e3 ♘d7. However, it seems that these old masters either examined this position by feeble gas-light or else they supposed that White would now have to succumb by playing 17 ♖ad1? ♘xe5 18 ♔xe5 ♖fe8+ 19 ♔f4 g5+. However, by modern reckoning White would have the better game, if he were to play consistently for a central position with 17 ♗d4. In view of the threat of 18 ♖ab1 a6 19 a4, Black's best reply is 17...a6; then there follows 18 ♖hg1 with the intention of weakening Black's position on the long dark diagonal.

14 ♔xe4

Chigorin takes a further risk; 14 ♔e2 would have been good enough for a draw after 14...♕h3 (not 14...exf3+ on account of 15 ♔f2 ♕h3 16 ♗f1!) 15 ♖d1 exf3+

---

1   4 fxe5 usually transposes to the game continuation after 4...♘xe4 5 d3 ♗b4. White has other possibilities at move 5, but none gives him any advantage.

(15...♛xf3+ is weak, because of 16 ♔e1! and White saves his bishop) 16 ♔f2 ♛xh2+ 17 ♔e3 ♛h6+ with perpetual check (for if 18 ♔e4 ♛h4+ 19 ♗f4, Black can play 19...cxb5)

14...♛g6+ 15 ♔e3 cxb5 16 ♗a3 ♞c6 17 ♛d5 ♛xc2 18 ♜ac1 ♛f5 19 ♜he1 ♜d8?! *(D)*

Black clearly cannot take the e-pawn because of 20 ♔f2, but 19...b4 would have been better and safer than the move played. After 20 ♗xb4 (20 cxb4 0-0 21 b5 ♜fe8 is in Black's favour) 20...♞xb4 21 cxb4 0-0 the exposed position of White's king together with his scattered pawns gives Black a considerable advantage. Thus in the event of 22 ♜ed1 (22 ♜c7 is weaker because of 22...♜ae8 23 f4 ♜d8 24 ♛e4 ♛h3+) 22...♜ae8 23 f4 ♛h3+ 24 ♛f3 ♛xh2 25 ♜d2 ♛h6 Black threatens both 26...♜xe5+ and 26...f6. The queen's great manoeuvrability comes into its own in situations like this.

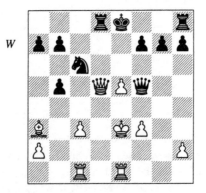

20 ♛xb5

20 ♗d6 also came into consideration, though 20...f6 would then have led to a difficult and unclear position.

20...a6

20...g5 could have been parried by 21 ♜cd1.

21 ♛b1

The queen must cover the d3-square and if 21 ♛f1, then Black could have carried out an artificial castling by means of ...♔d7-c8 and so made his advantage clear[1].

---

1   In fact 21 ♛f1 ♔d7 can be met by 22 ♛d3+ and White escapes into a playable ending. 21 ♛f1 is best answered by 21...♞xe5 and White cannot exploit the line-up on the e-file because his own king is so exposed.

21...♕g5+ 22 f4

White has to consent to this move, which exposes his king still further; 22 ♔f2? is not good on account of 22...♕h4+ 23 ♔f1 (neither 23 ♔e3 ♕h6+ nor 23 ♔g1 ♖d2 is any better) 23...♕h3+ 24 ♔f2 ♕xh2+ 25 ♔e3 ♕d2+ 26 ♔e4 g5 and Black wins.

22...♕g2 23 ♗d6

If 23 ♕e4 then 23...♕xa2! 24 ♗d6 ♔d7 and Black succeeds in consolidating the position of his king while remaining a pawn ahead. Also interesting is 23 ♕c2 ♕h3+ 24 ♔e4 f5+ 25 exf6 gxf6. The opening up of the e-file is of no help to White, since his king has nowhere to go; in view of the threat of mate he is forced to play 26 f5, on which 26...♘e5 wins.

23...♕h3+ 24 ♔e4

To engineer a possible escape for the king via d2 White would have to give up his h-pawn; moreover, there would also be a permanent danger of the exchange of queens. For this reason he prefers to embark on new adventures.

24...f5+ 25 ♔d5 *(D)*

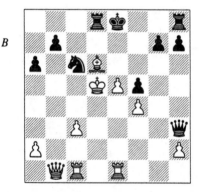

This position caused amazement among some of the spectators, who attempted to get the manager of the tournament to intervene, since it was clear that White's piece on d5 was his queen and that on b1 his king! The position is, of course, a strange one; what is also unusual is that within seven moves the white king has reached a1. Clearly, it is helped in this by Black, who checks unnecessarily instead of building up a mating net. Black played 25...♕g2+?, when the correct move was 25...♖c8!. In that case White's king would get into trouble on the c-file, which it would have to cross to extract itself from the scrape it has got into. The following variations illustrate the strength of the rook move and are at the same time instructive as regards play against an exposed king: 25...♖c8! and now:

1) White carries out a counterattack with his queen: 26 ♕xb7 ♕g2+ 27 ♔c5 ♘e7+ 28 ♔b6 ♖c6+ 29 ♔a7 ♕f2+ 30 ♔a8 0-0+ 31 ♗b8 ♖b6 and Black wins.

2) The white king tries to force its way through to the a1-corner; this gives rise to the most interesting point in the analysis. After 26 ♔c4 Black does not try any checking moves, but instead first consolidates his own position by 26...g6!!, having observed that White has no good move to make. If 27 ♖c2 or 27 ♕c2, then 27...b5+ 28 ♔b3 ♘d4+, while if 27 ♖cd1, then 27...♘d4+; if 27 ♖ed1 or 27 ♖f1, the ring is tightened by 27...♕e3, and if 27 ♕b6, then 27...♘a5+ 28 ♔d5 (or 28 ♔b4 ♕xh2!) 28...♕g2+ 29 ♔e6 ♕xa2+ 30 ♔f6 (or 30 c4 ♘xc4, etc.) 30...♖c6 31 ♕a7 ♖f8+ 32 ♔g7 ♖c7+! 33 ♗xc7 ♖g8+ 34 ♔f6 ♕f7+ 35 ♔g5 ♕e7+ and mates[1].

The possibility of 27 ♔b3 still remains. There is admittedly no mating net then, but with 27...♕xh2 Black obtains a material advantage and goes on to threaten both 28...♕xf4 and 28...♘a5+ followed by ...♘c4.

3) The white king tries to defy the danger of mate by advancing to b6. Black then has a number of continuations, the simplest of which seems to be 26 ♔c5 ♕xh2 27 ♔b6 ♕xf4 28 ♔xb7 (if 28 ♕b3, then 28...♕f2+ 29 ♗c5 ♕xc5+ 30 ♔xc5 ♘a5+ with a won ending) 28...♕c4 29 ♔xc8 ♘b4+ 30 ♔b7 ♕b5+ 31 ♔a7 ♘c6+ followed by 32...♔d7+ and mates.

The actual game took the following course:

25...♕g2+? 26 ♔c4 b5+ 27 ♔d3 ♕f3+ 28 ♔c2 ♕f2+ 29 ♔b3 ♖c8 *(D)*

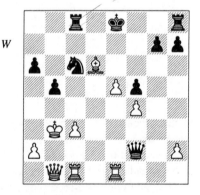

---

1   In this line Vuković fails to take his own advice and gives too many checks, which actually allow White to escape by 34 ♔h6! ♕xh2+ 35 ♔g5 ♕g3+ 36 ♔f6, etc. The correct continuation is 32...♕e6! and there is no way to meet the threat of 33...♖g8+ 34 ♔h6 g5+.

30 ♖c2

White obviously cannot play 30 ♕xf5 since then 30...♘a5+ leads to mate; instead, he gives up his f-pawn and then by retreating his king quickly to a1 safeguards his position.

30...♕xf4 31 ♔b2 ♘a5 32 ♔a1 ♕c4?

A further mistake; he could still have fought for a draw by 32...♕f3!. The square c4 is naturally more suitable for the knight.

33 e6 ♘c6

After 33...♖c6 34 ♕d1 ♘b7 35 ♗e5 Black cannot play 35...♖xe6 because of 36 ♗xg7 ♖g8 37 ♖xe6+ and White wins.

34 ♕d1 h5?

A terrible move; he should have played 34...♖d8.

35 ♖g1! ♖h7 36 ♖xg7! 1-0

Since if 36...♖xg7, then 37 ♕xh5+ followed by 38 ♕h8+ and White forces mate.

In addition to this strange game, I shall extract from the treasury of chess curiosities three more encounters which have particular relevance to the theme of a king's successful wandering. The series opens with a game between Hamppe and Meitner, in which the pursued king seeks asylum among the enemy pawns and is successful to the extent that the opponent cannot obtain anything beyond perpetual check.

Hamppe – Meitner
Vienna, 1872
Vienna Game

1 e4 e5 2 ♘c3 ♗c5 3 ♘a4

3 ♘f3, which was often played by Anderssen, is the soundest answer to 2...♗c5. Hamppe's move is of doubtful value because of the bishop sacrifice on f2.

3...♗xf2+

In return for the bishop, Black obtains a promising attack on the king, which is deprived of the right to castle.

4 ♔xf2 ♕h4+ 5 ♔e3

If 5 g3 then 5...♕xe4 6 ♕e2 ♕xa4 (not 6...♕xh1 because of 7 ♘f3 and 8 ♗g2) 7 ♕xe5+ ♘e7 8 ♕xg7 ♖g8 9 ♕xh7 d6 and Black has the better position.

5...♕f4+ 6 ♔d3 d5 *(D)*

7 ♔c3

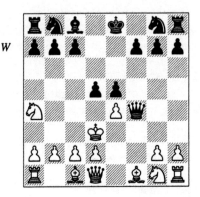

White plans b3 and ♔b2. If 7 ♘c3, then 7...♘f6! 8 ♕e1 (or 8 ♕f3 dxe4+ 9 ♘xe4 ♗f5 etc.[1]) 8...dxe4+ 9 ♔c4 whereupon Black should not continue with 9...♗e6+ 10 ♔b4 e3+ 11 ♔a3 ♘c6 since White replies with 12 b3 followed by ♔b2, but rather with 9...e3+! 10 ♔b3 ♘c6 11 a3 ♗e6+ and wins. This illustrates the method of countering a king's planned withdrawal to safety.

7...♕xe4 8 ♔b3

If 8 d4 then 8...♘c6 9 ♗b5 (or 9 b3) 9...exd4+ and Black has three pawns for his bishop as well as good prospects for a continuing attack on White's king or, indeed, his knight on a4.

8...♘a6 9 a3 (D)

9 c4? would be weak because of 9...b5!. Similarly, 9 ♗xa6 bxa6 10 c3 ♕xg2 11 ♕f3 (or 11 ♘e2 ♗g4 12 ♖e1 ♘e7!) 11...♗h3! is bad for White[2]. This is a typical example of an attack against a displaced king being deferred on the grounds that further action would only help the consolidation of the king's position. Thus, for example, after 9 ♗xa6 bxa6 10 c3, 10...♖b8+ would enable White to prepare a new home for his king on b2 by 11 ♔a3 and b3. Instead, Black directs his attack against the other flank and, while mowing down some pawns, tries to exploit the general lack of development of White's position.

9...♕xa4+!

Effective, and probably necessary, although it gives no more than a draw. If 9...♗e6 White would reply 10 d4! exd4 11 ♗xa6 bxa6 12 ♘f3 with the better prospects. Bilguer's *Handbuch* answers 9...♗e6 with 10 d3? d4+ 11 c4 dxc3+ 12

---

1   This line is only equal after 10 ♕xf4 exf4 11 ♔e2! ♘xe4 12 d3 followed by ♗xf4, restoring the material balance.

2   This is highly disputable after 12 ♕g3 ♕xh1 13 ♕xe5+ ♔f8 14 ♘xh3, and White could quickly develop a strong initiative.

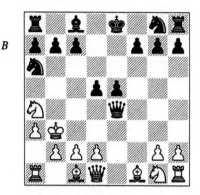

♔xc3 and considers that White retains the advantage. However, after 12...♕d4+ 13 ♔d2 ♘f6! 14 ♕c2 (if he stops 14...♘e4+ by 14 ♘c3, then 14...♘c5!) 14...0-0-0 15 ♘f3 ♕f2+ 16 ♔d1 ♘g4 Black has excellent chances based on ...e4 and ...♘e3+.

10 ♔xa4 ♘c5+ 11 ♔b4[1] a5+ 12 ♔xc5

If 12 ♔c3? then 12...d4+ 13 ♔c4 b6 14 ♔d5 f6 15 ♔c6 ♔d8, and the mating net is complete[2].

12...♘e7 13 ♗b5+ ♔d8 14 ♗c6! *(D)*

The only reply!

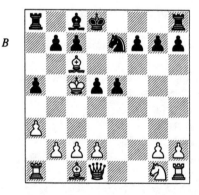

---

1   In his book *Draw!*, Wolfgang Heidenfeld offered some rather convincing analysis to prove that White could have won by 11 ♔b5!.

2   Heidenfeld pointed out that this line can be improved by 14 ♕f3 ♗e6+ 15 ♕d5 ♘e7 16 ♕xe6 fxe6 with an unclear position.

14...b6+ 15 ♔b5 ♘xc6 16 ♔xc6

Against 16 c3? or 16 ♔a4?, 16...♘d4 is decisive.

16...♗b7+ 17 ♔b5

He must not capture! If 17 ♔xb7? then 17...♔d7 18 ♕g4+ ♔d6 and White has no defence against 19...♖hb8#.

17...♗a6+ 18 ♔c6 ½-½

Black keeps up perpetual check with the bishop on b7 and a6. White's king must not venture to a4 because of ...♗c4 and then ...b5#.

An original ending to a king hunt!

The next game abounds in dramatic features and gives us an opportunity for some more remarks on the subject of attacking a king that has lost the right to castle.

Morphy – Barnes

Simultaneous Display against Five Masters, London 1859
Petroff Defence

1 e4 e5 2 ♘f3 ♘f6 3 ♗c4

Morphy regularly employed this against the Petroff; it does no more than leave the position evenly balanced.

3...♘xe4 4 ♘c3

A dubious gambit originating from Kieseritzky.

4...♘xc3 5 dxc3 f6!

A good, as well as necessary, move in this position.

6 0-0 ♕e7?!

After this White has approximately equal chances. Correct was 6...♘c6! 7 ♘h4 g6 8 f4 f5! with advantage to Black.

7 ♘h4 d6 8 ♕h5+ ♔d8 9 f4

9 ♘g6? fails against 9...♕e8.

9...♗e6 10 ♗xe6 ♕xe6 11 fxe5 dxe5 12 ♘g6

White regains the pawn, since if 12...♕e8?, then 13 ♕d1+! unpins the knight with gain of tempo.

12...♗c5+ 13 ♔h1 ♖e8 14 ♕xh7 ♕g8 15 ♕h5 ♘d7 16 b4?

A positional mistake, since he forfeits the chance of c4, without which his pawn attack is ineffective. 16 a4 was correct.

16...♗d6 17 ♗d2 ♕f7

Threatening ...♘f8.

18 ♕g4 ♕e6 19 ♕e4 ♘b6! *(D)*

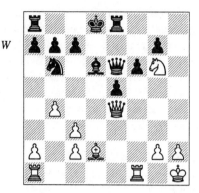

Owing to the weakness on c4, White's position has lost its sting. Morphy now decides to compromise his game still further by sacrificing his knight; there is probably nothing better.

20 ♕xb7 ♕g4 21 a4 ♖c8 22 ♖ad1 ♕xg6 23 ♗e3 ♘c4 24 ♕c6 ♕f7

Clearly not 24...♘xe3 because of 25 ♖xd6+ ♔e7 26 ♖d7+ ♔f8 27 ♕c5+.

25 ♗xa7 e4

25...♔e7 would also have been good, followed by ...♔f8 ('delayed artificial castling').

26 ♖d4 ♕h5

Black begins to have his threats. 27 h3 is obviously met by 27...♕e5, while if 27 g3, then 27...♖h8 28 h4 ♕e2, threatening mate by either 29...♕xf1+ or 29...♖xh4+. Morphy now finds the one reply which still offers resistance.

27 ♖f4! e3 28 g4 e2 (D)

28...♕h4 was probably even stronger.

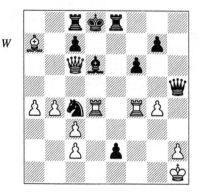

29 gxh5 e1♕+ 30 ♔g2 ♖e2+ 31 ♔h3 f5?

Black has drawn his opponent's king out of position but now, when he is faced with the task of producing a mating attack, he stumbles. 31...f5? only appears to tighten the net (that is, by the threat of 32...♕f1+ 33 ♖xf1 ♖xh2#); in fact it allows the king to escape via g5. 31...♕f1+ 32 ♖xf1 ♖xh2+ 33 ♔g4 ♘e5+ would also have been unsound, since after 34 ♔g3! ♘xc6+ White can liquidate by interpolating 35 ♖xd6+ cxd6 36 ♗b6+ and only then 37 ♔xh2.

31...♕xc3+ 32 ♖d3 (forced) 32...♕e5 33 ♕f3 ♔e7, etc. was one line which led to victory.

32 ♕xc4! ♕f1+ 33 ♔h4 ♖xh2+ 34 ♔g5 ♕g2+?

After this fresh mistake Black ought to have lost. 34...♕g1+ 35 ♖g4 ♕e3+ might still have resulted in a win[1].

35 ♖g4! *(D)*

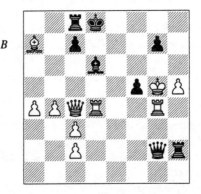

By sacrificing his rook White succeeds in blocking the g-file and thus obtaining a respite for his king in the comparative safety of g5. Naturally, the king is only secure there for one or two moves, but in the present position that is enough, for White also has some threats at his disposal.

The initiative now passes to White, and he should win quickly. The creation of a 'makeshift shelter' for one or two moves is often extremely important when the king is being pursued, always on the assumption, of course, that the counterattack made possible by the gain of time promises to be successful.

35...fxg4 36 ♕f7?

---

1   In fact, it wins rather easily after 36 ♔g6 ♕h6+ 37 ♔xf5 ♕xh5+ 38 ♖g5 ♖f2+ 39 ♖f4 ♖xf4+ 40 ♕xf4 ♕f7+. It follows that White should have played 32 ♖xc4! instead of 32 ♕xc4?, when the position would indeed have been unclear.

Fortune smiled on him earlier, but now he loses the game which he could have won, e.g. 36 ♖xd6+ cxd6 37 ♕g8+ ♔e7 (if 37...♔c7 or 37...♔d7, then 38 ♕f7+ ♔c6 39 b5#) 38 ♕xg7+ ♔e8 (or 38...♔e6 39 ♕f6+ ♔d5 40 ♕f7+! mating next move) 39 ♕g6+ ♔e7 (if 39...♔d7 then 40 ♕f7+ ♔d8 41 ♗b6+ ♖c7 42 ♕xc7+ ♔e8 43 ♕d8+ ♔f7 44 ♕f6+ ♔g8 45 ♕g6+ ♔f8 46 ♕xd6+, etc.) 40 ♕f6+ ♔e8 41 ♕e6+ ♔d8 42 ♗b6+ ♖c7 43 ♕xd6+ etc.

36...♕c6! 37 b5

If 37 ♕f8+ then 37...♔e8 38 ♖xd6+ cxd6 39 ♕xd6+ ♕d7 40 ♗b6+ ♔e8 41 ♕xh2 ♕e7+ and Black captures the bishop by further checking.

37...♕d7 38 ♖xd6 ♕xd6 0-1

Barnes played a number of games against Morphy; with his distinctive positional style, he was the most successful of all the British masters against that combinative genius.

Now comes the third and last example from the collection of curiosities – the game between Michelet and Kieseritzky, in which the hunted white king is not only saved but goes on actively to participate in the attack on his black colleague. The key to this success is the confinement of Black's queen in a most unusual 'cage'.

Michelet – Kieseritzky
Paris, 1845
King's Gambit Accepted

1 e4 e5 2 f4 exf4 3 ♘f3 g5 4 ♗c4 g4 5 ♘e5

Today the Muzio Gambit 5 0-0 is considered more promising.

5...♕h4+ 6 ♔f1 f3

The so-called Cochrane Gambit, which is favourable for Black.

7 d4 ♘f6 8 ♘c3 ♗g7

8...fxg2+ is also good.

9 g3 ♕h3+ 10 ♔f2 d6 11 ♘xf7 ♖f8 12 ♘g5 ♕g2+ 13 ♔e3 *(D)*

13...♗h6?

An unsound idea, since White can obviously counter it by ♔d3, after which the bishop will have done nothing but lose control of the long diagonal.

13...♘c6 was correct, and if 14 a3 then 14...♔e7 threatening 15...h6.

14 ♔d3 ♘c6 15 a3 ♗xg5 16 ♗xg5 ♘xe4

This sacrifice is incorrect, but Black's position was already inferior as a result of his mistake on the 13th move. White's king is quite happy on d3.

17 ♕e1 ♗f5 18 ♘xe4 f2 19 ♕e3 ♔d7 20 ♗d5 ♖ae8 21 ♖af1!

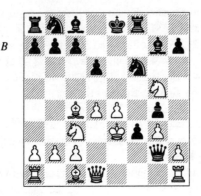

White actually encourages Black to carry out his threat to win the queen, producing an original riposte to it.

21...♗xe4+ 22 ♗xe4 ♖f3 23 ♕xf3! gxf3 24 ♗f5+

White now wins the other rook, leaving the black queen boxed in at g2. White conducts the ending with what is in effect an extra piece and, logically enough, takes his king into battle as well.

24...♖e6 25 d5 ♘e5+ 26 ♔e4 h5 27 dxe6+ ♔e8 28 ♗f6 h4 29 ♗xe5 dxe5 30 ♔xe5 hxg3 31 ♔f6 1-0

The final position deserves a diagram.

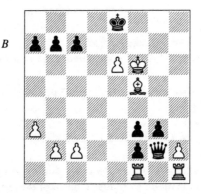

Black is lost, since he has no proper defence against ♗g6+ followed by e7+ and e8♕, etc. Black's play throughout this game is an example of how *not* to conduct an attack on a wandering king.

3 On castling and attacking the castled position in general

The origin of castling

Castling, the most distinctive move in the whole of chess, affects the nature of mating attacks in various ways and because of its importance in this connection, the general significance of the move is worth examining.

Castling is not of any great antiquity. It is also obvious that such a complex and distinctive operation as the modern castling move was not born in a day, but rather developed gradually from century to century with the evolution of the rules of the game themselves.

In the Indian game of chaturanga (pre-chess) there is no trace of the move, nor can it be found in the Arab shatranj. The first traces of any unusual or exceptional movement being made by the king, out of which the castling move evolved, are to be found in mediaeval European chess, which in its first stages can be described as the first and not very significant revision of shatranj towards providing the pieces with greater mobility. A historical source attesting to this first revision is a work by the Lombard monk Jacobus de Cessolis, in which are recorded the rules governing the movements of the individual chess pieces at the time. There it is stated that king, queen, and pawns have the right to make an initial move of two squares as well as the normal one. From this early reform the double opening step taken by the pawn survives to this day, while in the case of the queen it became obsolete when the piece was given its present powers of movement during the great reform of the game at the end of the fifteenth century. In the case of the king it was further developed and altered until it eventually took its present-day shape as castling.

There is extensive confirmation of the introduction of the king's move from other sources after Cessolis, though the particular conditions governing the move vary. The form most frequently recorded is that where the king moves like a knight ('*Freudensprung*'), with the limitation that it is not allowed to go beyond the second rank. The next form, which made its appearance in Italy in the sixteenth century, already included a movement by the rook in the same move – a step nearer to the castling of today. The king's use of the knight's jump disappears at this point and the rules state that the king is free to move from e1 to g1 or h1 and the rook from h1 to f1 or e1. This type of 'free castling' or 'Italian castling' persisted in Italy right up to the nineteenth century, when it was superseded by the present rules, which were introduced in France during the eighteenth century.

This short survey of the historical evolution of castling is a good illustration of the gradual development of the rules of chess and it makes it particularly clear that these rules have been changed and perfected with the desire of enriching the game; the general tendency towards giving the pieces more dynamic movement reflects the increased animation of social movements in Europe from the Middle Ages onwards.

In addition to this general line of development in the laws of chess, we also owe the introduction and eventual adoption of the castling move to the indirect influence of the great reform of the fifteenth century. This reform created a powerful queen out of the *fers* (which moved one square) and the modern bishop out of the *alfil* (which moved exactly two squares). In this new type of chess, with three long-range pieces, the fighting ability of the king declined; once in the days of pre-chess it had been the strongest piece of all. The king now became a hindrance with its slow movement, and its position in the centre of the back rank stood out immediately as a *fault in the game's structure*. On the one hand, it had to be safeguarded against the formidable new forces, and on the other it had to be removed from the centre so as not to hamper them. For this reason it was necessary for the king to get away from the centre as quickly as possible, and it was to this end that the king's double move was built on and transformed into the full castling move. Therefore, not only the development of this most distinctive move can be traced through the history of chess but also its logic: it exists as the necessary complement to the reform of the other pieces' movements. We start a game of chess today with the pieces placed in the ancient order which derives from chaturanga, and then we switch over by castling to a new position, which is better suited to the alterations made in the game's rules.

The dynamic and positional significance of castling

Chess moves in general can be looked at from the dynamic or the positional point of view, depending on whether we are considering them as part of an active combination or as static features.

The castling move without doubt powerfully increases the dynamic potential of a position. A player who has castled at once obtains a whole range of possibilities which he did not have before. He has increased the influence of the rook, cleared the square e1 for a possible attack along the e-file, and on top of this he has prepared the ground for the quick establishment of 'communication between the rooks', i.e. the entire clearing of the back rank, as a result of which the rooks cover each other or can combine together in attacks.

On the other hand, castling is also a positional move, and one which provides a particular element of permanency to the position. For it is unique and irrevocable; it can only be carried out once in a game, which means that the king will as a rule stay on the side on which it has castled. In special cases it can, it is true, travel with a greater or lesser degree of difficulty from its castled position to various parts of the board. Thus castling is only relatively irrevocable (unlike a pawn's move, which is absolutely so) but for practical purposes the king's position after castling is, at least until the arrival of the endgame, fairly definitely a permanent positional feature. Before castling, the king has three possible courses of action: to remain in the middle or to castle either to right or left. Once it has castled it no longer has any choice; it then has a definite shelter, a 'permanent address', a fact which the opponent naturally takes into account. It is certainly safer against attack, but it has at the same time committed itself positionally to one particular area of the board; thus the undoubted advantages of castling are offset by certain disadvantages.

Artificial castling

Chess also contains the term 'artificial castling', which involves a player creating a position the same as or similar to that reached after genuine castling. It is attained not by a single castling move but a series of moves by the king and the rook. In the continuation from the following diagram we shall encounter the simplest example of 'artificial castling.'

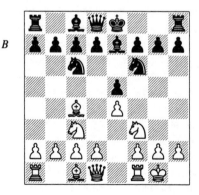

Black, to move, played:

1...♘xe4

White's best would now be 2 ♘xe4 d5 3 ♗d3 dxe4 4 ♗xe4, in which case the prospects would remain even. However, before taking the knight on e4 White decides to use his bishop to prevent his opponent from castling – an idea which, in this position, is faulty.

2 ♗xf7+ ♔xf7 3 ♘xe4

At first sight White's plan appears to have succeeded, since, as well as maintaining the material balance, he has prevented Black from castling. However, the further play shows that Black can carry out 'artificial castling' without difficulty and has made a clear gain in that he is left with strong pawns in the centre.

3...d5 4 ♘g3 ♖f8 5 d3 ♔g8

Now the superiority of Black's position is quite obvious, and one can easily appreciate the part played by 'artificial castling'; Black has admittedly expended three moves on it, but White has derived no advantage from this fact, since he has made three moves of even less value, i.e. ♗xf7+, ♘xe4, and ♘g3. In a sense, Black was castling while White was transferring his knight from c3 to g3.

The correct moment for castling

Beginners are often advised to castle as quickly as possible. This is a useful and sensible piece of advice in the majority of instances. Certainly, less experienced players offend against this general precept extremely often, postponing castling unnecessarily and as a result suddenly finding themselves in an awkward situation, by which time it is far too late to castle. The present writer once made a statistical survey of late castling using a number of simultaneous games and came to the conclusion that a common characteristic of so-called 'simultaneous massacres' (when the master wins all, or nearly all, of the games) was precisely the lateness of castling. Around the twelfth move of one such simultaneous display the situation was as follows: the master had castled on eighteen of the boards and not yet on two, while his opponents had castled on three boards but not on the rest. The result: 20-0 to the master – a real massacre! This is a typical example which indicates the disadvantages resulting from a delay in castling. In other simultaneous displays, where masters had a harder task and poorer results, the statistics on castling, taken around the twelfth to fifteenth moves, on the whole showed smaller discrepancies.

The general rule that one should castle as soon as possible is therefore quite in order, though it must at once be emphasized that there are also many exceptions to it. Every chess player of greater experience is well acquainted with those particular situations when it is correct to postpone castling or when it is altogether unnecessary. To make the matter clearer, I shall set out some situations of this kind and support them with examples:

1) *Castling is postponed* or not carried out at all, because some other *action* is more useful. This might be quite simply the capture of an opponent's piece, the spoiling of his position, or, indeed, an attack. If such an attack is sufficiently strong and profitable, the attacker often never castles, because he is victorious first. This kind of situation needs no particular examples.

2) *Castling is postponed, because for the time being it is still dangerous.* It is better to prepare it by removing the danger first, e.g. by exchanging the opponent's threatening pieces or by some other manoeuvre.

As an example of the dangers of castling too early, let us take the following variation of the Giuoco Piano.

1 e4 e5 2 ♘f3 ♘c6 3 ♗c4 ♗c5 4 d3 ♘f6 5 ♗g5 h6 6 ♗h4 d6 7 0-0?

At this point castling is premature and incorrect. There is a danger of Black's replying ...g5 and following up with a pawn attack against White's castled position; this danger ought to be averted first. 7 ♘c3 is a step in this direction; if Black continues with 7...0-0? 8 ♘d5 g5, then White can reply 9 ♘xg5! ♘xd5 10 ♕h5 hxg5 11 ♗xg5 with an overwhelming attack. Moreover, if Black answers 7 ♘c3 with 7...g5 8 ♗g3 and then ...♗g4 or ...h5!?, the situation is less dangerous because *White has not yet castled* and can therefore prepare to castle on the queenside, which is not threatened.

7...g5 8 ♗g3 h5! 9 ♘xg5 h4! *(D)*

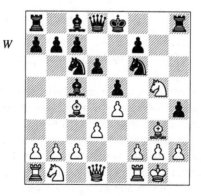

Black does not worry about the consequences of ♘xf7 but continues his attack consistently. In fact, he gives up his queen for the bishop on g3; this would not be a good exchange if White had not castled, but against the castled position the attack is decisive.

10 ♘xf7 hxg3 11 ♘xd8

If 11 hxg3, then 11...♕e7 12 ♘xh8 ♕h7 followed by ...♘g4, with a decisive attack.

11...♗g4 12 ♘f7 ♖xh2! 13 ♕d2 ♘d4 14 ♘c3 ♘f3+ 15 gxf3 ♗xf3 16 ♕h6 ♖g2+ 17 ♔h1 ♖xf2+ 18 ♔g1 ♖g2+ 19 ♔h1 ♖g1#

3) *The player does not castle at once* because, although he is able to castle on one side, he actually wishes to castle on the other side and needs to make further preparations. Alternatively, he delays until his opponent castles, and only then decides which side to castle. If he is aiming for an attack, he may decide to castle on the opposite side to his opponent; if he is aiming to forestall an attack, then he will more likely castle on the same side as his opponent.

There are many examples in the games of the masters of this kind of pause before castling. It is assumed, of course, that this pause does not entail any dangers. In open positions such dangers are more frequent than in closed ones.

The following situation will serve as an example of this pause before castling.

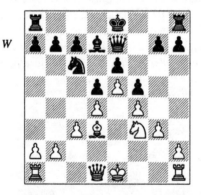

It is White's move and he may, if he wishes, castle short immediately. But he calculates as follows: after 1 0-0 Black will play ...0-0, and then how can I attack him? The pieces by themselves can achieve nothing in this blocked position; h3 and g4 still need to be played and must be prepared by ♕d2. But in the meantime Black will consolidate his position on the kingside (e.g. by means of ...g6 and ...♖f8-f7-g7) after which the attack will have lost its power. There is no doubt that for an attack based on g4, White's king is not well placed at g1, and it is better for that purpose to castle on the queenside and then deploy the rooks on the g- and h-files. However, if White chooses 1 ♕d2 and then 2 0-0-0, Black can play

2...0-0-0, whereupon the attack with g4 no longer applies; White will have to play a hasty b4, in which case it will be quickly seen that his king is badly placed on c1. Consequently, he must put off castling and wait. White therefore plays 1 ♕e2, and if 1...0-0, then 2 0-0-0, while if 1...0-0-0, then 2 0-0. He castles on the opposite side from Black in order to get the maximum freedom for carrying out his attack.

4) *Castling may be postponed,* and perhaps forgone forever, in certain positions where the centre is permanently blocked.

The reason for being able to postpone castling in such positions is, of course, that the pawns form an obstruction in the centre and so make it impossible to open the central files and diagonals without painful sacrifices. With the centre blocked, the kings are also safer in the middle, at least for some time. The logical course of attack in such cases tends to be on the unblocked flanks, and there are times when the king is more exposed by being in a castled position on the wing than in the middle, where it is protected by the blocked pawns.

A convenient example to illustrate this can be obtained by re-examining the above diagram, which we ought to do anyway because we left White's move 1 ♕e2 unanswered. Black's best reply also consists of a postponement of castling, e.g. 1...a6 or 1...♘d8. The postponement of castling is feasible for both sides in this position, and for a very obvious reason: the pronounced blockade in the centre. Attacks can only take place down the flanks and as a result the kings are at the moment relatively safe in the middle. Play from this position might develop as follows:

1 ♕e2 ♘d8 2 h3 ♘f7 3 ♕d2 0-0-0

It is less dangerous for Black to castle on the queenside now; if White plays 4 0-0, Black replies 4...♖dg8, threatening ...g5, while after 4 0-0-0 the danger of an attack on the flank disappears and Black can relax.

In this case the preliminary skirmish has in fact ended with castling, but there are blocked positions where castling does not occur at all and the kings stay permanently in the middle. Even in the above position White has the alternative of not castling and instead co-ordinating his rooks by ♔f2; later on he can even take his king up to e3.

5) *Castling is unnecessary, because the endgame is already not far off,* in which case the king is well placed in the middle of the board.

These cases too are not infrequent in master chess; we shall select two examples from opening theory, where the white king forfeits the right to castle as a result of the exchange of queens.

1 d4 d5 2 c4 e6 3 ♘c3 ♘f6 4 ♗g5 ♘bd7 5 e3 ♗e7 6 ♘f3 0-0 7 ♖c1 c6 8 ♗d3 dxc4 9 ♗xc4 ♘d5 *(D)*

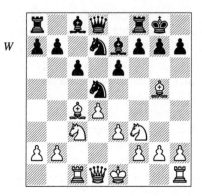

Capablanca's freeing manoeuvre in the Orthodox Defence to the Queen's Gambit.

10 ♗xe7 ♕xe7 11 ♘e4 ♕b4+ 12 ♕d2 ♕xd2+ 13 ♔xd2

This variation was played in a number of games from the 1927 World Championship Match between Capablanca and Alekhine. White does not worry about castling, as the position is approaching an endgame and the king is fairly safe in the middle of the board.

A second example is supplied by my analysis of a variation of the Slav Defence.

1 d4 d5 2 c4 c6 3 ♘c3 dxc4 4 e4 e5 5 dxe5!

In my *Modern Opening Theory* I suggested that this was better than 5 ♗xc4.

5...♕xd1+ 6 ♔xd1! *(D)*

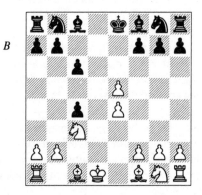

White could have retained his right to castle by playing 6 ♘xd1; however, it is better to use the king since castling is no longer necessary in this position, and it is more important that the knight should remain on c3. For example, after 6 ♘xd1 b5 7 a4 Black is not obliged to continue with ...b4, whereas after 6 ♔xd1 b5 7 a4 he has nothing better than 7...b4, whereupon White obtains the advantage by 8 ♘b1 ♗a6 9 ♘d2.

In this instance White, in playing ♔xd1, does not gain the 'centralizing tempo' which he did on the thirteenth move in the previous example, but he prefers to lose his chance to castle just to keep his knight on c3.

Many occasions for renouncing castling in this way arise in practice, but one should avoid taking the king too far afield. This comment applies to so-called 'queenless middlegames' and not to true endgames, in which the king is nearly always better placed in the centre. One should keep one's eyes open and weigh up the opponent's opportunities for an attack on one's king, for they can easily develop in 'queenless middlegames'. Safety from attack and a genuine prospect of making further piece exchanges – these are the two important criteria affecting a decision on the forfeiture of the right to castle.

The cases I have mentioned in which castling can be justifiably postponed or dispensed with are meant to induce the reader to think about the problem more deeply, for every rule in chess should be applied flexibly. To make a correct decision on exactly when to castle one needs considerable knowledge and experience.

Finally, one more hint: even in cases where there is justification for a delay in castling, it is still a good thing to have the opportunity to castle quickly on one side at least. When the pieces have been moved out on one side of the back rank, we have an opportunity to castle 'at hand', and this castling will cost just one tempo. However, if there is one piece which has still not left the back rank then obviously castling will cost us two tempi. Now there is a big difference between one tempo and two, if one's opponent can discover some concealed means for a sudden attack on the king before it has reached its castled residence! For this reason it is good policy to get ready to castle as soon as possible, and then consider whether it can still be put off for a while.

The basic elements of the attack on the castled king

The attack on the castled king is a particular type of mating attack, but in practice it is the most important, since castling takes place in the majority of games.

In considering an attack of this kind, we must begin with a general survey of the action involved, acquainting ourselves, on the one hand, with the basic characteristics of the actual *castled position* itself and, on the other, with the good and bad aspects of an attack on that position.

The castled position consists of the castled king and the protective pawns and also to a certain extent the pieces which are in the vicinity or in some other way connected with the formation.

This structure should be regarded as a *positional formation,* i.e. a group of pieces having one or more fairly permanent features. One could also go further and say that castled positions are, as a rule, *passive* rather than active positional formations, i.e. their more permanent feature stems ultimately from a certain immobility of the pieces, and not in their mobility, as is the case when the pieces are in strong positions. (This is, of course, the general rule, but in practice the castled position may also contain a piece in a strong position, for example a fianchettoed bishop.)

The passive nature of the castled position results from the lack of mobility of the king, and this is indirectly transferred to the other pieces in the position as well; the first to be affected are the pawns, which 'may not be moved, if the castled position is not to be weakened', and which are as a result made indirectly immobile. If they in fact move from their initial squares and so create weaknesses in the castled position, these weaknesses result from the reduced options entailed by the advance. (A pawn at h2 controls the square g3 and also has it in its power, by advancing, to govern g4, g5, g6, etc. If it moves to h3, then, out of its total number of actual or potential areas of control, it loses that over g3, and so loses part of its active potential.) Even the pieces associated with the castled position are affected to a certain extent by the general immobility of the formation, whether functionally because of the need for a certain square to be defended or spatially because of the difficulty involved in their centralization.

The structure and the degree of weakness of the opponent's castled position also influence the way in which the attacker employs his pieces in a mating attack. The variety here is extremely wide, ranging from lightning assaults to purely positional manoeuvres and from uncompromising charges to cautious preparations, in which the player really only flirts with an attack on the king in order to restrict his opponent's options. More will be said on these and similar points later on.

However, the basic weaknesses of the castled position which I have described also contain one positive feature which becomes apparent when an attempt is made to exploit them. This positive feature derives from the fact that the castled position is always a decentralized one, so that as a rule any attack on it demands a greater or lesser decentralization of the attacker's pieces. This factor is particularly important in that the main positional rule for normal play is that pieces should be centralized. There is, then, a *basic contradiction* between consistent centralization and an attack on the castled king, and it is here that the principal risk of such an attack lies. If the attack does not succeed, the fact that some of the attacker's pieces are out of position as a rule tells against the attacker.

The reader will come to understand the deeper significance of this argument in the final chapters of this book.

To understand the attack on the castled king we shall start with the basic factors involved, spatial, material and temporal (the method I applied in my *Introduction to Chess* and *School of Combinations*). It is true that in every action which takes place on the chessboard all these three factors can be observed together, since each move has its own spatial, material and temporal significance; however, the emphasis of one's actual observation may be in one case on the spatial, in another on the material, and in a third on the temporal, aspect. For this reason, the separation of the different factors is the most effective and the clearest method for teaching purposes.

The attack on the castled king in the past

At the time when modern chess was in its infancy, i.e. after the reforms of the rules in the last quarter of the fifteenth century, the attack on the castled king did not yet exist, or at any rate there was no trace of it in the games recorded. The castling move itself was at that time only in the process of being created (some were still using the mediaeval king's jump, while others were castling but in two moves – i.e. first ♖h1-f1, and then on the next move ♔e1-g1, etc.) and combinative technique – especially with the 'new pieces', the queen and the knight – was still fairly primitive, so that the decision in a game was usually reached by cruder methods than by attacking the castled king, e.g. by capturing on f7 before castling had taken place or simply by winning material. The first recorded instance of an attack on the castled king occurs in the so-called Paris MS., which originated about 1500, a more mature and fuller development of Lucena's work of 1497, the oldest printed book on modern chess. In the course of analysing an opening (one later given the name of Philidor Defence) the author arrives at the position at the top of the following page:

Black, to move, plays:

1...g5! 2 ♘h2 h5

He uses his pawns to carry out an attack on the king, a plan suited to this position as it takes advantage of White's weakness on h3.

3 f3?

A mistake, which Lucena makes 'in accordance with the thought of his times'. White could have defended himself satisfactorily if he had immediately played 3 b5!.

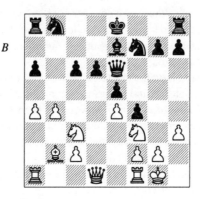

3...♘h6 4 b5 ♖g8 5 ♕e2?

A further mistake. White should at once have played 5 bxc6 ♘xc6 6 ♕d5 ♕d7 7 ♗a3, when Black, pinned down at c6 and g8, would have had to refrain from going straight ahead with ...g4 and consolidate his position first.

5...g4 6 fxg4 hxg4 7 ♘xg4?

Poor defensive technique! After 7 ♔h1 Black would have had a difficult task, for 7...gxh3 would not do any good because of 8 ♕h5+ followed by ♕xh3.

7...♘xg4 8 hxg4 ♖xg4 9 bxc6 ♘xc6 10 ♘d5 ♗d8 *(D)*

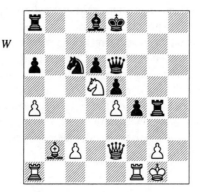

11 c4?

White could have put up more resistance by 11 ♖a3. No real advantage would come of 11 ♕c4 because of 11...♔d7. Naturally, 11 c4? is very weak and quite inappropriate, since it does nothing to help the defence and only obstructs the diagonal for the white queen.

11...♖a7 12 ♖f2 ♖h7 13 ♕d1? ♕h6?!

Black's technique is poor too. After 13...♖gh4 14 ♖f1 ♕g6!, White would be caught in a mating net.

14 ♔f1 ♕h5 15 ♕f3 ♕g6 16 ♕d3 ♖h1+?

The manuscript follows on from here with 17 ♔e2 ♖xa1 18 ♗xa1 ♖xg2 and concludes: 'Black has the better prospects'. To all appearances the author was mainly concerned with the win of a pawn, forgetting that the primary aim of an attack on the castled king is mate! By 16...♖g3 17 ♕c2 ♕g4 18 ♔e1 ♗a5+ the matter could have been brought to an end considerably more quickly.

The advance in technique in attacking the castled king was extremely slow throughout the sixteenth century, and it was only at the beginning of the seventeenth that Greco in his manual indicated some combinations which, though new then, now strike modern minds as nothing more than elementary tricks. As an example of the technical level reached by Greco, let us look at a continuation from his book.

1 e4 e5 2 ♘f3 ♘c6 3 ♗c4 ♗c5 4 0-0 ♘f6 5 ♖e1 0-0 6 c3 ♕e7?

Greco had not yet realized the importance of keeping control of the centre and gives Black this weak move instead of the correct 6...d6.

7 d4 exd4 8 e5!

This is even stronger than 8 cxd4[1].

8...♘g4 *(D)*

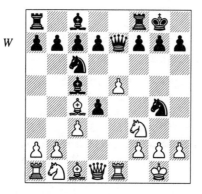

---

1   As we shall see, this comment is incorrect. After 8 cxd4 White has a clear advantage, since Black has no compensation for White's central control. The move 8 e5 is a mistake which gives Black at least equality.

9 cxd4?

Weakly played. By 9 ♗g5 (an intermediate move!) 9...♕e8 10 cxd4 White would have obtained a winning position. (Greco and other authors right up to the middle of the nineteenth century did not see the intermediate move 9 ♗g5, so that 8 e5 came to be regarded in the textbooks as a mistake![1])

9...♘xd4! 10 ♘xd4 ♕h4

This is Greco's trick. White has two exposed spots, at h2 and f2.

11 ♗e3

Greco naturally also gives the continuation 11 ♘f3 ♕xf2+ followed by 12...♕g1+ and a smothered mate by the knight at f2.

11...♕xh2+ 12 ♔f1 ♕h1+?!

In carrying his attack further Greco does not notice all the finesses. 12...♘xe3+ followed by ...d6 would have been better here[2].

13 ♔e2 ♕xg2 14 ♖g1 ♘xe3 15 ♔xe3?

This way White loses two valuable pawns, and Greco concludes his analysis with **15...♗xd4+ 16 ♔xd4 ♕xf2+ 17 ♔c3 ♕e3+ 18 ♗d3 ♕xe5+**, with advantage to Black.

Instead of 15 ♔xe3?, the correct continuation is 15 ♖xg2 ♘xd1 16 ♘f5, when Black must find the reply 16...d5! 17 ♘xg7 ♗h3!, if he is to retain the better prospects (though even here there is still some uncertainty after 18 ♖g3 ♗xf2 19 ♖xh3 dxc4 20 ♘d2, etc.). If he played 16...♘xb2 17 ♘h6+ ♔h8 18 ♘xf7+, he would have to consent to a draw, since 18...♖xf7 is probably not a good idea[3].

In step with the general advance in chess skill there can also be seen an advance in the technique of attacking the castled king, first with Philidor and then, particularly, with Morphy. The romantic reaction which followed led to the

---

1   Black should meet 9 ♗g5 by 9...dxc3!. After 10 ♗xe7 ♗xf2+ 11 ♔f1 cxb2 12 ♘c3 (12 ♘a3 ♗e1 also favours Black) 12...♗xe1 (12...bxa1♕ 13 ♕xa1 ♗xe1 14 ♘d5 is unclear) 13 ♘d5 ♘xe7 14 ♘xe7+ ♔h8 Black has a clear advantage in view of the threats of 15...bxa1♕ and 15...♘e3+. White's strongest move is 9 b4!, but an analysis of the resulting complications (which lead to a roughly equal position) would take us too far afield. Perhaps those old analysts knew a thing or two after all!

2   A baffling comment, as after 12...♘xe3+ 13 fxe3 d6 14 ♘f3 White starts to consolidate his extra material. Greco's continuation appears best to me.

3   After 18...♖xf7 19 ♗xf7 b6!, followed by ...♗a6+ and developing the rook, Black is virtually winning – three pawns for the exchange and a pair of active bishops is surely too much.

development of a number of particular types of sacrificial attacks, but without in general reaching Morphy's level. Steinitz was concerned with perfecting defensive technique, and his influence on the style of the period was slowly beginning to make the attack on the castled king fade from master chess. Lasker, too, the new World Champion, was even in his youth already turning away from forcing such attacks, preferring to aim at perfection in the endgame. At the end of the century, however, there were three great masters who defended the thesis of attacking chess and who in doing so clearly showed themselves to be supporters of the attack on the castled king. These were Chigorin, Tarrasch and Pillsbury, each of whom in his own way helped to enrich the technique of attack. Chigorin illustrated particularly the power of the positional sacrifice in his games; Tarrasch's thesis was that the rapid development of the pieces and a strong centre were the basic requisites for an attack on the castled king; while Pillsbury created a kind of synthesis of the attacking style and the positional and endgame play of Steinitz and Lasker. In other words, the American grandmaster showed how a rapid switch can be made from attack to a simplification which gives the better ending. In this way all the basic elements of a perfected technique for attacking the castled king were set out, and after a short period of stagnation in the first two decades of the present century there followed the real blossoming of the dynamic style with the arrival of Capablanca and Alekhine. This development is still relevant to the theme of the attack on the castled king today, and more will be said about it at the end of the book.

4 Mating patterns

Spatial relationships in a mating attack can be observed by examining mating patterns, focal-points, and the roles played by the ranks, files, and diagonals. In this chapter we shall be concerned with mating patterns. This choice has a practical justification in that mating patterns can be more easily remembered than the ways leading up to mate. For this reason mating patterns, even though they occur only at the very end of a mating attack, are fundamental for practical purposes because of the excellent mnemonic assistance which they provide to the player.

Our first concern is for the most common mating patterns; these hardly ever occur in the middle of the board, but they are very frequent in the castling area, i.e. near the king's position on the edge of the board.

Typical mates without enemy pieces

There are a very large number of typical mates of this kind and most of them are elementary, so we shall consider only a few examples. (For the sake of greater clarity the diagrams are shown without the white king.)

In the first position White, to move, has a choice between two typical mates:

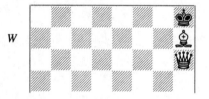

1) **1 &g6+ &g8 2 &h7+ &f8 3 &f7#.**
2) **1 &f5+ &g8 2 &e6#.**

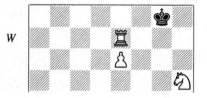

In this position there are again two possible mates, depending on how Black replies.

If **1 ♘f6+ ♚h8**, then **2 ♖h7#** (the so-called Arab mate, because it is recorded in Arabic manuscripts of the ninth century). If **1 ♘f6+ ♚f8**, then there follows **2 ♖f7#**, a mating pattern which is worth remembering.

Another mate which should be known is this one with two knights, but if there are no other pieces on the board then it cannot be forced.

Typical mates with enemy pieces

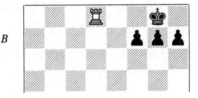

The so-called back-row mate by the rook (or queen) is one of the most typical mating patterns.

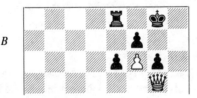

Of the fairly large number of typical mates with queen and pawn this one is given first. Black is to move; he cannot escape mate, since he is threatened by 1 ♕h6 and 2 ♕g7#. If he plays 1...♚h7, then 2 ♕h4+ and 3 ♕h6, etc. If Black had a pawn on h7 he would have the defence 1...♚h8 2 ♕h6 ♖g8.

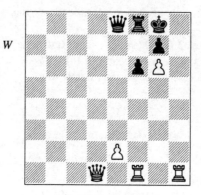

Damiano's Mate

This is a position from the book (1512) by Damiano, a Portuguese apothecary, one of the first authors in the literature of European chess. White mates in five moves.

1 ♖h8+ ♔xh8 2 ♖h1+ ♔g8 3 ♖h8+ ♔xh8 4 ♕h1+ ♔g8 5 ♕h7#.

The rook sacrifices were naturally introduced to make the essential point clear: the queen must reach the h-file with gain of tempo.

The pattern of Damiano's mate can be seen more clearly in the following examples.

1 ♕h5 ♗e7 2 ♕h7+ ♔f8 3 ♕h8#.

In this case a bishop has been placed on f8 and also a pawn on d6, with the result that the bishop can only move to e7, where it blocks the king's escape. The general theme of Damiano's mate, the pattern of which is characterized by a black pawn on g7 and a white pawn or bishop on g6, can be subjected to numerous variations.

The following diagram serves as a memory aid for mates with queen and rook: Black, to move, cannot avoid mate; if he plays 1...♔g7, then 2 ♕h6+ and 3 ♕h7#

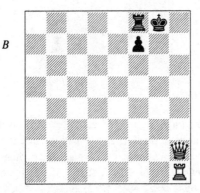

or 3 ♕h8#, while if 1...f6, then 2 ♕h7#. If Black has another pawn on g7 he can save himself from immediate mate by 1...f6, while if he has one on g6 he can extricate himself by 1...♚g7.

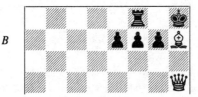

Of the mates with queen and bishop this position is worth remembering.

Black cannot save himself from mate, but if he plays 1...g6, White does not reply 2 ♗xg6+ (which is answered by 2...♚g7, and Black's king slips away) but 2 ♕h6, in which case there is no remedy against mate.

Smothered Mate

The smothered mate with queen and knight is a celebrated one: **1 ♘f7+ ♚g8 2 ♘h6+ ♚h8** (or 2...♚f8 3 ♕f7#) **3 ♕g8+! ♖xg8** (or 3...♘xg8) **4 ♘f7#.**

This position falls into category of typical mates, and it is useful to know the mating patterns which arise if Black tries to parry the threat of ♕h7#, e.g. with **1...♖b8**. If there is a black pawn on e7 or if the square is otherwise occupied by Black, then there follows **2 ♕h7+ ♔f8 3 ♕h8#**; if this is not so, mate can be achieved, for example, by **2 ♕xf7+ ♔h8 3 ♘e6 ♖g8 4 ♕h5#**.

Of the various attacking positions with queen and knight this scheme is also well worth remembering. On **1 ♘f6+**, Black replies **1...♔h8** and if **2 ♘h5+**, then **2...f6**.

If **1...♔g7**, White has a double check with **2 ♘e8+** (in some cases, depending on the arrangement of the other pieces, **2 ♘h5+** may be stronger) and after **2...♔h6 3 ♕f4+ g5 4 ♕f6+ ♔h5 5 ♘g7+** White only needs a pawn on g2 or h2 to force mate.

Greco's Mate

This position is also worth knowing; Black is forced to play **1...h6**, after which he is mated by **2 ♗xf7+ ♔h8 3 ♕g6! hxg5 4 ♕h5#**.

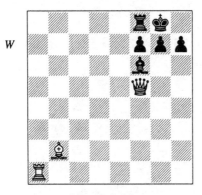

In the case of mating patterns with rook and bishop one should first of all get to know the above position. It is Black's move and he must try to parry ♖g5#; this cannot be achieved by 1...h6, because of 2 ♖xh6, which leaves him with no way out. So **1...♖c8 2 ♖g5+ ♔f8 3 ♖g7!**, and now too mate is unavoidable, for Black is unable to free the square d7 in time to provide the king with an escape square. If he did not have, for instance, the pawn on c6, he could play 3...♗c6 4 ♖xh7 ♔e8 and then 5 ♖h8+ could be met by 5...♔d7. One could replace Black's bishop and c6-pawn by a white pawn on c6 and a black one on c7; mate would still be unavoidable[1].

Morphy's Mate

The pattern of this mate with rook and bishop becomes clear in its final stage.

1 ♕xf6 gxf6 2 ♖g1+ ♔h8 3 ♗xf6#.

1   In the diagram position, Black can avoid mate by 1...♖a8 2 ♖g5+ ♔f8 3 ♖g7 ♖a4 4 ♖xh7 ♖g4. It is true to say that this defence is not often available in practical situations, but it is worth bearing in mind the idea of 'defending from behind' because it is often overlooked.

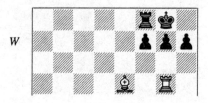

Morphy's Concealed Mate

A similar mating pattern occurs in this diagram: **1 ♖xg7+ ♔h8 2 ♖xf7+** (not 2 ♖g1+ because of 2...f6) **2...♔g8 3 ♖g7+ ♔h8 4 ♖g1+ ♖f6 5 ♗xf6#**.

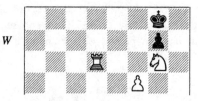

1 ♖d8+ ♔f7 (or 1...♔h7 2 ♖h8#) **2 ♖f8#** is a typical mating pattern well worth remembering.

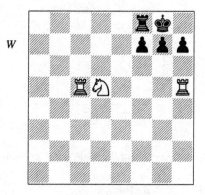

Anastasia's Mate

1 ♘e7+ ♔h8 2 ♖xh7+ ♔xh7 3 ♖h5#.

(The name comes from W. Heinse's novel *Anastasia and chess* (1803), in which this mate is recorded.)

Here the continuation ends with a typical mating pattern with a rook and pawn.

1 ♕g5 ♔h8 2 ♕h6 ♖g8 3 ♕xh7+ ♔xh7 4 ♖h1#.

'Blind swine'

If it is White's move, he mates with 1 ♖g7+, 2 ♖h7+, and 3 ♖bg7#. If Black is to move and plays **1...♖fd8**, White can neither force mate or even win. That is to say, after 2 ♖g7+ ♔h8 3 ♖h7+ ♔g8 4 ♖bg7+ ♔f8 5 ♖b7, Black simply plays 5...♔g8, 'questioning' the white rook and countering the threat of mate. (It depends of course on the distribution of the other pieces whether White can in fact win. In this position he can easily mate if he has a pawn on h4, for he plays 6 h5 followed by 7 h6, 8 ♖bg7+, and 9 ♖h8# – a mate which is worth remembering. In this line Black's pawn on f6 is actually a help to White. If it were not there, Black could get a draw after 6 h5 by playing 6...♖a6!.)

The pair of rooks which 'grunt out check' on the seventh rank but cannot get a sight of mate were once nicknamed *'blind swine'* by Janowski.

An acquaintance with typical mating patterns is extremely useful when making a quick survey of the board in an actual game. The addition of further material to the position can be especially useful, for then one can see which changes help to prevent mate and which enrich the mating patterns in new situations.

Less usual mating patterns

Of the large number of less usual, and even exotic, mating patterns, I have chosen ones which bear some nickname or which can easily be given one.

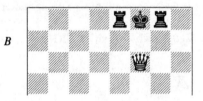

Epaulette Mate

The epaulettes are, of course, the two black rooks on the king's shoulders. The next mate also gets its name from its outward appearance.

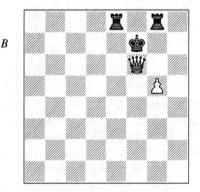

'Swallow's tail'

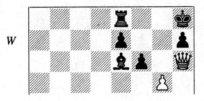

Pawn Mate

1 g6 ♗g8 2 g7#. On 1 g6 ♔g8 2 ♕xh7+ ♔f8 we get yet another mating pattern with 3 g7+ ♔f7 4 g8♕# (mate with two queens).

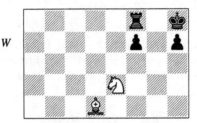

1 ♘xf7+ ♔g8 2 ♘h6#. Or **1 ♘g6+ ♔g8 2 ♘e7#.**

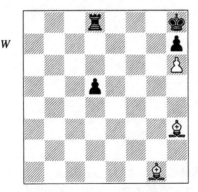

Mate with Two Bishops

1 ♗e6 d4 2 ♗h2 and **3 ♗e5#.**

This could also be called Rubinstein's mate, after the famous game Rotlewi-Rubinstein, in which mate with two bishops was the basic motif of the attack.

Boden's Mate

This position is from the game Schulder-Boden, London 1853[1], in which the following mate with two bishops was recorded for the first time; it is not uncommon after castling queenside. Black plays: **1...♛xc3+! 2 bxc3 ♝a3#**.

Pillsbury's Mate

1 ♖xg7+ ♚h8 2 ♖g8+! ♚xg8 3 ♖g1+ and mate.

This is really a variation on Morphy's mate, contrived in such a way that it is the rook which mates and not the bishop, which is under attack from Black's rook.

_____

1   In the original book this example was incorrectly given as Macdonell-Boden, 1869 and Black's rook on e8 was missing.

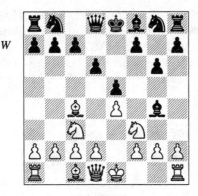

Legall's Mate

Legall was Philidor's teacher and this position arose in the game Legall-St Brie, Paris 1750. The moves leading up to the diagram were **1 e4 e5 2 ♘f3 d6 3 ♗c4 ♗g4 4 ♘c3 g6?** and Legall now played: **5 ♘xe5! ♗xd1?** (5...♗e6 would have been better) **6 ♗xf7+ ♔e7 7 ♘d5#**. (This is of course a case of an attack before castling, but the example is given here for purely practical reasons.)

The next mate is similar to Greco's, but differs in that the attacker (here Black) opens the h-file not only for his opponent but also for himself. It arose in the game Anderssen-Max Lange, Breslau 1859 after **1 e4 e5 2 ♘f3 ♘c6 3 ♗b5 ♘d4 4 ♘xd4 exd4 5 ♗c4 ♘f6 6 e5 d5 7 ♗b3 ♗g4 8 f3 ♘e4 9 0-0 d3 10 fxg4?**[1] *(D)*

Max Lange's Mate

---

1   10 ♕e1! would have favoured White.

Play proceeded as follows: **10...♗c5+ 11 ♔h1 ♘g3+ 12 hxg3 ♕g5 13 ♖f5 h5!** and now if 14 ♖xg5, then 14...hxg4+ and mate; in the game White played **14 gxh5** but resigned after **14...♕xf5 15 g4 ♕f2 0-1**.

The next position arose in the game Réti-Tartakower, Vienna 1910 after the moves **1 e4 c6 2 d4 d5 3 ♘c3 dxe4 4 ♘xe4 ♘f6 5 ♕d3 e5 6 dxe5 ♕a5+ 7 ♗d2 ♕xe5 8 0-0-0 ♘xe4** *(D)*

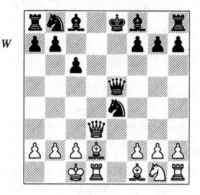

Réti's Mate

The game concluded: **9 ♕d8+! ♔xd8 10 ♗g5+ ♔c7** (or 10...♔e8 11 ♖d8#) **11 ♗d8#**.

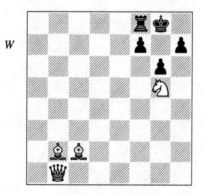

Blackburne's Mate

For this mate the attacker needs three minor pieces (two bishops and a knight) and usually a queen as well, which is sacrificed.

1 ♕h1 h5 2 ♕xh5! gxh5 3 ♗h7#. This mating pattern is named after Blackburne, who was the first to mate in this way.

5 Focal-points

The series of examples examined in the chapter on mating patterns has given us a good idea of the difficulties a defender encounters when his forces (especially the pawns in front of his castled king) are poorly placed and when the attacker's one aim is to fill the various 'holes and cracks' in the weakened enemy defences with his own pieces and thus obtain an even tighter grip. It follows from this that the squares in the immediate vicinity of the king, where the drama of the mating attack usually reaches its climax, play a special role. If the attacker threatens mate or actually mates on these squares, they are *mating focal-points,* but if he only harries the king from them or uses them as points from which to break into the castled position, they are called *strategic* or *auxiliary focal-points.* It may be that there is more than one mating focal-point, and in that case we speak of *compound focal-points.* If there are many focal-points (both mating and strategic) on squares of the same colour, we speak of a *network of weak squares.*

Generally speaking, every focal-point is a *weak square* in the defender's territory and a potentially strong one for the attacker. In addition to the focal-points there are also other squares in the castling area which have a specific function, e.g. *blocked squares,* particularly those occupied by the defender's pawns, and also any weak squares on which the attacker can safely post his pieces.

As an illustration of this, take the following position (which we have already seen earlier). Here we have the following scheme:

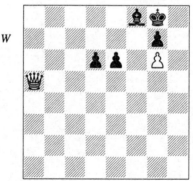

- mating squares: g8 and f8;
- mating focal-points: h7 and h8;
- auxiliary focal-point: h7 (after Black parries mate by ...♗e7)
- attacker's strong squares: f7, g6 and h7;
- blocked squares: g7 and later e7.

The focal-point at g7

As usual, when referring to specific squares we assume that White is the attacker. It is understood that if Black is the attacker, then the discussion applies equally to the square g2.

The most important focal-points where castling kingside is concerned are g7 and h7, since these squares are more accessible to the attacker than the others in the castling area. Of the two, h7 is the more frequent object of attack (since it comes under fire from the bishop operating from d3, a natural point of development, while the king's knight can reach g5, for example, more easily than f5 or h5). However, *attacks against g7 are the more dangerous.* The reasons for this are very simple: the queen can mate more easily from g7 than h7 (owing to the king's ability to flee to f8), but as well as this, a weakness on g7 usually brings with it two more on f6 and h6, while one on h7 generally only entails a single extra one at g6. Every player of any experience is well acquainted with this fact and knows that ...g6 involves a greater weakening than ...h6. On the other hand, h7 is usually harder to defend than g7, which the king's bishop can support in two ways (from f8 or f6).

The next position illustrates a typical example of an action against the square g7:

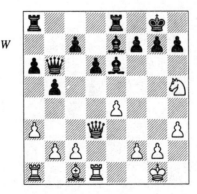

White, to play, has excellent prospects for an attack on g7. His knight is already observing the square, while his queen and bishop are in a position to threaten it in one move. An extremely useful point is the fact that the queen has the choice of attacking from either c3 or g3. Nevertheless, the situation is not quite as simple as that, and White must be prepared to sacrifice his bishop on h6 if he is to obtain a winning position; by simply playing 1 ♕g3, White would only gain a relatively small advantage, e.g. 1...g6 2 ♗g5 ♕c5 3 ♘f6+ ♗xf6 4 ♗xf6, when Black can counter with 4...h6 followed by ...♔h7. Only 1 ♗h6! guarantees complete success; the main reason why it is better to move the bishop rather than the queen is that in order to attack g7 the bishop has only the one move to h6, whereas the queen has a choice between c3 and g3. Thus the bishop enters the fray first, while the queen waits to see which will be better, depending on Black's reply. Thus:

1 ♗h6! g6

If 1...gxh6, then 2 ♕c3 f6 (if 2...♗f8, then 3 ♘f6+ leads to a quick conclusion) 3 ♕g3+ ♗g4 (otherwise the queen mates on g7) 4 ♕xg4+ ♔f7 5 ♕g7+ ♔e6 6 ♘f4+ ♔d7 7 ♘d5 followed by 8 ♘xf6+. In this variation the queen is most effective if it goes first to c3 and then to g3.

If 1...♗f8, then White plays 2 ♗xg7 ♗xg7 3 ♕g3 ♔f8 4 ♕xg7+ ♔e7 5 ♕g5+ ♔f8 6 ♖d3 or 6 ♘f6.

2 ♕c3 f6 3 ♘xf6+ and White wins, for after 3...♗xf6 4 ♕xf6 Black has no defence against mate on g7.

In order not to be unfair to Black, who tends to suffer in books such as this, here are some actual cases where White came to grief on the analogous square – g2.

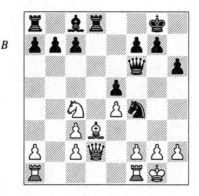

B

This position arose in the game Coria-Capablanca, Buenos Aires 1914. Black, to move, attacks g2:

1...♗h3! 2 ♘e3 ♗xg2 3 ♘f5

White played this in desperation; if 3 ♘xg2 ♕g5 4 f3, Black plays 4...♘h3+ and wins White's queen – a typical trick in positions such as this.

3...♗xe4 4 ♘g3 ♘h3#.

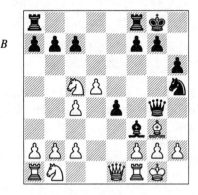

This position is taken from Field-Tenner, New York 1933. It is Black's move.

1...♘f4 2 ♘xe4[1] ♕h3! 0-1

The attack on g2, with its threat of mate, is carried on regardless. White resigned since he sees that 3 gxh3 is followed by 3...♘xh3#.

The following position arose in the game Boleslavsky-Ufimtsev, Semi-finals USSR Championship, Omsk 1944. The Soviet master and geologist Ufimtsev, playing Black, overcame his great opponent as follows:

1...♘e4! 2 ♕a5

After 2 ♗xb6 ♘xd2 White cannot play 3 ♘xd2 because of the attack on g2, so he would lose either his bishop on b6 or his knight on f3.

2...♖hg8 3 ♘e1

Not 3 ♗xb6 because of 3...♖xg2+ 4 ♔h1 ♖xh2+ 5 ♘xh2 ♘xf2#.

3...♖xg2+ 4 ♘xg2 ♘d2!

Black threatens 5...♖xg2+ 6 ♔h1 ♖xh2+ 7 ♔g1 ♖h1#. If 5 f3, then 5...♕xe3+ wins.

---

1   It is interesting to note that White cannot save himself, even with another second move, e.g. 2 ♘d3 ♘e2+ 3 ♔h1 ♗xg2+ 4 ♔xg2 ♕f3+ 5 ♔h3 exd3 6 ♕d2 g5 or 2 ♕e3 ♘xg2 3 ♕d2 ♘f4.

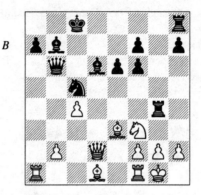

5 ♕d5 ♗xd5 6 cxd5 ♕xb2 7 ♗xd2 ♕xa1 8 ♗f3 ♗xh2+ 0-1

White has escaped being mated, but has to surrender owing to the great material losses he has suffered.

The next two games illustrate the attack on the castled king, with g2 (or g7) as the focal-point.

Vygodchikov – Alekhine
Correspondence Game, 1908/9
Ruy Lopez

1 e4 e5 2 ♘f3 ♘c6 3 ♗b5 a6 4 ♗a4 ♘f6 5 0-0 ♗c5

The Møller Variation, against which White can gain a slight advantage by playing 6 c3. In continuing 6 ♘xe5, as he does here, White makes the defence somewhat easier for Black.

6 ♘xe5 ♘xe5 7 d4 ♘xe4! 8 ♖e1 ♗e7 9 ♖xe4 ♘g6 10 ♘c3?!

10 c4 is stronger.

10...0-0 11 ♘d5 ♗d6 12 ♕f3 f5?

Instead of this weak move, correct is 12...b5! 13 ♗b3 ♗b7 with the better prospects for Black.

13 ♗b3! ♔h8

13...fxe4 is impossible because of 14 ♘e7+ ♔h8 15 ♘xg6+ and 16 ♕h3+. Alekhine now has an inferior position.

14 ♖e2 f4 *(D)*

15 c4?

The beginning of a bad plan. It admittedly brings White material gains but at the same time exposes him to a relentless attack on his castled position. Correct

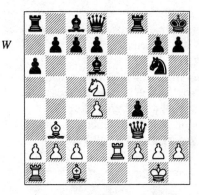

was 15 ♗d2 c6 (after 15...♘h4 16 ♕h5 f3 White can happily reply 17 ♖e4) 16 ♗b4! ♗xb4 17 ♘xb4 d5 18 ♖ae1 and White has the advantage[1].

15...c6 16 c5?

A further mistake; 16 ♘c3 would have been preferable.

16...♗b8 17 ♘b6 d5!

Now all Black's pieces come into play except the rook, and this Alekhine logically gives up, for he does not need it.

18 ♘xa8 ♘h4 *(D)*

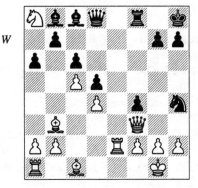

19 ♕c3

If 19 ♕h5 then 19...g6 20 ♕h6 ♗g4 threatening both 21...♗xe2 and 21...♘f5[2].

---

1   Vuković's line loses a piece after 17...a5 18 ♘d3 a4 19 ♗c4 d5, so the move actually played is probably best.

19...f3 20 ♖e5

In an attempt to contain Black's attack, White gives back some of the extra material, but there is no longer any way out.

20...♗xe5 21 dxe5 ♘xg2

Naturally, Black takes on g2 with the knight and not the pawn, for he does not want to block the square g2, which is to be the focal-point of the attack.

22 ♕d4 ♕d7 23 e6 ♕xe6 24 ♗d2 ♕g6 25 ♗c2

White gives up still more, but the destruction is not halted!

25...♕xc2 26 ♔h1 ♕g6 27 ♖g1 ♗h3 28 ♘b6 *(D)*

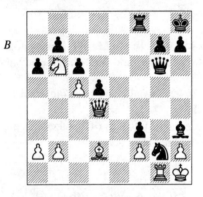

28...♘f4

Black no longer plays for mate but instead simplifies to obtain a winning position.

29 ♖xg6 ♗g2+ 30 ♖xg2 fxg2+ 31 ♔g1 ♘e2+ 32 ♔xg2 ♘xd4 0-1

Alekhine – Lasker
Zurich, 1934
Queen's Gambit Declined, Orthodox Defence

1 d4 d5 2 c4 e6 3 ♘c3 ♘f6 4 ♘f3 ♗e7 5 ♗g5 ♘bd7 6 e3 0-0 7 ♖c1 c6 8 ♗d3 dxc4 9 ♗xc4 ♘d5 10 ♗xe7 ♕xe7 11 ♘e4

Alekhine's move; it is equally as good as 11 0-0.

11...♘5f6 12 ♘g3 e5

---

2   Alekhine gave 20...♘f5 followed by 21...♘xd4 in his notes. Indeed, after Vuković's 20...♗g4, White may play 21 ♖e5! ♗xe5 22 dxe5, threatening 23 ♗xf4, when Black's attack collapses.

12...♛b4+ 13 ♕d2 ♕xd2+ is sounder, with a queenless middlegame, which Capablanca drew as Black in seven games against Alekhine in their 1927 World Championship Match.

13 0-0 exd4 *(D)*

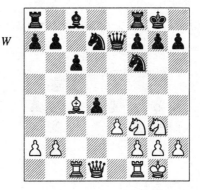

14 ♘f5

This move is slightly weaker than the straightforward 14 exd4, which poses Black problems.

14...♕d8 15 ♘3xd4 ♘e5 16 ♗b3 ♗xf5 17 ♘xf5 ♕b6

Unnecessarily misplacing the queen. Correct was 17...g6 18 ♘d6 (or 18 ♕d6 ♖e8) 18...♕e7, when Black can put up a good defence.

18 ♕d6 ♘ed7 19 ♖fd1 ♖ad8 20 ♕g3 *(D)*

The decisive battle for the focal-point g7 begins.

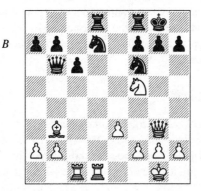

20...g6 21 ♕g5 ♚h8

White threatened 22 ♖d6; if 21...♛b5, then 22 ♞e7+ ♚g7 23 ♛xb5 cxb5 24 ♖c7 is in White's favour.

22 ♞d6 ♚g7 23 e4!

A strong move, which not only prepares e5 but also clears the third rank so that White can bring a rook into the attack.

23...♞g8 *(D)*

This hastens the end, but 23...♞e8 was just as inadequate in view of 24 ♞f5+ followed by 25 ♛e7[1].

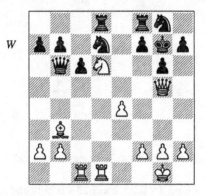

W

24 ♖d3! f6

If 24...h6, there follows the other variation of Alekhine's elegant combination: 25 ♞f5+ ♚h7 26 ♞xh6 f6 (or 26...♞xh6 27 ♖h3) 27 ♞f5! fxg5 28 ♖h3+ mating.

25 ♞f5+ ♚h8 26 ♛xg6! 1-0

Since 26...hxg6 is answered by 27 ♖h3+ and mate.

A pointed end to a game which contained some typical manoeuvres in the struggle by the queen and knight for the focal-point g7.

Further examples of play against the focal-point g7 are contained in the chapter on fianchettoed positions.

The focal-point h7

While the attacker cannot easily target g7, the square h7 is often exposed to danger even in the opening stages of a game, although attacks based on h7 as a focal-point are generally not so dangerous as those aimed at g7. This important point has already been noted, together with the reason for it, i.e. the fact that the

---

1   24 ♞xb7, winning a piece, is even more convincing.

king can escape from g8 to f8, whereas to avoid the threat of the queen on g7 the king has to travel further (to e8 or e7). Because of this, the main task involved in attacks on the focal-point g7 is the 'clearing' of that square, while the possible escape of the king is a minor worry. In attacks on h7 the 'clearing' is usually the easier task, while the attacker's main preoccupation is *to stop the king escaping;* this means essentially that he should have a new focal-point in view, if the attack is to be successful. In other words, the possible escape of the king turns the primary focal-point h7 into a secondary one, so that a new, real focal-point becomes necessary. It is worth keeping this important fact in mind, since in practice the majority of possible attacks on h7 founder precisely on the king's use of the simple defensive expedient of running away.

These factors, which apply to most attacks on h7, are well illustrated by the following example.

W

White, to move, begins with **1 ♕b1!**. Black's queen has to guard the square e8, and so has only two replies:

1) **1...♕d7 2 ♖e7!** (after 2 ♖xe8+? ♕xe8 3 ♕h7+ ♔f8 White's attack comes to a dead end, since the black king has e7 to escape to) **2...♕xe7** (2...♖xe7 has the same effect, while if 2...♕d8, then 3 ♕h7+ followed by 4 ♖xf7#) **3 ♕h7+ ♔f8 4 ♕h8#**.

2) **1...♕c6 2 d5 ♕c8 3 ♖xe8+** (this is all right now, but 3 ♖e7? would not do because of 3...♗xg5) **3...♕xe8 4 ♕h7+ ♔f8 5 d6**, and Black cannot avoid mate next move by 6 ♕h8#.

White's combination, then, has two variations, and the point of each is to deprive Black's king of an escape to e7, either by blocking it or playing d6. The square h7 appears here as a secondary focal-point, while the crucial factor in the combination is the mate when the king reaches f8.

There is in fact such an abundance of attacks against the castled king with a real or secondary focal-point at h7, and they differ so widely, that an attempt to systematize them would take us too far afield; let us be content with a few general examples, and then deal in more detail with 'the classic bishop sacrifice on h7', which in practice is the most important kind of attack on the focal-point h7.

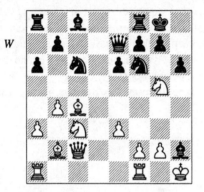

This position arose in Szabo-Kotov, Groningen 1946. It is White's move, and he effects the 'clearing' of the focal-point h7 by eliminating the knight on f6:

1 ♘d5! exd5 2 ♗xf6 ♗f5

The only reply, though an inadequate one.

3 ♕xf5 g6

White now continued with **4 ♕xg6+ fxg6 5 ♗xd5+ ♖f7 6 ♗xe7** and won on the basis of his material advantage, but **4 ♗xe7 gxf5 5 ♗xf8** would have been even clearer.

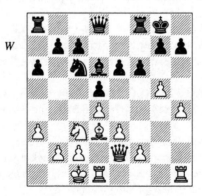

Here we have a straightforward example of the creation of a mating position by directing the queen and a pawn against the focal-point h7, followed by a typical new mate after the black king has escaped.

1 ♗xh7+ ♔xh7 2 ♕h5+ ♔g8 3 g6 ♖e8 4 ♕h7+ ♔f8 5 ♕h8+ ♔e7 6 ♕xg7#.

In this position Black aims to drive White's rook from f4 and then proceed with ...g3, creating a threat against h2. He plays:

1...♗e5 2 ♘xe5

If 2 d4 ♗xf4 3 ♗xf4, Black continues 3...g3 4 ♕f3 ♕h2+ 5 ♔f1 ♕h1+ 6 ♔e2 ♘f6 7 ♕xg3 ♗g4+ 8 ♔e3 ♕c1+ 9 ♔d3 ♕f1+ 10 ♔c2 ♕xc4 and wins.

If 2 ♕f3 ♗xf4 3 ♕xf4 ♕e1+ 4 ♔h2 (both 4 ♗f1 ♖h7 and 4 ♕f1 ♕xf1+ 5 ♔xf1 ♖h7 are in Black's favour) 4...♘f6! 5 ♘xh8, Black wins by 5...g3+ 6 ♕xg3 ♘g4+.

2...dxe5 3 ♖f7

If 3 ♖f1, Black plays 3...0-0-0 and then ...g3, forcing mate. At once 3...g3 would not be good because of 4 ♗f7+ and 5 ♕h5.

3...g3

This move is now playable; indeed, it is obligatory, since after 3...0-0-0 4 d3 g3 Black is a tempo behind with his attack; White then has the following defence, a characteristic one in such positions: 5 ♗e3 ♕h2+ 6 ♔f1 ♕h1+ 7 ♗g1, and Black's attack has come to nothing.

4 ♕f3 ♗g4! *(D)*

A typical method of preparing the mating net; one should not check if this only simplifies the opponent's defence. It should be noted that checking at h2 and then h1 loses a tempo. Black's aim is to oblige the white king to move to f1 of its own free will, and then give check with the queen directly at h1, without stopping at h2.

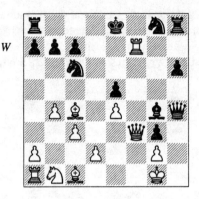

5 ♖f8+ ♔d7 6 ♖f7+

If 6 ♕f7+, then 6...♘ge7, while 6 ♗e6+ is answered by 6...♗xe6! 7 ♖xa8 ♘f6! 8 ♖xh8 ♕h2+ 9 ♔f1 ♕h1+ 10 ♔e2 ♗g4 and wins. Lastly, 6 ♕d3+ is simply met by 6...♘d4.

6...♘ge7 7 ♕e3 ♖af8 and Black wins easily, for example after 8 ♔f1 ♖xf7+ 9 ♗xf7 ♖f8.

For our final example in this section let us examine the main line of the Møller Attack in the Giuoco Piano. In this White's attack, involving the sacrifice of a knight on h7, is so strong – or weak – that the game ends in a draw.

1 e4 e5 2 ♘f3 ♘c6 3 ♗c4 ♗c5 4 c3 ♘f6 5 d4 exd4 6 cxd4 ♗b4+ 7 ♘c3 ♘xe4 8 0-0 ♗xc3 9 d5

Møller's strengthening of the attack; 9 bxc3 used to be played, whereupon Black obtains the advantage by 9...d5.

9...♗f6!

The best reply.

10 ♖e1 ♘e7 11 ♖xe4 d6

If 11...0-0, then 12 d6 is reckoned to give White good prospects.

12 ♗g5 ♗xg5 13 ♘xg5 0-0[1] 14 ♘xh7 ♔xh7 15 ♕h5+ ♔g8 16 ♖h4 f5 *(D)*

Instead of 16...f5 Bogoljubow suggested and experimented with 16...f6, which is weaker.

In the position after 16...f5, White must try to justify the sacrifice of the knight. Admittedly, he controls the square h7, but, at the same time, he cannot prevent the black king from escaping via f7 when it is checked. If the game is continued correctly, White can only obtain perpetual check, not mate. Both 17

---

1   Current theory reckons 13...h6 to be best, when White is struggling for equality.

♕h7+ (variation A) and 17 ♖h3 (B) lead to a draw, while the rest end in a win for Black. These other, poorer, continuations are given under (C) and (D).

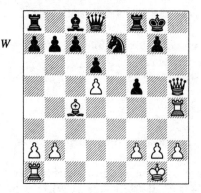

A) 17 ♕h7+

This is the oldest method, tried out in innumerable games and ending in a draw.

17...♔f7 18 ♖h6

18 ♖e1 is not good because of 18...♘g6 19 ♖h6 ♕g5, etc.

18...♖g8 19 ♖e1 *(D)*

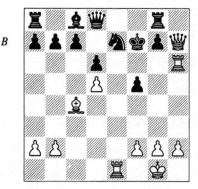

19...♕f8

Maroczy, and later Bogoljubow, tried to find a win for Black at this point with 19...♔f8 but further analyses have shown that White has a draw by 20 ♖h3! ♗d7 (if 20...f4 then 21 ♖h4 is in White's favour) 21 ♖he3 ♘c8 22 ♗d3 g6 (if 22...♘b6, White wins by 23 ♗xf5 ♘xd5 24 ♗xd7! ♘xe3 – or 24...♕xd7 25

♖f3+ – 25 ♗e6 ♔e7 26 ♖xe3) 23 h4 ♖g7 24 ♕h8+ ♔g8 25 ♕h7, repeating moves. Possibly one could also play for a win here with 25 ♕h6+ ♔f7 26 ♖e6.

20 ♗b5

20 ♗e2 is weaker, since after 20...♔e8 Black's king escapes to d8.

20...♖h8

20...c6? is bad because of 21 dxc6 while if 20...a6?, then 21 ♖ee6 axb5 22 ♖hf6+ with advantage to White.

21 ♕xh8 gxh6 22 ♕h7+ ♔f6 23 ♖xe7! ♕xe7 **24 ♕xh6+**, and White forces perpetual check.

B) 17 ♖h3

White's other sound continuation, discovered by Keres.

17...f4!

According to Keres, all other moves give White the advantage.

18 g4 fxg3 19 ♕h7+ ♔f7 20 ♕h5+ ♔g8 21 ♕h7+ with perpetual check.

Against 20...g6 Keres gives 21 ♕h7+ ♔e8 22 ♖xg3 and White stands better, but Black can improve by 21...♔f6 22 ♕h4+ ♔f7 and draws. Black would probably not be able to venture on 22...g5 23 ♕h6+ ♘g6 24 ♖h5 gxf2+ 25 ♔xf2 since if 25...♔e5+ White can boldly play 26 ♔e3.

Now we examine White's weaker continuations.

C) 17 ♗e2? ♖e8! 18 ♖e1

18 ♕h8+ ♔f7 19 ♗h5+ is not sufficient for a draw on account of 19...♘g6.

18...♔f8 19 ♗b5

Or 19 ♕h8+ ♘g8!.

19...♗d7 20 ♖e6 ♘g8! and White's attack is driven back[1].

D) 17 ♖e1? ♘g6! 18 ♖h3 *(D)*

18...♖f6!

18...f4 is weaker because of 19 ♖e6 and so is 18...♘f4?, e.g. 19 ♕h7+ ♔f7 20 ♖he3 ♘g6 21 ♕h5 followed by ♖e7+, etc[2].

---

1   At the end of this line 21 ♕xf5+ ♘f6 22 ♗xd7 ♕xd7 23 ♖xf6+ wins for White, so Black must search for an improvement earlier. 17...♘g6 18 ♕h7+ ♔f7 19 ♖h6 ♘f4 20 ♗h5+ ♘xh5 21 ♕g6+ ♔g8 22 ♕xh5 gxh6 23 ♕g6+ with a draw may well be Black's best, so 17 ♗e2 probably doesn't deserve a question mark.

2   However 21...♕f6 seems to defend, e.g. 22 ♖e7+ ♔g8 or 22 ♖e6 ♗xe6 23 ♖xe6 ♕xb2 24 ♕xg6+ ♔g8. Therefore White should prefer 21 ♖g3! ♕f6 22 ♖e6! ♗xe6 23 dxe6+ ♔e8 24 ♖xg6 with advantage.

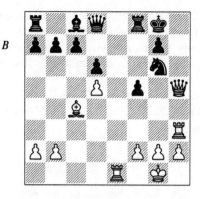

19 ♖g3

This is relatively the best way out for White. 19 ♖e6 ♗xe6 20 ♕h7+ ♔f8 21 dxe6 d5 is inadequate for White, and he loses.

Keres played 19 ♕h7+ ♔f7 20 ♖e6 in several correspondence games and he gives this continuation in his handbook *Theorie der Schacheröffnungen*. Nevertheless, Black can then win by 20...♘f8 21 ♕h5+ g6, etc. This simple continuation was, strangely enough, not noticed by Keres's 'correspondence customers', and Euwe also fails to record it in his opening works, giving instead a draw by 20...♗xe6? 21 dxe6+ ♖xe6 22 ♗xe6+ ♔xe6 23 ♕xg6+ ♕f6 24 ♖e3+, etc.

19...♘e5

The only reply. 19...♔f7? 20 ♖e6! is in White's favour, for he wins back his sacrificed piece and keeps up his attack.

20 f4

Neither 20 ♖xe5 dxe5 21 d6+ ♗e6 nor 20 ♕g5 ♕f8 leads anywhere.

20...♘f7 21 ♖ge3 ♗d7

White's attack has come to a halt and Black has an adequate defence, for example if 22 ♖e7, then 22...♘h6 followed by 23...♖f7.

The reader will find further examples concerning the focal-point h7 in the next chapter, which deals with *the classic bishop sacrifice*. These examples provide a typical illustration of the part played by the square h7 as a mating and secondary focal-point.

The auxiliary focal-point f7

Mention has already been made of the vulnerability of the square f7 before castling, and now we shall examine the part played by an assault on that square after the king has castled. First of all, it should be remarked that the square f7 is only in exceptional cases the focal-point in the true sense, i.e. the square from which mate is effected. However, it is very often an auxiliary focal-point, which is attacked either in order to drive the king away from g8 or, by means of a sacrifice, to draw the king on to the actual square itself.

The following position from the game Tylor-Koltanowski, Hastings 1930 arose after the moves **1 d4 ♘f6 2 ♘f3 d6 3 ♘c3 ♘bd7 4 e4 e5 5 ♗c4 ♗e7 6 0-0 0-0 7 ♕e2 exd4 8 ♘xd4 ♖e8** (D).

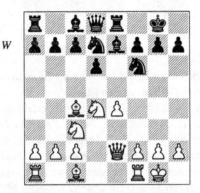

White, by attacking f7, drew Black's king out from the safety of its castled position.

9 ♗xf7+! ♔xf7 10 ♘e6

Making use of the familiar feature of the hemmed-in queen.

10...♔xe6 11 ♕c4+ d5 12 exd5+ ♔f7

The king cannot advance to e5 because of 13 ♕f4# nor to f5 because of 13 ♕d3+ with a mating attack, while if 12...♔d6, there follows 13 ♘b5+ ♔e5 14 ♖e1+ ♔f5 15 ♕d3+ ♔g4 16 ♕h3#.

13 d6+

After 13...♔f8 the king has returned to its shelter, but now the trouble over the hemmed-in queen reappears: 14 dxc7 and Black loses, since after 14...♘b6 15 cxd8♕ ♘xc4 16 ♕d4 the old white queen dies but a new one comes to life.

Black therefore played **13...♘d5**, but after **14 dxe7 ♖xe7 15 ♘d5** his position was hopeless.

The following position from the game Burn-E. Cohn, Breslau 1912 illustrates a faulty attack on f7. It was White's move and he played:

1 ♘xf7!?

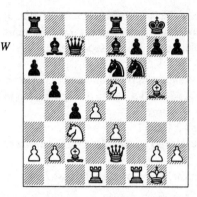

Malicious old men said that this was the only sacrifice ever risked by the cautious master Burn in his whole chess career. To this observation one might add, 'and even then it wasn't correct', as will shortly be seen.

1...♔xf7 2 ♕h5+ ♔g8?

This presents White with a tempo, which is decisive. After the correct 2...♔f8! one cannot see how White's attack can succeed, for example 3 ♗xf6 ♗xf6 4 ♕xh7 ♖ac8! 5 d5 ♘g5 6 ♕h8+ ♔e7, and Black can defend himself satisfactorily.

3 ♗xf6 ♗xf6 4 ♕xh7+ ♔f8 5 d5

Black now loses, since if he moves his knight, White plays 6 ♖xf6+.

5...♕e5 6 dxe6 ♕xe3+ 7 ♔h1 ♕xe6 8 ♗g6 1-0, for at the very least Black loses the exchange, e.g. after 8...♕g8. The alternatives 8...♖ec8 9 ♖de1, 8...♖e7 9 ♖de1! ♕g8 10 ♖xf6+ gxf6 11 ♕xe7# and 8...♕c6 9 ♕h8+ ♔e7 10 ♖fe1+ are even worse for Black.

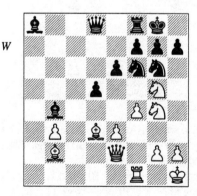

This position arose in the game Capablanca-R. Illa, Buenos Aires 1911. White's combination contains a thrust against the focal-point f7 as a preparation for the decisive action based on the real focal-point at h7.

1 ♗xf6!

Interesting, though inadequate, is the alternative possibility 1 ♘xf6+? gxf6 2 ♕h5 fxg5 3 ♕h6 d4! 4 ♗xd4 e5 5 ♗xe5 f6 6 ♗xg6 ♕d7, and White loses a piece without getting enough in return[1].

1...gxf6 2 ♘h6+ ♔g7 3 ♘hxf7

Gaining an important tempo by the attack on the e-pawn.

3...♕e8 4 ♕h5

The capture on f7 has helped to weaken the b1-h7 diagonal, on which lies the real focal-point at h7.

4...fxg5 5 ♕h6+! ♔g8

If 5...♔xf7, then 6 ♕xh7+ ♔f6 7 ♗xg6 ♕xg6 8 fxg5+ ♔e5 (or 8...♔xg5 9 h4+!) 9 ♕c7+ ♔e4 10 ♖xf8 and White wins.

6 ♘xg5 1-0

Black presumably saw 6...♕e7 7 ♗xg6 hxg6 8 ♕xg6+ ♕g7 9 ♕xe6+ ♔h8 10 ♖f3, and decided to abandon resistance[2].

Black might have tried to continue with 6...♖f7 7 ♗xg6 hxg6 8 ♕xg6+ ♔f8 9 ♘xe6+ ♔e7, admittedly without any real prospects of survival, e.g. 10 ♖c1! ♗d6 11 ♘g5, etc.

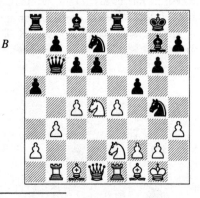

B

---

1   In fact this line is also winning for White, since at the end White can continue 7 ♗xf6 ♖xf6 (7...hxg6 8 ♕xg6+) 8 ♗xh7+ ♔f7 9 ♗g8+ ♔xg8 10 ♕xf6 with the decisive material advantage of ♖+4♙ v 2♗.

2   Vuković overlooks the mate in two by 10...♕a1+, but of course White had several genuine winning lines, e.g. 10 ♕h3+ ♔g8 11 ♘e6.

This position occurred in the game Najdorf-Ivkov from the last round of the tournament at Mar del Plata 1955.

Black, to move, correctly decided to sacrifice his knight on f2, obtaining two pawns and a powerful attack against the exposed white king:

16...♘xf2! 17 ♔xf2 ♖xe4 18 ♗b2 ♘c5 19 ♔g1!

White finds the best defence and withdraws his king to h1. If White had tried to retain his material advantage with 19 ♔f3?, the answer would have been 19...♘e6 20 ♘c2 ♘g5+ 21 ♔g3 ♗xb2 22 ♖xb2 ♕c5! with a decisive attack.

19...♘e6 20 ♔h1 ♘xd4 21 ♘xd4 ♖xd4!

Not 21...♖xe1? 22 ♕xe1 ♗xd4 because of 23 ♕e8+ ♔g7 24 ♕e3! c5 25 ♕e7+ ♔g8 26 ♗xd4 cxd4 27 c5 followed by 28 ♗c4+ and White wins.

22 ♗xd4 ♕xd4 23 ♕xd4 ♗xd4

Black has re-established the material balance and is rather the better placed; after a few more moves he settled for a draw, since that was all he needed for first place.

Janowski and Soldatenkov – Lasker and Taubenhaus
Consultation Game, Paris, 1909
Danish Gambit

1 e4 e5 2 d4 exd4 3 c3 dxc3 4 ♗c4 cxb2 5 ♗xb2 ♘f6?!

Better is 5...d5 6 ♗xd5 ♘f6 and if 7 ♗xf7+ then 7...♔xf7 8 ♕xd8 ♗b4+, etc.

6 e5 ♗b4+ 7 ♘c3 ♕e7 8 ♘e2 ♘e4? *(D)*

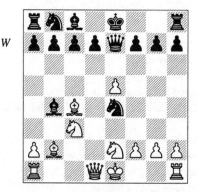

This leads to the exchange of the only two minor pieces Black has developed, which inevitably adds to White's advantage in development. 8...♘g4 was worth considering, and even 8...♕xe5 would have been better than the move played.

9 0-0 ♘xc3 10 ♗xc3 ♗xc3 11 ♘xc3 0-0 12 ♘d5! ♕xe5

Black would also be in difficulties after 12...♕d8 13 ♕h5 d6 14 f4 but there would at least be a hope of recovery then, whereas the course actually taken holds no prospects whatever.

13 ♖e1 ♕d6 14 ♕h5 c6

White threatened 15 ♘xc7 ♕xc7 16 ♕xf7+ ♖xf7 17 ♖e8#. Both 14...h6 15 ♖ad1! and 14...♘c6 15 ♖e4! were bad for Black, while if 14...g6, then 15 ♕h6 ♘c6 16 ♖e4 with an irresistible attack.

15 ♘c7 g6

15...♕xc7 provokes a catastrophe on the focal-point f7, i.e. 16 ♕xf7+ and 17 ♖e8#.

16 ♕h6 ♕xc7 *(D)*

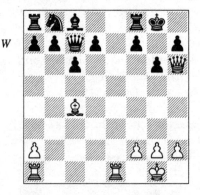

17 ♗xf7+!

The assault on f7 is now carried out as effectively by the bishop as it was by the queen in the variation above.

17...♔xf7 18 ♕xh7+ ♔f6

The partnership finished off the game as follows:

19 ♕h4+[1] ♔g7 20 ♖e7+ ♖f7 21 ♕d4+ ♔f8[2] 22 ♕h8+ ♔xe7 23 ♖e1+ ♔d6 24 ♕e5#.

Lasker came to grief in several games against Janowski through accepting sacrifices against his own principles. It is possible that Lasker was riled by the touch of impudence which can be seen in Janowski's moves and of which there was even more in his behaviour as a whole.

---

1   19 ♕e7+ ♔f5 20 ♕xf8+ mates more quickly.

2   Or 21...♔g8 22 ♖e8+ ♖f8 23 ♖xf8+ ♔xf8 24 ♕f6+ ♔g8 25 ♖e1, etc.

Complex focal-points

Just as a successful combination derives essentially from the multiple effects of single moves, so attacks on the castled king are also more likely to succeed if they are built up with the assistance of threats against a number of different squares. We shall find that in many attacks of this kind the attacker tries to corner the king by creating a second or even a third focal-point. There have already been cases of such complex focal-points in previous examples, but we shall now examine the matter more closely.

We have already mentioned the part played by secondary focal-points and by the combination of this kind of focal-point with a real one. However, here we will examine only the combining of two or more real focal-points, i.e. squares from which a player either actually mates or could do so in a variation. These real complex focal-points can be divided up as follows:

1) The focal-points are adjacent squares of different colours (e.g. g7 and h7).

2) The focal-points are nearby squares of the same colour (e.g. h7 and f7).

3) The focal-points are of the same colour and make up a whole complex or network of squares (e.g. f6, g7 and h8).

In general, one or more of the attacker's pieces control both focal-points, while the rest, in the course of the attack, transfer their influence from one focal-point to the other, preferably in the shortest time possible (i.e. one move). As far as simultaneous influence over two squares of different colours is concerned, for practical purposes only the queen comes into consideration, and in exceptional cases the rook; but if the focal-points are of the same colour, both the knight and, in particular, the bishop are effective. All the pieces are capable of transferring the attack from one focal-point to the other, though the bishop is unable to do this if the focal-points are of different colours. The bishop is, however, well suited to the case of focal-points of the same colour, while when the focal-points belong to the third group, it is indeed the classic piece by which the whole network is dominated.

When play is based on focal-points of different colours, the attack may be switched rapidly from one of the squares to the other. However, the commoner and more important cases are those in which there are two separate stages, the attack on the first focal-point being exhausted before the player transfers it decisively to the second. This transfer is often combined with a transformation of the mating pattern. An example of this is given in the following diagram *(D)*.

White, to move, begins with a sharp threat against the focal-point g7.
1 f6 ♚h8

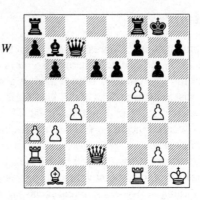

In order to be able to meet 2 ♕h6 by 2...♖g8. 1...♕c6 is weaker because of 2 ♖f3[1] and Black has only made his position worse.

2 ♕h6 ♖g8

White can clearly go no further in his threats against g7, but a new opportunity now offers itself – a rapid preparation for mate on h7, for which the queen is already excellently placed; all that is needed is to bring a rook on to the h-file.

3 ♖f3! ♗xf3

Forced, since there was a threat not only of 4 ♖h3 (against which, for example, 3...♕c6 would have helped[2]) but also of 4 ♕xh7+ and 5 ♖h3#.

4 gxf3 d5

The new threat of a queen sacrifice followed by ♖h2# wipes out Black's defence. White does not play 5 ♖h2 now, in which case Black would give up his queen for the rook, but **5 f4**, when Black can only stave off mate for a move or two by sacrificing his queen at f4.

In the following diagram we have an instructive example of play using focal-points of different colours. The threat against the focal-point h7 is replaced by one against g7. Then comes the decisive moment in the main variation – a sudden simultaneous attack on h7 and g7. In one sub-variation there even appears a third focal-point at f7.

1 ♖h1 ♔g8!

By 1...♗xg3+ 2 ♔e2 Black would only make the defence more difficult for himself. In playing 1...♔g8! he attempts to defend by running with his king, i.e. he surrenders h7 to White and hopes for the continuation 2 ♕xh7+? ♔f8 3 ♕h8+

---

1   2 ♕h6 forces immediate mate.
2   I cannot see why it would have helped.

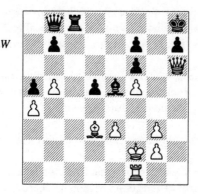

⌂e7, which leads to a complete consolidation of the black king's position; the tables are then turned and Black threatens ...⌐c3 followed by play on the queenside against the weak spots in White's camp. Therefore, White does not capture on h7, but hits on a manoeuvre to open up the d3-h7 diagonal by the lethal f6.

2 ⌐h5!

The passive 2 ⌐h3 would be weak, while 2 ⌐h4? is clearly no good because of 2...⌂xg3+ and 3...⌂xh4.

The text move threatens 3 ⌐g5+ fxg5 4 f6 with the double threat of 5 ⌐g7# and 5 ⌂xh7+ ⌂h8 6 ⌂g6+ ⌂g8 7 ⌐h7+ ⌂f8 8 ⌐xf7#. This main variation, culminating in simultaneous threats against h7 and g7 can, it is true, be countered by 2...⌐d6, but that allows 3 ⌐xh7+, 4 ⌐h8+, and 5 ⌐xc8, when White is a rook up. After 2...⌂xg3+ 3 ⌂e2 Black can do nothing in the face of ⌐g5+ and f6. However, he discovers a subtle defence, which is typical for such positions.

2...⌐c7 *(D)*

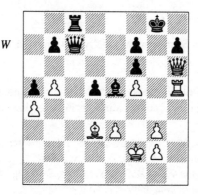

This protects the third focal-point at f7, which is important as the final mating square in the combination beginning with 3 ♖g5+; thus after 3...fxg5 4 f6 ♗xf6 5 ♗xh7+ there is no mate. But White still has one trump card left.

3 b6!

Attacking Black's queen, which is overloaded with duties at the key square c7: it is obliged to guard the rook (against the possibility of ♕xh7+ and ♕h8+) and also watch the square f7. Black therefore played:

3...♕d7

If 3...♗xg3+, White would in this case have to play 4 ♔f3![1].

4 ♖h4

A simple move and one which shows that Black's queen has yet another function – to maintain control of the b8-h2 diagonal. There is now an irresistible threat of ♖g4+; 4...♗xg3+ 5 ♔xg3 ♕d6+ 6 ♔f3 ♕f8 is useless due to 7 ♕xh7#.

An excellent example of the shift of threats from one focal-point to another, and at the same time a lesson in the troubles facing a piece which is overburdened with different functions.

W
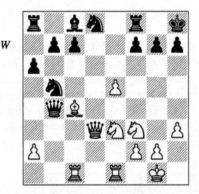

In this position, from Szabo-van Scheltinga, Hilversum 1947, White won in interesting fashion.

1 ♘g5 g6 2 ♘d5

White's first move, with its attack on h7, forced a weakening on the long diagonal, and his subsequent manoeuvres aim to bring the queen to that diagonal.

---

[1]   Black should try 3...♕c1!, creating serious counter-threats and preventing 4 ♖g5+ fxg5 5 f6 because of 5...♖c2+ 6 ♗xc2 ♕xc2+, followed by 7...♕g6. White should continue 4 ♖h4 ♖c2+ 5 ♗xc2 ♕xc2+ 6 ♔g1 ♕xf5 7 ♕h5 with a large advantage, but of course there is no mate.

2...♕a3 3 ♗xb5 axb5 4 ♖c3 ♕a5 5 e6! ♘xe6 6 ♖xe6 ♗xe6 7 ♕d4+ f6 8 ♘xf6

Now White threatens to decide the issue by ♘h5+ and mate at the focal-point g7. Black's only answer is to attack the white queen.

8...♕b6 9 ♕e5 ♕d6 10 ♖xc7! 1-0

After 10...♕xe5 the attack returns to the original focal-point at h7 in the shape of 11 ♖xh7#.

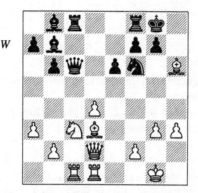

This position arose in the game V. Vuković-Endzelins from the match between Yugoslavia and Latvia at the 1936 Munich Olympiad. White first obtained freedom of action for himself by blocking the long light diagonal.

1 d5! exd5

If 1...♘xd5, then 2 ♕g5 g6 3 ♗xg6, etc.

2 ♘e2 ♕e6 3 ♗xg7! ♔xg7 4 ♕g5+ ♔h8 5 ♕h4+

White checks from h4 rather than h6 to give Black the chance to make a mistake. Endzelins did in fact fall for it and played **5...♔g7?**; this was followed by **6 ♘d4**, and Black lost his queen, since ♘f5+ leads to a terrible catastrophe on the focal-point g7. The rest of the actual game is of no interest (it finished **6...♖g8 7 ♕g5+ ♔f8 8 ♘xe6+ ♔e7 9 ♘g7 ♖xg7 10 ♕xg7 ♖g8 11 ♖e1+ 1-0**), but what does interest is an analysis of Black's more tenacious reply 5...♔g8 *(D)*.

Rellstab in his book of the tournament states that White would then have to satisfy himself with perpetual check, but this is not correct. Admittedly, after 6 ♘d4 ♖xc1! 7 ♖xc1 ♕e5 8 ♘f5 Black has the reply 8...♘e4!, an interesting example of a move with a double defensive purpose with reference to the focal-points h7 and g7, around which White's attack revolves. Further attempts, e.g. by 9 ♕g4+ ♔h8 10 f3, are dangerous for White because of 10...♗c8!, while other short-cuts also have obstacles in their way. It was, however, White's intention to

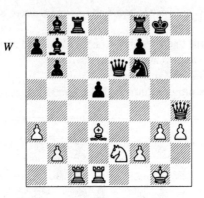

take the rook with his queen, and this would in fact have won the game, as the following analysis shows:

6 ♕g5+ ♔h8 7 ♕h6+ ♔g8 8 ♘d4 ♖xc1 9 ♕xc1! ♕e5 10 ♘f5

There is now an attack on the two focal-points h7 and g7, combined in some variations with another on f7.

If Black plays 10...♘e4, there follows 11 ♗xe4 dxe4 12 ♕g5+ ♔h8 13 ♖d7! when Black has no proper defence against the threat of 14 ♕h6+ and 15 ♘e7+ winning his queen, e.g. if 13...♖e8, then 14 ♕h5+ ♔g8 15 ♕xf7+ mating.

10...♘h7 11 ♕h6 ♖e8

The only way to meet the threat of 12 ♘e7+ and 13 ♕xh7#.

12 ♘d6! ♗xd6

Neither 12...♘g5 13 ♘xe8 nor 12...♖e7 13 ♗xh7+ ♔h8 14 ♘f5 hold out any hope for Black.

13 ♗xh7+ ♔h8 14 ♗g6+ with the final mate on f7.

Into the second group fall focal-points of the same colour which do not qualify as 'a network of squares'. The most typical case is that of h7 and f7, and in the next example we shall examine the most typical attack by the queen and bishop against these two squares.

In the following diagram White begins with:

1 ♕h5

He is threatening to sacrifice his bishop on h6 because all the essential preconditions for such a sacrifice have been fulfilled, as will be seen from the following analysis. We shall examine those replies by Black which lead to the characteristic formation of white queen on h6 and bishop on the b1-h7 diagonal. We shall leave aside the replies 1...♕e6 and 1...f6, the first of which is bad because of 2 ♗f5 and the second because of 2 ♕g6.

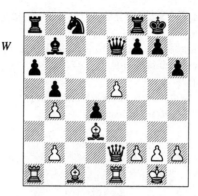

First of all, the naïve capture 1...♕xb4?. This is defeated by the sacrifice 2 ♗xh6 gxh6 3 ♕xh6, threatening mate on h7. This could be parried by 3...♖e8, but Black then has to pay for the unprotected focal-point at f7 after 4 ♗h7+ ♔h8 5 ♗g6+ ♔g8 6 ♕h7+ ♔f8 7 ♕xf7#.

We have seen that the square f7 must be protected by the queen, since the rook on f8 has to move after the sacrifice, which suggests 1...♘b6 or 1...♘a7. These too are answered by 2 ♗xh6 gxh6 3 ♕xh6, and if 3...♖e8, then 4 ♕h7+ and 5 ♕h8#; nor is there any future in 3...f6 4 exf6 ♖xf6 5 ♖xe7 ♖xh6 6 ♖xb7.

Black realizes that his queen is not well placed on e7 because it blocks this escape square and thus enables White to mate with his queen on h8. Black can try to move his queen away, but in such a way that it still protects the focal-point f7: 1...♕c7 2 ♗xh6 gxh6 3 ♕xh6 ♖e8 (or 3...f6 4 exf6, with the decisive threat of 5 ♖e7) 4 ♖ac1 ♕d7 5 ♗h7+ ♔h8 6 ♗f5+ and White wins the queen.

From this it can be seen that Black's queen could not even have gone to d7 on the first move.

We can now cut our speculation short; there only remain 1...♖e8 and 1...♖d8. That 1...♖d8 is no good can be seen after 2 ♗xh6 gxh6 3 ♕xh6, since then 3...♕e6 cannot be played because of 4 ♕g5+.

Thus we arrive at the main variation:

1...♖e8

After this move the sacrifice of the bishop on h6 is somewhat more complicated, but it is still White's best continuation. On the other hand, 2 ♗f4 is also good; less useful here (as on the first move) is 2 ♕g4 because of 2...♔h8 3 ♕xd4 ♖d8 4 ♕c3 ♘b6 and Black can hold his own.

2 ♗xh6 gxh6 3 ♕xh6 ♕e6

This is the right reply. After 4 ♗h7+ ♔h8 White now gets nowhere by 5 ♗g6+, while the other discovered checks fail because White's queen is attacked by Black's; furthermore, if 5 ♕h5, Black has the reply 5...♔g7 6 ♗f5 ♕h6 with an adequate defence.

White's later play is interesting, even if it is no longer as typical of this kind of attack as the possibilities cited hitherto.

4 ♕h7+ ♔f8 5 ♗f5 *(D)*

White's queen is now best placed where it is, on h7; further checks would only make it easier for Black to defend himself.

5...♕c6

After 5...♕d5 6 ♕h6+ Black cannot play 6...♔g8 due to 7 ♗h7+ and 8 ♗e4+, while 6...♔e7 7 ♗e4 wins the black bishop, for 7...♕d7 is defeated by 8 e6.

5...♕b6 is of no use either, since 6 ♖ac1! leaves Black without a reasonable reply, e.g. if 6...♘e7, then 7 e6 fxe6 8 ♗xe6 is quickly decisive.

6 ♗e4 ♕b6 7 ♗xb7 ♕xb7 8 e6 and White wins.

The threat is 9 ♕h8+ ♔e7 10 exf7+ and the reply 8...♘d6 fails against 9 e7+ and 10 ♕h8#.

This analysis shows what great power there is in the formation of queen at h6 and bishop at d3 when combined with a rook at e1 and a pawn at e5. The various operations connected with the focal-points h7 and f7 are well worth remembering, since opportunities to use them arise frequently in actual games. Since the defender must move his rook from f8 when mate is threatened at h7, it is clearly a decisive factor whether or not the focal-point f7 is protected by other pieces. An alternative defence involves ...f6 or ...f5, but the success of such a reply depends on the other features of the position, which must be carefully assessed.

The main feature of the third group is the network of weak squares of the same colour; here the attacker's bishop is, as a rule, the piece which controls the focal-points permanently, while the others are used for manoeuvring purposes. It should be noted that control over a network of squares is also an important factor in positional play, but in attacks on the castled king it is particularly effective. The reason for this is a positional one, since control over a network is often of a fairly permanent nature. The most essential precondition is to 'clear' the network not only of the influence of the opponent's bishop (either by eliminating it or driving it away) but also of possible resistance from the opponent's pawns at important points in the network.

When the attacker has 'cleared' the network and fixed the position, the attacking operation proper follows; the squares which are candidate focal-points can easily be determined, while the other squares in the network may serve as secondary focal-points or else as strong squares for the attacker to post his pieces on.

In the above diagram the network of dark squares is already 'cleared' and covered by White's bishop, which is firmly installed at f6. The network consists of the squares f6, g7 and h8, and also the connected squares f8 and h6. The squares g7 and h8 are candidates as focal-points, f6 is a strong square for the attacker's pieces while f8 and h6 can serve as secondary focal-points or strong squares. All this concentration of white power encircles the unfortunate black king, which has no real prospect of extricating itself from the net and escaping to the queenside, since e7 is also controlled by White. Black does not even have a dark-squared bishop to provide resistance on the network, and because of the blocked position in the centre he cannot undertake a counterattack; he is confined to defending himself. The only minor piece he has left is a knight, but this piece can in fact exercise considerable defensive influence in positions of this kind.

If White's domination is based on a dark-square network, Black still has one thing on which he can logically rely – the solid structure of his position on the light squares. In some such cases the success of an attack depends on the ability to break down resistance on the light squares by means of a sacrifice. This feature appears in the analysis of the above position, which, by virtue of its simplicity and its typical character, will well repay study.

It is Black's move, and his first concern is to provide a defence against White's manoeuvre ♕d2-h6, which threatens to bring about disaster on the focal-point g7. Various attempts at defence by Black and attacking stratagems by White, all of them typical and consequently instructive, will now be examined in a series of continuations.

A) 1...h6

Black is contemplating a defensive system with his king on h7 and his knight on g8, which could be reached after, say, 2 ♕d2 ♔h7 3 ♖e3 ♘e7 4 ♖h3 ♘g8. White can then assert his superiority by 5 ♗g5 h5 6 g4, but 1...h6 can be better punished as follows:

2 ♖e3! ♔h7 3 ♖h3 ♘e7 4 ♖xh6+! ♔xh6 5 ♕g4 ♔h7 6 ♕h3+ ♔g8 7 ♕h8#.

Here we see the part played by the focal-points at h6 and h8.

B) 1...h5 2 ♕d2 ♔h7 (D)

Forced, as White threatened mate by 3 ♕h6; if 2...♔f8, then 3 ♕h6+ also mates.

W

3 ♕g5

The simplest answer, as it prevents ...♘e7 for a decisive tempo. Also good is 3 g4, for 3...hxg4 is met by 4 ♕g5 and mate. If 3 ♖e3, Black can defend himself more stubbornly with 3...♘e7 4 ♖h3 ♘f5 5 g4 ♘h6 followed by 6...♖g8.

3...♖c7 4 ♖e3 ♘e7 5 ♖h3 ♘f5

Otherwise White mates by 6 ♖xh5+!.

6 g4 罝g8

Or 6...ᐁh6 7 罝xh5, etc.

7 gxf5 gxf5 8 罝xh5#.

In this example it is the resistance on the light squares that is overcome.

C) 1...豐e8

Black's queen is hoping to defend from f8.

2 罝e3 豐f8 3 罝h3 h6 4 豐d2 ⚊h7 5 ⚊g5 h5 6 豐e2 ᐁe7 7 罝xh5+! gxh5 8 豐xh5+ ⚊g8 9 ⚊f6 ᐁg6 10 罝e1, and Black has no answer to the threat of 罝e3-h3 followed by 豐h8+ and mate.

This is an important mating pattern in such positions.

D) 1...ᐁe7 2 豐d2 豐e8

Or 2...ᐁf5 3 g4 ᐁg7 4 豐h6 ᐁe8 5 罝e3, threatening both 6 罝h3 and 6 豐xh7+.

3 罝e3 豐f8 4 罝h3 罝c7

This position can also arise in variation C.

5 豐g5 b5 6 豐h4

White may also play 6 g4, 7 罝h6, and 8 豐h4.

6...h5 7 豐g5 ⚊h7 8 罝xh5+! gxh5 9 豐xh5+ 豐h6 10 豐xf7+ and mate.

Yet another instructive mating pattern!

E) 1...⚊f8

The black king tries to slip out of the net via e8.

2 豐d2 ⚊e8 3 豐h6 ᐁe7 *(D)*

Or 3...ᐁd8 4 豐xh7 豐a4 5 豐g8+ ⚊d7 6 豐f8 with a decisive attack on the new focal-point at e7.

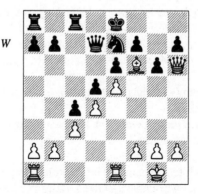

4 ♕xh7 ♕a4 5 ♖e3

At this point White gains nothing from checking, but must instead bring his rook to f3.

5...♕c2 6 ♖f3 ♕xb2 7 ♖f1 ♕a3

This parries the threat of 8 ♗xe7, but now 8 ♗g5 ♘f5 9 g4 decides the game.

In this variation the black king wriggled out to the edge of the network of weak dark squares, but even there he met his fate, its cause being the last square in the network, e7.

We shall not leave the above diagram yet, because a feature of very great practical importance should be pointed out. This is the benefit derived by White from the action of his rook on the h-file. Without an opportunity of making the manoeuvre ♖e3-h3, White cannot take Black's position by storm, because he lacks a threat against h7; if this does not exist, Black does not have to weaken his position, since he can easily ward off the threats against g7 alone. So even in this case, where there is a definite 'same-colour network', there is still a part to be played by alternative focal-points on squares of different colours (h7 or f7), and this applies in most practical cases. The weaknesses on the squares of the network are usually only the *more* sensitive ones, which does not mean that squares of the other colour will necessarily be safe – the king may succumb on them too!

We have noted the important part played by the rook on the h-file in the variations above, and we shall now go on to examine how positions of this kind can be exploited if there is no chance of employing a rook. Suppose that we move White's h-pawn from h2 to h4 in the above diagram; this gives a new situation of a type which often arises in practice, for the h-pawn is frequently advanced during the game. The pawn's being on h4 considerably blunts White's attack, and 1 h4? in the diagrammed position would be a poor move. Nevertheless, even with the pawn on h4 White has the better game, although he can only exploit his advantage slowly and Black retains chances of attacking on the queenside. Indeed, if Black's position on that side were a little further advanced, one could conclude that he would be able to preserve the balance. However, as things stand White is still the stronger, and we shall examine one continuation arising out of the new situation.

The modified diagram (with the pawn on h4) is given on the following page.

1...b5 2 ♕d2 ♕e8 3 ♖e3

In this case too White's rook belongs on h3, even though his attack along the h-file is only a 'thing of the future'.

3...♕f8 4 ♖h3 a5

4...h5 would be to White's advantage, since it would simplify his task of opening up the g- and h-files, for example 5 g4 hxg4 6 ♖h2 a5 7 h5 followed by 8 hxg6

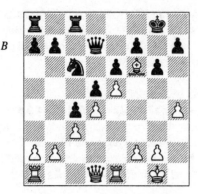

B

(but not 8 h6? because of 8...♔h7, and Black is at once in a safe position!) with a decisive attack.

5 h5 b4 6 g3

White's plan, a typical one in positions of this kind, is to play ♔g2 and then ♖ah1. The immediate 6 hxg6 would be weaker, for Black would reply 6...fxg6 opening up the second rank for defensive purposes. White must first of all post his heavy pieces in their assault positions and only then venture on hxg6.

6...a4 7 a3!

Otherwise Black obtains good prospects with ...a3.

7...bxc3 8 bxc3 *(D)*

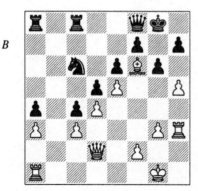

B

8...♘a5

A raid by a black rook along the b-file will not succeed, since both rooks are needed to defend the second rank, as can be seen from the following variation: 8...♖ab8 9 ♔g2 ♖b3 10 ♖ah1 ♖c7 11 ♕g5 ♖xa3 (or 11...♕xa3 12 ♕h6 ♕f8 13

♕xh7+ ♔xh7 14 hxg6+ ♔xg6 15 ♖h5 and mate) 12 hxg6 fxg6 13 ♖xh7 ♖xh7 14
♕xg6+ ♔g7 15 ♗xg7 ♕xg7 16 ♕e8+ and White wins. Black could, it is true,
play 11...♖b2, in which case the above combination would not work; however, it
would not stop the manoeuvre ♖h4-f4.

9 ♕g5 ♘b3 10 ♖e1 ♖c7

Clearly, 10...h6 is bad because of 11 hxg6.

11 ♔g2 ♖aa7 12 ♖eh1 ♖ab7 13 ♖h4! ♖d7 14 ♖f4 ♖dc7

Black is unable to parry the combination which White has prepared. If White
had previously made an incorrect exchange on g6, ...♕e8 would now be the answer to everything; in the present position this move would be answered by 15
♕h6 ♕f8 16 ♕xh7+ ♔xh7 17 hxg6+ ♔xg6 18 ♖g4+ ♔f5 19 ♖h5+ ♔xg4 20
♖g5#.

15 hxg6 fxg6 16 ♕xg6+! hxg6 17 ♖h8+ ♔f7 18 ♗d8+ and White finally
wins.

It is well worth remembering this analysis, especially the method of delaying
the attack with the h-pawn is and how the winning position is prepared by a calculated deployment of the pieces. The reader will be reminded of this extremely
important practical technique in the section on the role of the rook files in the attack on the castled king.

As for the part played by the network of weak squares in attacks on the castled
king, one more diagram and one interesting master game will be given as examples.

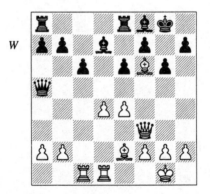

This position is from the game Euwe-Flohr, Amsterdam 1939. White's bishop
has reached the square f6, but the network is still guarded by the opponent's
dark-squared bishop, which is preparing to effect a delayed fianchetto by ...♗g7.
For this reason forceful play by White is indicated.

1 ♖c5!

With the idea of eliminating the dark-squared bishop. If Black plays 1...♗xc5, then 2 dxc5 uncovers an attack on the bishop at d7, which Black cannot defend, e.g. if 2...♕c7, the manoeuvre ♕e3-h6 is decisive.

1...♕xa2 2 ♖h5! e5

If 2...gxh5, then 3 ♕g3+ wins, while 2...♗g7 is answered by 3 ♗xg7 ♔xg7 4 ♖xh7+ ♔xh7 5 ♕xf7+, followed by 6 ♖d3. Also interesting is 2...h6 3 e5! ♔h7 4 ♕e3 ♕xb2 5 ♖d3 ♕b1+ 6 ♗f1 g5 (if 6...gxh5, then 7 ♕e4+ and 8 ♕g3+ wins; otherwise Black is mated by 7 ♖xh6+ ♗xh6 8 ♕xh6+ ♔xh6 9 ♖h3#) 7 ♕e4+ ♔g8 8 ♖xg5+ hxg5 9 ♖h3, etc. The move played parries the threat of 3 ♕h3.

3 dxe5 ♗e6 4 ♕f4 ♕xb2 5 ♗f1 ♗e7

He still cannot play 5...♗g7, because of 6 ♗xg7 and 7 ♕h6+.

6 ♕h4

Euwe notes in his commentary that Black's queen is fairly well placed on b2 (by controlling f2 and f6 it prevents ♕h6 being played at once) and cites as more precise 6 ♖b1 ♕d4 (if 6...♕xb1, then 7 ♕h6) 7 ♖b4! ♕d8 8 ♕h4, etc. 6 ♖d3 would also win more quickly than the move played.

6...♗c5!

The great defensive master's last trump: 7 ♖xh7? is now no good because of 7...♕xf2+. Even so, Black is lost; the process merely takes a little longer.

7 ♖h6 a5

If 7...♗g4, then 8 ♖d3 with the threat of 9 ♖e3!.

8 ♖d3 ♗xf2+

Otherwise White will play 9 ♖f3.

9 ♕xf2 ♕xf2+ 10 ♔xf2 *(D)*

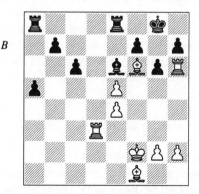

10...a4

The situation now becomes critical; White must get his rook to h3 before Black's pawn promotes to a queen.

If 10...♖a6, there is insufficient time for 11 ♗e2 because of ...♖b6-b3, nor is 11 ♖f3 ♖b6 12 ♖f4 strong enough owing to 12...g5! 13 ♖f5 ♖c8, and the black king escapes to d7. Strongest, after 10...♖a6, is 11 g4 ♗xg4 12 ♗h3!, etc.

11 ♗e2

White can also win by 11 g4 ♗xg4 12 ♗h3. After the text move Black cannot reply 11...a3 because of 12 g4 a2 13 ♖xh7, so he tries to prolong the game by a desperate rook sacrifice.

11...♖a5 12 g4 ♖xe5 13 ♗xe5 ♗c4 14 ♖dh3 ♗xe2 15 ♗f6 ♖e6 16 e5 ♗xg4 17 ♖xh7 ♖xf6+ 18 exf6 1-0

The rook has no difficulty in controlling the pawns, e.g. 18...♗xh3 19 ♖xh3 b5 20 ♖c3 b4 21 ♖xc6 b3 22 ♖b6, etc.

Pilnik – Najdorf
Mar del Plata, 1942
Caro-Kann Defence

1 e4 c6 2 d4 d5 3 ♘c3 dxe4 4 ♘xe4 ♘f6

Sounder is 4...♗f5 or 4...♘d7 followed by ...♘gf6.

5 ♘xf6+ exf6

The doubling of the pawns on the f-file represents a slight weakness in Black's position whichever pawn he recaptures with.

6 c3 ♗d6 7 ♗d3 0-0 8 ♕h5

Black could answer this with 8...f5 (9 ♗xf5? g6) and so ward off White's attack without weakening his castled position. Indeed, 8...f5 not only avoids weakening Black's position, it also falls in with his correct positional plan, i.e. the front f-pawn is used to control squares on the e-file, while the back one (at f7) stays at home and guards any weaknesses which the front one leaves behind it. If the front pawn is exchanged in some tussle over a square, Black has got rid of the doubled pawns and the fear of an inferior ending.

8 ♕c2 was sounder.

8...g6

Though less precise than 8...f5 this is still not a mistake.

9 ♕h4 (D)

9...c5?

Fundamentally inappropriate, since White is stronger on the queenside and in particular has a firm hold on d4. Black should have left any operations on the queen's wing to White and instead prepared for ...f5 and ...♘d7-f6, but without

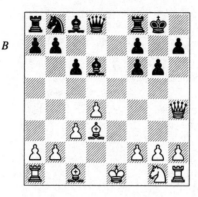

exchanging queens and without relinquishing the d8-h4 diagonal to White. Correct, therefore, was 9...♘d7 10 ♘e2 ♗e7! 11 0-0 f5 12 ♕g3 ♘f6, etc.

10 ♘e2 ♘c6 11 ♗h6 f5?

Black should have played 11...♖e8. At this point ...f5 is weak.

12 ♗g5!

By exchanging queens White could have obtained the better endgame prospects. However, why should he play for an endgame when he has the opportunity to gain control of the diagonal h4-d8, thereby obtaining the necessary conditions for an attack on the castled king based on a network of weak dark squares?

12...♕b6

The diagonal cannot be defended: if 12...♗e7, then 13 ♗xe7 ♘xe7 14 dxc5 ♕xd3 15 ♕xe7 while 12...f6 13 ♗c4+ ♔h8 14 ♗h6 is equally unacceptable[1].

13 0-0 cxd4 14 cxd4 *(D)*

14...♖e8

Some commentators have marked this move out as the decisive mistake and have suggested 14...♗e6 (preventing ♗c4), but this would make the win easier, e.g. 15 ♗f6 ♖fe8 (or 15...h5 16 ♕g5 ♔h7 17 d5 ♗xd5 18 ♗xf5) 16 ♘f4! ♘xd4 (precluding 17 d5; if 16...♗xf4 17 ♕xf4, Black will find himself unable to defend the focal-point g7, having given up his dark-squared bishop) 17 ♘h5 ♘c6 18 ♗c3 ♗e5 (18...♗e7 comes to the same) 19 ♘f6+ ♗xf6 20 ♗xf6 h5 21 ♕g5 ♔h7 22 ♗e2 and White decides the game by ♗xh5.

In this analysis, as in other phases of this game, it should be noted that a method has been used which we have already seen in the variations arising from

---

1   It is hard to see why this latter line is unacceptable. Black may continue with 14...♖e8, threatening 15...♖e4, and thanks to the move ...f6 Black's kingside dark squares are not especially weak.

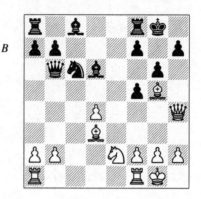

B

the diagram on page 109; namely, in creating threats against a dark-square net-work, White repeatedly makes use of sacrifices on squares of the other colour. These sacrifices fulfil the task of breaking up clusters of pawns which otherwise impede the attacker's access to the weak squares on the network itself. The link-age between the operations on the networks of different colours should be noted; on one network the intention is to keep the attacking pieces in the strongest and most permanent positions possible, while on the other they are sacrificed when the situation demands.

It should finally be pointed out that, instead of the move played, 14...♛xb2? would have been bad because of 15 ♖fb1 ♛a3 16 ♖b3 ♛a5 17 ♗f6 ♖e8 18 ♗c4, when White's prospects for an attack are greatly improved.

15 ♗c4 h5 *(D)*

There was a threat of 16 ♗xf7+ ♚xf7 17 ♛xh7+ ♚e6 18 d5+ ♚xd5 19 ♖ad1+. If 15...♗e6, then 16 d5 would naturally follow.

W

16 ♖ae1?

After this move Black gains drawing chances. In such an attractive position one would expect to find a safe and clear way to victory. White here has all the necessary ingredients for success: control over a dark-square network; advantage in development; two pieces to break up the cluster on the light squares (bishop at c4 and knight at e2); and as well as all this, a pawn in the centre that prevents Black from using his e5 square as a post for his pieces!

Stronger and simpler would have been 16 ♗f6!, as the following lines show:

1) 16...♗e7 17 ♕g5 ♗xf6 18 ♕xg6+.

2) 16...♗e6 17 d5 ♗xd5 18 ♗xd5 ♖xe2 19 ♕g5 ♔f8 20 ♖ae1![1] ♕b5 (or 20...♘d4 21 ♕h6+ ♔e8 22 ♗xc6, etc.) 21 ♗f3 ♖xe1 22 ♖xe1 ♘e5 23 ♕h6+ ♔e8 24 ♗xe5 and 25 ♕h8+.

3) 16...♖e4 17 ♕g5 ♔f8 18 ♘c3!, and the black rook has no good square to go to: 18...♖xd4 is inadequate because of 19 ♖fe1, while 18...♖g4 is answered by 19 ♕h6+ ♔e8 20 ♗xf7+ ♔xf7 21 ♕g7+ ♔e8 (or 21...♔e6 22 d5#) 22 ♖ae1+ and mate is unavoidable.

16...♖e4 17 ♘f4 ♕xd4 18 ♖xe4 fxe4?

This pawn blocks the fourth rank to White's advantage. Black should have played 18...♕xe4, when 19 ♘xg6 ♕xh4 20 ♘xh4 leads to an ending in which White is the better placed, but Black can still salvage a draw by 20...♗e6 21 ♗d3 (or 21 ♗e2 ♔g7! when 22 ♗xh5 fails against 22...f6 and 23...♖h8) 21...f4 threatening both the a-pawn and 22...♔g7 followed by 23...f6.

19 ♘xh5!

Breaking up Black's light-square complex.

19...gxh5 20 ♗f6! ♕c5

Forced; if 20...♕xc4 then White wins by 21 ♕xh5 while if 20...♗e5 then 21 ♕g5+ is decisive.

21 ♖d1! ♔f8 *(D)*

The only reply. If 21...♗e6 then 22 ♖d5! ♕xc4 (or 22...♗xd5 23 ♕xh5) 23 ♕g5+ ♔f8 24 ♖xd6 and mates, while 21...♗e7 22 ♖d5 ♗xf6 loses to 23 ♕g3+.

22 b4!

Obliging the knight to abandon its watch on d8. That White's bishop on c4 is still 'taboo' can be seen from 22...♕xc4 23 ♕xh5 ♔e8 24 ♖xd6 ♕c1+ 25 ♖d1, and Black loses his queen.

---

1   This move is refuted by 20...♕xf2+!! and Black forces mate himself. However, Vuković's attacking plan is basically correct, except that White has to exercise a little more care: 20 ♕h6+ ♔e8 21 ♕g7 ♘d8 22 ♖ae1 and now 22...♕xf2+ 23 ♖xf2 ♖xe1+ 24 ♖f1 ♗c5+ fails, because after 25 ♗d4 the bishop is defended.

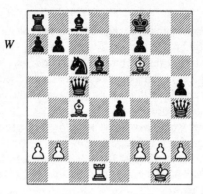

22...♘xb4 23 ♕g3! ♗g4

Clearly the only answer, for 23...♗xg3 cannot be played on account of 24 ♖d8#.

24 ♖xd6 ♘d3

Or 24...♕xc4 25 ♕f4 and mates.

25 ♗xd3 ♕c1+

Not 25...exd3 because of 26 ♕f4.

26 ♗f1 ♖c8 27 h3 ♕xf1+ 28 ♔h2! ♕c1 29 hxg4 hxg4 30 ♕xg4 ♕h6+ 31 ♔g3 ♖c3+ 32 f3 1-0

The first part of this tense game is instructive as an example of the gradual creation of the preconditions necessary for an attack on the castled king, while from the twelfth move onwards, by which time White's control of the dark-square network is assured, the course of the game and its analysis provide many useful lessons on how to carry out an attack of this kind.

6 The classic bishop sacrifice[1]

This sacrifice deserves a chapter to itself, because it is the oldest and most explored of all the sacrifices involved in the attack on the castled king and also because it provides particularly good illustrations of the role of h7 and f7 as mating and secondary focal-points.

The earliest instance of the sacrifice of the bishop on h7 followed by ♘g5+ occurs in Gioacchino Greco's handbook of 1619, but the first systematic review of it was made by E. Voellmy in his article 'On attacking the castled king' in the *Schweizerischen Schachzeitung* in 1911. Some writers give it the name of Greco's sacrifice, for which there are some grounds, while others call it Colle's sacrifice, for which there is in fact no justification, as Colle never played a good game which contained the sacrifice in spite of the fact that he often used it. I think the term 'classic bishop sacrifice' more appropriate, since this indicates both its early origins and also the basic simplicity of the idea underlying it.

Greco reaches the position below in his handbook after making six not particularly intelligent moves.

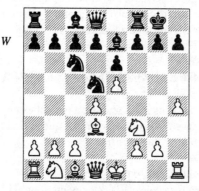

Now comes the blow: **1 ♗xh7+! ♔xh7 2 ♘g5+ ♔g8** (if 2...♗xg5, then 3 hxg5+ ♔g6 4 ♕h5+ ♔f5 5 ♕h3+ ♔g6 6 ♕h7#; 2...♔h6 3 ♘xe6+ costs Black his queen; thirdly, after 2...♔g6 3 h5+ there is a choice between 3...♔h6 4

---

1 More commonly called the *Greek Gift* sacrifice, although the reason for applying this term specifically to the sacrifice on h7 is unclear.

♘xe6+ and 3...♔f5 4 g4#) **3 ♕h5 ♖e8** (or 3...♗xg5 4 hxg5 f5 5 g6) **4 ♕h7+ ♔f8 5 ♕h8#.**

Let us now consider the next, rather more natural, position, where the classic sacrifice is again successful.

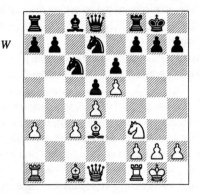

1 ♗xh7+ ♔xh7 2 ♘g5+

Here, as in other examples of the classic bishop sacrifice, there are *three main variations* arising from the sacrifice, i.e. those beginning with ...♔g8, ...♔h6, and ...♔g6. These three variations must be carefully examined on every occasion, for if any one of them contains a loophole, the whole combination falls to the ground.

1) variation with ...♔g8

2...♔g8 3 ♕h5 ♖e8 4 ♕xf7+ ♔h8 5 ♕h5+ ♔g8 6 ♕h7+ ♔f8 7 ♕h8+ ♔e7 8 ♕xg7#.

This variation contains, as its main feature, a typical example of an attack using h7 and f7 as secondary focal-points with the queen finally mating on g7, a common enough pattern after this sacrifice.

2) variation with ...♔h6

2...♔h6 3 ♘xe6+ and 4 ♘xd8, etc.

This naturally succeeds because Black's queen is on d8, but even with the queen on a5 the move 2...♔h6 would have no prospects. In that case White would win by, e.g. 3 ♕g4 ♖h8 (otherwise ♕h4+ and ♕h7#) 4 ♘xe6+ and 5 ♕xg7#.

3) variation with ...♔g6

2...♔g6 3 h4

This is the strongest move here; in other cases ...♔g6 may be best met by ♕g4. Black's reply is forced.

3...♖h8 4 h5+! ♖xh5 5 ♕d3+ f5 6 exf6+ ♔xf6 7 ♕f3+ ♔e7 8 ♕f7+ ♔d6 9 ♕xh5 and White wins.

One could now produce a series of examples, pursuing different variations according to the various elements in each position, but it is more to the point at once to pose the question as to *how to judge the correctness of the sacrifice,* first with reference to White's position and then to Black's.

Necessary conditions for the classic bishop sacrifice

White must firstly have a queen, a bishop and a knight. The light-squared bishop must be able to reach h7 in order to force the tempo of the attack, though it is not essential that it should put Black in check or take a pawn in so doing. The knight should be within easy and safe reach of the square g5, and the queen within reach of h5, though in some cases it is enough for it to be able to get to some other square on the h-file.

As far as *Black's* position is concerned, there should be two pawns standing intact at f7 and g7 (g7 may on rare occasions be occupied by a bishop instead of a pawn); the h-pawn should be on h7 (on h5 in exceptional cases), but it may be that there is no h-pawn at all. The position of Black's queen on d8 and a rook on f8 points to, but does not absolutely guarantee, the correctness of the sacrifice. What is more important is that Black's knight should not be able to reach f6 and that neither his queen nor bishop should be able to occupy the h7-b1 diagonal unharmed.

These are the basic conditions which need to be taken into account. In the examples which follow we shall examine to what extent each of these conditions is fulfilled; the positions are chosen in such a way as to show which is the *critical* continuation in each example, i.e. the one that is in doubt because a certain condition is apparently unfulfilled.

The variation with ...♔g8 is critical

In the following position the sacrifice is correct:
   1 ♗xh7+ ♔xh7 2 ♘g5+ ♔g8
   The continuation 2...♔h6 obviously fails; while if 2...♔g6, then 3 ♕d3+ ♔f6 (3...f5 4 ♕g3! wins, for Black cannot play 4...♔f6 because of 5 ♖xe6#) 4 ♕e4 threatens both 5 ♘h7+ and 5 ♘xe6, and 4...♔e7 does not work because of 5 ♕xe6+ fxe6 6 ♖xe6#.
   3 ♕h5 ♘f6
   An example of the defence of the focal-point h7 by the knight, but in this case

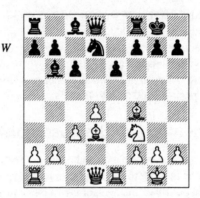

White's position is strong enough (thanks to the activity of his bishop on f4 and rook on e1) to withstand the loss of time.

4 ♕h4 ♖e8

If 4...g6, then 5 ♕h6!, followed by 6 ♗e5 and ♖e3-h3, wins, while 4...♗c7 would be met by 5 ♗e5, etc.

5 ♗e5 ♕e7

If 5...♔f8, then 6 ♕h8+ and 7 ♕xg7 is decisive.

6 ♖e3 ♗d8 7 ♖h3 and White mates.

In the position in the next diagram an important condition regarding the ...♔g8 variation has apparently not been fulfilled, since the diagonal from c8 to f5 is open to Black's bishop. However, White has the possibility of ♕e4+ as well as other active factors in his favour, and therefore the sacrifice still succeeds.

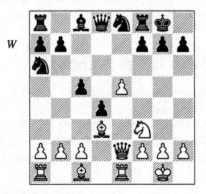

1 ♗xh7+! ♔xh7 2 ♘g5+ ♔g8

Both 2...♔h6 and 2...♔g6 are bad, the latter being met by 3 ♕e4+ f5 4 ♕h4 f4 5 ♕h7+ ♔xg5 6 h4+ ♔g4 7 f3+ ♔g3 8 ♕g6+ ♔xh4 9 ♔f2, etc.

3 ♕e4!

But not 3 ♕h5? ♗f5!.

3...f5 4 ♕h4 ♖f7 5 ♕h8+![1] ♔xh8 6 ♘xf7+ ♔g8 7 ♘xd8 and White wins.

Here the boxed-in position of Black's rook and the possibility of ♕e4+ followed by ♕h4 fully compensate for the absence of one of the basic conditions.

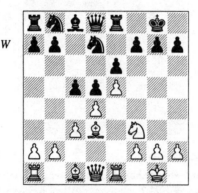

In this position Black has an extra tempo in which to defend himself after ...♔g8 because his rook is already on e8, but White's position is so strong in other respects that his sacrifice still leads to a successful breakthrough.

1 ♗xh7+ ♔xh7 2 ♘g5+ ♔g8 3 ♕h5 ♘f8

A difficulty for Black is that he cannot defend the f7-square; if, for example, 3...♕e7, then 4 ♕h7+ and 5 ♕h8# while if 3...f6, then 4 ♕f7+ ♔h8 5 ♖e3, etc.

4 ♕xf7+ ♔h8 5 ♖e3 and White wins.

These three examples represent only a small section of a large number of possible cases in which the crucial continuation is ...♔g8. How large the variety of these positions is and how sensitive they are to minute changes can be illustrated by the following observation: if, in any of the previous three diagrams, White's h-pawn is moved to h4, the bishop sacrifice is no longer correct. In the first two diagrams (on page 124) this is because the queen is prevented from getting to h4, while in the diagram above it is because White's rook can no longer create threats along the h-file. Having the pawn on h4 rather than h2 is an obstacle in the variation with ...♔g8; on the other hand, we shall see how it assists White in the variation with ...♔g6.

---

1   5 e6 is even stronger, when 5...♕xg5 is forced to avoid mate.

The variation with ...♔g6 is critical

Here the critical continuation is ...♔g6, while that with ...♔g8 involves less difficulty.

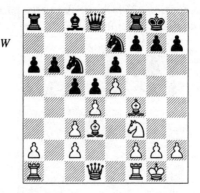

W

1 ♗xh7+ ♔xh7 2 ♘g5+ ♔g6

If 2...♔g8 3 ♕h5 ♖e8, White should keep his eyes well open and stop himself from charging in with 4 ♕xf7+?, since then Black has an adequate defence in 4...♔h8 5 ♕h5+ ♔g8 6 ♕h7+ ♔f8 7 ♕h8+ ♘g8 8 ♘h7+ ♔f7. The finesse lies in not taking the pawn on f7 but playing 4 ♕h7+! ♔f8 5 ♕h8+ ♘g8 6 ♘h7+ ♔e7 7 ♗g5+ f6 8 ♕xg7#!

3 ♕g4! f5 4 ♕g3 ♔e8 5 h4!

Only now does White play this move and force ...♖h8; after the earlier 3 h4 ♖h8 4 ♕g4 f5 5 ♕g3, Black could have countered with 5...♕g8.

5...♖h8 6 ♘xe6+ ♔f7 7 ♕xg7+ ♔xe6 8 ♕f6+ ♔d7 9 ♕d6#.

This is a characteristic outcome of the continuation ...♔g6; with the king on g6, the pawn on h4 is an assistance to White, as it usually is when Black adopts this defence.

In the next case White has no pawn on e5, but the presence of his rook on the open e-file ensures success against ...♔g8. In the variation with ...♔g6 White is made to work for victory.

1 ♗xh7+ ♔xh7 2 ♘g5+ ♔g6 3 ♕g4 f5

If 3...♔f6, then 4 ♕h4 ♖h8[1] 5 ♕f4+, etc. is strongest.

---

1   Here 4...♔g6 is much stronger, when White has nothing better than to repeat moves. Thus White should instead meet 3...♔f6 by 4 ♘e4+ ♔e7 5 ♕xg7 dxe4 (the only chance) 6 ♗g5+ ♔e8 7 ♗xd8 ♖xd8 8 ♖xe4 with a winning position.

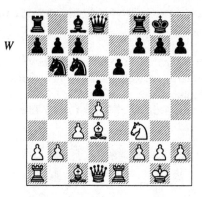

4 ♕g3 f4

4...♔f6 is answered by 5 ♘xe6.

5 ♗xf4 ♔f5 6 h3!

White must be careful; on 6 ♕d3+ Black has 6...♔f6.

6...♕e8

There is no future in 6...e5 because of 7 dxe5.

7 ♘h7 ♕h5 8 ♕d3+ ♔xf4 9 g3#.

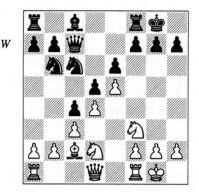

1 ♗xh7+ ♔xh7 2 ♘g5+ ♔g6

In this instance White has no dark-squared bishop, which is what usually rules out the continuation ...♔h6, but even so White can win after 2...♔h6 by 3 ♕g4, threatening an immediate ♕h4+. However, ...♔g8 is also a critical continuation, owing to the protection which Black's queen gives to the focal-point f7. Nevertheless, after 2...♔g8 3 ♕h5 ♖e8 4 ♘df3 ♘d8 5 ♘h4 ♘d7 6 ♕h7+ ♔f8 7 ♖ae1 White's attack is too strong and Black cannot extract his king, for example

7...♗e7 8 ♘g6+ fxg6 9 ♕xg7+ ♘f7 10 ♘xf7 ♕b6 11 ♘d6+ ♔d8 12 ♘xe8 ♔xe8 13 ♖e3, etc.

3 ♕g4 f5 4 ♕h4

The absence of Black's queen from d8 makes this move possible. Black is now obliged to sacrifice in return, since otherwise White will decide the issue with 5 ♕h7+ and an eventual mate.

4...♘xe5 5 dxe5 ♕xe5 6 ♘df3 ♕c7 7 ♖ae1 and White wins.

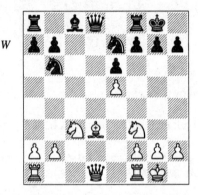

This position differs fundamentally from those considered so far and touches on some new aspects of the sacrificial combination.

1 ♗xh7+ ♔xh7 2 ♘g5+ ♔g6

If 2...♔h6, both 3 ♘xf7+ and 3 ♕g4 ♘f5 4 ♘ce4 lead to victory. Instead of the dark-squared bishop White has the knight on c3 as an active supporting piece, which proves its value in numerous variations. Consider, for example, 2...♔g8 3 ♕h5 ♕d3, where the fact that White has the move 4 ♘ce4 is decisive.

3 ♕g4 f5 4 exf6

4 ♕g3 is not so strong in this position.

4...♔xf6

An obviously important point here and in similar positions is that Black loses his queen after 4...gxf6 5 ♘xe6+, etc.

5 ♘ce4+ ♔e5 6 f4+ ♔d5 7 ♕d1+ ♔c6 8 ♖ac1+ ♔b5 9 ♖c5+ mating quickly.

The variation with ...♔h6 is critical

This continuation is usually difficult for the attacker if he does not have a second bishop and has his h-pawn at h4, and is consequently without the possibility of ♕g4 and ♕h4+.

Here is an example:

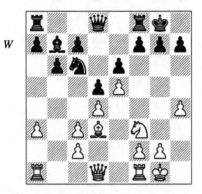

1 ♗xh7+ ♔xh7 2 ♘g5+ ♔h6

Against either of the other continuations White wins easily, but against the text move he has to work hard; victory cannot be forced here, though he has a promising attack.

3 f4!

This is probably White's strongest move. After 3 ♕d2 ♕e7! White can re-establish material equality by 4 ♘xe6+ and 5 ♘xf8, but Black is then the better placed.

3...♘e7 4 h5 g6 5 hxg6 ♘xg6 6 ♕g4 ♔g7 7 f5! exf5 8 ♖xf5

White's threats include 9 ♖xf7+ and 9 e6, as well as 9 ♕h5, so he should win. If 8...♗c8, then 9 ♕h5 is decisive.

Declining the sacrifice

One of the necessary conditions for the success of the classic bishop sacrifice, as of any sacrifice at all, is the opponent's inability to obtain an advantage by rejecting the sacrifice altogether. The attacker must therefore consider what will happen if his opponent plays ...♔h8 and does not take the bishop. The following diagram shows an example of this.

1 ♗xh7+?

Instead of trying to sacrifice his bishop (which is incorrect in this position, since Black can successfully decline it) White should have played 1 ♗e2 with the intention of making use of his pair of bishops and centralizing his knight by ♘d4.

1...♔h8! 2 ♘g5

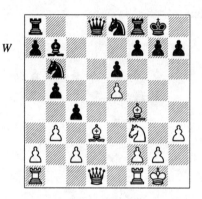

The bishop has nowhere to retreat to, while if 2 ♕e2, then 2...♗xf3 3 ♕xf3 ♔xh7, i.e. Black accepts the sacrifice as soon as he has eliminated White's knight, for without that White's attack is worth nothing.

2...♕xd1 3 ♖fxd1 g6!

White now has no satisfactory defence against the threat of ...♔g7 and ...♖h8, and this gives Black the better prospects.

A practical criterion for the sacrifice

We shall now attempt to establish a practical rule for positions of the type given on pages 122-129, a means by which players can orientate themselves quickly and fairly accurately. Positions similar to that on page 121, i.e. with a rook on h1 and pawn on h4, will be left aside for the time being and will be dealt with in chapter 7. It should also be remarked that in the positions on pages 122-129 the basic condition that the defender should not be able to reject the sacrifice unscathed was fulfilled. It should further be added that the arrangement of Black's pieces in those positions did not depart greatly from the normal, while White, in addition to the essential light-squared bishop, the queen, and the knight on f3, had at his disposal *a number of other supporting pieces* to sustain his attack. Listed in categories, these were:

Pawn at e5 and bishop at c1 on pages 122, 124 (bottom) and 125;
Pawn at e5 and bishop at f4 on page 126;
Pawn at e5 and knight at d2 on page 127 (bottom);
Pawn at e5 and knight at c3 on page 128;
Pawns at e5 and h4 on page 129;
Rook at e1 and bishop at f4 on page 124 (top); and
Rook at e1 and bishop at c1 on page 127 (top).

As can be seen, the principal supporting pieces are the pawn at e5 and the bishop on the diagonal c1-f4, followed by the knight on d2 or c3 and the rook on the open e-file. There may be a few other such supporting pieces (e.g. a rook on f1, if the f-file is open) which have not been provided with examples, but the reader will already have seen the basic idea – as a rule *at least two active support-ing pieces are necessary*, if the classic bishop sacrifice is to bring the attacker success.

This is a simple practical criterion and should help the player to get his ap-proximate bearings. To make this survey of the sacrifice and the structure of its necessary conditions as clear as possible, White has been made the attacker in all the examples; if Black carries out a sacrificial attack on h2, naturally all that has been said applies analogously.

To provide further material on the classic bishop sacrifice three master games will now be examined. The first belongs to the post-war era and provides an ex-ample where the sacrifice is quite correct. In the second the young Capablanca sacrifices on h7, but the analysis shows the existence of a loophole in the varia-tion with ...♔g6 which his opponent failed to notice. In the third, Colle sacrifices and wins both the game and the Brilliancy Prize, even though in fact two of the variations are unsound!

Kottnauer – Kotov
Match, Prague vs Moscow, Moscow 1946
Queen's Gambit Declined, Semi-Slav Defence

1 c4 e6 2 d4 d5 3 ♘c3 c6 4 ♘f3 ♘f6 5 e3 ♘bd7 6 ♗d3 dxc4 7 ♗xc4 b5 8 ♗d3 a6 9 e4 c5 10 e5 cxd4 11 ♘xb5 axb5

Nowadays 11...♘xe5 is more commonly played and analysed. 11...♘g4 is not so good because of 12 ♘bxd4 ♘gxe5 13 ♗e4 when White has the advantage.

12 exf6 ♛b6 13 fxg7

The incisive quality of this variation is rapidly lost if White continues 13 0-0 gxf6 14 ♗e4 ♗b7 15 ♗xb7 ♛xb7 16 ♘xd4 ♖g8 17 ♛f3. Black can then simplify the position and reach an ending by 17...♛xf3 18 ♘xf3 ♖g4! in which the chances are approximately even.

13...♗xg7 14 0-0 0-0 15 ♛e2 ♘c5? *(D)*

According to modern analysis the classic bishop sacrifice is correct at this point and therefore 15...♘c5? should be censured; instead, the correct continua-tion is 15...♗b7 16 ♗xb5 (the sacrifice at h7 does not work here because of the defence provided by ...♘f6 in the ...♔g8 variation) 16...♗xf3 17 gxf3 ♘c5 and if 18 a4 or 18 ♗c4, then 18...e5 with good positional compensation for the pawn.

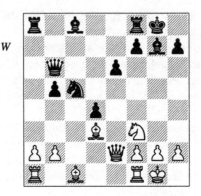

16 ♝xh7+!

Here is an example of the classic bishop sacrifice on h7 in a position which differs from those examined hitherto. First of all, a bishop, and not a pawn, is on g7, while Black's queen is on b6 and not on d8. Let us now look at the conditions for success in each of the variations. Clearly, ...♔h8 does not come into consideration at all, nor does moving the king to h6, but the variation with ...♔g8 gives rise to a few doubts, since the bishop's presence on g7 prevents the well-known harrying of the king by ♛h8+. We shall see later on how really critical this variation is and that White's success hangs on a thread. The ...♔g6 variation presents an even harder prospect, for White has only one of the supporting pieces mentioned above (bishop at c1) at his disposal and still needs an extra tempo to make up the necessary pair with ♜e1. Furthermore, Black's queen is not imperilled on b6 by the battery of queen on g4 and knight on g5, as is the case when it is on d8; moreover, Black's considerable strength in the centre and on the queenside opens up the possibility of defending by returning the material and exploiting the positional compensation obtained for it. According to our scheme, then, the continuation ...♔g6 represents a danger to White, and we should have to doubt the success of the attack if it were not for one more factor which helps White: the fact that a bishop, and not a pawn, stands at g7 means that an attack on that square entails the loss of a piece and not of a pawn. While the bishop on g7 helps Black in the ...♔g8 variation, with ...♔g6 it acts as a drawback which compensates for the deficiencies in White's position already referred to. These points will be best illuminated by further analysis.

16...♔xh7 17 ♞g5+ ♔g6

Let us now consider the alternative continuation, 17...♔g8. After 18 ♛h5 ♜d8 19 ♛xf7+ ♔h8 all the commentators (including the author in his *Modern Opening Theory*) have given a win for White by 20 f4 ♛b7 21 ♜f3?. However, there is a flaw in this, in that Black can embark upon 21...♕xf7 22 ♘xf7+ ♔g8 23 ♘xd8, obtaining excellent compensation for the exchange, e.g. 23...♗d7 24 b4 ♘a4 25 ♘b7 ♗c6 26 ♘c5 (or 26 ♘a5) 26...♗xf3 27 gxf3 d3 28 ♖b1 ♘c3 and Black wins the c1-bishop at the very least. This scotches the idea of 21 ♖f3?; a better move, therefore, is 21 ♕g6, though after 21...♔g8 22 ♖f3 ♕e7 23 ♖h3 ♔f8 (otherwise 24 ♖h8+!) White only has a draw by 24 ♘h7+ ♔g8 25 ♘g5, etc. If he plays for a material advantage with 24 ♖h8+? ♗xh8 25 ♘h7+ ♕xh7 26 ♕xh7, then 26...♗g7 brings his attack to a standstill, after which Black's threats make themselves felt.

These variations, however, do not comprise a full coverage of 17...♔g8; instead of 20 f4 White has a better move, i.e. 20 ♗f4!. Here is an analysis:

1) 20...♘d7 21 ♘xe6 wins.
2) 20...♘d3 21 ♕g6! picks up the knight.
3) 20...♕b7 fails against 21 ♗c7.
4) 20...e5 21 ♗xe5 ♕h6 22 ♕e7! ♗e6 23 ♗xg7+ ♕xg7 24 ♕xc5 winning.
5) 20...♖a7 21 ♕g6 ♔g8 22 ♗e5 ♕b7 (the queen must defend the bishop on g7, since otherwise White plays 23 ♕h7+ followed by ♗xg7+ and ♕h8+) 23 ♖ac1 ♘a6 24 ♖xc8! ♕xc8 (or 24...♖xc8 25 ♗d6! and there is no defence against 26 ♕h7#) 25 ♕h7+ ♔f8 26 ♗xg7+ ♖xg7 27 ♕h8+ ♖g8 28 ♕f6+ and 29 ♕f7#.

As can be seen, a considerable analytical effort was needed to overcome a defence built round the fianchetto, and more will be said about this in a separate chapter.

18 ♕g4 f5 19 ♕g3 *(D)*

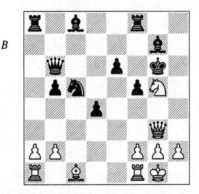

A critical stage of the game. It is now evident that the position of his bishop at g7 is an embarrassment to Black, since there is an immediate threat of ♘xe6+ with a double attack on g7 and f8.

In the actual game Black played 19...♔f6, but that move, like 19...♗f6, does not cause White as much difficulty as 19...♖f7!, as the following variations show:

1) 19...♗f6 20 ♘xe6+ ♔f7 21 ♘xf8 ♔xf8 22 ♕g6 ♘e4! (Black's strongest defence; White cannot now play 23 f3 because of 23...d3+ 24 ♔h1 d2 and Black has at least equal chances[1]) 23 ♗h6+ ♔e7 24 f3 d3+ 25 ♔h1 ♘f2+ 26 ♖xf2 ♕xf2 27 ♕h7+ ♔e6[2] 28 ♕g8+ ♔e5 29 ♕e8+ ♔d4 30 ♕c6, with advantage to White.

2) 19...♖f7! (this move was suggested by Kovaliev, who considered that it saved Black's game, but his analysis did not take into account the important intermediate move 20 b4!) 20 b4! and now:

2a) 20...♘d7 21 ♘xe6+ ♔h7 (or 21...♔f6 22 ♘c7! and White wins) 22 ♖e1 ♘f6 23 ♘g5+ ♔g8 24 ♘xf7 ♔xf7 25 ♖e7+ ♔xe7 26 ♕xg7+ ♔e6 27 ♗g5 and White's attack cannot be withstood.

2b) 20...♘a4 21 h4! e5 22 h5+ ♔f6 23 ♖e1 ♖e7 24 ♗f4 exf4 25 ♘h7+ ♔f7 26 ♖xe7+ ♔xe7 27 ♕xg7+. White's attack is extremely strong and the advance of his h-pawn must be decisive. This analysis does not exhaust the position entirely but it does illustrate White's excellent chances.

19...♔f6 20 ♗f4! *(D)*

Keres had already analysed 16 ♗xh7+ and its consequences before this game took place. At this point he gave the continuation 20 ♕h4? on which Black plays

---

1   This is a considerable exaggeration. After 25 fxe4 dxc1♕ 26 ♖axc1 White has a material advantage and a strong attack – indeed this line seems clearer than 23 ♗h6+.

2   27...♔d6 is a much better defence. After 28 ♗f8+ ♔e6 29 ♕g8+ ♔e5 White is deprived of the check on e8 and so the position remains unclear.

20...♖h8 and White gets no more than perpetual check. Kotov knew of this analysis, which explains why he went in for 15...♘c5?. Now Kottnauer shows that White has a stronger move than 20 ♕h4? and in doing so demonstrates that not even the analysis of great masters is always reliable.

20...♔e7

If 20...♘d7 White wins at once by 21 ♘xe6 ♕xe6 22 ♖ae1 ♕d5 23 ♕g5+ ♔f7 24 ♖e7+.

21 ♖ac1 ♖a7

If 21...b4, which rules out an attack by 22 b4, White plays 22 ♘h7[1] ♖f7 23 ♕g6 with the decisive threat of 24 ♘g5.

22 ♖fe1 ♗d7

If 22...♗f6 White wins by 23 ♘h7 ♖f7 (or 23...♘e4 24 ♖xe4) 24 ♘xf6 ♖xf6 25 b4 etc.

23 b4 ♘a6 24 ♘xe6 ♗xe6 25 ♕xg7+ ♖f7 26 ♗g5+ ♔d7 27 ♕h8 ♕b8 28 ♕xd4+ 1-0

Capablanca – Molina
Buenos Aires, 1911
Queen's Gambit Declined, Orthodox Defence

1 d4 d5 2 c4 e6 3 ♘c3 ♘f6 4 ♗g5 ♘bd7 5 e3 c6 6 ♘f3 ♗e7 7 cxd5 ♘xd5 8 ♗xe7 ♘xe7

Black's opening play is not to be taken as a model; on 7 cxd5 the reply 7...exd5 would have been better, and at this point he should certainly have played 8...♕xe7 instead of recalling his knight.

9 ♗d3 c5 10 0-0 0-0 11 dxc5?!

This move only has a point if the sacrifice on h7 is correct, otherwise it makes it easier for Black to equalize. Since the sacrifice is unsound, 11 ♖c1 would have been the right course.

11...♘xc5 12 ♗xh7+?!

The young victor from San Sebastian naturally does not consent to make a peaceful move like 12 ♗e2 against an Argentine amateur. However unsound the sacrifice is, his opponent will see to it for himself that his own position is spoilt...

12...♔xh7 13 ♘g5+ ♔g6 *(D)*

---

1   Somewhat more convincing is 22 ♗c7! ♕c6 (forced, as the queen must defend both c5 and d6) 23 ♘xe6! ♗xe6 24 ♕xg7+ ♔e8 25 ♕e5 with an easy win. The move 21...♖a7 is designed partly to prevent ♗c7.

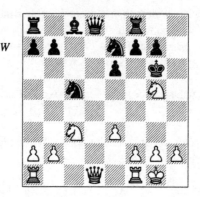

Black is correct to choose the ...♔g6 variation and the reader – armed with the guidance given a few pages back – will notice that White's chances of success in this case are dubious, since he does not have the two necessary supporting pieces, but only one, and a fairly weak one at that (the knight on c3).

14 ♕g4 f5

As a lover of fine combinations from his earliest youth, Capablanca here quotes the following continuation: 14...e5? 15 ♘e6+ ♔f6 16 f4! e4 (or 16...♘c6 17 ♕g5+ ♔xe6 18 f5+ ♔d7 19 ♖fd1+ ♘d4 20 ♕xg7 when White will get one piece back and have three pawns for his knight plus a winning attack against Black's exposed king) 17 ♕g5+ ♔xe6 18 ♕e5+ ♔d7 19 ♖fd1+ ♘d3 20 ♘xe4 ♔c6 21 ♖xd3 ♕xd3 22 ♖c1+ and mate in a few moves.

15 ♕g3 ♔h6?

This game has entered the anthologies as one of Capablanca's famous feats because commentators have passed this obviously incorrect move by in silence. By 15...♔f6! Black could have shown that the bishop sacrifice was unsound. White can then still exert some pressure (after 16 ♖ad1 ♗d7 or 16 b4 ♘a6), but he has not got the time to strengthen his attack decisively, since Black threatens to consolidate his position (e.g. 16 e4 g6 or 16 f4 ♖h8). White must therefore take the exchange by 16 ♘h7+ with the result that his attack comes to a halt, leaving him without sufficient compensation for Black's material advantage[1].

In addition to 15...♔f6!, another move which is better than the one played is 15...f4, which would force White to play for a draw, i.e. 16 exf4 ♘f5 17 ♕g4 ♘h6 18 ♕g3 ♘f5, etc[2].

---

1   This comment is unjustified, since after 15...♔f6 16 ♖ad1 ♗d7 White wins by
      17 b4 ♘a6 18 e4.
2   This comment is correct, so both 15...♔h6 and 15...f4 should lead to a draw.

16 ♕h4+ ♔g6 17 ♕h7+ ♔f6

If 17...♔xg5 then 18 ♕xg7+ ♔h5 (or 18...♘g6 19 f4+) and White obtains a mating attack by 19 f4 or 19 ♘e2.

18 e4!

In order, on 18...♖h8, to have the reply 19 e5+ ♔xg5 20 f4+, etc. If 18...e5, then 19 ♖ad1 ♕e8 20 ♖d6+ is strong.

18...♘g6 (D)

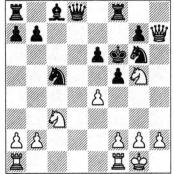

19 exf5?

This makes it easier for Black to defend himself and throws away the opportunity of e5+; it is uncertain whether White now has the advantage or not. Capablanca in his commentary correctly notes that 19 exf5 was not the best move, but he recommends instead 19 f4?, which would not have been good either; Black replies 19...♕d4+ (Capablanca only gives 19...fxe4? 20 ♖ad1 ♕b6, when White wins with 21 ♖d6) 20 ♔h1 ♘xe4 21 ♘cxe4+ fxe4 22 ♖ad1 ♕a4, and White's attack begins to wane; moreover, Black threatens 23...♖h8[1].

Correct would have been at once 19 ♖ad1, with the following variations:

1) 19...♕b6 is simply met by 20 exf5.

2) 19...♘d3 20 f4 ♕d4+ (if 20...♖h8, then 21 e5+ wins) 21 ♔h1 ♘f2+ (or 21...fxe4 22 ♘cxe4+ ♔e7 23 ♕xg6) 22 ♖xf2 ♕xf2 23 e5+ ♔e7 24 ♕xg7+ ♔e8 25 ♕c7 and mates.

3) 19...♕e8 20 f4 fxe4 21 ♘cxe4+ ♘xe4 22 ♘xe4+ ♔e7 (or 22...♔f5 23 ♘g3+[2] ♔f6 24 ♘h5+, etc.) 23 ♘d6 and White wins.

---

1   White has no trouble forcing a draw at the end of this line, for example by 23 ♖c1 or 23 b3, but he cannot gain the advantage.

2   23 ♕h3+ ♔xe4 24 ♕d3# is quicker.

4) 19...♛xd1 20 ♜xd1 ♜h8 21 e5+ ♚xg5 22 h4+ and White wins.

19...exf5 20 ♜ad1 ♞d3!

Against other moves 21 ♞d5+ would be decisive; but White is now really threatened with ...♜h8 and has to withdraw his queen, which means that the strongest weapon in his attack has been beaten back.

21 ♛h3 ♞df4?

Black throws away his chance. With 21...♞gf4 (22 ♛h4 ♜h8) he could have given White a lot of trouble and perhaps even won the game.

22 ♛g3 ♛c7 23 ♜fe1 (D)

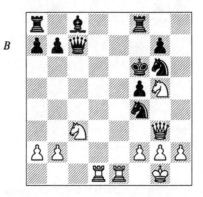

23...♞e2+?

This loses a piece, but Black would probably lose whatever he played[1]. Thus if 23...♗e6, then 24 ♜xe6+ ♞xe6 25 ♞d5#, while if 23...♗d7, White simplifies the position by 24 ♞d5+! ♞xd5 25 ♞h7+ ♚f7 26 ♛xc7 ♞xc7 27 ♜xd7+ ♚g8 28 ♞xf8 ♞xf8 29 ♜xc7.

24 ♜xe2 ♛xg3 25 ♞h7+

The famous intermediate move!

25...♚f7 26 hxg3 ♜h8 27 ♞g5+ ♚f6 28 f4 1-0

This game, here given a proper critical commentary for the first time, provides yet another blow against the legend of 'the infallible Cuban'.

Another interesting point is that Capablanca often undertook attacks against the castled king in his earlier years, but extremely rarely as he became older. This was to a certain extent the result of the progressively greater ability of his

---

1   The strongest defence is 23...♜d8!, which prevents 24 ♞b5 owing to 24...♞e2+.
     In this case White would have a draw at best.

opponents and a general rise in standards, but it was perhaps even more because of a gradual waning of enthusiasm under the weight of increasing self-criticism. Unlike Capablanca, Alekhine played in his own style from his youth right till the end, accepting the risk of difficult attacks against the castled king even against strong opponents.

Colle – O'Hanlon
Nice, 1930
Colle System

1 d4 d5 2 ♘f3 ♘f6 3 e3 c5 4 c3 e6 5 ♗d3 ♗d6 6 ♘bd2 ♘bd7 7 0-0 0-0 8 ♖e1 ♖e8

This does little harm, but 8...♕b6 is better, according to theory.

9 e4 dxe4 10 ♘xe4 ♘xe4 11 ♗xe4 cxd4 12 ♗xh7+? (D)

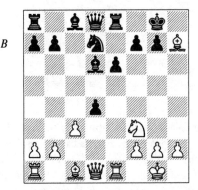

A great lover of the classic sacrifice, Colle here too is unable to control his temperamental penchant for sacrifice, though even at a quick glance it is apparent that the presence of Black's knight on d7 is a danger in both the main variations, while a valuable tempo is saved in the ...♔g8 variation by the rook's being on e8. Correct would have been either 12 ♘xd4 or 12 cxd4[1].

12...♔xh7 13 ♘g5+ ♔g6

So far all is well, since in the event of 13...♔g8 the sacrifice is half correct, that is, White can obtain a draw. After 13...♔g8 14 ♕h5 ♘e5 15 ♖xe5 ♗xe5 16 ♕xf7+ White can get perpetual check, but no more than that. Black is no better off if he tries a different line in this variation, e.g. 14...♕f6 (instead of 14...♘e5)

---

1   As we shall see, Vuković is far too pessimistic about this sacrifice.

15 ♕h7+ ♔f8 16 ♘e4 ♕e5 17 cxd4, whereupon 17...♕xh2+ is forced, for 17...♕d5 is not feasible because of 18 ♕h8+ ♔e7 19 ♗g5+ f6 20 ♕xg7+, with a massacre of Black's pawns[1].

14...♘f6? is very weak indeed on account of 15 ♕xf7+ ♔h8 16 ♖e4.

14 h4 (D)

Obviously, this is the only continuation which can present Black with any difficulties; 14 ♕g4 holds out no prospects here because of the reply 14...f5 15 ♕h4 ♘f6.

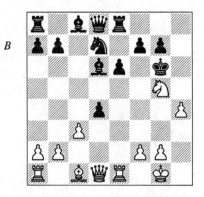

14...♖h8?

The decisive mistake. Black was probably only reckoning on 15 ♕d3+ f5 16 ♖xe6+ ♘f6, and did not see that White also had 15 ♖xe6+!. Correct was 14...f5! 15 h5+ (or 15 ♘xe6 ♕xh4 16 ♘f4+ ♗xf4 17 ♖xe8 ♕h2+ 18 ♔f1 ♕h1+ 19 ♔e2 ♕xd1+ 20 ♔xd1 ♗e5! and Black stands better) 15...♔f6 16 ♕xd4+ ♗e5 17 ♖xe5[2] ♘xe5 18 ♘h7+ ♔f7 19 ♘g5+ ♔g8 20 ♕xe5 ♕d1+ when Black is the exchange ahead and should win.

15 ♖xe6+! ♘f6 (D)

---

1   First of all, Vuković's line 13...♔g8 14 ♕h5 ♘e5 15 ♖xe5 ♗xe5 16 ♕xf7+ is
     not a draw, but a forced win for White after 16...♔h8 17 ♕h5+ ♔g8 18 b3, and
     the arrival of the bishop on a3 completes the mating net. His other suggestion,
     14...♕f6 15 ♕h7+ ♔f8 16 ♘e4 ♕e5 is in fact Black's best defence, but even
     here White need not take the draw, but can very well play for a win by 17 f4!
     ♕d5 18 c4 ♕c6 19 f5!. After 19...♘f6 20 ♘xf6 gxf6 21 ♗g5!, for example,
     White has an extremely dangerous attack. Thus Colle's sacrifice gives White a
     very promising attack even against perfect defence, so Vuković's acerbic com-
     ments regarding Colle's play (see page 121) seem rather unjustified.

If 15...fxe6 then 16 ♕d3+ wins, e.g. 16...♔h5 17 g4+ followed by a quick mate or 16...♔f6 17 ♕f3+ ♗f4 18 ♕xf4+ with a slightly delayed, though still relentless, pursuit ending in mate.

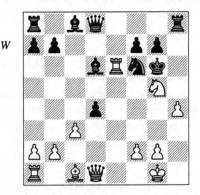

16 h5+ ♔h6
Or 16...♖xh5 17 ♕d3+ and 18 ♕h7#.
17 ♖xd6 ♕a5 18 ♘xf7+ ♔h7 19 ♘g5+ ♔g8 20 ♕b3+ 1-0

We have used this game to illustrate a case where the classic bishop sacrifice was incorrect. The tournament jury, however, awarded it the First Brilliancy Prize. This was immediately after Alekhine's reign of terror at San Remo and before the Carnival.

---

2   17 ♕h4! is a huge improvement which leaves Black defenceless, e.g. 17...♕a5 (17...♔e7 18 ♕b4+ ♔f6 19 f4 ♗c7 20 ♕d4+ e5 21 ♕c4 mates) 18 f4 ♗c7 19 ♘xe6+ ♔f7 20 ♘g5+ ♔f8 21 ♖xe8+ ♔xe8 22 ♕e1+ ♔f8 23 ♕e6 ♕c5+ 24 ♗e3 ♕e7 25 h6 and wins.

7 Ranks, files and diagonals in the attack on the castled king

An action in the vicinity of the castled king can be carried out by any of the pieces, but the long-range ones, the queen, rook, and bishop, are the most effective. They can attack from a distance along the ranks, files, and diagonals. The line concerned has to be 'captured,' i.e. one's own long-range piece has to be placed on it, confrontation by the opponent's corresponding piece has to be overcome, and the line has to be 'cleared' of all enemy influence. Outposts lie on such lines; batteries and pins take place along them. In a mating attack the line may finally witness the execution, i.e. checkmate. In this chapter we shall consider in turn the part played in the attack on the castled king by the ranks, files, and diagonals and reveal some typical operations involving them.

The weakness of the back rank

Of operations on the ranks, the first class to be considered is that aimed at a weakness on the back rank. A few practical examples will help.

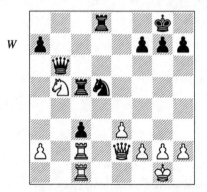

This position is from Bernstein-Capablanca, Exhibition Game, Moscow 1914. It is White's move, and he ought to have realized that because of his weakness on the back rank Black's pawn on c3 was 'taboo'. He should therefore have played 1 ᐁd4, but he decided not to, and the result was a disaster on his back rank.

1 ♘xc3? ♘xc3 2 ♖xc3 ♖xc3 3 ♖xc3 ♕b2! 0-1

But not 3...♕b1+? 4 ♕f1, in which case 4...♖d1 is impossible because of Black's weakness on his own back rank. However, the move 3...♕b2, typical of Capablanca, solves the problem completely: White resigned, for he is unable to take the queen and his own rook and queen are threatened; if 4 ♕d3 or 4 ♖d3, then 4...♕a1+ wins.

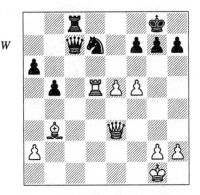

This position is from Mikenas-Maroczy, Folkestone 1933. White, to move, advanced his e-pawn to exploit Black's weakness on the back rank.

1 e6 ♘b6 2 e7 ♖e8 3 ♖d8! ♖xd8 4 e8♕+ and mate next move.

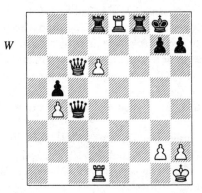

In this position, which occurred in the game Najdorf-Julio Bolbochan, Mar del Plata 1948, White exploited Black's back-row weakness by an operation in which his passed pawn played a typically prominent part.

1 ♖xd8! ♖xd8

If 1...♛xc6, then 2 ♖xf8+ ♚xf8 3 d7 and White wins.

2 ♛b6 ♖f8

This loses at once, but Black could not have lasted long in any case, e.g. 2...♛c8 3 d7 ♛a8 (or 3...♖xd7 4 ♛e6+) 4 ♛e6+ ♚h8 5 ♖e1 h6 (or 5...g6 6 ♛f6+ ♚g8 7 ♛xd8+ ♛xd8 8 ♖e8+) 6 ♛g6 ♖g8 7 h3 (preparing an escape hole in order to threaten ♖e8) 7...♛d8 8 ♛f7 ♚h7 9 ♖e8 and White wins.

3 d7 ♖f1+ 4 ♚g1! 1-0

Since after 4...♖xg1+ 5 ♚xg1 Black cannot halt the d-pawn.

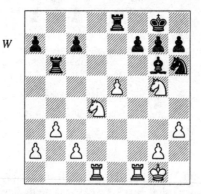

This position is from the game Alekhine-E. Cohn, Stockholm 1912. White, to move, must try to retain his extra pawn. A 'realistic' tournament player would quietly play 1 ♖fe1 c5 2 ♘df3 and if 2...♗xc2, then 3 ♖c1, or if 2...f6, then 3 exf6 ♖xe1+ 4 ♘xe1, etc. However, this seemed too limp a solution to the young Alekhine, who wanted to keep Black's knight in its corner at h6 a little longer; in a typically 'incisive' way he defended the pawn on e5 indirectly, or rather 'sold it for the back rank', and this is in fact as good a method as that given above.

1 c4 ♖xe5 2 c5!

A little more spice; if 2...♖xc5, then 3 ♘de6 wins a rook.

2...♖a6?

He could have put up more resistance by 2...♖f6, for 3 ♘f5 does not achieve much because of 3...♚f8. Correct would be 3 ♘gf3!, against which Black must play 3...♖e8, but not 3...♖xc5? on account of 4 ♘f5!, when White wins the exchange at the very least[1].

3 ♘de6?

This only leads to a small material advantage, whereas he could have won convincingly by 3 ♘b5![2], which is equally effective in stopping Black's rook from returning to the back rank (with the help of ♘xc7) but at the same time does not leave the knight *en prise* at e6. This point is demonstrated by the following variations:

1) 3...♔h8 4 ♖d8+ ♘g8 5 ♘xf7+ ♗xf7 6 ♖xf7, and Black loses his knight while White's on b5 remains intact.

2) 3...f6 4 ♘xc7 ♖xa2 5 ♖d8+ ♗e8 6 ♘xe8 ♔f8 7 ♘xc7+ ♔e7 8 ♖e8#.

3...♔h8

The only reply.

4 ♖d8+ ♘g8 *(D)*

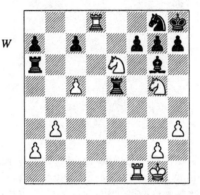

5 ♘xc7

White cannot play 5 ♖xf7 because of 5...♖axe6, while if 5 ♘xf7+ ♗xf7 6 ♖xf7 ♖axe6 7 ♖ff8 White merely regains the piece he has lost – that is the difference between the knight's position on b5 and e6. Even more instructive is the fact that 5 ♖fd1? will not work because of 5...♖axe6! 6 ♘xe6 fxe6, and there is no mate (by ♖xg8+ and ♖d8+) since Black has freed the square f7.

---

1 An interesting moment. After 2...♖f6 3 ♘gf3 ♖e8, as Vukovic gives, it is hard to see what White has gained in return for surrendering his extra pawn. Of course, White retains a positional advantage, but this is far from conclusive. Curiously, in the English edition of his best games collection, Alekhine does not mention 2...♖f6, but in his *Deux Cents Parties d'Echecs* he gives "On 2...♖f6, White wins by 3 ♘f5!, etc.". Probably both 3 ♘gf3 and 3 ♘f5 are wrong; the strongest line is 3 ♘c6! ♖e8 (3...♖xf1+ 4 ♔xf1 ♖e8 5 ♖d7 is also very bad) 4 ♘e7+ ♔f8 5 ♖fe1!, threatening 6 ♘xg6+, and Black's position is hopeless (5...♗f5 6 g4 or 5...♗c2 6 ♖d2).

2 Vukovic is absolutely correct about 3 ♘b5!, a move which goes unmentioned by Alekhine.

5...Rxa2 6 Rfd1

Now that Black already has a rook at a2, 6 Nxf7+ Kxf7 7 Rxf7 is answered by 7...Ree2, while if 6 Rxf7, then 6...Rxg2+ 7 Kf1 Rgxg5 8 Rff8 Rgf5+.

6...f6 7 Rxg8+ Kxg8 8 Rd8+ Be8 9 Nxe8 Kf8 10 Nd6+ Ke7 11 Re8+ Kd7 12 Rxe5 fxe5 13 Nc4 Kc6 14 Ne4 (D)

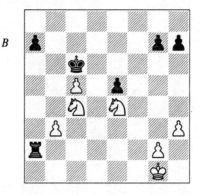

One might now say 'and White won after another twenty moves', for this position no longer has anything to do with the difficulties on the back rank, but it is worth remarking that the task is a difficult one, so difficult indeed that Alekhine went astray and after **14...Ra1+ 15 Kf2 Kd5 16 Kf3 a5** played **17 Ke2?** (17 Ncd2 was correct). This was answered by **17...a4!** (not 17...Kxe4? on account of 18 c6!), after which White, objectively speaking, should not have got more than a draw. Alekhine, however, did not submit to 18 Nc3+ Kxc5 19 Nxa4+ Kd4 but went on to risk **18 Ncd2? a3 19 b4 Rc1!** and so reached a losing position. Play continued **20 Kd3 a2 21 Nb3 Rd1+ 22 Kc2 a1Q 23 Nxa1 Rxa1 24 Nc3+,** at which stage Black could have won by 24...Kc4! 25 c6 Ra7! 26 b5 Rc7. Instead, he spoilt his position by playing **24...Kc6?** The finish ran: **25 Kd3 Rf1 26 g3! h5 27 Kc4 h4 28 b5+ Kd7 29 gxh4 Rf4+ 30 Kd5 Rxh4 31 c6+ Kc7 32 Kc5! Rxh3 33 b6+ Kb8 34 Nb5 1-0**

Combinations based on the weakness of the back rank are usually of short duration and matters come quickly to a head. This has been shown by the examples given above, and others, equally short-lived, could easily be added to them. However, just as success may come quickly, so too failure can suddenly occur as a result of a lightning counter-stroke which removes the weakness from the opponent's back rank. As an example of such a turning-point let us examine the next position.

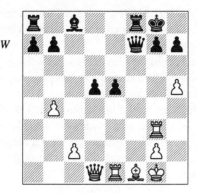

Flohr, when he was White in this position from a simultaneous display played in Leningrad during 1933, continued:

1 ♖xe5

and left his opponent to think it over.

1...♕f2+

Both Flohr and the commentators thought that Black, in making this move, had fallen into a trap, but in fact he has nothing better. For example, if 1...♗e6, then 2 ♕e1 ♖ae8 (or 2...♗f5 3 ♖e7) 3 ♗b5 ♗d7 4 h6! (not 4 ♖f3 because of 4...♕xh5) 4...♗xb5 (if 4...g6, White wins with 5 ♖f3) 5 ♖xg7+ ♕xg7 6 hxg7 ♖f1+ 7 ♕xf1 ♗xf1 8 ♖xe8+ and White wins[1].

2 ♔h2 ♕xf1?!

This is a comparative mistake only, since Black's game is now lost in any case. 2...♕f4 would have offered more resistance.

3 ♕xd5+ ♔h8

If 3...♕f7, White wins by 4 ♖e7!.

4 ♖f3?

This was intended to be the decisive stroke, but in fact it is a mistake. White would easily have won by 4 h6, and if 4...g6, then 5 ♖f3; alternatively, if 4...gxh6 then 5 ♖e8, after which mate is unavoidable. This variation shows the correct way to exploit the weakness on the back rank, while 4 ♖f3? was inadequate as Black had the reply 4...♗e6!, when by returning the extra piece he could have got rid of the weakness on his back rank with tempo and reached a drawn position. As it was, however, he played **4...♖xf3?**, and everything was immediately put

---

1   In this line 4...♕f6! favours Black after 5 ♖xg7+ ♔h8 or 5 hxg7 ♖xe5, so White should prefer 3 h6 g6 4 ♖ge3 d4 (4...♗d7 5 ♖f3) 5 ♖f3 ♕d7 6 ♖xf8+ ♔xf8 7 ♗b5 and wins.

right: White replied **5 ♕xf3**, and Black with good reason resigned **(1-0)**.

This example shows what vigilant care needs to be taken with combinations aimed at a weakness on the back rank.

In connection with this back-row weakness, something should also be said about the so-called 'escape hole', i.e. the gap made by moving a pawn with the sole purpose of eliminating the danger of mate on the back rank or at least of freeing the rook guarding the rank. On the other hand, such a move, like any pawn move in front of the castled king, represents a weakening of the position, and it is a question here of correctly assessing whether the advantages involved outweigh the weaknesses or *vice versa*. This is one of the numerous double-edged features of chess.

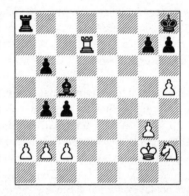

As an example of the sensitivity of the connection between the weakness of the back rank and that of the 'escape hole' the above position is instructive.

It is Black's move, and if it were not for his weakness on the back rank, the problem would be an extremely straightforward one: White's pawns on the queenside would fall one by one. Thus it is a question of first averting the danger on the back rank and only then making the time to 'pick off' the pawns. Let us create an 'escape hole' for the king.

1...h6?

A mistake? Yes, and a bad one, for Black is now faced with a new weakness on g6. The other 'hole', 1...g6, is no good either, since White can get an easy draw by 2 ♘g4 (with the threat of ♘f6 and mate on h7) 2...♖f8 (or 2...♗f8 3 h6) 3 h6 ♖f5 (the only move; for if 3...b5, 4 ♖d5 is a strong reply, while 3...♔g8? is not good on account of 4 ♖g7+ and 5 ♘e5) 4 ♖d8+[1] ♖f8 (4...♗f8? 5 ♘e3 and 6

---

1   White would even stand to win after 4 ♘e3!, winning the c4-pawn for nothing.

♘xc4) 5 ♖d7 followed by a repetition of moves.

Also weak is 1...♗f8? 2 ♘g4 ♖xa2 3 h6! gxh6 4 ♘f6 ♗g7 5 ♖d8+ ♗f8 6 ♖d7!, again with a draw by repetition.

2 ♘g4 ♖xa2 3 ♘e5 ♔g8 4 ♖d8+ ♗f8

Or 4...♔h7 5 ♘g6, mating.

5 ♘xc4 b5

Or 5...♔f7 6 ♖b8.

6 ♘e5 ♖xb2 7 ♘g6 ♖xc2+ 8 ♔f3 ♖c3+ 9 ♔g4 ♖c4+ 10 ♔h3 ♔f7 11 ♖xf8+
and Black must lose.

As we have seen, the 'escape holes' did not work; in this position they represent too great a weakness, so the only correct continuation is 1...♔g8!, which removes the danger on the back rank without weakening the pawn position. What is more, Black must also avoid moving his pawns if White continues with his sharpest reply, 2 h6! (since if 2...gxh6, White can draw by 3 ♘g4). He should instead play the solid 2...♗f8, after which he can reap his pawn harvest with ...♖xa2, etc. Another typical variation is 2 ♘g4 (instead of 2 h6) 2...♖xa2 3 ♘e5 ♖xb2 4 ♖d8+ ♗f8 5 ♘d7 ♖xc2+ 6 ♔f3 ♔f7. Now one can appreciate the significance of White's lack of an outpost for his knight – he wins the bishop by 7 ♘xf8 but Black, with 7...b3, wins the game[1].

The sensitivity of 'escape holes' of this kind can best be seen if White's pawn on h5 is moved to h4. Then, as well as 1...♔g8, Black may also play 1...h6, a fact of which the reader may convince himself by his own analysis.

The weakness of the second rank

The second rank, on which the pawns stand at the start of the game, is generally as weak as the back rank; the pawns stand on it but do not protect it. There is, however, a difference, in that the second rank is harder to 'clear' prior to its being used by a rook or queen because the pawns tend to get in the way, just as trees in a forest tend to obstruct a clear view. Consequently, weaknesses on the second rank most frequently appear on individual squares or focal-points, and it is rarer to find a general weakness affecting the whole rank. The latter phenomenon,

---

1   This is all rather confusing. After what Vuković considers to be Black's best continuation, 1...♔g8 2 ♘g4 ♖xa2, White can play 3 h6 forcing 3...♗f8 (or else perpetual check), but after 1...♗f8 2 ♘g4 ♖xa2, which Vuković condemns on account of 3 h6, Black can reach exactly the same position by playing 3...♔g8!. The truth of the matter is that 1...♔g8 and 1...♗f8 work equally well, because neither weakens the kingside pawn structure.

which concerns us here, is generally described as 'a rook on the seventh rank', but it would be more accurate to speak of a strongly-placed queen or rook on the opponent's second rank.

This kind of situation is on the whole exploited for positional purposes (to put pressure on the pawns and capture them or else to prevent the opponent from moving his king into the centre), but the position of a queen or rook on the seventh rank can also be useful in an attack on the castled king, where a 'clearing up' operation is often of decisive importance.

A weakness on the second rank often goes hand in hand with a weakness on the back rank. The following combination of Rubinstein's makes effective use of both ranks.

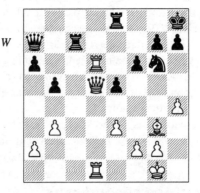

This position occurred in the game Rubinstein-Maroczy, Gothenburg 1920. White's first act was to advance his pawn to h6 and so create the necessary conditions for an attack on the seventh rank.

1 h5 ♘f8 2 h6!

White now threatens 3 ♗h4, which would also be decisive in the event of 2...gxh6.

2...♘g6 3 ♕e6!

Now White takes advantage of the weakness of the back rank to penetrate with his queen; 3...♖xe6 is met by 4 ♖d8+, while if 3...♖ce7, then 4 hxg7+.

3...♖f8 4 ♖d7

The position is ripe for the rooks to take possession of the seventh rank. Black is now forced to play 4...gxh6, after which the 'clearing' of the rank is complete.

4...gxh6 5 ♗h4! 1-0

The threat of ♗xf6+ compels 5...♘xh4, but then White achieves total domination of the seventh rank (by 6 ♕e7 followed by mate on h7).

The reader should note the methodical character of this combination and especially the part played by the 'clearing-up' operation.

In this position from the game Nimzowitsch-Capablanca, New York 1927, Black's rook is already on the seventh rank, but its bite is not yet fully felt because of the pawn in the way at f2. To obtain complete control over the rank, Black sacrifices a pawn, which enables him to double rooks.

1...e5! 2 ♗xe5 ♖dd2 3 ♕b7 *(D)*

If 3 ♕f1, Black's strongest line is 3...♕d5 4 ♗f4 (or 4 ♗d4) 4...♕f3 5 ♕g2 ♕xg2+ 6 ♔xg2 ♖xf2+ 7 ♔h3 (or 7 ♔g1 ♖g2+ 8 ♔h1 ♖xh2+ 9 ♔g1 f6) 7...h5! 8 ♖h1 ♗e7 9 ♖ac1 g5 and White loses his bishop owing to the threat of ...g4#.

If 3 ♖f1, then 3...♕xe3! is decisive (4 ♗f4 ♖xf2), since White cannot take the queen for fear of being mated by the rooks.

These two alternatives are instructive illustrations of the use of rooks on the seventh rank.

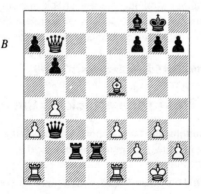

3...♖xf2 4 g4 ♕e6 5 ♗g3 ♖xh2! 6 ♕f3

If 6 ♗xh2, then 6...♕xg4+ 7 ♔h1 ♕h3 and White is mated, for he cannot defend both the focal-points g2 and h2 with his queen.

6...♖g2+ 7 ♕xg2 ♖xg2+ 8 ♔xg2 ♕xg4 and Black won as a result of his material superiority.

The last example in this group is meant to take the reader away from the usual pattern.

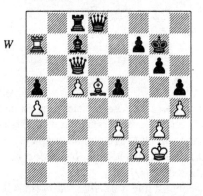

W

In this position from the game Flohr-Stoltz, Warsaw 1935, White has some pressure on the seventh rank but lacks reinforcements. Thus after 1 ♗c4 ♔f8 2 ♗a6 Black has the reply 2...♗b8![1], and the position resolves itself into an ending with bishops of opposite colours. This is not enough for White, and he sees that a successful invasion is possible on the sixth, rather than the seventh, rank.

1 ♗xf7! ♔xf7 2 ♖a6! ♗d6

Otherwise Black cannot stop the mating attack starting with ♕xg6+. If 2...♕g8, then 3 ♕d7+ mates, while 2...♗b6 is weaker than the text move on account of 3 ♕xb6 ♕xb6 4 cxb6 ♖b8 5 ♖xa5 and White goes on to win Black's e-pawn.

3 ♕d5+ ♔g7 4 ♖xd6 ♕e8 5 ♖e6 ♖xc5 6 ♕b7+ 1-0

The role of the files in the attack on the castled king

Of all the long-range actions, the most important in attacking the castled king is the vertical one on the open file. It is important because it is easier to 'clear' a file

---

1   Although 2 ♕b7, and only then 3 ♗a6, wins a piece for nothing.

than a rank, and it is useful because being placed on an open file is 'the best way for a rook to be employed'.

There are four ways of establishing a rook (or queen) on an open (or half-open) file:

1) the file is already open from one end to the other or to an opposing piece and all that is needed is for the rook to be brought on to it.

2) the rook is posted in front of one of its own pawns (e.g. the king's rook is manoeuvred via e1 and e3 to h3 in front of the pawn on h2).

3) the pawn in front of the rook advances and is sacrificed to open up the file.

4) the pawn in front of the rook leaves the file by making a capture.

The further operations of the rooks on the file are similar to those which take place when control is assumed of any line (constructing outposts, clearing, capturing pieces, squares, and focal-points, etc.).

As a first general example of the part played by the files in an attack on the castled king, let us examine a famous game of Rubinstein's.

P. Johner – Rubinstein
Teplitz-Schönau, 1922
Queen's Gambit Declined

1 d4 d5 2 c4 e6 3 ♘f3 a6

Modern theory does not rate this move very highly. White obtains a sound and useful position by exchanging on d5.

4 cxd5 exd5 5 ♘c3 ♘f6 6 ♗g5 ♗e7 7 e3 0-0 8 ♗d3 c6 9 ♗xf6

The normal and objectively best course for White here is to prepare a so-called minority attack, e.g. after castling kingside and playing ♖ab1 he advances his pawns to b4 and a4, continuing with b5 and bxc6 in order to weaken Black's pawn formation. Another way is to play on Black's weaknesses at c5 and b6 after exchanging the dark-squared bishops. Johner, a player with an incisive style, does not fancy these positional schemes and chooses a third way: castling on the opposite side and making an attack on the castled king, which is not a bad plan, but allows Black equal chances.

9...♗xf6 10 ♕c2

After eliminating Black's knight at f6, White induces a weakening of Black's castled position.

10...h6 11 0-0-0

First 11 h3 would have been better, and only then 0-0-0, with the further plan of ♖dg1, g4, h4 etc. The text move permits Black to divert White's g-pawn from its file by playing ...♗g4 and ...♗xf3, after which the danger of the thrust g5 is averted.

11...♗g4! 12 h3 ♗xf3 13 gxf3 *(D)*

Admittedly, White now has an open g-file, but Black is not weak on this file, since the g7-square is excellently covered. Here the g-file is of less value than the possibility of g4-g5, which White enjoyed before the exchange on f3. If Black's pieces had been differently arranged, the opening of the g-file might have been a good thing, but as it is Black's weakness is at h6, not g7; the result is that the opening of the file has considerably blunted White's potential attack on the kingside. This instructive point should be remembered, since similar positions often occur in practice.

13...a5?

The great Akiba is dozing at this point, and is not far from falling into an inferior position. The move 13...a5? did not appeal to Grünfeld or Becker, the conscientious authors of the tournament book, though they missed the essential point of the situation and recommended 13...♘d7, which is equally weak.

The position can be briefly summed up as follows: gxf3 has undoubtedly blunted the direct attack on the castled king, but it has given an added sharpness to the central position, where White threatens e4-e5 (naturally, after strengthening d4 by means of ♘e2 and perhaps ♗f5). If White manages to play e5, a turning-point in the situation is reached and White, on the basis of his power in the centre and his expulsion of the bishop from f6, obtains a strong attack, in which the open g-file also comes in very useful. Turning-points of this kind can be very instructive.

There still remains the question what Black ought to have played in order to prevent or hinder White's central advance. The answer is given by the following

analysis: 13...b6! 14 ♘e2 ♖a7 15 ♔b1 (after 15 e4 dxe4 White could not continue with 16 fxe4 because of 16...♗xd4 while after 16 ♗xe4 White would not be
able to drive the enemy bishop away from f6; note also that since there was a
threat of 15...c5, there is no time for further preparations, e.g. by 15 ♗f5)
15...♖c7 16 ♗f5 c5! and Black has the better prospects; on 17 dxc5 he naturally
plays 17...bxc5, while if 17 ♕d2, he makes the consistent reply 17...♘c6!, without having anything to fear from 18 dxc5 bxc5 19 ♕xd5?, since by 19...♕b8 he
can build up a powerful attack against White's king position. The essence of this
analysis lies in Black opening up files by ...b6 and ...c5. We shall see how Black
returns to this motif later on in the game and by opening up these files finally set-
tles the issue.

14 ♔b1

More precise would be 14 ♘e2 immediately, but even against the move played
it is too late for Black to play ...b6, etc., because he has lost a tempo by playing
13...a5?.

14...♘d7 15 ♘e2 ♕b6 16 ♗f5 ♖fd8 *(D)*

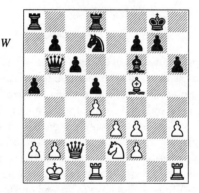

17 ♗xd7?

White misses the opportunity to advance his e-pawn to e5; after 17 e4! dxe4
18 fxe4 ♘f8 19 e5 ♗e7 20 ♖hg1 White's advantage is obvious. The exchange on
d7 makes Black's task easier.

17...♖xd7 18 ♘f4

If White attempts to prepare e4 by 18 ♖d3, etc., Black has ...♖ad8 to exert sufficient pressure on White's pawn at d4. For this reason White decides on an attack against the castled king with pieces alone, unaided by an aggressive central
pawn formation, and as a result his prospects of success are not so great.

18...♖d6 19 ♖hg1 ♔h8 20 ♖g4 ♖g8 21 ♖dg1 ♕c7 22 ♘d3!

After a series of necessary defensive moves Black has begun preparing ...b6 and ...c5, and White realizes that he cannot endanger Black's position by operations with his pieces down the flank without the support of his central pawns. Thus if 22 ♘h5 b6 23 ♕f5, which the commentators in the tournament book recommended, Black simply plays 23...♕e7 and finally carries out his threat with 24...c5. Thus White was correct to decide to centralize his knight on e5.

22...b6 23 f4 c5! *(D)*

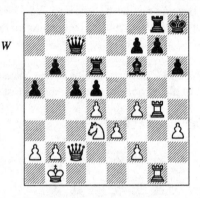

Black gives up a pawn with the aim of opening up the b- and c-files and so promoting an attack on the castled king. The sacrifice is absolutely correct; White should have declined the poisonous gift and instead of 24 dxc5? played 24 ♘e5!, in which case the position would have been approximately level. The official commentators showed that against the continuation 24...c4 White then has 25 ♕a4 with the idea of playing 26 ♕b5; against this 25...b5 26 ♕xb5 ♖b6 (or 26...♖b8) is of no avail because White thwarts all Black's designs with 27 ♘xf7+. After 24 ♘e5 it would perhaps be best for Black to play 24...♖b8! 25 ♕b3 ♖c8, in which case White would have to defend himself with 26 ♖c1. At this point 26 ♕b5 is no good because of 26...cxd4, while in the event of an attack by 26 ♕c2 ♔g8 27 ♕f5 Black has an interesting counterattack based on a 'heavy barrage' along the c-file: 27...cxd4! 28 ♘xf7!? ♖c6 29 ♘xh6+ ♔f8 30 a3 ♖c1+ 31 ♖xc1 ♕xc1+ 32 ♔a2 d3 and wins.

24 dxc5? bxc5 25 ♕xc5 ♖c6 26 ♕a3

If 26 ♕xd5, then 26...♖d8 27 ♕e4 (or 27 ♕f5 g6) 27...♕b7!, with the double threat of 28...♖xd3 and 28...♖c1+, is decisive.

26...♖c8!

Black has two files on which to attack and he decides on the c-file, since then things move even more quickly than after 26...♖b8.

27 ♖d1

If 27 ♖4g2, then 27...♗xb2 is also decisive.

27...♗xb2! 28 ♔xb2

White cannot take with his knight because of 28...♖c1+ and mate, while if 28 ♕xb2 then 28...♖b6 29 ♖c1 ♖xb2+ 30 ♔xb2 ♕b6+ 31 ♔a1 ♕f6+ 32 ♔b1 ♖c3 and Black wins.

28...♖c3!

First of all Black forces White's queen to abandon its defence of the square c3.

29 ♕a4 ♖c2+ 0-1

30 ♔a3 ♕d6+, 30 ♔b1 ♖b8+ and 30 ♔a1 ♕c3+ are all hopeless for White.

In this game and its notes we can see the various degrees of significance which open files can have. Firstly, there was White's open g-file, which was shown to be ineffective without support from another quarter; nevertheless, the notes pointed out its value as soon as White's pawn was advanced to e5. Then followed Black's manoeuvres to open up the b- and c-files, described firstly in the commentary and later actually put into practice at a critical stage of the game. Once the c-file had been opened by means of a sacrifice, the formidable power of the rooks on the file eventually brought the attacker victory.

The attack along the h-file

Using a rook to control an open h-file is one of the classic methods of attack after castling kingside, and so a number of examples will be devoted to it.

Firstly, we have an instance of a rook exercising control from h3, in front of the h2-pawn.

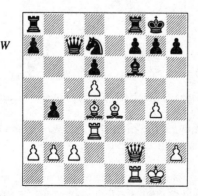

This diagram comes from Rödl-Sämisch, Swinemünde 1931. White plays:

1 ♗xh7+

A sacrifice of the bishop which might be termed 'semi-classic', this draws the king out to h7 so that the rook can get to h3 with gain of tempo; at the same time defence by ...h6 is excluded. It could also be put like this: the temporal factor here requires that the operation of 'clearing' h7 be carried out before posting the rook on the h-file.

1...♔xh7 2 ♖h3+ ♔g8 3 ♗xf6

White removes the bishop from f6 to allow his queen to move immediately to h4.

3...♘xf6 4 ♕h4 ♕c5+ 5 ♖f2 ♘h5

Since the f-pawn is blocked, this is the only possible way of averting mate.

6 ♕xh5 f6 7 g5 ♕xd5

To stop the fatal thrust g6. If 7...♖fe8, the quickest results are attained by 8 gxf6.

8 ♕h7+ ♔f7 9 ♖xf6+ 1-0

If 9...♔e7 10 ♕xg7+ ♖f7 11 ♖xf7+ ♕xf7, then 12 ♖e3+ is decisive.

Next we have an example of a complex sacrificial combination based on an explosive opening of the h-file.

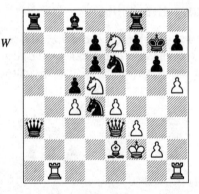

White (P. Schmidt) mated Black (K. Richter) in spectacular style:

1 ♕h6+

Drawing the king into the fire of the battery of rook and h-pawn. If 1 hxg6, Black would relieve his position by exchanging queens.

1...♔xh6 2 hxg6+

Discovered check, or 'a salvo from the battery of rook and pawn', or, lastly, the pawn on h5 as a kind of outpost – three names for the same thing.

2...♔g5 3 ♖h5+!

With this sacrifice White lures the king into the fire of a new battery – bishop and pawn!

3...♔xh5 4 f4+ ♘xe2 5 ♘f6+ ♔h6 6 ♖h1+ ♔g7 7 ♘e8+ ♖xe8 8 ♖xh7+ ♔f6 9 ♖xf7#

This is also an instructive example with reference to weaving the mating net: White is the master of the h-file, but he still needs to deprive the black king of squares on the g-file. The most difficult to deal with is g5, but White solves that problem with his third and fourth moves.

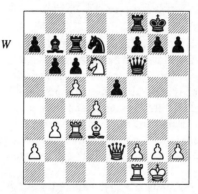

W

This example, from the game Toth-Szigeti, Budapest 1946, shows us an execution of Anastasia's mate on the h-file.

1 ♗xh7+ ♔xh7 2 ♖h3+ ♔g8 3 ♕h5 ♕h6

To all appearances Black has parried the attack on the h-file, but now comes the unexpected point.

4 ♘f5! ♕xh5 5 ♘e7+ ♔h7 6 ♖xh5#

One of the most important types of attack along the h-file is that which involves the doubling of the heavy pieces on the file, threatening mate at h8. If the enemy king's flight squares on the second rank are occupied by its own pawns, then the attacker must concentrate his effort on doubling his heavy pieces as rapidly as possible and mate his opponent at the focal-point h8. However, if the king has a square to escape to or there is a threat to get one by moving the g-pawn or f-pawn, attention must be turned to this possible means of defence. The most economical formation against this, as far as the use of attacking material is concerned, is one with an assault pawn at g6 and a defending one at g7. The continuations from the following diagram are devoted to this typical formation (with colours reversed).

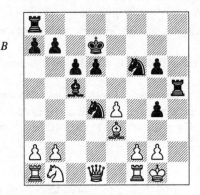

In this example Black is the attacker. He has already sacrificed his queen in order to reach this position, his intention being to mate White's king with a rook on h1. Doubling rooks is not a problem for Black in this position, but he is involved in a struggle for f2, which is important as a flight square for the white king. There are two methods of handling this: the king can be allowed to get out and a mating net then woven round it, or the formation with the pawn at g3 and doubled rooks can be set up. Both courses lead to success in this position, and both do so in two ways, so that in all Black has four lines which lead to victory. Here they are:

A) 1...♖ah8 2 f4

The only reply; if 2 g3, White is mated by the rooks; if 2 f3, then 2...g3.

2...♖h1+

This is the 'mating net' method; 2...g3 allows White to reply 3 ♛xh5.

3 ♔f2 ♘xe4+ 4 ♔e1 ♖xf1+ 5 ♔xf1 ♖h1+ 6 ♗g1 ♖xg1+ 7 ♔xg1 ♘f3+ 8 ♔f1 ♘g3#.

In this variation the doubled rooks have disappeared, but the 'doubled knights' are not to be overlooked.

B) 1...♘e2+ 2 ♛xe2 ♖ah8 3 f4 g3 4 ♛xh5 ♗xe3+ 5 ♖f2

Some players are more hurt by forced moves of this kind than by mate itself.

5...♘xh5 6 ♔f1 gxf2 7 ♔e2 f1♛+ 8 ♔xf1 ♘g3+ 9 ♔e1 ♖h1#

Let us now look at the two continuations which use the method based on the ...g3 formation.

C) 1...♘e2+ 2 ♛xe2 ♖ah8 3 f4 ♗xe3+ 4 ♛xe3 ♘xe4!

This controls f2 and draws the queen away from the defence of g3.

5 ♛xe4 g3

By means of a series of diversions Black has now established the necessary conditions for the success of the pure formation of doubled rooks plus pawn on g3 against pawn on g2. To avoid mate White would now have to give up nearly all his material: 6 ♕e7+ ♔xe7 7 ♖e1+ ♔d7 8 ♔f1 ♖h1+ 9 ♔e2 ♖e8+, after which 10...♖exe1 leads to a further harvest on the back rank.

D) 1...♖h7 *(D)*

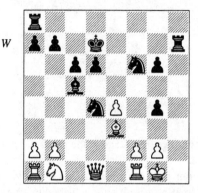

Finally, there is also the possibility of the rook retiring from h5 so that the queen cannot take it after ...g3.

2 f4

If 2 g3, we get the following entertaining variation: 2...♘f3+ 3 ♕xf3 gxf3 4 ♗g5 ♘xe4 5 ♗h4 ♘xg3! 6 ♗xg3 ♖ah8 mating. An example of 'clearing up' on the h-file[1].

2...g3 3 ♖f3

Or 3 ♕e1 ♘e2+ 4 ♕xe2 ♖ah8, etc.

3...♖ah8 4 ♖xg3 ♖h1+ 5 ♔f2 ♘xe4#

In the above diagram doubling rooks was an easy task, but the crux lay in controlling the squares which the king might use for its escape. However, there are cases where the problem lies in actually doubling the rooks on the intended file. As a rule a necessary condition for this is that the attacker's back rank should be clear of other pieces so that the rooks can be moved at will. When the rooks on a given rank cover each other, they are said to be 'united'. Naturally, being 'united' can also apply to a queen and rook. The continuation from the following diagram is instructive in this context.

---

1   There is no argument about Vuković's first three lines, but in variation 'D' White can play 2 ♗xd4 ♖ah8 (after 2...♗xd4 3 ♖e1 ♖ah8 4 ♔f1 the king slips out) 3 ♕xg4+! ♔c7 4 ♕h3 ♖xh3 5 gxh3 ♗xd4 6 ♘c3, escaping into an ending in which he is only slightly worse.

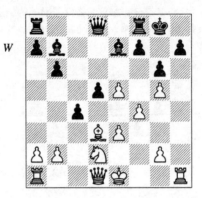

The diagram represents a critical stage in the game Krogius-Niemelä, Lovisa 1934.

White is in a precarious position, even though his pawn formation is sound and he has an open h-file. If he withdraws his bishop to c2, Black has the strong reply 1...d4, while 1...♗xg5 is also worth considering. If 1 ♕g4 cxd3 2 ♕h4 (2 ♕h3 h5 3 gxh6 {3 g4 ♗c8!} 3...d4! is in Black's favour) 2...h5 3 g4, Black plays 3...♔g7! 4 gxh5 ♖h8 5 h6+ ♔h7, and White's attack is beaten back. Black's defensive plan against the idea of using the white g-pawn to break open the h-file is worth remembering, since there are often opportunities for such play in practice.

Taking into account all the difficulties described, White decided to strike immediately with his rook at h7; Black failed to discover the correct reply.

1 ♖xh7! cxd3?

It is true that Black could not take the rook because of 2 ♕h5+ ♔g8 3 ♕h6 cxd3 4 ♔f2, after which he has no satisfactory defence against ♖h1. However, it was also not a good idea to take the bishop; the precious tempo should have been expended on breaking up White's pawn formation, which is in fact the decisive factor in White's success on the h-file. Thus 1...♗xg5! would have been correct. In that case two of White's pieces are threatened and if 2 ♔f2, then Black can play 2...♔xh7; 2 ♖h3 can be met by 2...♗c8 and then ...♗h4+, while if 2 fxg5, then either 2...♕xg5 or 2...♔xh7. By sacrificing on g5 Black eliminates White's control of h6, and in some variations he captures with his queen on e5, thereby covering the square h8 in the manner of a fianchettoed bishop.

2 ♔f2! *(D)*

Uniting the rooks on the back rank above all else! In fact, the chief value of this kind of move derives from the characteristic dual control which it provides. That is, by playing 2 ♔f2! White opens up the square h1 both for the queen and the a1-rook, whereas after, for example, 2 ♕g4? only the queen would be brought into action and the a1-rook would be left behind. The inadequacy of 2 ♕g4? is shown by the following continuation: 2...♔xh7 3 ♕h4+ ♔g8 4 ♔f2 f6! 5 e6 (if 5 exf6, Black plays 5...♗xf6, enabling his king to wriggle out via f7) 5...fxg5 6 ♕h6 ♗f6 and Black has defended himself; e.g. if 7 ♕xg6+ ♗g7 8 ♖h1, then 8...♖f6, while if 7 ♖h1, then 7...♕e7 8 ♕xg6+ ♕g7, etc.

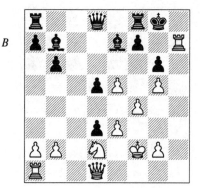

2...f6

If 2...♔xh7, then 3 ♕h1+ ♔g8 4 ♕h6 leaves Black without a defence against 5 ♖h1 (for 4...f6 is no good on account of 5 ♕xg6+). The white queen must be brought to h6, and it makes no difference whether it goes via h1 or h4 (as both ♕g4-h4-h6 and ♔f2, ♕h1-h6 take three tempi), but in the case of the a1-rook, the continuation 2 ♔f2! is better than 2 ♕g4?, which does nothing to bring it into action.

Finally, it should be mentioned that a delayed sacrifice at g5 is also of no avail, e.g. 2...♗xg5 3 ♕h1 ♗f6 (or 3...f5 4 e6! ♗f6 5 ♕h6 ♕e8 6 ♖h1 and 7 ♖h8+) 4 ♕h6! followed by 5 ♖h1 and 6 ♖h8+.

3 ♕h1 1-0

For if 3...♕e8 or 3...fxe5, then 4 ♕h6 is decisive.

The formation with rook on h1 and pawn on h4

Of the various formations on the h-file the most important in practice is undoubtedly that with a rook on h1 and pawn on h4. It is a good representative example of battery attacks with rook and pawn which are created when the pawn captures an opposing piece and thereby opens up the file for the rook. This situation is often engineered by placing another attacking piece on the square covered by the pawn, creating threats which induce or oblige the opponent to take it. There are two other methods of exploiting the formation of rook and pawn – one is to simply advance the pawn, the other involves switching the rook on to another file (e.g. with rook on h1 and pawns at h4 and g2, moving the rook to h3 and then to g3).

Here are a few examples of these ideas.

W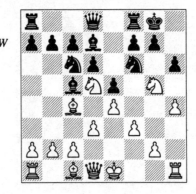

In this position we see a formation in which preparations have already been made for the opening of the h-file after the capture of the knight at g5. It is true that White, to move, currently has no very sharp threats, but he reckons correctly that he can quickly strengthen his position; in the meantime, he puts his trust in the efficacy of hxg5 if Black takes the knight.

1 c3 hxg5?

We shall examine this weak move in order to get to know the various typical combinations which occur when the h-file is opened in such circumstances. Correct was 1...a5!, stopping b4. White would then probably play 2 g4 to exclude the possibility of ...♘f6-h5-g3. Thus, the game could go on for a few more moves with the knight on g5 *en prise,* until the critical moment came to decide on the exact significance of the knight's position: either White's attack would break through, or Black would take the knight without any ill-effects to himself, or thirdly White might simply withdraw the knight from g5.

2 hxg5 ♘xd5 3 ♗xd5 ♗e6

If 3...g6, then 4 ♔e2! (a characteristically quiet move by the king to unite the heavy pieces on the back rank) 4...♔g7 5 ♖h7+! ♔xh7 6 ♕h1+ ♔g8 7 ♕h6 ♘e7 8 ♗d2 ♘xd5 9 ♖h1 followed by mate.

4 f4! ♖e8

This seems to provide the most resistance. If 4...g6, then 5 f5 ♗xd5 6 f6 ♗e6 7 ♕f3 and White can easily organize a mating attack.

5 ♕h5 ♔f8 6 ♗xe6 ♖xe6

Or 6...fxe6 7 g6 ♘e7 8 f5 exf5 9 ♗g5, etc[1].

7 f5 ♖e8 8 g6 ♔e7 9 ♗g5+ and Black either loses his queen or is mated, e.g. 9...f6 10 ♗xf6+ gxf6 11 ♕h7+ ♔f8 12 ♕f7#.

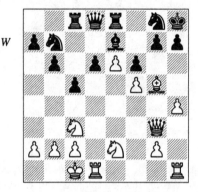

W

This position arose in the game Boden-Bird, London 1869. White played a move which made clear his ardent wish that Black should take the bishop on g5.

1 ♘f4 fxg5?

Black takes the bishop, even though there is no danger at the moment. He could have played, for example, 1...a6 2 ♘cd5 b5 3 h5, after which there is a real threat of ♘g6+. This can be parried by 3...h6, and if 4 ♘g6+, then 4...♔h7[2].

2 ♘g6+!

A typical method of 'clearing' the file before the battery opens fire with hxg5.

2...hxg6 3 hxg5+ ♘h6 4 gxh6 ♗g5+ 5 ♔b1 ♗xh6

If 5...gxh6, then 6 ♘e4 ♗g7 (or 6...♔g8 7 ♖xh6 ♗xh6 8 ♕xg6+ ♗g7 9 ♕f7+ mating) 7 ♖xh6! ♔xh6 8 ♘xg5! ♕xg5 (or 8...♔g7 9 ♘e4) 9 ♖h1+ ♕h5 10 ♕xg6#.

6 ♕xg6 ♖e7 7 f6 ♕e8 8 f7 ♕f8 9 ♖xh6+ gxh6 10 ♖h1 ♖xe6 11 ♕xe6 ♔h7 12 ♘e4 ♖c7 13 ♘g5+ and mates.

The diverse character of the formation with rook on h1 and pawn on h4 is well illustrated by the following examples where the rook is switched from the h- to

---

1   In this line, Black can still resist with 7...♔e7, so White should prefer 7 ♕h8+ ♔f7 8 g6+ ♔xg6 9 ♕h5+ ♔f6 10 fxe5+, winning immediately.

2   Although White then wins easily by 5 ♘gxe7 ♘xe7 6 ♗xf6 gxf6 7 ♘xf6+ ♔h8 8 ♕f4 ♘g8 9 ♘xg8 ♔xg8 10 f6.

the g-file. In this case the rook is potentially active on two files at the same time and develops great power as a result.

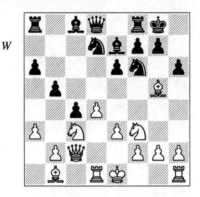

The above position arose in the game Vuković-Dr Vajda, Debrecen 1925. Black had just threatened White's bishop by ...h6, and White replied:

1 h4!

If Black accepts the sacrifice, then after 1...hxg5 2 hxg5 g6 3 gxf6 ♘xf6 4 ♘e5 White obtains an attacking position without having to surrender any material.

1...♖e8 2 ♘e5 ♗b7

Consistently refusing the gift offered him on g5, Black hopes to persuade the bishop eventually to retreat. However, he is in any case in a poor position, as a result of his premature advance ...c4 earlier in the game. With his pawn on c5 Black would still have some say in the centre, and a central action is usually a valuable antidote against an attack on the castled king. With the pawn on c4, Black is only able to undertake slow operations on the queenside, and they are not sufficient to counterbalance White's attack.

3 ♖h3!

A manoeuvre designed to bring the rook into the game as quickly as possible; it is characteristic of the formation with rook on h1 and pawn on h4.

3...♘f8

Black lacks a good answer to the threat of ♗xh6. After 3...♗xg2 4 ♖g3 his situation deteriorates still further, while if 3...♔f8, then 4 ♗xh6 gxh6 5 ♘xf7 ♔xf7 6 ♕g6+ ♔f8 7 ♕xh6+ ♔f7 8 ♗g6+ ♔g8 9 ♖g3 leads to mate.

4 ♗xh6! *(D)*

4...♘h5

If 4...gxh6, then 5 ♖g3+ soon decides the issue.

5 ♕e2 g6

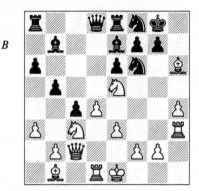

Or 5...♗xg2 6 ♕xh5 g6 7 ♖g3, etc.

6 g4 ♘g7 7 h5 ♗f6

Black gives up a second pawn, but he can do nothing to save his position. After **8 hxg6 ♗xe5 9 gxf7+ ♔xf7 10 dxe5 ♕a5** White played **11 e4** and won in ten more moves, but the finish might have been even more abrupt with 11 ♗xg7 ♔xg7 12 g5 followed by ♕h5.

The h-file in connection with the classic bishop sacrifice

The analysis of the classic bishop sacrifice, to which we devoted particular attention in an earlier chapter, must now be supplemented by cases where such a sacrifice is combined with an attack along the h-file. This arises when White has a rook on h1 and pawn on h4, the pawn acting as a support for the knight on g5. We shall examine two examples from master chess in which the h-file is opened up.

The following position comes from the game Steinitz-Golmayo, Havana 1888, and arose after the moves:

1 e4 e6 2 d4 d5 3 ♘c3 ♘f6 4 e5 ♘fd7 5 f4 c5 6 dxc5 ♗xc5 7 ♘f3 0-0 8 ♗d3 ♘c6? *(D)*

Steinitz at this point played:

9 h4

White could have played immediately 9 ♗xh7+ ♔xh7 10 ♘g5+ ♔g6 11 ♕d3+ f5 and then 12 ♕g3 ♕e8 (against other queen moves, 13 ♕h4 is decisive) 13 ♘xe6+ ♔f7 14 ♘c7[1] ♕d8 15 ♘xa8 when White has the upper hand.

---

1   In this line 14 ♘xg7! ♖g8 15 ♘xe8 ♖xg3 16 e6+ is decisive.

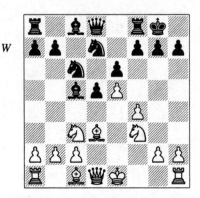

Steinitz rejected the idea of the sacrifice because on the twelfth move he had reckoned only on 12 ♘xe6? ♛a5 13 ♘xf8+ ♘xf8 14 ♛xd5 ♗e6, which would indeed have been favourable for Black.

9...f6

White would have had a harder task after 9...h6, although even then he could have gained the advantage by 10 ♘g5. Given that this is a typical continuation, let us examine a few variations:

1) 10...hxg5 11 ♗h7+! ♚xh7 12 ♛h5+ ♚g8 13 hxg5 f5 14 g6 and mate.

2) 10...♘dxe5 11 fxe5 ♘xe5 12 ♗h7+ ♚h8 13 ♗f4 ♘g6 14 ♗d2 and White is the better placed[1].

3) 10...♘b4 11 ♗h7+ ♚h8 12 ♛h5 ♛e7 13 ♗d2 f5 (if 13...♖e8 then 14 ♗g6 while against 13...♘c6 or other such moves White plays 14 0-0-0) 14 ♛g6 ♘xc2+ (also in White's favour is 14...♛e8 15 ♘xe6, etc.) 15 ♚d1 ♘xa1 16 ♗g8! followed by mate with the queen on h7[2].

---

1   This contention seems highly dubious. After 13...♘c4, attacking b2 and threatening 14...e5, White is clearly worse. Black has two central pawns for the piece, White's king is trapped in the centre and his pieces are hopelessly tangled up on the kingside. Therefore White should prefer 12 ♘f3, with a double-edged position.

2   There is also a fair degree of wishful thinking in this line, for example after 14...♛e8 15 ♘xe6 ♘xc2+ 16 ♚d1 (16 ♚e2 ♛xe6!) 16...♛xg6 17 ♗xg6 ♘xa1 the queens are exchanged and White is a whole rook down. He can regain the exchange easily enough, but rounding up the a1-knight is far from easy – the assessment must be that Black is better. All these lines illustrate the point that Vuković himself makes: launching an attack without first completing your development is a risky business.

10 ♘g5! fxg5 (D)

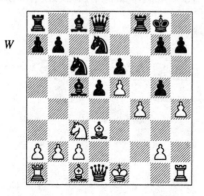

11 ♗xh7+!

The sacrifice is both correct and necessary; after 11 hxg5 Black would have the reply 11...g6 12 ♖xh7 ♘dxe5 13 fxe5 ♗f2+, etc.

The fact that the knight is sacrificed on g5 first and then the bishop on h7 makes no difference to the actual structure of the combination; the order of moves is conditioned by temporal factors.

11...♔xh7 12 hxg5+ ♔g8 13 ♕h5 (D)

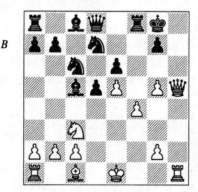

13...♘dxe5

Otherwise 14 g6 is decisive[1].

---

1   Here Black misses 13...♘cxe5! 14 fxe5 ♕c7!, when it is hard to see how White can continue his attack.

14 fxe5 &f5[1] 15 g4 &xe5+ 16 &d1 &e3

If 16...&d7, then 17 ♕h8+ &f7 18 &f1+ &e7 19 ♕xg7+ &d6 20 ♘b5#, while if 16...&f8, then 17 &f4.

17 &xe3 &xe3 18 ♘b5! *(D)*

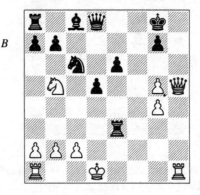

In the preceding note we gave a line ending with ♘b5#; now the same move serves to tighten the mating net, which Black had attempted to cut through by 16...&e3 (freeing the c5-square for the king's escape!).

18...&f3

The alternatives were 18...&f8 19 ♕h8+ &f7 20 &f1+ followed by mate and 18...&e5 19 ♕h7+ &f8 20 &f1+, etc.

19 g6 1-0

It is the formation with pawn on g6 against pawn on g7 (which has already been discussed) that is finally decisive. The part played by the knight on b5 is evident in several variations, as well as in the final position, e.g. if 19...&f8, then 20 ♕h8+ and 21 ♕xg7+, etc.

Alekhine – Asgeirsson
Reykjavik Simultaneous Display, 1931
French Defence

1 e4 e6 2 d4 d5 3 ♘c3 ♘f6 4 &g5 &e7 5 &xf6 &xf6 6 ♘f3 0-0 7 &d3 &e8?!

An unnecessary loss of time; correct is 7...c5 at once.

---

1   In this position 14...♕c7 is less effective, as 15 &f4! &xf4 16 ♕h8+ &f7 17 g6+! &e7 18 ♕xg7+ gives White a very dangerous attack – Black needs a defensive knight on d7.

8 e5 &e7 9 h4 c5?! *(D)*

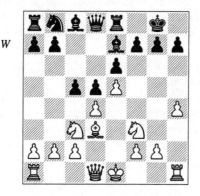

White has prepared for the sacrifice of his bishop on h7 by 9 h4, and the reply 9...c5 does nothing to stop it. Relatively best was 9...f5! 10 exf6 (after 10 ♘e2 c5 11 c3 White is the better placed, but his attack is delayed and Black is not without counterplay) 10...&xf6. The situation is then easier for Black, for as a result of the exchange on f6 an extremely important attacking unit has disappeared, namely White's pawn on e5. Sacrifices in this position are therefore not worthwhile; after 11 &xh7+ &xh7 12 ♘g5+ &g8 13 ♕h5 Black has an adequate defence in 13...♕d7, while if 11 ♘g5, he can play 11...&xg5 12 hxg5 ♕xg5! 13 &xh7+ &f8, and White's attack is not worth much owing to his weakness in the centre and the activity of Black's queen, especially on the dark squares[1].

The last continuation can also be brought about by a different series of moves: 11 ♘g5 &xg5 12 &xh7+, when Black should not play 12...&xh7 (in which case 13 hxg5+ and 14 ♕h5 is extremely strong) but 12...&f8! 13 hxg5 ♕xg5, ending with the position described above. These possibilities are worth getting to know well, since we are dealing with a typical position. Particularly important is the significance of Black's ...f5 in this kind of position: if White does not take the pawn at once *en passant*, the sacrifice on h7 is prevented directly; while if he takes it, then it is indirectly thwarted or at any rate made weaker, since White's pawn has disappeared from e5.

It is also worth noting that to avert the sacrifice entirely by ...h6 or ...g6 is not a good thing in this position. If 9...h6, White plays 10 ♘e2 followed by c3 and

---

1   This is not so. After 14 ♕f3+ &e7 (14...♕f6 15 &g6) 15 ♖h5 ♕f6 16 ♕g3 ♕xd4 (or else 17 0-0-0, with a massive lead in development without any sacrifice by White) 17 ♖d1 ♕f6 18 &g6 ♖f8 19 ♖f5 Black's queen is trapped.

attacks in a different way (e.g. by means of ♗b1 and ♕d3 he forces a weakening of the square g6 or, alternatively, he plays g4, etc.); in this connection it is important to note that ...f5, if played later on, would create a new weakness on g6. If 9...g6, White can immediately play 10 h5, but still better is first 10 ♘e2, etc.

10 ♗xh7+!

The sacrifice is correct, even though it demands extremely precise and high-quality play from the attacker.

10...♔xh7 11 ♘g5+ ♔g8

11...♔g6 would be hopeless here; the formation comprising rook on h1 and pawns on h4 and e5 is a formidable weapon against it, e.g. 11...♔g6 12 ♕d3+ f5 13 h5+ ♔xg5 14 ♕g3+ and 15 ♕g6#.

12 ♕h5 ♗xg5

He must!

13 hxg5 ♔f8 14 g6!

This move puts a spoke in Black's defensive plans. He would lose quickly after 14...fxg6 15 ♕xg6, while if 14...cxd4, White can win either by 15 gxf7 or 15 ♕h8+ ♔e7 16 ♕xg7 ♖f8 17 ♕f6+ ♔d7 18 g7 ♖g8 19 ♖h8 ♕e8 20 ♘xd5 ♘c6 21 ♕h6.

14...♔e7 15 gxf7 ♖f8 *(D)*

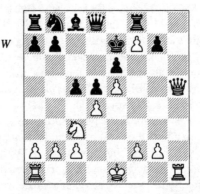

16 0-0-0 *(D)*

Alekhine the player and Alekhine the commentator failed to see that Black could have saved himself after this move. 16 dxc5! was both necessary and good in order to prevent Black from taking the initiative in the centre. This is underlined by the following variations:

1) 16...♘d7 17 0-0-0 ♕a5 (if 17...♖xf7 White wins by 18 ♘xd5+ and 19 e6, while if 17...♘xc5, then 18 b4) 18 ♕g5+ ♔xf7 19 ♖h7 ♖g8 20 ♘xd5! ♕xa2 (if

20...exd5 then 21 e6+ ♔xe6 22 ♕xd5+ and 23 ♕xg8 wins, while if 20...♕xc5, then 21 ♕h5+ ♔f8 22 ♘f4 wins) 21 ♕e7+ ♔g6 22 ♕xe6+ ♘f6 23 ♖xg7+ mating.

2) 16...♘c6 17 0-0-0 ♕a5 (or 17...♖xf7 18 ♕g5+ ♔d7 19 ♕g6 ♘xe5 {19...♕e7 transposes to line 3} 20 ♖xd5+ exd5 21 ♕d6+ and 22 ♖h8+, etc.) 18 ♕g5+ ♔xf7 19 ♖h7 ♖g8 20 ♕f6+ ♔e8 21 ♕g6+ ♔e7 (if 21...♔f8, then 22 ♖h4 wins, while if 21...♔d8, then 22 ♘xd5) 22 ♖xg7+ ♖xg7 23 ♕xg7+ ♔e8 24 ♖h1! ♘e7 25 ♖h7 ♕xc5 26 ♘a4! ♕c7 (or 26...♕b4 27 ♕f7+ ♔d8 28 c3!) 27 ♕f7+ ♔d8 28 ♕f8+ mating.

3) 16...♖xf7 17 ♕g5+ ♔d7 18 ♕g6 ♕e7 (defending the rook and parrying the threat of ♘xd5) 19 0-0-0 ♘c6 (if 19...♔c7, then 20 ♘b5+ and 21 ♘d6, while if 19...♔c6, then 20 ♖xd5) 20 ♕g4! ♔c7 21 ♘b5+ ♔b8 22 ♘d6 ♖f8 23 ♖h7 ♘xe5 (if 23...♖g8, then 24 ♖dh1 followed by ♖h8, etc.) 24 ♕g3 ♕f6 25 ♖xg7 ♕f4+ (should Black attempt to free himself with 25...♗d7, White wins by 26 ♕xe5 and 27 ♖xd7) 26 ♕xf4 ♖xf4 27 ♖h1 ♖f8 28 ♖hh7 and mate on b7.

These variations do not exhaust the possibilities of the position, but they give a good illustration of the strength of White's game after 16 dxc5.

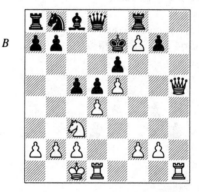

B

16...a6?

An example of the inadequacy of passive defence. 17 ♘b5, which is what Black was afraid of, is by no means White's principal threat and is only effective in conjunction with a strong initiative. Alekhine is also at fault in his commentary when he claims that ♘b5 represented a threat after 16 0-0-0.

Instead of 16...a6? Black should have played 16...cxd4! and thus exploited the extra tempo in the centre, e.g.:

1) 17 ♘b5 ♘c6 and now:

1a) 18 f4 ♖xf7 19 ♘d6 and now Black has a satisfactory defence in 19...♕f8![1].

1b) 18 ♘d6 ♘xe5 (this gives back material and at the same time eliminates White's threats) 19 ♘xc8+ ♖xc8 20 ♕xe5 ♕c7, and Black's position is in no way inferior.

1c) 18 ♕g5+ ♔d7 19 ♕xg7 b6! 20 ♘d6 ♗a6 21 f4 d3 and Black obtains counterplay, e.g. if 22 c3 or 22 cxd3, then 22...♘d4, while ♘e8 can always be answered by ...♔e7.

2) 17 ♖xd4 ♘c6 18 ♖f4 (sacrifices at this point are insufficient to break through) 18...♔d7 19 ♖g4 ♕e7 20 ♖xg7 b6 and against any further activity by White on the kingside Black has enough counterplay based on ...♘d4 and eventually ...♖ac8 and ...♕c5.

17 dxc5!

Now all is well again, and the position is won.

17...♘d7 18 ♖xd5! ♕a5

If 18...exd5 then 19 ♘xd5+ ♔e6 20 ♘f4+ ♔e7 21 e6! ♘f6 22 ♕e5 and mates.

19 ♕g5+ ♔xf7 20 ♖h7 ♖g8 21 ♖d4!

There are a number of 'subsidiary solutions' here, but 21 ♖xd7+? ♗xd7 22 ♘e4 does not work because of 22...♕e1#.

21...♕xc5 22 ♖xd7+

But now, of course, this way is all right!

22...♗xd7 23 ♘e4 ♕b4 24 ♘d6+ ♔f8 *(D)*

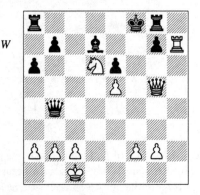

25 ♕f6+ gxf6 26 ♖f7#.

In the past commentators used to end their work on games like this by praising the winner, but does not the loser in some way deserve credit too? Is it not he who

---

1   Not so, as White wins by 20 ♕g5+ ♔d7 21 ♘xf7 ♕xf7 22 ♖h7 and the g7-pawn falls.

'fulfils the ardent desires' of the attacker, as is done in this case by the good-natured matador from Ultima Thule...?

Diagonals in the attack on the castled king

Tartakower thought it suitable to bestow epithets of the following kind on the files: a-file – positional; b – covetous; c – far-sighted; d – prosaic; e – dangerous; f – tempting; g – sacrificial; and h – contentious. He might also have invented something similar (even if he in fact did not) to apply to the ranks. But the diagonals? Well, they are all somehow equally 'elegant, subtle, far-sighted', etc. On the *long* diagonals (a1-h8 and a8-h1) more kings have already died than in the whole of the world's history; more tragedies have been played out on the *classic* diagonals (b1-h7 for White and b8-h2 for Black) than in all the world's theatres, and on the *developing* diagonals (a2-g8 and a7-g1 respectively) there have been more mistakes made than in a large library full of books. Now that we have started on nicknames and epithets, let us bestow on the diagonals a4-e8 and h4-d8 (from White's point of view; a5-e1 and h5-d1 from Black's) the name of *pinning diagonals*. The reader can think over for himself how much material he has already lost on them.

Just as the rook is the piece suited for play on open files and ranks, so the bishop is the master of the diagonals, indeed they are his *raison d'être*. At all stages of the game, and especially in an attack on the castled king, marshalling bishops on the diagonals demands great skill. A player's skill, in fact, is often demonstrated by his play on the diagonals, and the impression is then given that 'the slender bishop is subtler than the stout rook'. Putting facetiousness aside, let us now look at the relationship between the lines commanded by the rook and the bishop's diagonals.

In the first place, it should be stressed that the fundamental difference does not lie in the number or importance of the squares on the files or diagonals, nor in the weight of operations on them. The differences arise only from the different values of rook and bishop and also from the part played by pawn moves in opening up or blocking a line.

It is harder to sacrifice the more valuable rook than the bishop, and the order of value is even more relevant when it comes to pinning: exchanging a bishop for a pinned rook wins the exchange, while bishop for knight is tit-for-tat, but a rook can only gain from pinning a piece when it takes the queen. The other difference is still more explicit: it is comparatively easy to open up or close a diagonal by the normal advance of one's pawns, but achieving the same object on a file means that the pawn has to make a capture, and this naturally depends on the disposition of one's opponent's pieces; hence, there may be considerable difficulty in opening up a file. If, on the other hand, it has to be closed, an outpost as a rule has to be established; on the diagonals, however, outposts are the exception, since the 'open-shut' game is easily carried out by the pawns. It is in this, ultimately, that the whole 'subtlety and far-sightedness' of the diagonal lies. We shall open a series of examples with a case of pinning on a diagonal. The pinning here is in fact a temporary episode within the whole operation of 'clearing up' on the diagonal, and the end comes with the line being completely breached when the pinned piece is captured.

W

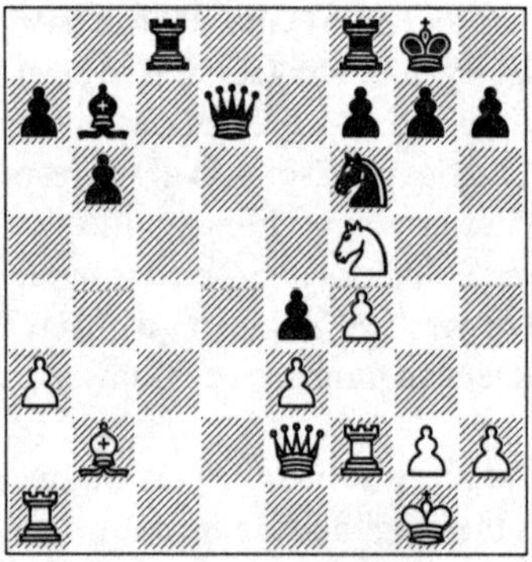

This position comes from the game Tolush-Renter, Estonian Championship 1945. It is White to move.

1 ♘xg7

This draws Black's king out to g7 and at the same time opens up the diagonal of the white bishop on b2.

1...♔xg7 2 ♖d1 ♕e7

If 2...♕e6, then 3 f5.

3 ♕g4+ ♔h8 4 ♖d7

In this way White wins the enemy bishop, but the correct method of exploiting the position would have been to aim consistently for a breakthrough on the square f6, e.g. 4 ♕g5 ♖c6 5 f5 ♖g8 (or 5...♖d8 6 ♖e1 and if 6...♖dd6, then 7 ♕h6 followed by ♖f4 wins; otherwise the manoeuvre ♖f4-g4 is at once decisive[1]) 6 ♕h6 ♗c8 7 h4 b5 (Black has no better move; for example, ...♖g7 and ...♘e8 will not save him because of f6) 8 h5 a5 9 ♖fd2 b4 (the combination which White has

1 Black might defend by 6...♖dd6 7 ♕h6 ♕d8, and if 8 ♖f4 then 8...♖d1. In view of the uncertainties of this approach, Tolush's method appears sounder.

prepared by advancing his h-pawn to h5 is also decisive against other moves) 10 ♖d6 ♖xd6 11 ♖xd6 ♕xd6 12 ♗xf6+ ♕xf6 13 ♕xf6+ ♖g7 14 h6 and White mates.

4...♕e6 5 ♕g5 ♖c6 6 ♖xb7 and White won in due course.

An important point is that, in addition to 'clearing' one's opponent's pieces from a diagonal, cases also occur where one's own pieces prevent it being opened. It is extremely difficult to resuscitate a diagonal on which one has a blocked pawn of one's own. Structurally, it is a similar problem to that of opening a file where a pawn blocks the path of a rook, and it is usually solved in the same way, i.e. by sacrificing a piece on a square controlled by the pawn. Here is an example.

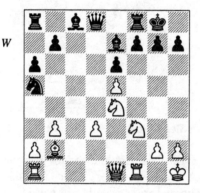

This position occurred in the game Alexander-Szabo, Hilversum 1947. White pitched his knight into f6 with check so as to bring the long diagonal back to life.

1 ♘f6+! gxf6

If 1...♔h8, then 2 ♕h4 is very strong[1].

2 ♕g3+ ♔h8 3 exf6 ♗xf6 4 ♘e5!

White threatens 5 ♖xf6, 5 ♘xf7+ and indeed 5 ♕h4 (5...♗xh4 6 ♘xf7+ and 7 ♘h6#. Black no longer has any defence.

4...♗xe5 5 ♗xe5+ f6 6 ♖xf6 1-0

Since if 6...♖xf6, 7 ♖f1 is decisive.

The 'clearing' of the long diagonal was a victory for the bishop.

---

1   2 ♕h4 allows the defence 2...♕xd3. Instead, 2 ♕e4 is correct, when 2...gxf6 3 exf6 followed by ♘g5 forces mate.

As far as play on the diagonals is concerned, the strength of the central squares on the given diagonals is particularly important. These squares can assist the attacker in setting up outposts, in transferring pieces, and in other operations. Thus one should, as a rule, aim to have such squares protected or even over-protected. This is one of the maxims of positional play, and we shall see in the next example how Black pays for ignoring this maxim and how the attack on the castled king suddenly erupts.

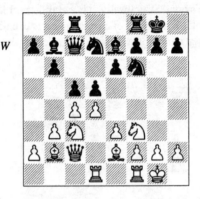

This position arose in Stoltz-Guimard, Groningen 1946. White played:

1 dxc5 ♘xc5?

A mistake, since it surrenders to White control over the important central squares d4 and e5, which means that the long diagonal occupied by his bishop on b2 is already as good as opened up (considering the gain of tempo by ♘b5, which White always has in hand). Black should have played either 1...bxc5 or 1...♗xc5.

2 ♘b5 ♕d8

2...♕b8 is not good here because of White's grip on e5, e.g. 3 ♗e5 ♕a8 4 ♘c7, and Black loses the exchange.

3 ♘xa7

Black will, it is true, win back the a-pawn, but White will have succeeded, without loss of time, in strengthening the position of his knight at b5 (...a6 is no longer possible).

3...♖a8 4 ♘b5 ♖xa2 5 ♕b1 ♖a8 6 ♘g5

Suddenly the course of the game turns against Black's castled position; White threatens ♗xf6 followed by mate on h7.

6...h6?

Black should have consented to a further weakening of the diagonal by 6...g6, for that would have meant less trouble for him than the text move[1].

7 ♗xf6 hxg5 8 ♗e5

By threatening ♗c7, White installs his bishop with gain of tempo at e5, a square that is now firmly under his control. His next intention is to play ♕b2, after which the bishop's whole manoeuvre takes on the purpose of clearing the diagonal.

8...♕c8 9 ♕b2 dxc4

If 9...f6, which the tournament book (by Euwe and Kmoch) considers correct, White wins a pawn: 10 ♗d6 ♖e8 (or 10...♕d7 11 ♗c7 ♖a6 12 ♗f3, etc.) 11 ♗xe7 ♖xe7 12 ♘d6 ♕c6 13 ♘xb7 ♖xb7 14 cxd5 exd5 15 ♖xd5, and Black is in difficulties on a fresh diagonal (a2-g8).

10 ♗xc4

Not 10 ♗xg7? because of 10...♕c6.

10...♕c6 11 f3 *(D)*

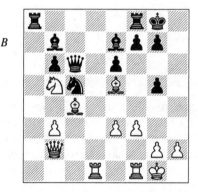

11...♗a6

The tournament book gives this a question mark and suggests 11...f6; however, after 12 ♗d6 ♖fe8 13 b4 ♘a4 14 ♕b3 ♔h8 15 ♗xe7 Black loses his e-pawn.

12 ♘d4

Making use of the other square Black surrendered with 1...♘xc5?. White has now created a battery consisting of queen and knight.

12...♕b7 13 ♗xa6 ♖xa6 14 ♗xg7!

The various operations on the diagonal are concluded by a bishop sacrifice, the aim of which is to lure the king into the line of fire. Black did not submit to

---

1   6...♘ce4 is perhaps the most sensible. Black blocks the b1-h7 diagonal without creating a further weakness on the kingside.

this and played **14...Ĕfa8**, losing after a further sixteen moves. However, we are only interested in the continuation 14...♔xg7, which is followed by 15 ♘xe6+ ♔g6 16 ♕g7+ ♔f5 17 ♘d4#. The plan also works with 15 ♘f5+, in which case mate is achieved by 17 g4#.

The next example is devoted to the problem of recognizing strong diagonals and combining their 'clearing' with an effective use of the bishop.

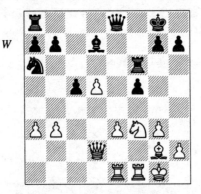

Here we have a position from the game Lundin-Tartakower, Groningen 1946. It is clear that White is the better placed, and that Black is weak on the a2-g8 diagonal, but it is less obvious that the white bishop will put in such a quick appearance on that diagonal and that the game will be decided on the b1-h7 diagonal. White won as follows:

1 e4! fxe4

Otherwise e5 is too strong.

2 ♘g5 Ĕxf1+ 3 ♗xf1!

The bishop is on its way to c4, the knight on g5 is already casting glances in the direction of f7, and the threats on the e-file see to it that the initiative remains in White's hands.

3...♕g6 4 d6

This opens the diagonal with gain of tempo (the threat is ♕d5+ and then ♕xb7).

4...Ĕf8 5 ♗c4+ ♔h8 6 ♕d5 h6

If 6...♗c6, then 7 ♘f7+ ♔g8 8 ♕xc6! bxc6 9 ♘e5+ ♔h8 10 ♘xg6+ hxg6 11 Ĕxe4 g5 12 ♗xa6, etc.

7 ♘f7+ ♔h7 8 ♘e5 ♕e8 9 ♕xe4+ ♗f5 10 ♕xb7 ♘b8 11 ♗f7 ♕d8 12 ♕f3 ♕f6 13 g4 ♗b1 14 ♕d1!

Now Black's bishop does not have a single square left on the b1-h7 diagonal. Black lost the exchange and the game a few moves later.

Here is an example showing the strength of two bishops working together.

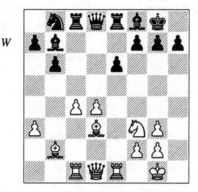

White offers a pawn in order to open up the long diagonal for his b2-bishop.
1 d5! ♘d7

Black does not accept the sacrifice. After 1...exd5 2 ♖xe8 ♕xe8 3 ♘g5 both 3...g6 4 ♗xg6! fxg6 5 ♕d4 and 3...h6 4 ♗h7+ ♔h8 5 ♕h5 give White a decisive attack.

2 dxe6 ♖xe6 3 ♖xe6 fxe6 4 ♕c2 ♗xf3

4...g6 is met by 5 ♕c3, while if 4...h6, then 5 ♗h7+ ♔h8 6 ♘h4.

5 ♗xh7+ ♔h8 6 gxf3

Having gained a pawn and weakened Black's position, White won the game in ten more moves.

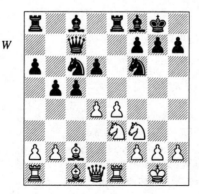

In this position, which arose in Geller-Kotov, USSR Championship (Moscow) 1955, White sacrificed a pawn to obtain control of the long diagonal and thereby gain the possibility to break through with a winning attack.

16 b3! ♘b4 17 ♗b1 ♘xe4?

Black accepts the pawn sacrifice, a decision which not only costs him a series of tempi but also causes him to yield control of the long diagonal to White.

18 ♗b2 ♗b7 19 d5 c4 20 bxc4 bxc4 21 ♗xe4 ♖xe4 22 ♘g5 ♖e7 23 ♕h5 h6 24 ♘f5! ♖xe1+ 25 ♖xe1 hxg5

25...g6 fails against 26 ♕xh6! ♗xh6 27 ♘xh6+ ♚f8 28 ♘h7#. If 25...c3, White wins by 26 ♖e7! cxb2 27 ♘xh6+[1].

26 ♖e3 ♗c8

There was a threat of 27 ♖h3 f6 28 ♕g6, etc. If 26...f6, then 27 ♕g6! (not 27 ♗xf6 because of 27...♕f7!) 27...g4 28 ♘h6+ ♚h8 29 ♘xg4, etc. If 26...g4, then 27 ♘h6+ gxh6 28 ♕xg4+ with mate in three moves.

27 ♗xg7! ♗xg7 28 ♖e8+ 1-0

For 28...♗f8 is answered by 29 ♖xf8+ and 30 ♕h8#.

---

1   After 26 ♖e7, Black has the surprising defence 26...♗xd5!, when 27 ♖xc7 cxb2 28 ♕d1 ♗xa2 promotes the pawn. Therefore, 26 ♘e7+ ♕xe7 27 ♖xe7 ♗xd5 28 ♘xf7! is better, when White should win.

8 Pieces and pawns in the attack on the castled king

Our examination of the attack on the castled king has so far (in chapters 4-7) been mainly directed towards the spatial aspect of the attack, and it is now time to examine the parts played by particular pieces and the significance of material sacrifices. Some of these points have already been touched on, so in this chapter we shall concern ourselves only with certain themes where the material aspect is paramount and which have not yet been fully dealt with.

The queen in the attack on the castled king

The queen is undoubtedly the most important piece in the attack on the castled king, and indeed without it such an attack rarely comes into consideration. Admittedly, it is not impossible to undertake a direct attack without the queen, but the necessary conditions for it cannot easily be created.

The queen's great mobility, its main characteristic, is a useful factor in the attack on the castled king, but its effectiveness at short range is even more striking. If it is in occupation of the focal-point g7, the enemy king on g8 has every square taken from it; moreover, if it is protected on that focal-point and the focal-point itself has been cleared of the influence of the opposing pieces, then the king is mated. The queen is, as it were, 'made for focal-points', and particularly for play on compound focal-points. Therefore, the queen's chief strategy in an attack on the castled king consists in playing on the focal-points and discovering ways in which to attack as effectively as possible at close range. Thus the queen, which in an endgame on an open board feels such an aversion towards the opponent's king that it will not allow it nearer than two paces away, is filled in attack with some kind of dark desire and dreams only of how it can steal into the castled dwelling and there fold the king in a close and deadly embrace.

The reverse side of the queen's positive characteristics is its great material value; this means that the queen is not lightly sacrificed and is not as a rule given up for smaller gains, such as preventing castling or clearing a focal-point. However, there are a number of different kinds of queen sacrifice which occur in the attack on the castled king; these can be reduced in the main to two fairly sharply differentiated types: the case where the sacrifice forces mate, 'check upon check', as it were, and the case where it produces a great positional weakness on the opposing side.

There are also unusual and curious queen sacrifices; we shall give three examples as variations on this theme, ranging over a period of 40 years.

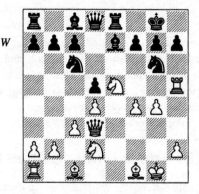

In this position, from the game Fox-Bauer, Washington 1901, White, to move, set his opponent a trap.

1 ♘dc4 dxc4?

Black in his greed accepted the sacrifice, which he should have refused.

2 ♕xg6!

A correct sacrifice of the queen, which forces the opening of either the h-file or the a2-g8 diagonal.

2...hxg6

Or 2...fxg6 3 ♗xc4+ ♚f8 4 ♘xg6+ and 5 ♖h8#.

3 ♘xg6 fxg6 4 ♗xc4+ ♚f8 5 ♖h8#

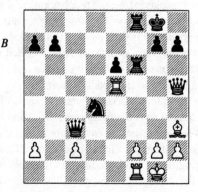

A position from the game Lewitzky-Marshall, Breslau 1912. Marshall won renown in the following way:

1...♖h6 2 ♕g5 ♖xh3 3 ♖c5

White saw that 3 gxh3 would not do because of 3...♘f3+ and intended, on 3...♕a3, to play 4 ♖c7, etc[1].

However, Black took him by surprise with:

3...♕g3!! 0-1

4 hxg3 ♘e2# and 4 fxg3 ♘e2+ 5 ♔h1 ♖xf1# fail at once, while after 4 ♕xg3 ♘e2+ 5 ♔h1 ♘xg3+ 6 ♔g1 ♘xf1 7 gxh3 ♘d2 White is left a knight down.

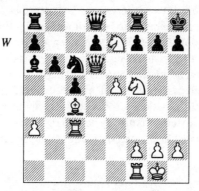

W

This position is from a blindfold game of Alekhine's at Tenerife in 1945 (Alekhine-Supico) and acts as a counterpart to Marshall's combination above. Alekhine, in playing

1 ♕g6!

forced Black to resign **(1-0)**. If Black does not take the queen but plays instead 1...♖g8, White wins by 2 ♕xh7+ and 3 ♖h3#; if Black plays 1...hxg6 the rook mates immediately, while if 1...fxg6, then 2 ♘xg6+, and again the rook mates on h3.

Lovers of curiosities will have noticed the common square (g6 or g3) on which the queen is sacrificed on all three occasions. The curious side of these examples should not distract one from noticing what is typical in them: in all these cases the attacker has a number of other pieces at his disposal, all in the strongest aggressive positions, while only his queen is somehow 'underemployed'. As a result, it is given the task of breaking up the position by sacrificing itself. The situation is that although the pieces are in very aggressive positions, they cannot

---

1   Although even this fails after 4...♘e2+ 5 ♔h1 ♖xh2+ 6 ♔xh2 ♕d6+, etc.

settle the issue by themselves since, if they are sacrificed, their aggressive formation also disappears. It is therefore left to a less committed piece to carry out the work of destruction, and in these cases this is none other than the queen. Usually, however, the reverse applies: the other pieces are sacrificed, while the queen reaps the harvest.

The heavy pieces in the attack

The examples in chapters 4-7 have shown us various kinds of operations on the part of the rook, the bishop, and the knight on lines and focal-points, and no further illustrations of the use of these pieces in an attack on the castled king need be given. Only one special case remains to be dealt with, and that is the attack on the castled king carried out by the heavy pieces (queen and rooks) alone. The main feature of this kind of attack can be summed up as the task of *overcoming the clumsiness of the rooks*. The attacker must aim to make his own rooks active and force his opponent's into passivity. A rook's mobility depends essentially on its ability to switch its control suddenly from one file to another and, in particular, from a file to a rank. Or, in the terminology used in my *Introduction to chess* (2nd ed., p. 171), the rook must have corresponding strong squares at its disposal. Here are a few examples:

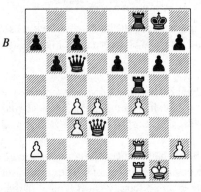

This position is from the game Winter-Capablanca, Ramsgate 1929. Black, to move, played:

1...♔h8

Black threatens 2...g5, which would not have been good at once because of 2 ♖g2. White is now obliged to weaken his pawn position by moving his h-pawn.

2 h4 ♖h5 3 ♖h2 ♖hf5

After 'feeling about' a little Black reverts to the former position.

4 ♖hf2 ♕d6 5 ♕e3 ♕d8 6 ♕xe6

A disagreeable exchange, but White has nothing better. If 6 ♖h2, then 6...♕f6, while if 6 ♕g3, then 6...♕f6 followed by ...c5.

6...♕xh4 7 ♕e3

On 7 ♕e4, which would have provided better resistance, Black would have replied 7...♕g3+ followed by 8...♕xc3, but not 7...♖g5+? because of 8 fxg5 ♕xe4 9 ♖xf8+ and White mates.

7...♖h5

It is patently clear that Black's rooks are active and White's passive.

8 ♖g2 ♕h1+ 9 ♔f2 ♕h3! 10 ♕g3

White has no satisfactory defence. If he exchanges queens, he loses a pawn, while if 10 ♖g3, then 10...♕h2+ followed by 11...♕xa2.

10...♕e6 11 ♔g1 ♕xc4 12 ♖e1 ♕f7 13 ♖f2 ♖f5 14 ♖e4 g5 0-1

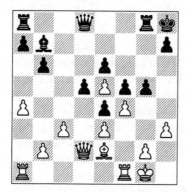

This position is from the game Rubinstein-Alekhine, Dresden 1926[1]. Black played:

1...gxf4 2 ♖xf4

2 exf4 is no better, since Black can continue 2...♕h4 with the double threat of 3...♖xg2+ and 3...♕xh3.

2...♕g5 3 ♗f1 ♕g3!

Black compels the king to go to h1 so that he can play ...♕g3 with gain of tempo on the sixth move!

---

1   In the original book, this position was incorrectly given with Black's bishop on c8 instead of b7. The analysis has been modified to take account of this correction.

4 ♔h1 ♕g7 5 ♕d4 ♗a6! 6 ♖f2 ♕g3! 7 ♖c2 ♗xf1 8 ♖xf1 ♖ac8

By threatening to break through at c4, Black gains a tempo for doubling rooks. Alekhine now uses his heavy pieces to force home the final attack.

9 b3 ♖c7 10 ♖e2 ♖cg7 11 ♖f4 ♖g6! *(D)*

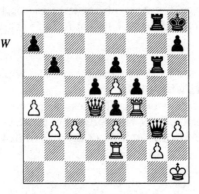

Black threatens ...♖h6, ...♖xh3+ and ...♕g1#. If White plays 12 ♖f1, the plan of 12...♖h6 followed by sacrificing at h3 is again in order, for the rook on f1 is unprotected; moreover, if it is moved (e.g. to a1) then 13...♖xh3+ still succeeds because the queen can follow up with a decisive check at f3.

In his book, *My Best Games of Chess 1924-1937,* Alekhine mentions another reply, 12 ♕d1, and claims that 12...♖h6 leads to an original *zugzwang* position; this is not correct (because Black has the strong threat of 13...♕g7 14 ♕d4 ♖xh3+, etc.), but it is true inasmuch as White's rooks cannot move; they provide a perfect illustration of 'the rook's clumsiness'.

After 12 ♕d1 ♖h6 White would have to play 13 ♕a1 (not 13 c4 because of 13...d4!), in which case the strongest reply is 13...a6! (creating another threat, i.e. ...b5-b4 followed by ...d4; if 13...♕g7, then 14 c4 is possible). Now White's front e-pawn is lost, but he can still offer some resistance by 14 ♖f1. Black, however, must not take the e-pawn while White's queen is on a1; he does better with 14...b5 15 axb5 axb5, after which one can speak of a type of *zugzwang* position, since White cannot prevent the situation of his pawn on e5 from deteriorating still further. If 16 b4 (or 16 ♕d1 or 16 ♕e1), Black takes the pawn on e5, after which he should win.

In the actual game White gave up a pawn in a different way and lost as follows: **12 ♕b4?! ♖h6 13 h4 ♕g7!** *(D)*

Stronger than the prosaic 13...♖xh4+. The black queen retires and at the same time creates the threat of ...♖g6, a typical case of a tripled formation with a rook

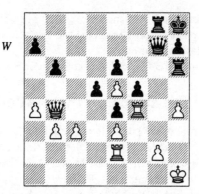

in front of the queen. The reader should note the mobility of Black's heavy pieces, which allows such rapid and useful regroupings to be made. In the course of the game and its variations up to this point two pairs of corresponding strong squares for Black stand out, namely, g6 and h6 for the rook, and g3 and g7 for the queen.

14 c4 ♖g6 15 ♕d2 ♖g3!

After all the different formations on the squares described, here is yet another: the rook now tries out the square g3 and threatens ...♖h3+.

16 ♕e1 ♖xe3 0-1

If 16 ♔g1, Black had planned to play 16...d4! 17 exd4 e3 18 ♕c2 ♖h3, and White is helpless against 19...♕g3.

Alekhine won the Brilliancy Prize for this game. How light those heavy pieces were in his hands!

After these examples, which are typical of the style of the two world champions, here is a little light entertainment.

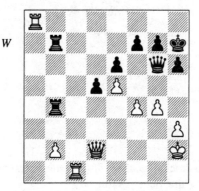

It is the finish of the game Bernstein-Kotov, Groningen 1946. Black, having greedily and needlessly snapped up a pawn (he had just played ...♖e4xb4 instead of the correct ...♖c4) lost as follows:

　1 ♖cc8 ♕e4 2 ♖h8+ ♔g6 3 f5+ exf5 4 ♕xh6+! gxh6 5 ♖ag8#

The sacrifice in the attack on the castled king

Before we turn to the role of the pawns in the attack on the castled king, a few general remarks must be made about sacrifices in the castling area. Certain combinative elements are present in the case of every sacrifice, though these sacrifices may be of widely diverging types. However, the typical sacrifice in the castling area is the one which is closely influenced by the special characteristics of that area, namely the castled king and the pawns in front of it. The typical sacrifice either changes the structure of the pawns, or aims to draw the king on to a square where it can be attacked, or else helps to create a focal-point. We have already met examples of the last two types in the course of discussing focal-points, particularly in the case of the classic bishop sacrifice. Here our principal interest is the pawn structure and the possibility of altering it by means of a sacrifice. A sacrifice can either simply annihilate one of the pawns in front of the king, or it can deflect the pawn on to another file, or finally it can cause it to be blocked.

The main use of the sacrifice in the attack on the castled king is to eliminate the pawns in the castling area, and a number of examples will be devoted to this. But first of all, let us examine two examples where the emphasis is on spoiling the pawn structure by deflecting or blocking the pawns.

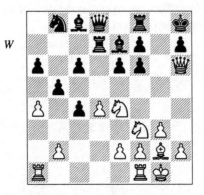

This position comes from an analysis of the game Capablanca-Nimzowitsch, Bad Kissingen, 1928. White mates as follows:

1 ♘fg5! fxg5

Deflecting the pawn from f6.

2 ♘f6!

Blocking the f7-pawn.

2...♗xf6 3 ♗e4

and Black has no way of stopping mate on h7.

White here overcame the resistance of Black's f-pawn on the diagonal b1-h7 by making sacrifices which deflected one pawn and blocked the other.

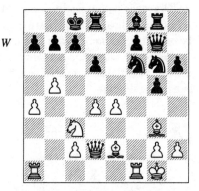

This position arose in the game Steinitz-L. Paulsen, Baden-Baden 1870. It is White's move, and he is faced with the task of finding the most effective attacking plan against Black's castled position. To this end he played:

1 b6!

White gives up a pawn in order to weaken Black's castled position and open up the a- and b-files. This kind of pawn sacrifice is instructive and typical. Its advantage lies in the fact that Black has no way of blocking the pawn structure but is forced to capture in order to avoid getting into worse difficulties.

1...axb6 2 ♖xf6!

The castled position has been effectively weakened and the situation is ripe for the further thrust a5, that being the logical method of following up 1 b6!, but Steinitz sees that, before playing a5, he can strengthen his attack still further by sacrificing the exchange.

2...♕xf6 3 ♗g4+ ♔b8 4 ♘d5 ♕g7 5 a5

Now the force of this move is even greater than before.

5...f5

If 5...b5, then 6 a6 b6 (or 6...bxa6 7 ♕a5 ♕xd4+ 8 ♗f2) 7 a7+ ♔b7 8 ♘xc7 ♔xc7 (or 8...f5 9 ♘e6) 9 ♕c3+ ♔b7 10 ♗d7 with a decisive attack.

If 5...c5, then White plays 6 axb6 ♕xd4+ 7 ♕xd4 cxd4 8 ♘c7 followed by 9 ♖a8#.

6 axb6 cxb6 7 ♘xb6 ♘e7

Black must parry the threat of 8 ♕c3.

8 exf5 ♕f7 9 f6! ♘c6

Or 9...♕xf6 10 ♕c3 ♘c6 11 ♖a8+ ♔c7 12 ♘d5#.

10 c4 ♘a7 11 ♕a2 ♘b5 12 ♘d5 and White won after **12...♕xd5 13 cxd5 ♘xd4 14 ♕a7+ ♔c7 15 ♖c1+ ♘c6 16 ♖xc6#.**

One further remark must be made before passing on to the destructive sacrifice: a sacrifice and the operations following it must have the *aim of creating a focal-point,* especially if the opponent has some active counterplay at his disposal. The next diagram shows an example where the attacker wrecks his opponent's castled position and regains the material he has sacrificed, but is still unsuccessful because he cannot create a focal-point.

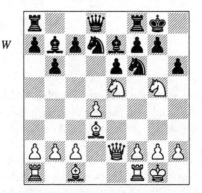

This position is from the game Colle-Tartakower, Niendorf 1927. White is excellently placed here and ought to continue with 1 ♘h3, but Colle, the lover of sacrifices, cannot resist the temptation and offers material in a position which is still insufficiently prepared.

1 ♘exf7? ♖xf7 2 ♘xe6 ♕c8 3 ♗g6 ♘f8 4 ♗xf7+ ♔xf7 5 ♘xg7

All these captures have been made on different squares, none of which qualifies as a candidate for a focal-point. No wonder that Black develops a counterattack that ensures sufficient counterplay.

5...♗a6 6 c4 ♕g4 7 ♕xg4 ♘xg4 8 ♘f5 ♗xc4 9 ♖d1 h5

The position is balanced and the game ended in a draw after a further 17 moves.

The destructive sacrifice

We have already referred to the annihilation of the pawns in front of the castled king as the most important or at any rate predominant result of sacrificial operations. It would be more exact to say that the destruction of these pawns is the most common combinative element of sacrifices in the castling area. Most players tend to pay more attention to the material aspect than to the temporal one, but the most decisive consequence of the destruction of pawns is that the departed pawns can no longer affect the game. This is a permanent positional factor by means of which many combinations are sustained, even when all may not have been in order on the temporal side. It is very important to spot the opportunities for making a destructive sacrifice, and in many positions the attacker is shown the way by simply calculating what would happen if his opponent were not to have a certain pawn.

We shall look at a number of examples which illustrate typical destructive sacrifices.

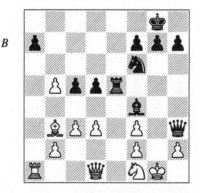

This position arose in a match game between Loyd and Delmar in 1879. It is Black's move, and he must act quickly if White is not to break through by b6 or ♖xa7. Various attempts like ...♖g5+ or ...♖h5 meet with resistance, and only the immediate capture of the pawn at h2 ensures mate.

1...♗xh2+! 2 ♘xh2 ♖g5+ 3 ♘g4 ♖h5 4 ♘h2 ♕xh2+ 5 ♔f1 ♖e5 and mate by ...♕h1# is unavoidable.

The destructive sacrifice on g7 (or g2) is particularly dangerous, and we shall examine one out of the rich collection of this type.

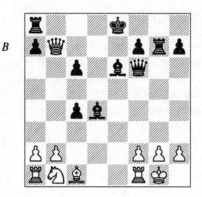

This position arose in the game Shumov-Jaenisch, St. Petersburg 1849. Black, to move, concluded the game as follows:

1...♖xg2+ 2 ♔xg2 ♕g6+ 3 ♔h1 ♗d5+ 4 f3 ♗xf3+ 5 ♖xf3 ♕g1#

We shall now go on to look at cases of successive sacrifices, whereby two of the pawns in front of the castled king are eliminated. It is often easy to spot sacrifices of this kind if the position is looked at in the light of our thematic criterion: what would the situation be if the pawns were not there? Let us take the next diagram, for example.

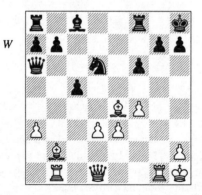

In this position, from the game Keller-Rohaczek, Vienna 1937, it is White's move, and he has an easy task if he imagines Black's position without the pawns on h7 and g7 and realizes that White then mates with his queen on h5 and rook on g1. The operation is then extremely simple.

1 ♗xh7 ♔xh7 2 ♕h5+ ♔g8 3 ♖xg7+ ♔xg7 4 ♖g1+ and mates.

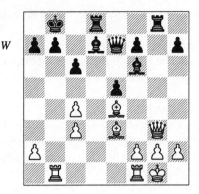

This position is from a correspondence game between Luprecht and Schulz played in the United States in 1946. Here it is a question of removing Black's pawns on a7 and b7 from in front of the king. If these pawns did not exist, a build-up with a rook on b1 and a queen on e3 would give White an irresistible mating attack. The solution is therefore simple.

1 ♗xa7+ ♚xa7 2 ♕e3+

First, the queen is brought nearer with gain of tempo and then the second pawn is annihilated.

2...♚b8 3 ♖xb7+ ♚xb7 4 ♖b1+ ♚c7

Or 4...♚c8 5 ♕a7, when either the queen mates at b7 or the rook at b8. Mate is also inevitable after 4...♚a8 5 ♕b6.

5 ♕b6+ ♚d6 6 c5+ ♚e6 7 ♕b3#

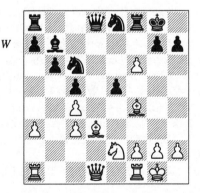

A more complex instance of a double destructive sacrifice is provided by the finish to the game Lilienthal-Najdorf, which was awarded the First Brilliancy

Prize at the Saltsjöbaden Interzonal tournament in 1948. In the above position, White continued:

1 fxg7!

This eliminates the pawn on g7 (in this case the sacrifice does not take place on that square but indirectly at f4). Black accepts the sacrifice in order not to be left a pawn down.

1...♖xf4 2 ♘xf4 exf4 3 ♗xh7+!

Eliminating the pawn on h7 as well – by a direct sacrifice. Beyond that, in fact, there is no mate in sight. However, Black's weakness on the second rank and the power of the manoeuvre ♖ad1-d7, by which it must be exploited, are evident.

3...♔xh7 4 ♕h5+ ♔xg7 5 ♖ad1 (D)

5...♕f6

Black has three minor pieces for a rook and two pawns, but his knights are badly placed, whereas the position is just right for White's rooks.

With 5...♕f6, Black attempts to lessen the force of the attack by returning some material, but he is unsuccessful because his knights continue to find themselves on awkward squares. Other lines were no better, e.g.:

1) 5...♘d4 6 cxd4 cxd4 7 ♖fe1! ♘f6 8 ♕e5 ♔f7 9 ♖xd4 and White wins.

2) 5...♘d6 6 ♕g4+ ♔f7 7 ♖fe1 ♗c8 8 ♕xf4+ also wins.

3) 5...♕c8 (if 5...♕e7, then 6 ♖fe1, while if 5...♕c7, then 6 ♕g4+ and 7 ♖d7) 6 ♖fe1 ♘f6 7 ♕g5+ ♔f7 8 ♖d6 ♕h8 9 ♖ee6 is also decisive.

6 ♖d7+ ♔f8 7 ♖xb7 ♘d8

Or 7...♘d6 8 ♖h7 ♘f7 9 ♖xf7+ ♕xf7 10 ♕h8+ ♕g8 11 ♕f6+ followed by 12 ♕xc6 and White wins.

8 ♖d7 ♘f7 9 ♕d5 ♖b8 10 ♖e1 f3 11 ♖e3! 1-0

If 11...♘g5, then 12 h4 ♘h3+ 13 gxh3 ♕g6+ 14 ♕g5 is decisive.

Of the various sacrificial devices to eliminate two pawns in front of the castled king, the sacrifice of both bishops on h7 and g7 is particularly worth noting. One of the oldest examples of this occurred in the game Lasker-Bauer, Amsterdam 1889. The opening moves were:

1 f4 d5 2 e3 ♘f6 3 b3 e6 4 ♗b2 ♗e7 5 ♗d3 b6 6 ♘c3 ♗b7 7 ♘f3 ♘bd7 8 0-0 0-0 9 ♘e2 c5 10 ♘g3 ♕c7 11 ♘e5 ♘xe5 12 ♗xe5 ♕c6 13 ♕e2 a6? *(D)*

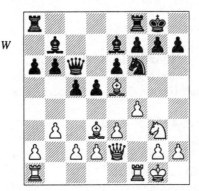

In this position, after Black's mistaken last move, Lasker worked out a combination which involved the sacrifice of both bishops; to this end he first of all forced the deflection of Black's knight.

14 ♘h5! ♘xh5

14...c4 also results in a quick finish, e.g. 15 ♘xf6+ ♗xf6 (or 15...gxf6 16 ♕g4+ ♔h8 17 ♕h4 cxd3 18 ♗xf6+ ♗xf6 19 ♕xf6+ followed by ♖f3-g3, etc.) 16 ♗xh7+ ♔xh7 17 ♕h5+ ♔g8 18 ♗xf6 gxf6 19 ♖f3 with a quick mate.

15 ♗xh7+! ♔xh7 16 ♕xh5+ ♔g8 17 ♗xg7! *(D)*

The dark-squared bishop gives itself up just like its colleague on the light squares, and it is left to White's queen and rook to make use of the files thereby opened. If now 17...f6, then 18 ♖f3 wins.

17...♔xg7 18 ♕g4+ ♔h7 19 ♖f3 e5

To prolong the game by sacrificing his queen; clearly, there is no other possibility.

20 ♖h3+ ♕h6 21 ♖xh6+ ♔xh6 22 ♕d7 ♗f6 23 ♕xb7 and White won the game in a few moves.

Here are two more examples of this type.

Nimzowitsch – Tarrasch

Preliminary event, St Petersburg 1914
Queen's Gambit Declined, Tarrasch Defence

1 d4 d5 2 ♘f3 c5 3 c4 e6 4 e3 ♘f6 5 ♗d3

Correct here is 5 cxd5.

5...♘c6 6 0-0 ♗d6 7 b3 0-0 8 ♗b2 b6 9 ♘bd2 ♗b7 10 ♖c1 ♕e7 11 cxd5 exd5 12 ♘h4 g6 13 ♘hf3 ♖ad8 14 dxc5?

Better is 14 ♖e1 and then ♘f1.

14...bxc5 15 ♗b5 ♘e4 16 ♗xc6 ♗xc6 17 ♕c2 ♘xd2! 18 ♘xd2 d4 19 exd4 *(D)*

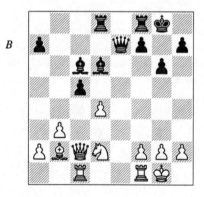

19...♗xh2+!

The beginning of the sacrificial combination.

20 ♔xh2 ♕h4+ 21 ♔g1 ♗xg2 22 f3

If White accepts the second sacrifice by 22 ♔xg2, then 22...♕g4+ 23 ♔h2 ♖d5 is decisive.

22...♖fe8 23 ♘e4 ♕h1+ 24 ♔f2 ♗xf1 25 d5 f5 26 ♕c3 ♕g2+ 27 ♔e3 ♖xe4+ 28 fxe4 f4+ 29 ♔xf4 ♖f8+ 30 ♔e5 ♕h2+ 31 ♔e6 ♖e8+ 0-1

For if 32 ♔d7, then 32...♗b5#.

Alekhine – Drewitt
Portsmouth, 1923
Sokolsky Opening

1 ♘f3 d5 2 b4 e6 3 ♗b2 ♘f6 4 a3 c5 5 bxc5 ♗xc5 6 e3 0-0 7 c4 ♘c6 8 d4 ♗b6 9 ♘bd2 ♕e7 10 ♗d3 ♖d8 11 0-0 ♗d7 12 ♘e5! ♗e8 13 f4 ♖ac8 14 ♖c1 ♘d7 15 ♘xc6 ♖xc6 16 c5 ♘xc5 17 dxc5 ♗xc5 18 ♖f3 ♗xa3? 19 ♖xc6 ♗xc6 *(D)*

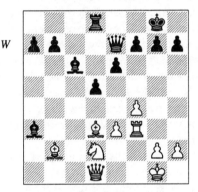

20 ♗xh7+!

The beginning of a well-prepared combination involving two bishop sacrifices.

20...♔xh7 21 ♖h3+ ♔g8 22 ♗xg7 1-0.

If 22...♔xg7, then 23 ♕g4+ and mate, while after 22...f6 23 ♗h6 ♔f7 24 ♕h5+ Black's king cannot extricate itself from the mating net.

The pawns in the attack on the castled king

These examples of destructive sacrifices have shown us a procedure for dealing with the opponent's pawns, and now we shall examine the part played by the attacker's pawns in the attack on the castled king. The part is a very varied one, reflecting, as it does, the rich possibilities inherent in the pawn's movements. The pawns are, above all, the pieces which cost one the least to sacrifice in one's efforts to weaken the enemy position; they are also excellent at harrying one's opponent's pieces as well as helping to support one's own on focal-points or strong squares. In all these cases the positive characteristics of the pawn are to the fore. The other side to the use of pawns in an attack on the castled king is a logical consequence of their negative characteristics, namely their limited mobility and the impossibility of reversing their moves. The attacker's pawn needs, on average, three moves before it can have a direct effect on the opposing castling area itself; also, the attacker cannot transfer it from one file to another at will, but only when opposing units are so placed as to come into its line of fire. Equally inconvenient is the other aspect of the pawn's negative characteristics: in advancing, it weakens the squares which it leaves behind it, and if the attack does not succeed, serious positional weaknesses may become evident in the attacker's position. The irreversibility of pawn moves may also lead to a general blockade, which in turn produces a rigid position and complicates the attack. However, the pawn still has one more positive characteristic which can on some occasions help the attacker: the promotion of the pawn into a piece on the opponent's back rank may be the attacker's last trump at the critical stage of an attack.

Thus all the different aspects of the pawn's special characteristics find their expression in an attack on the castled king, and the picture becomes still more varied when we fill in the spatial side of pawn operations in this kind of attack. Here is a brief summary of a pawn's role in the attack on the castled king.

1) The attacker's pawn (with or without a sacrifice) forces the opponent to weaken his castled position.

2) It serves to create combinative elements in attack (e.g. by deflecting or attracting the opponent's pieces or opening up files).

3) It forms part of an attacking formation (e.g. in the formation with a rook on h1 and a pawn on h4 or as a support to a piece on a focal-point).

4) A particular example of such an attacking formation which should be mentioned is the pawn centre; as a rule, this serves either generally to confine the opponent or to provide the basis for an attack on the castled king.

5) The pawn advances independently on the flank in order to drive an enemy piece away or to take control of a square. An advance of this kind is usually called a bayonet attack.

6) Two or three attacking wing pawns advance against the opponent's castled position in a frontal formation (a pawn avalanche or roller).

7) The pawn moves up into the castling area as a straightforward attacking unit against the enemy king.

8) The pawn advances into the castling area (with or without an attack on the king) in order to be promoted, after which it can carry on the attack in its new role.

These various types of action are usually interrelated in practical play, and single moves often combine two or more such functions. Indeed, when the process is observed as a whole over the space of a few moves, the continuous transition from one type to another is virtually the rule, except in the case of point 4 (centre pawns). As an example of the kind of progressive changes which can take place in the role of a pawn attack let us look schematically at 'the career of an h-pawn', move by move.

h3: the pawn advances and drives an opposing piece from g4. This could be termed a 'little bayonet' (cf. point 5);

h4: it makes up a set formation in conjunction with a rook on h1 (point 3); this is followed by g4, and we have a frontal formation (point 6);

h5: it threatens to open up the h-file by capturing an enemy pawn at g6 (potentially under point 2); Black therefore counters by blocking the position with ...g5, but as a result weakens the pawn structure in front of his king (point 1);

h6: it acts as a support for an attack against the focal-point g7 (point 3);

h7+: Black has warded off the threats on g7, but now the pawn turns to direct attack (point 7);

h8♕: the pawn promotes to a queen and carries on the attack (point 8).

Every chess player will admit that such a career on the part of an h-pawn is in no way exceptional but is, on the contrary, a typical illustration of the many-sidedness of a pawn's role in an attack on the castled king.

Examples have already been given of the aspects of a pawn's activity listed under points 1-3 and 7-8, so we shall restrict ourselves in this chapter to a survey of those under points 4-6.

The role of the pawn centre

The centre pawns have the task of controlling important squares and preventing the opposing forces from using them. As a result the pawn centre is the main weapon in the struggle for an advantage in development and space. However, in addition to the general positional function of restricting the opponent, the pawn centre also acts as a basis for an attack on the castled king. Firstly, the overall restriction imposed on the opponent makes it difficult for him to deploy his pieces and so indirectly assists the attacker's plans; in addition, each of the centre pawns directly controls the outer squares of the castled position. Thus, on e5, the e-pawn controls the important square f6, and on e6, the square f7; a similar control is exercised against the queenside castling position by the d-pawn (the squares c6 and c7).

We have already seen a number of fine examples of the influence of a centre pawn in an attack on the castled king, and especially the part played by the pawn on e5 in the classic bishop sacrifice. In this section we shall examine the more general situation, where a central formation has the functions both of a restricting agent and also of a direct controller of squares in the castling area. From the profusion of practical examples of this kind we shall take one in which the attacker's centre is particularly dynamic.

Tarrasch – Alekhine

Bad Pistyan, 1922

Blumenfeld Counter-Gambit

1 d4 ♘f6 2 ♘f3 e6 3 c4 c5 4 d5 b5 5 dxe6?

Preparing to accept the gambit offered by Black with 4...b5. Nowadays it is well known that it is not worth accepting this gambit and that it is best to play 5 ♗g5, in order to maintain the centre pawn at d5.

5...fxe6 6 cxb5 d5

Black's great strength in the centre more than compensates for the minus pawn.

7 e3 ♗d6 8 ♘c3 0-0 9 ♗e2 ♗b7 10 b3 ♘bd7 11 ♗b2 ♕e7 12 0-0 ♖ad8 13 ♕c2 e5 14 ♖fe1 *(D)*

White has no satisfactory defence against the growing threat of ...e4. If 14 e4, the strongest continuation is 14...d4 15 ♗c4+ ♔h8 16 ♘d5 ♗xd5 17 ♗xd5 ♘xd5 18 exd5, after which 18...e4 follows with even greater effect.

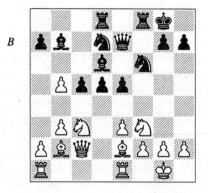

14...e4

Now both aspects of the influence exerted by Black's pawn mass in the centre can be clearly seen: White is restricted, and at the same time the pawn on e4 deprives his knight of the square f3.

15 ♘d2 ♘e5 16 ♘d1

A laborious defence; this knight has to cover f2, while the other goes to f1 to defend h2.

16...♘fg4 17 ♗xg4 ♘xg4 18 ♘f1 ♕g5

This move is aimed against the square g2; Black's plan is to advance the d-pawn and open the long diagonal for the b7-bishop.

19 h3 ♘h6 20 ♔h1 ♘f5 21 ♘h2 *(D)*

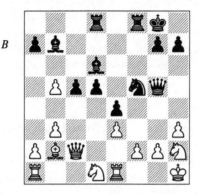

21...d4!

Black's central mass makes another vigorous contribution to the attack. The d-pawn now advances to d3, where it controls White's support square e2. If 22 exd4 e3, both 23 fxe3 and 23 ♖g1 are answered by 23...♕g3!.

22 ♗c1 d3

Still better is 22...♘g3+ 23 ♔g1 d3, for then 24 ♕c4+ can be met without loss of tempo by 24...♗d5.

23 ♕c4+ ♔h8 24 ♗b2 ♘g3+ 25 ♔g1 ♗d5 26 ♕a4 ♘e2+ 27 ♔h1 ♖f7 28 ♕a6 h5 29 b6 ♘g3+ 30 ♔g1 axb6 31 ♕xb6 d2 32 ♖f1 ♘xf1 33 ♘xf1 ♗e6 34 ♔h1 ♗xh3 35 gxh3 ♖f3 36 ♘g3 h4 37 ♗f6 ♕xf6 38 ♘xe4 ♖xh3+ 0-1.

It is an irony of fate that the person to experience the might of the centre in this game should have been Tarrasch, a great devotee of the centre and a noted exponent of central pawn strategy. Such drastic examples of an action by the whole central mass in the attack on the castled king will not be found in contemporary master practice. The technique of playing against the centre has been so perfected that one can no longer succeed by the single expedient of following the pattern of the game above. Masters no longer accept gambits like the Blumenfeld; on all occasions they examine the extent of the compensation or the possibility of play against the centre, either by counterattacking it with pawns, or by exerting a restraining pressure on it with their pieces. The central formations which occur nowadays in master chess are not as a rule so uncompromisingly lethal as this one, but instead tend to be critical and sensitive formations, which demand an extremely precise use of the pieces if they are not to become weak and collapse. As a result of this characteristic sensitivity of central formations in the games of present-day masters, the temporal aspect of such actions has also altered, and nowadays one rarely sees a full pawn centre being maintained for many moves; it usually appears as a transitory feature, a phase of the game which is immediately followed either by an attack on the castled king or some other action. The following game provides an illustration of this kind of temporary, flexible centre and of a rapidly developed attack on the castled king.

Keres – Fine
Ostend, 1937
Queen's Gambit Declined, Semi-Tarrasch Defence

1 ♘f3 d5 2 d4 ♘f6 3 c4 e6 4 ♘c3 c5 5 cxd5 ♘xd5

5...exd5 would lead into the Tarrasch Defence proper. After the text move, the game develops along independent lines.

6 e4 ♘xc3 7 bxc3 cxd4 8 cxd4 ♗b4+

Black's dark-squared bishop is exchanged in order to simplify the position further. Each exchange, as a rule, helps to diminish the power of the pawn centre and increases the significance of a queenside majority, which Black has here. Because of this, theory regards this position as approximately equal.

9 ♗d2 ♗xd2+ 10 ♕xd2 0-0 11 ♗c4 ♘d7?

This move is considered weak by present-day theory. Better is 11...♘c6 12 0-0 b6 13 ♖fd1 ♗b7.

12 0-0 b6 13 ♖ad1 ♗b7 14 ♖fe1 ♖c8 15 ♗b3 ♘f6

An attempt to put pressure on the centre and induce e5, after which Black can play ...♘d5. However, White can leave his pawn on e4 for the time being and first strengthen his position in readiness for an attack on the castled king. The weak side of 15...♘f6 stems precisely from the possibility of gaining a tempo by attacking the knight with e5; without this White would have no advantage. In the very line Black used here to simplify the position (moves 6-9) the exchange of the f6-knight, the piece exposed to attack by e4-e5, is an essential part of Black's whole system; now, however, a knight appears again on f6 and with it the attacking motif e5.

Even so, 15...♘f6 is not a mistake, for other moves are no better; the bad move has already been made – 11...♘d7?. It is true that the commentator Reinfeld mentions 15...♕f6 in his book on Keres, continuing with 16 e5 ♕h6? 17 ♕xh6 gxh6, according to the pattern of the game Reshevsky-Fine, Hastings 1937; in that game, however, Black's knight was on c6 and his queen's rook on d8, so that his simplifying manoeuvre was in order. In this position, though, White would continue 18 d5 exd5 19 ♗xd5 ♗xd5 20 ♖xd5 ♘c5 21 ♖d6, and the pawn on h6 begins to totter, since 21...♔g7 or 21...♘e6 is answered by 22 ♘h4 followed by ♘f5.

16 ♕f4 ♕c7 17 ♕h4 ♖fd8 (D)

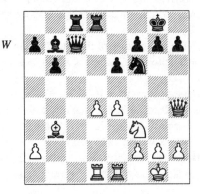

18 ♖e3?

White's pawn centre, which has now been standing on the board for a number of moves, provides a typical illustration of the sensitivity of such formations. The crisis has been mounting from move to move, and the question now is whether the time is ripe for e5 or whether the position still needs reinforcing. White cannot wait much longer, since Black has a strong card to play on the queenside, namely ...b5 and ...a5, etc. Keres decides on reinforcement and in doing so makes a mistake. Correct was 18 e5 immediately; reinforcement would perhaps also have worked, but in the shape of 18 ♖d3.

After 18 e5 there are two main ways open to Black (lines 3 and 4 below):

1) 18...♗xf3? is bad due to 19 exf6, when the threat of 20 ♕g5 wins a piece.

2) 18...♘e8 is not good, e.g. 19 ♘g5 h6 20 ♘xe6 fxe6 21 ♗xe6+ ♔h7 22 d5 with a large advantage for White.

3) 18...♘d5 19 ♘g5 h6 20 ♘e4 ♘c3 (otherwise 21 ♘d6) 21 ♘xc3 (21 ♘f6+ is probably insufficient in view of 21...♔h8) 21...♕xc3 22 ♖e3 ♕b4 (if 22...♕c6, then 23 ♖g3) 23 ♖g3 ♔h8 24 ♕g4 (24 ♗c2 is also good) 24...♕f8 25 h4 ♖c7 26 f4 ♖cd7 (alternatives are 26...g6 27 h5 and 26...♗d5 27 f5) 27 f5 exf5 28 ♕xf5 ♖xd4 29 ♖xd4 ♖xd4 30 e6 with advantage to White.

4) 18...♘d7 19 ♘g5 ♘f8 20 ♖e3 h6 21 ♘h3 and White has a promising attack.

18 ♖d3 may be even stronger than the move which we have just examined, for with his rook on d3 White threatens e5 immediately. Thus 18...b5 is answered by 19 e5 and if 19...♘d7, then 20 ♘g5 ♘f8 21 ♘xh7 ♘xh7 22 ♖h3[1], while if 19...♘d5, then 20 ♘g5 h6 21 ♘e4 followed by ♘d6. After 18 ♖d3 Black would have to play 18...h6, in which case 19 e5 ♘d5 20 ♘d2 gives White the advantage.

All these continuations serve to illustrate my thesis on the critical nature of the full pawn centre; objectively, White's success was quite possible, but one imprecise move (18 ♖e3?) and everything has evaporated, as we shall see.

18...b5!

Now e5 is no longer a threat (because of the double attack after 19 e5 ♘d5 20 ♘g5 h6) and so Black is able to make progress on the queenside.

19 ♖de1 a5 20 a4 b4? *(D)*

While this is positionally attractive, it allows the initiative to slip out of Black's hands, with the result that White comes back into the game with prospects which are worth a draw at least. Black should have played 20...bxa4 21 ♗xa4 h6 when White's attack would have petered out: 22 e5? (22 g4 does not work because of 22...♕f4 while if 22 h3, Black plays 22...♕c4 23 ♗b3 ♕b4) 22...♘d5 23 ♖e4 ♘e7 24 ♖g4 ♗xf3 25 gxf3 ♘f5 with advantage to Black.

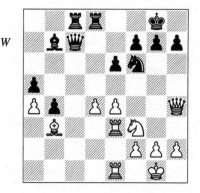

21 d5!

The immediate 21 e5 was not good, but it becomes favourable when preceded by d5, for then the black knight's access to the d5-square is blocked, while

---

1   Black can defend by 22...♗e4! 23 ♕xe4 ♘g5, winning the exchange. Thus 21 ♖g3 is a better attacking attempt, with an unclear position.

the e-file and the a2-g8 diagonal are opened up. An instructive way of using a flexible centre!

21...exd5

21...e5 will not do because of 22 ♘g5 h6 (otherwise 23 ♘xh7) 23 d6!.

22 e5 *(D)*

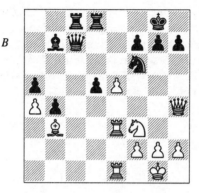

22...♘d7?

A mistake, after which White's initiative takes on new force. A draw could have been salvaged by 22...♘e4! 23 e6 fxe6 24 ♖xe4 dxe4 25 ♗xe6+! ♔h8! 26 ♘g5 h6 (26...g6 is weaker on account of 27 ♗f7 h5 28 ♗xg6 when White has an extremely promising attack) 27 ♘f7+ ♔h7 28 ♘g5+ ♔h8 29 ♘f7+ with perpetual check. If, instead of 25...♔h8, Black plays 25...♔f8?, the situation turns in White's favour, e.g. 26 ♕xh7! ♕c3 (if 26...♕f4, then 27 ♘h4 is decisive, while 26...♕e7 is no use because of 27 ♗xc8) 27 ♕g8+ ♔e7 28 ♕f7+ ♔d6 29 ♗xc8 ♗xc8 (if 29...exf3, then 30 ♕e7+ is decisive; 29...♕xc8 fails against 30 ♖d1+ ♔c5 31 ♕e7+, while if 29...♖xc8, then 30 ♖d1+ ♔c6 31 ♕e6+ ♔c5 32 ♕d6+ and 33 ♘d2+) 30 ♖xe4!, when White has a decisive attack.

Keres in his commentary continues 22...♘e4! 23 e6 fxe6 24 ♖xe4 dxe4, but instead of going on with 25 ♗xe6+!, he gives 25 ♘g5?, which is weaker, since strangely enough the knight is better placed on f3 than g5 when Black's king goes to f8. The critical line then is 25...♕c3! 26 ♗xe6+ ♔f8! 27 ♕f4+ ♔e7 28 ♕f7+ ♔d6 29 ♕f4+, whereupon Black need not settle for a draw by perpetual check with 29...♔e7, for he has instead 29...♔c5! 30 ♖c1 ♔b6 31 ♗xc8 e3! 32 ♕xe3+ ♕xe3 33 fxe3 ♖xc8 34 ♖xc8 ♗xc8 and his b-pawn costs the knight its head. An interesting reversal, with Black's king being saved by White's weakness on the back rank!

23 ♘g5?! *(D)*

Keres did not notice the stronger move 23 ♘d4! either during the game or in his commentary. Moving the knight to g5 keeps up the tempo of the attack but leads to no more than a skirmish on the focal-points h7 and f7, whereas moving it to d4, although less immediately forceful, opens up the more productive prospect of play against the focal-point g7, which is quite clearly the weakest point in Black's castled position.

After 23 ♘d4! Black is virtually obliged to continue 23...♘f8 24 ♗c2 ♘g6 25 ♗xg6 fxg6 when 26 ♘e6 wins the exchange, leaving him with insufficient compensation in return. Black's other continuations are weaker, e.g. 23...♘c5 (23...♘xe5? 24 ♖xe5 ♕xe5 does not work because of 25 ♕xd8+) 24 ♘f5 ♘e4 (if 24...♘xb3, White wins by 25 ♕g5) 25 ♖xe4 dxe4 26 ♕g5 ♔f8 (or 26...g6 27 e6 ♗d5[1] 28 ♗xd5 followed by ♘e7+ and ♘xd5, etc.) 27 ♕xg7+ ♔e8 28 e6 fxe6 29 ♕g8+ and 30 ♕xe6#.

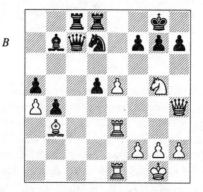

B

23...♘f8?

The move which loses the game. Correct was 23...h6 after which there is some doubt whether White can win. Keres carries on from 23...h6 with, among other continuations, 24 e6 hxg5 25 exf7+ ♔xf7 26 ♖e7+ ♔g8 27 ♕h5 (if 27 ♕xg5 or 27 ♕d4, Black plays 27...♕c3, while 27 ♖xg7+ ♔xg7 28 ♕xg5+ is insufficient on account of 28...♔h8 when White has not got the time to play ♖e7) 27...♕c3? after which White obtains the advantage by 28 ♕f7+ and 29 ♖7e3. However, instead of 27...♕c3?, Black can play 27...♕f4!, and after 28 ♖xd7 (alternatives are 28 g3 ♕f5 and 28 ♕g6 ♕f6) 28...♖xd7 29 ♖e8+ ♕f8! 30 ♖xf8+ ♔xf8 White not only cannot win but even has the worst of it. The analysis can admittedly be

---

1   Black can unexpectedly turn the tables by 27...♕c3! 28 exf7+ ♔h8, but White
     can improve just before: 27 ♘e7+ ♔f8 28 ♕f6 wins.

improved at the beginning, for 24 e6 can be replaced by 24 ♘xf7 followed by 25 e6+, but it is no longer clear that White has the advantage. Finally, one might consider trying 24 f4 hxg5 25 ♕xg5, but this loses its power after 25...♕b6 26 f5 ♘f8, since Black can meet 27 f6 with 27...♘e6, threatening, in addition to the queen, 28...♖c3.

All these variations arising from the position on the twenty-third move provide instructive illustrations of how to spot the correct focal-point. The analysis of 23 ♘d4! showed a typical attack on g7 ending in success for White, whereas in the continuation after 23 ♘g5?! h6! a consistent attack could not be built up against any focal-point; White's operations instead took on the character of an attempt to destroy the black king's pawn cover, and as a result Black obtained open lines for his pieces as well as the time in which to organize his defences.

24 ♘xh7 ♘xh7 25 ♖h3 ♕c1 *(D)*

A desperate move, but Black no longer has an adequate defence. White could also have played 26 ♕xd8+ now and won by virtue of being the exchange ahead, but he prefers to seek a mating attack, which brings even quicker success.

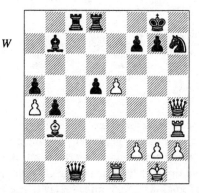

26 ♕xh7+ ♔f8 27 ♖e3 d4 28 ♕h8+ ♔e7 29 ♕xg7 ♖f8

Or 29...♗d5 30 ♕f6+ ♔f8 31 ♗xd5 ♖xd5 32 e6.

30 ♕f6+ ♔e8 31 e6 1-0

For 31...dxe3 is defeated by 32 exf7+ ♔d7 33 ♕e6+, and if 33...♔c7, then 34 ♖xc1+, or if 33...♔d8, then 34 ♕d6#.

The bayonet attack

The term 'bayonet attack' is used to designate the advance of one of the attacker's pawns on the side of the board facing the opposing castled position, as a result of which the pawn drives off one of the opponent's pieces or creates a sharp threat of some kind. A typical example of the bayonet attack is the move g4, whereby White prepares the advance g5 and an attack on Black's knight at f6. The following examples show us some typical cases of the bayonet attack.

The following position arose in Keres-Petrov, Estonia-Latvia Match, 1939 after the moves **1 e4 e6 2 d4 d5 3 ♘d2 dxe4 4 ♘xe4 ♘d7 5 ♘f3 ♗e7 6 ♗d3 ♘gf6 7 ♕e2 ♘xe4 8 ♗xe4 ♘f6 9 ♗d3 c5 10 dxc5 ♕a5+ 11 ♗d2 ♕xc5 12 0-0-0 0-0 13 ♘e5 b6** *(D).*

W

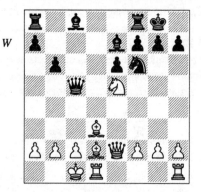

White now played:
14 g4! ♗b7

Black attempts to halt the further advance of White's pawn by indirect means, namely, by attacking the rook on h1. The other possible replies were no better; White's position is already so powerful that a bayonet attack is fully justified. If 14...h6, White would continue 15 h4, threatening g5 with even greater effect; against 14...g6 he would not play 15 g5 immediately (since Black would reply 15...♘h5), but 15 h4 followed by h5. Finally, if 14...♗d6 then 15 f4 is very strong.

15 g5!

White does not worry about his rook, since if 15...♗xh1, he can dictate matters with 16 gxf6 ♗xf6 (or 16...gxf6 17 ♕g4+ ♔h8 18 ♖g1 ♖g8 19 ♘xf7#) 17 ♘d7 ♕c6 18 ♘xf6+ gxf6 19 ♕g4+ ♔h8 20 ♕h4 f5 21 ♕f6+ ♔g8 22 ♖g1+ ♗g2 23 ♗h6 and mates.

15...♘d5 16 ♖hg1

Black could have answered 16 ♘d7 with 16...♕c7 17 ♘xf8 ♘f4! forcing simplification.

16...♕c7 *(D)*

In the event of 16...♘b4 Yudovich gave the following combination: 17 ♗xb4 ♕xb4 18 ♖g4 ♕c5 19 ♗xh7+ ♔xh7 20 ♖h4+ ♔g8 21 ♕h5 ♗xg5+ 22 ♕xg5 f6 23 ♕xg7+! ♔xg7 24 ♖g1+ and mates.

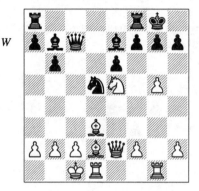

17 ♖g4

Keres does not carry his attack to its logical conclusion, i.e. by the sacrifice 17 ♗xh7+ ♔xh7 18 ♕h5+ ♔g8 19 f4 threatening ♖g4-h4. This attacking position is strong enough to guarantee victory, although it still demands precise play. Instead of 19 f4, Horowitz gives the weaker continuation 19 ♖g3 ♕xe5 20 ♖h3 and shows that 20...f6 then parries White's attack.

After the text move Black should have played 17...f5 18 gxf6 ♗xf6, whereupon White would have been left with only a slight advantage.

17...g6? 18 ♖h4 ♗d6 *(D)*

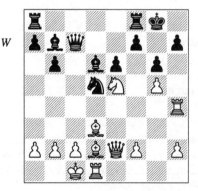

So as to answer the threatened 19 ♖xh7 with 19...♗xe5!.

19 ♘g4

Thanks to Black's error the attack has again got under way, and the game now 'plays itself'.

19...♖fc8 20 ♔b1 b5 21 ♖g1 ♗e7 22 ♘h6+ ♔f8 23 ♘xf7 ♗c5 24 ♖xh7 ♗d4 25 ♕xe6 ♗g7

White now played **26 ♘d6** and won in a few moves. By 26 ♘h8 he could have forced Black to resign at once.

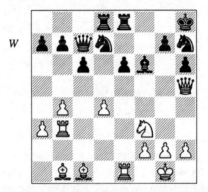

This position is from the game Alekhine-Weenink, Prague 1931. In this case too White produces the bayonet in the form of:

1 g4!

Alekhine, in *My Best Games of Chess 1924-1937,* says of this move: 'This little pawn threatens by its further advance to set on fire the black king's residence – and cannot possibly be stopped from that dark design.'

1...♕d6 2 ♗g6

Black had intended to meet 2 g5 with 2...♕d5, but the intermediate move 2 ♗g6 puts paid to that idea.

2...♖f8 3 g5!

The bayonet has its point in both the bishop on f6 and the pawn on h6, and nothing can be done about it.

3...♗xd4

If 3...♕d5 4 gxf6 ♖xf6, White cannot exchange queens, it is true, but he has 5 ♖d3 ♘hf8 6 ♗f7, holding on to the booty he has won.

4 gxh6 ♘df6 5 hxg7+ ♔xg7 6 ♕h6+ ♔h8 7 ♘xd4 ♕xd4 8 ♗b2 1-0.

Black's only possible attempt at resistance, 8...♕d7, is defeated by 9 ♖d3 ♕g7 10 ♗xf6 and mate in three moves.

The pawn avalanche

The formation composed of two or three neighbouring pawns on the same rank is often called a 'phalanx' in chess literature, but when such a phalanx attacks it can also be suitably described as an 'avalanche' or 'roller'. An attack based on a pawn avalanche generally entails even more positional commitments than the bayonet attack, as it involves advancing two pawns instead of only one. On the other hand, the avalanche's power is also greater than that of the bayonet, for an avalanche drives all the enemy pieces before it and offers more attacking possibilities.

When attacking by means of a pawn avalanche, it is usually important that one's opponent should be unable to retaliate in the centre or on the other wing. This is, admittedly, a general condition for any kind of attack on the castled king, but in the case of an attack using pawns it applies even more strictly, since one is more restricted positionally and the actual process of advancing pawns is slower than play with pieces, with the result that one's opponent has greater opportunities for counterplay. The next example will show us a case where the conditions for an attack using the avalanche are favourable.

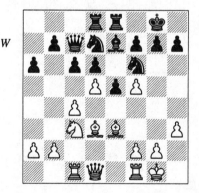

W

This position is from the game Schlechter-Tarrasch, Monte Carlo 1903. It is White's move.

1 g4

The use of the avalanche attack is well justified in this position. Black has no counterplay worth speaking of either on the queenside or in the centre, so that the risk White accepts in being committed to deciding the game on the kingside is not great. Moreover, White already has a pawn at f5, which is in fact in his way at the moment. When the g-pawn moves up to its aid within just two moves, there is considerable prospect of the position's being loosened up a little and that the f-pawn will acquire a dynamic potential.

1...♘c5 2 ♗b1 a5 3 ♔h1 ♘fd7 4 g5 f6?!

4...♘f8 would probably have been better. Moves which weaken the position, such as ...f6, should not be resorted to unless absolutely necessary. After 4...♘f8 5 ♕f3 Black would, of course, already be compelled to play 5...f6.

5 h4 ♗f8?

Certainly weaker than 5...♘f8; on his next move Black puts the bishop back on e7 and so loses two tempi. However, even after 5...♘f8 White's attack would be overwhelming.

6 ♖g1 ♗e7 (D)

Tarrasch was not a master who would lightly agree to the loss of a tempo, but in this case he was clearly convinced that his original plan had no prospects. This is evident from White's threat (Black's bishop is still on f8) 7 ♕g4 (not 7 ♕h5 followed by 8 g6? because of 8...h6, and Black would be saved by the blocked position[1]) 7...♔h8 8 ♗xc5 dxc5 9 ♘e4, when Black's defences give way under the pressure against the squares f6 and d6.

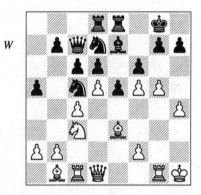

7 ♕h5 ♘f8 8 ♖g3 ♖a8

There are no useful moves that Black can make in his cramped position. After, for example, 8...♘cd7 9 ♖cg1 ♖c8 10 ♘e4 he finds himself in a sad state, without a satisfactory defence against the threat of 11 gxf6 ♗xf6 12 ♕h6.

9 ♗xc5 dxc5 10 d6! ♕xd6

---

1   In fact the plan of ♕h5 and g6 should also bring success, as after the reply ...h6 White can break through in King's Indian style by ♗xh6 followed by g7, with a crushing attack.

If 10...♗xd6, then 11 gxf6 is decisive.

11 ♘e4 ♕d8 12 ♖d1 1-0. Black cannot prevent the collapse of the weak point f6. If 12...♘d7, then 13 gxf6 ♗xf6 14 ♖xd7 ♕xd7 15 ♘xf6+.

In this example three phases in White's attack should be noted. The first is the creation of the advancing pawn avalanche, the second consists of the deployment of White's pieces, and the third is the actual execution or breakthrough.

The avalanche alone cannot, as a rule, be decisive, and its greatest enemy is the danger of blockade. Combating this danger depends for the most part on piece play, and this takes two main forms: allowing the position to be blocked and then breaking it up by sacrificing a piece; or first sacrificing the piece and then pushing forward with the pawn avalanche without any fear of its being blocked. In the following games we shall see these methods being applied; destroying the enemy pawn cover is essentially the main combinative element.

Rubinstein – Teichmann
Vienna Match (4), 1908
Queen's Gambit Declined, Orthodox Defence

1 d4 d5 2 c4 e6 3 ♘c3 ♘f6 4 ♗g5 ♘bd7 5 e3 ♗e7 6 ♘f3 0-0 7 ♕c2 b6

7...c5 is better.

8 cxd5 exd5 9 ♗d3 ♗b7 10 0-0-0 c5 11 h4 c4? *(D)*

Logically, Black must attack on the queenside, but his plan is too slow. Before he can set up the avalanche formation with pawns on c4 and b4, White will have a flourishing attack since his pieces are more active than Black's. Correct was 11...cxd4 in preparation for ...a6, ...b5 and ...♖c8; that would have constituted a more powerful threat.

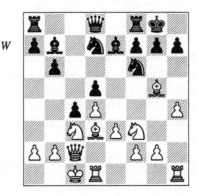

12 &f5 &e8

Kmoch, in his fine book on Rubinstein, thinks that even here ...a6 and ...b5 would have been better, but the black pawn can hardly reach b4, since after 12...a6 13 g4 there is an immediate threat of &xf6 followed by g5, picking up the booty on h7. If, for example, Black plays 13...g6 then 14 &xd7 followed at once by &h6 gives White a strong initiative.

The text move prepares the way for ...&f8, so White immediately takes the knight on f6 to prevent this.

13 &xf6 &xf6 14 g4!

Thus a 'small avalanche' is formed on the fourth rank. Soon it will become 'great' on the fifth, and finally 'terrible' when it reaches the sixth *en masse*.

14...&d6 15 g5 &e4 16 h5

The fifth rank has been reached without Black having moved an inch on the queenside.

If Black now plays 16...&xg5, there follows 17 &xg5 &xg5 18 &xh7+ &f8 19 h6! gxh6 20 &dg1, etc.

16...&e7 17 &dg1 a6 *(D)*

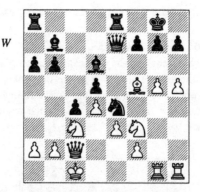

Black reckons that nothing is threatened and devotes a tempo to his slow counterattack on the queenside. Admittedly, White would get nowhere by moving his pawns at this point: if 18 h6, the position is blocked by 18...g6; while if 18 g6, then 18...fxg6 followed by ...h6. However, White has another device, namely the sacrifice of his bishop, which enables the pawns to go ahead happily and without any fear of being blocked.

18 &xh7+! &xh7 19 g6+ &g8

Or 19...fxg6 20 &xe4 dxe4 21 &g5+ and if 21...&g8 then 22 &xc4+ or if 21...&h6, then 22 &f7+ &xf7 23 hxg6+ mating.

20 ♘xe4

In fact superfluous. The immediate 20 h6 was simpler, and if 20...fxg6 then 21 ♖xg6 while if 20...f6, then 21 hxg7.

20...dxe4

If 20...♕xe4, then 21 gxf7+ is decisive.

21 h6 *(D)*

The avalanche has come down on Black's pawns, which can no longer offer any help by blocking the position. Carried away by the spectacle on the board, Kmoch adds two exclamation marks, which I am unable to do, since I can see another continuation which is simpler, stronger, and even more 'Rubinstein-like' than h6, in that it links the combination with a positional breakthrough in the centre: 21 ♘g5! ♗d5 (the f-pawn must not be moved because of 22 ♕xc4+) 22 gxf7+ ♗xf7 23 f3! ♗d5 (otherwise fxe4 and e5) 24 h6 ♖ac8 (or 24...g6 25 ♖h4) 25 fxe4 ♗xe4 26 h7+ ♔h8 27 ♕xe4! ♕xg5 28 ♕xe8+ and White wins[1].

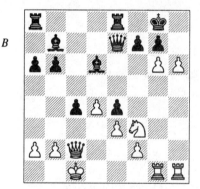

B

21...f6?!

This makes White's task easier, though the game would not have been saved by the more stubborn move 21...fxg6. 21...exf3 would have been even weaker, e.g. 22 gxf7+ ♕xf7 23 hxg7 with threats against h8 and h7.

After 21...fxg6 Kmoch shows that 22 ♖xg6? is weak (because of 22...exf3, and Black gains too much material in return for his queen). He gives the following line as good for White: 22 ♘h4 g5 23 ♘g6 ♕f6 24 h7+ ♔f7 25 h8♕ ♖xh8 26 ♘xh8+. However, the situation is somewhat doubtful after 26...♔e7, for while

---

1 However, this line is also not conclusive as instead of 23...♗d5 Black can create confusion by 23...c3, when White's plan of fxe4 followed by e5 starts to look too slow.

White is extracting his knight from the corner, Black works up a counterattack, e.g. 27 ♕e2 c3! 28 ♕h5 (or 28 bxc3 ♗a3+ followed by ...♕f5) 28...cxb2+, and if 29 ♔b1, then 29...♗a3, while if 29 ♔xb2, then 29...♕xf2+, etc.

22 hxg7 exf3 *(D)*

The queen can be saved by 22...♕e6 but then 23 ♖h8+ followed by 24 ♖h7+ and 25 ♖gh1 leads to a mating attack.

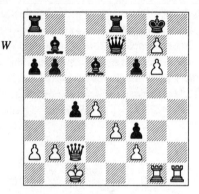

23 ♖h8+ ♔xg7 24 ♖h7+ ♔g8 25 ♕f5 c3

Or 25...♕e6 26 ♕h5, etc.

26 ♖xe7 1-0

For if 26...♖xe7, then 27 ♕xf6 is decisive.

König – H. Weiss
Vienna, 1919
Queen's Pawn Game

1 d4 e6 2 c3 d5 3 ♗f4 ♘f6 4 e3 c5

Here it is Black who is playing the Queen's Gambit, while White is building up his position according to the pattern which Black uses in the Semi-Slav Defence, to which the move ♗f4 is a useful addition. This is an example of a so-called inverted opening, in which White plays Black's system with a tempo in hand.

5 ♗d3 ♘c6 6 ♘d2 ♗e7?!

Black has obviously lost his bearings and is not aware that he is 'really White'; passive moves of this type do not fit in with the active position of his central pawns. Correct was 6...♗d6.

7 ♘gf3 0-0 8 ♘e5! ♖e8?

Black does not appreciate the real nature of the position and is not taking measures to obtain counterplay at the right time by means of an outpost on one of the central squares. He even surrenders control of the important e4 and e5 squares to White, and as a result suddenly comes up against the storm of an attack on his castled king. The correct course was 8...cxd4 9 exd4 ♘xe5 10 dxe5 ♘d7 11 ♕h5 f5! when Black can meet 12 f3 by 12...♕c7 and 12 g4 by 12...♘c5 13 ♗c2 ♘e4.

9 g4! *(D)*

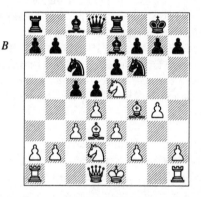

Throughout the opening stage of the game the conditions required to justify a 'bayonet attack' have been gradually accumulating. One group of these conditions has already been noted in the shape of Black's inferior moves and his lack of concern to control at least one of the important squares e5 and e4. The other group can be revealed by an analysis of the structure of White's position. This is clearly distinguished by good piece play together with a modest but sound pawn formation in the centre. Indeed, its essence lies in the very soundness of the formation c3, d4, and e3, with the strong protection which it gives to the square d4. If this solidity in the centre did not exist, Black would be able at the last moment to organize a counterattack in the centre as an answer to White's attack on his castled king.

His security against such a central counterattack – generally the main weapon in an active defence against an attack on the castled king – gives White great freedom in his attack on the castled position and is basically the main justification for the move 9 g4!.

9...♘xe5

If 9...♘d7 White will continue with g5 as in the game.

10 dxe5 ♘d7 11 g5! ♘f8

If 11...♗xg5, then 12 ♕h5 h6 13 ♖g1 ♗xf4 14 exf4 ♔f8 15 ♕g4 g6 16 ♗xg6. If 11...♕c7, then 12 ♗xh7+ ♔xh7 13 ♕h5+ ♔g8 14 g6 fxg6 15 ♕xg6 ♖d8 (or 15...♖f8 16 ♕xe6+ ♖f7 17 ♕xf7+ and 18 e6+) 16 ♖g1 ♗f8 17 ♘f3 followed by ♘g5.

12 h4 ♗d7 13 ♕g4 ♗c6 14 0-0-0 b5

This simplifies White's task, though better moves would not help Black very much.

15 h5 c4 16 ♗xh7+!

No sooner has White's pawn avalanche established itself on the fifth rank than he carries out the characteristic piece sacrifice, which breaks up the castled position and prevents a defensive blockade from being set up.

16...♘xh7 17 g6 ♘g5 18 ♘e4! ♘xe4 19 gxf7+ ♔xf7 20 ♕g6+ ♔f8

His position also soon collapses after 20...♔g8 21 h6 ♗f8 22 ♖dg1 ♖e7 23 ♕h7+! ♔xh7 (or 23...♔f7 24 hxg7) 24 hxg7+ ♔g8 25 ♖h8+ ♔f7 26 g8♕+, etc[1].

21 h6 ♗f6 22 hxg7+ ♗xg7 23 ♖h8+ ♗xh8 24 ♗h6+ ♔e7 25 ♕h7+ and mate next move.

Tolush – Kotov

USSR Championship, Moscow 1945
Sicilian Defence, Scheveningen Variation

1 e4 c5 2 ♘f3 e6 3 d4 cxd4 4 ♘xd4 ♘f6 5 ♘c3 d6 6 g3

It is more usual to play either 6 g4 or 6 ♗e2 at this point, which perhaps give White somewhat greater scope for attack than 6 g3.

6...♘c6 7 ♗g2 ♗d7

Another plan would have been 7...♘xd4 and then ...♗d7, in order to play the bishop to c6. White now withdraws his knight from d4 and so makes it difficult for Black to further the development of the c8-bishop.

8 ♘de2! a6 9 0-0 b5 10 a3 ♕c7 11 h3 ♗e7 12 ♔h1 0-0 13 g4

The preparation of a bayonet attack is justified in this position, for Black is still quite a long way from starting a counterattack by ...d5.

13...♔h8?

Not to the point; better is 13...♖fd8.

14 ♘g3 b4 15 axb4 ♘xb4 16 g5

Black has made a start to his preparations for the thrust ...d5, but White's attack is faster. White does not play 16 e5 here, as Black can then reply 16...♘fd5.

---

1   In fact, White ends up material down after 26...♔e8 27 ♕xf8+ ♔d7, etc., so he should prefer 23 hxg7 ♗xg7 24 ♖h7 ♕c7 25 ♖gh1, followed by mate.

16...♘g8 *(D)*

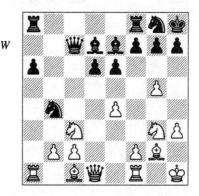

17 f4

A pawn attack on the kingside is a valuable weapon for White in the Scheveningen Variation, while Black's best response is a counter-stroke in the centre by ...d5. Black is somewhat behind in preparing for this thrust, and consequently White is able to set in motion his pawn attack. 17 ♗e3 was, by the way, also solid and good.

17...♗c6?

A weak move, which considerably helps White in regrouping his forces, because 18 ♘ce2! now immediately threatens c3. Correct was 17...♖fd8 preparing ...d5.

18 ♘ce2! ♗b5 19 ♗d2 d5

19...♘xc2? would not have worked because of 20 ♖c1 ♖ac8 21 ♗c3! ♘e3 22 ♕d4.

20 ♗c3!

Black has in fact managed to play ...d5, but White has made good use of the time and now, besides his bayonet (the pawn on g5), he also has a 'long sabre' in the shape of his dark-squared bishop on the long diagonal!

20...dxe4 21 ♘h5 f6 22 ♘xg7! *(D)*

Grandmaster Tolush, himself an officer, uses his weapons well. After the 'bayonet' and the 'sabre', here comes a suicide 'bomb'. The sacrifice is correct and characteristic of an attack based on a pawn avalanche.

22...♗xe2

The correctness of the sacrifice has its basis in the powerful threat of ♘d4, as can be seen in the following variation: 22...♔xg7 23 ♘d4! ♗c4 (or 23...♕d7 24 ♗xe4 and if 24...♗c6 in order to prevent 25 ♕h5, then 25 ♘xc6 ♕xd1 26 ♖fxd1

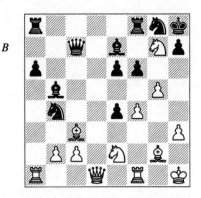

B

②xc6 27 ♗xc6 ♖a7 28 ♖d7, when White picks up another pawn and makes his task easy) 24 ♗xe4 ♖fd8 25 ♕h5 ♔f8 26 ♕xh7 with a decisive attack.

Also interesting is 22...♖ad8 23 ②d4 ♖xd4, when 24 ♕xd4 is not very effective because of 24...♔xg7, and White does no more than win back the sacrificed material. However, if 23...♖xd4, White has the fine reply 24 ♕g4!, which prevents 24...♔xg7 and creates the threat of 25 ②xe6 followed by 26 g6!. No answer to this has been found for Black.

Aware, therefore, of the force of ②d4 Black first of all takes the knight on e2 and then accepts the sacrifice.

23 ♕xe2 ♔xg7 24 ♗xe4 ②d5 25 ♕h5 ♖fd8

If 25...♖f7 then 26 g6 hxg6 27 ♕xg6+ ♔f8 28 ♖g1 and White wins.

26 ♖g1 ♗c5 27 gxf6+ ♔f8 *(D)*

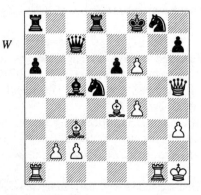

W

28 ♖xg8+! ♔xg8 29 ♗xh7+ ♔f8

If 29...♕xh7 then 30 f7+! is decisive.

30 ♕g6 ♘xf6 31 ♕xf6+ ♕f7 32 ♕h6+ ♔e7 33 ♕g5+ ♔d7 34 ♕xc5 ♕xh7 35 ♖d1+ ♔e8 36 ♕c6+ ♔f8 37 ♗b4+ ♔f7 38 ♕c7+ ♔g6 39 f5+! ♔h6 40 ♕f4+ ♔g7 41 ♕g5+ 1-0

For 41...♔f7 is answered by 42 ♕e7+ and mate in three more moves.

This game won the First Brilliancy Prize at the tournament.

Concluding remarks

Before we conclude this discussion of the role of the pawns in the attack on the castled king, we must warn the reader of the immense diversity of practical cases which resist all attempts to embrace them within a set of rules. Our acquaintance with certain rules should not lead us to handle the game in a routine fashion; the particular characteristics of every position must always be thoroughly examined from one move to the next.

In connection with pawn attacks, there are two cases worth mentioning which often arise in practice. In one case the position requires a rigid, positional use of the pawns in attack, and in the other the position is not at all suitable for the co-operation of the pawns and consequently the attack is better carried out by the pieces alone. For these two cases some suitable examples will now be given.

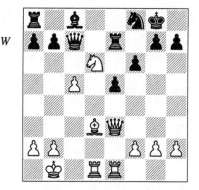

This position is from the game Steinitz-Marco, Nuremberg 1896. White is the more aggressively placed but Black's position is fairly solid, especially in the centre, where White lacks a pawn base. The diagonal a2-g8 may become danger-ous for Black, but it is not so yet, for if ♗c4+, Black can play ...♗e6. Nor are the conditions favourable for an attack with the 'bayonet' or 'avalanche' here; there-fore, another way has to be found to strengthen White's position, one which is es-sentially of a purely positional nature. Steinitz finds it: he advances his f-pawn to f5, where it restricts Black; the fact that this leads to a blocked position is a good thing, since Black's f-pawn can then be fixed at f6 and subsequently 'rolled up' by g4 and g5. This is a clear positional plan, which leads to the destruction of Black's pawn chain and thence to a real attack on his castled king. There is no bayonet or avalanche here, though pawn moves are still the decisive means of attack.

1 f4! ♗d7

Black wants to get his bishop to c6, since it cannot settle on the diagonal a2-g8 because of f5. If 1...♗g4, then 2 ♖d2 followed by h3 is strong, while 1...g6 would be a voluntary weakening of the castled position.

2 f5 ♗c6 3 ♗c4+ ♔h8 4 g4 b6

Black has no satisfactory answer to g5. If 4...h6 5 h4 ♘h7, we get 6 g5 fxg5 7 hxg5 and then either 7...♘xg5 8 ♕xg5 and 9 ♖h1+ or 7...hxg5 8 ♕h3, threatening 9 ♕xh7+.

5 g5 fxg5 6 ♕xg5 h6

Otherwise f6 follows.

7 ♕h5 bxc5 8 ♘f7+ ♔h7 9 ♘g5+ ♔h8 10 f6 gxf6 11 ♕xh6+ ♘h7 12 ♘xh7 ♖xh7 13 ♕xf6+ ♖g7 14 ♖xe5 1-0

As our second concluding remark we cited the case where the player has a choice between attacking with his pawns and attacking with his pieces. Every practical player will have experienced the difficulty of such a choice, and an immense amount of time has been consumed in master chess on such decisions. The trouble is that it is difficult to set up any general rule, since everything depends on the particular characteristics of the situation concerned. Before discussing this question any further, let us take an example, and then, by varying the pawn structure, try to penetrate to the heart of the problem.

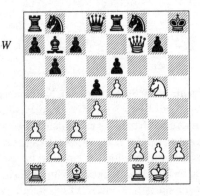

It will be easy for the reader to see that this position has arisen as the direct result of a classic bishop sacrifice. It is clear that White must aim to get a rook on to the h-file, and the only question is how to do it. One way would be f4 and then ♖f3-h3, and the other ♖e1-e3-h3. The first is faulty and allows Black to draw, while the second is correct and leads to a win for White. The position is such that only the pieces can cope with the task; the pawns should stay at home to avoid getting in the way. The following variations prove this assertion.

1) 1 f4? ♕d7

Of course, Black must on no account play 1...♖e7?, since 2 ♖f3 would result in the loss of his rook.

2 ♕h5+ ♔g8 3 ♖f3

White has nothing better. After 3 g4 g6 4 ♕h3 ♘h7 5 ♘f3 ♘c6 6 ♘h4 ♘e7 White is still unable to play f5 as planned, while Black obtains counterplay by ...c5, etc. Also good for Black is 3 f5 exf5 4 ♖xf5 ♕xf5 5 ♕xe8 ♘c6.

3...g6 4 ♕h4 *(D)*

Or 4 ♕h6 ♕g7.

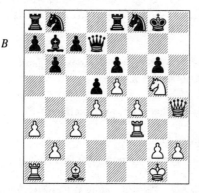

B

4...♘h7

This forces a draw. It is of no importance to our thesis whether Black can now play for a win, e.g. by 4...♕g7 followed by ...♘c6 and ...♘e7 or ...♘d8, etc.

5 ♖h3

White cannot avoid the exchange of knights; if 5 ♘h3, Black gets time to bring out his queen's knight and set up a complete defence.

5...♘xg5 6 ♕h8+ ♔f7 7 ♖h7+[1] ♘xh7 8 ♕xh7+ ♔f8

White now has to keep up perpetual check by 9 ♕h8+ ♔f7! 10 ♕h7+, but if the unfortunate pawn on f4 were not there, he would be able to mate by ♗h6+, etc.

2) 1 ♖e1! *(D)*

Not 1 ♖d1 because of 1...♗a6! 2 ♖e1 ♗d3 followed by ...♗h7, etc.

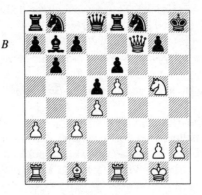

1...♕d7 2 ♕h5+ ♔g8 3 ♖e3 g6 4 ♕h4 ♕g7

If here 4...♘h7, then 5 ♖h3 ♘xg5 6 ♕h8+ would win. In this line 5...♖e7 is met by 6 ♕h6 ♖g7 7 ♘xh7 ♖xh7 8 ♕xg6+ ♖g7 9 ♕h5 ♖h7 10 ♗h6 ♘c6 11 ♕g6+ ♔h8 12 ♗g5 and 13 ♗f6+.

5 ♖h3 ♘bd7

Against anything else White's bishop decides the game by reaching f6, e.g. 5...♘c6 6 ♘f3 ♘h7 7 ♗h6 ♕d7 8 ♗g5, etc.

6 ♗d2

Opening the way for the other rook, for which the f-file, for instance, has attractions.

6...c5 7 ♖e1 cxd4 8 cxd4 a5

8...♖ac8 does not work at once because of 9 ♖f3 ♖e7 10 ♗b4.

9 b4

A simple device to hinder ...♖ac8; 9...a4 is answered by 10 b5, and the white bishop gains control of b4. Black now tries to put up a stand with ...♖e7 and ...♘h7.

9...♖e7 10 ♕g4 ♗c6 11 ♕e2

Black is tied up on the kingside, and White's best plan consists of trebling on the h-file. White carries out the necessary regrouping in such a way that not only is Black's bishop prevented from penetrating but also his rook's invasion along

---

1   Here Vuković overlooks that White can mate in two by 7 ♕f6+. However, his thesis is basically correct, because the stronger move 4...♕g7 casts doubt on White's attack.

the c-file is deferred; at the same time, he over-protects the e5-square as a precaution against any desperate sacrifices.

11...♗b7 12 ♖h4 ♗a6 13 ♕e3 ♗b5 14 ♖c1 a4 15 ♖c3 ♖ee8 16 ♕e1! ♖ac8 17 ♖ch3 ♖c2 18 f4 (D)

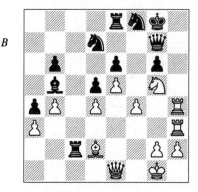

Only now, when his rooks are ready for the lethal blow on the h-file, can White touch his pawns.

18...♖ec8 19 ♖h6 ♗d3 20 ♕h4 ♖c1+ 21 ♔f2 ♖f1+ 22 ♔g3 and Black cannot prevent mate by ♖h8+.

In comparing these two variations, the reader cannot but recognize the essential feature of the position that condemns 1 f4? to failure but brings victory to the attack carried out by the pieces. The move f4 obstructs both the diagonal for the bishop on c1 and the f-file for the rooks, and so limits the possibilities of action along the very two lines on which Black is weak. His weakness on the f-file can be seen at a glance, and it is not difficult to deduce (on examining the diagrammed position) that he will also be weak on the dark squares, since he will be unable to postpone ...g6 for long. After f4 White is left with only his domination of the h-file, whereas if he does not play it, he also has the f-file and a line of action for his bishop, and it is the combination of all these factors that gives him victory.

We shall now *vary the position of the pawns in front of White's king* in the above diagram, so as to train our eyes to be keener in spotting the various finesses contained in this kind of position.

First let us suppose that **White's f-pawn** is already on **f4** (instead of f2) and that it is White to move. Now, of course, 1 ♖f3 will win at once, but if this possibility is excluded, e.g. by White's having his **h-pawn** on **h3**, what then? Even so, White wins – by **1 f5! exf5** (otherwise f6 is decisive) **2 ♖xf5**, and Black has no answer to the two threats of 3 ♖f4 and 3 ♕h5+ ♔g8 followed by either 4 ♘f7 or

4 ♖xf8+ ♔xf8 5 ♕h8+ and the queen mates on g7. If, for example, 2...♕d7, then 3 ♕xf8+, while if 2...g6, then 3 ♖f4 ♕xg5 4 ♕xe8.

The pawn on f4 wins in this case precisely because it disappears and in doing so immediately opens up the f-file with disastrous consequences for Black.

Let us now try a variation with the **h-pawn** at **h4** (rather than h2) *(D)*.

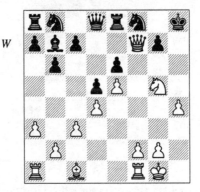

This position is fairly promising; White has his f-file and the bishop's diagonal is free as in variation '2', but the h-file has to be opened up by advancing the h-pawn. All White has to do is induce ...g6, after which the task of line opening is made easier and a blocked position averted.

White's best is **1 ♖e1 ♕d7 2 ♕h5+ ♔g8 3 ♖e3** (forcing ...g6, since it threatens ♖f3 and ♖xf8+; thus if 3...♘c6 4 ♖f3 ♘d8, then 5 ♖xf8+ ♔xf8 6 ♕h8+ ♔e7 7 ♕xg7+ ♘f7 8 ♘xf7 ♖g8 9 ♕h7 and White wins) **3...g6 4 ♕g4 ♘h7 5 ♘h3**, when he has good prospects.

If White's **h-pawn** is on **h3**, 1 h4 comes into consideration, with the idea of reaching a similar system to the one above, but with a tempo less.

With **White's g-pawn on g3** (rather than g2) the problem is more difficult, since the pawn is only in the way there. Perhaps White ought to give perpetual check at once. If 1 ♖e1, Black plays 1...♘c6, after which 2 ♖e3 does not work because of 2...♕xg5, while after 2 g4 ♕d7 3 ♕h5+ ♔g8 4 ♖e3 g6 5 ♕h4 ♕g7 Black's defences are already in quite good shape.

Things are different with the **g-pawn at g4** (which is, admittedly, impossible after the classic bishop sacrifice, but that does not matter here) *(D)*.

In this case the third rank is clear for the rook, and in addition the pawn at g4 also lends force to the thrust f5. As well as the method starting with 1 ♖e1 (on the pattern of variation '2'), still more successful here is **1 f4** (threatening ♖f3) **1...♕d7 2 ♕h5+ ♔g8 3 f5** and White must win. Here, finally, we have a case

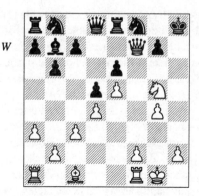

where an attack using the pawns is correct. One tiny change in the position and already the choice between attacking with pieces or with pawns has swung in favour of the pawns. Such is the sensitivity of the attack on the castled king, and it is now clear how difficult it is to create any more definite rule on this point! Still, I shall attempt to conclude the chapter with a series of tips – which will naturally apply only generally.

Ten Practical Tips

1) It is an essential condition for any attack on the castled king that the opponent should not be able to counterattack in the centre or on the other side of the board, or rather that his counterattack should not be dangerous and not develop fully before the attack on the castled king. An attack using pawns usually progresses more slowly than one with pieces, since it often contains moves without any immediate threat. So, before embarking on a pawn attack, one should beware particularly of the possibility of a counterattack by one's opponent.

2) A central pawn blockade prevents or limits counterattacks and so makes a pawn attack on the castled king easier.

3) One should always examine whether a promising attack can be made by the pieces alone, and if it can, the pawns should be left 'at home'.

4) As a rule, it is difficult for pawn assaults to succeed against unweakened castled positions, since the possibilities of blockade are very great. A preliminary action by the pieces is necessary to produce a weakening of the castled position or to remove the possibility of a later blockade when the pawns advance.

5) Every blockade in the castling area radically changes the character of the position, for it affects the activity of individual pieces and the whole nature of the play which follows.

6) One's own pawns usually constitute a great obstacle to one's rooks; if a position is characterized by the opponent's weakness on the files, the rooks are important pieces and pawns have no business on these files, except when their advance actually helps to clear a file. Rooks can be particularly usefully deployed on the third rank, if it is clear of pawns (an example of this was provided by the variations arising from the diagram on p.224).

7) A pawn storm generally increases the risk of an inferior endgame. If other elements in the position are also weighted against an endgame, the added risk entailed in an attack on the castled king is acceptable. However, if the player has the necessary conditions for a good endgame, he must make certain that his assault with the pawns will be successful, for otherwise it represents a real risk.

8) A player who already has an advanced pawn facing his opponent's castled position but which somehow gets in his way (e.g. a pawn on f5) must contemplate advancing the adjacent pawn, so that the lone pawn can be made an active component of an avalanche. Every advanced pawn presents a pretext for an avalanche and draws its neighbour towards it. This is least so in the case of an advanced h-pawn and most so if the pawn is on f5.

9) Attacks on the castled king in general, and those using pawns in particular, should always be judged on the basis of an assessment of the position as a whole. The placing of the pieces, the situation in the centre and on the other side of the board, positional strengths and weaknesses, how far the position is blocked, the prospects for the endgame – all these come into the reckoning which an experienced player must make before deciding to use his pawns in an attack on the castled king.

10) Cautious before opening his attack, the player must be incisive, consistent, and merciless once he has set out on his attacking course. For an insufficiently justified attack is not helped by belated doubts, but only by resourcefulness in the struggle to provide one's opponent with the most difficult task possible.

9 The attack on the fianchettoed and queenside castling positions

Up till now we have, on the whole, based our examination of the various aspects of attacking play on the ordinary kingside castling position. The fianchettoed and queenside castling positions present certain special characteristics, which affect the particular forms of attack used against these types of position.

The attack on the fianchettoed king position

The term 'fianchetto' (from the Italian, meaning 'little flank') denotes a bishop being developed on the flank (on g2, b2, g7 or b7), and if a player castles behind such a fianchetto formation, we talk of a fianchettoed king position.

Castled positions of this kind have their own particular good and bad sides; these will be examined on the basis of Black's kingside fianchetto position, which occurs in the Dragon Variation of the Sicilian, and the King's Indian and Grünfeld defences.

The good aspect of the position is, above all, its considerable capacity to resist attack along the diagonal b1-h7, thanks to the pawn formation, f7, g6, and h7; nor are the squares f6 and h6 too weak, for they are covered by the bishop on g7. The bishop is also well concealed against attacks and possibilities of exchange, while in many cases the defence is assisted by its ability to cover not only the squares f6 and h6 but also the possible mating square h8. Finally, the fianchettoed position is also suited for those operations in which the g-pawn disappears, as in the following well-known manoeuvre: Black plays ...f5, and then, on White's reply exf5 he coolly continues ...gxf5, with the aim of strengthening his position in the centre. Without the bishop on g7 such play would be risky because of the opening of the g-file, but it often succeeds with the fianchettoed bishop, since the bishop defends Black's king on the g-file about as well as a pawn does.

The weak aspect of the fianchettoed position lies in the fact that the position of the g-pawn at g6 simplifies the attacker's task in opening up the h-file by the advance of his h-pawn; there is also a danger that the fianchettoed bishop may be exchanged either for its opposite number or some other enemy unit. Without the bishop the castled position becomes weak and vulnerable and the squares previously covered by the bishop form a typically weak network.

Naturally, an attack on the fianchettoed king position is generally directed against these weak spots, and consequently, the *assault by the h-pawn* and actions aimed at *the exchange of the fianchettoed bishop* are the principal weapons in the attack against such a position.

First, we shall give simple examples of two typical operations: namely, the elimination of the fianchettoed bishop and the breaking up of the pawn structure in front of it.

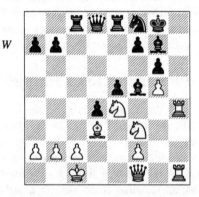

The first position is from the game Richter-Abramavicius, Hamburg 1930. It is White's move, and he sacrifices both his rooks for the fianchettoed bishop in order to be able to conclude the game by an attack on the weakened dark-square network.

1 ♖h8+ ♗xh8 2 ♖xh8+ ♔xh8 3 ♕h1+ ♘h7 4 ♘f6 ♔g7

Or 4...♕xf6 5 gxf6 ♗xd3 6 ♕h6 ♖xc2+ 7 ♔d1 ♖g8 8 ♘g5 and mates.

5 ♕h6+ 1-0

The following position occurred in the game Szilagyi-Szabo, Budapest 1946. Black, to move, broke up the pawn chain h2-g3 by a sacrifice and proceeded to decide the game on a network of squares of the opposite colour to that of the fianchettoed bishop.

1...♖xh2! 2 ♔xh2 ♘g4+ 3 ♔g1 ♗xg3 4 ♖e2

White loses, whatever the continuation, because of his weakness on the corresponding focal-points h2 and f2. Mate can be postponed only by a severe 'letting of blood'. After 4 ♘f3 exf3 5 ♗xf3 ♕h4 6 ♖e2 ♗f2+ 7 ♔f1 ♘h2+ 8 ♔g2 ♕g3+ 9 ♔h1 ♕xf3+ Black still mates with 10...♕g3+ and 11...♕h3#.

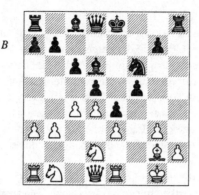

4...♛h4 5 ♘f1 ♝f2+ 6 ♖xf2 ♛xf2+ 7 ♔h1 ♛b2 0-1
For White loses either his rook or his queen.

Where there is a fianchettoed king position there is naturally no opportunity to sacrifice the bishop on h7; moreover, many other forms of sacrifice, typical enough in the case of normal castling, are out of the question against the specific structure of the fianchetto. A form of sacrifice which can be designated as characteristic in the case of a fianchettoed king position is that of the knight on f5. An example of such a sacrifice is provided by the next diagram.

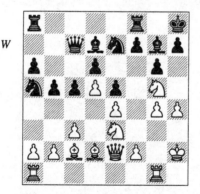

This position arose in the game Alexander-Pachman, Hilversum 1947. Against Black's fianchettoed king position White has a knight aggressively placed at g5, a 'little avalanche' of pawns on g4 and h4, a rook on g1 and his queen covering some useful squares. Nevertheless, to 'unlock' Black's solid position a sacrifice is necessary.

1 ♘f5!

Given the favourable supporting conditions, this typical 'anti-fianchetto' sacrifice is absolutely correct. From f5 the knight controls the squares g7 and h6 and has the intention, above all else, of eliminating the fianchettoed bishop. If Black does not accept the sacrifice but plays, for example, 1...♖ae8, White continues 2 ♘xg7 and then 3 f4 with good prospects, while if 1...♗f6, then 2 ♘h6. The acceptance of the sacrifice leads at once to a critical situation for Black as the reply gxf5 leads to a very dangerous attack, while the f5-square is well covered, and consequently there is no danger of Black making a counter-sacrifice on it.

1...gxf5 2 gxf5

In positions of a similar nature one is often faced with the question whether it is better to take on f5 with the g-pawn or the e-pawn. The answer depends on the various characteristics of the position; one takes with the g-pawn, if the opening of the g-file or the diagonal d1-h5 brings with it a decisive advantage, while in playing exf5 one takes into account other possible advantages, namely, freeing the square e4 (on which a knight, for example, can take up a strong position) or opening the b1-h7 diagonal for the bishop, or perhaps to keep in reserve the continuation g5. In this particular case the g-pawn is obviously indicated, since there is an immediate threat of ♕h5.

2...f6

If 2...h6, then 3 ♕h5, threatening 4 ♘xf7+ as well as 4 f6. If 2...♘g8, Black does not get as far as consolidating by ...♘f6 because of 3 ♘xh7 ♔xh7 4 ♖xg7+ ♔xg7 5 ♖g1+.

3 ♘xh7 ♗e8 *(D)*

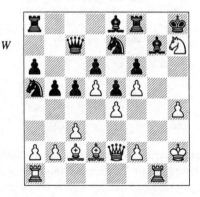

The only defence as the queen must not be allowed to reach h5.

4 ♖xg7!

The fianchettoed bishop's head has to roll!

4...♔xg7 5 ♘xf8 ♔xf8 6 ♗h6+

When the fianchettoed bishop vanishes from the board, its opposite number usually becomes extremely powerful.

6...♔f7 7 ♕h5+ ♘g6

If 7...♔g8, then 8 ♖g1+ ♘g6 9 ♖xg6+ ♗xg6 10 ♕xg6+ ♔h8 11 ♕xf6+ ♔h7 12 ♕g6+ ♔h8 and either 13 f6 or 13 ♗g5.

8 fxg6+ ♔g8 9 ♕f5 and White won in a few moves.

The importance of removing the fianchettoed bishop at the correct moment in this kind of attack is shown by the next position, one which I reached in an analysis of the Dragon Variation of the Sicilian in my book, *Contemporary Opening Theory*.

W

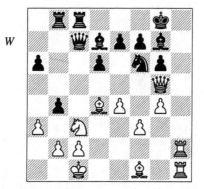

In my book I examined **1 ♕h4**, following it up by 1...bxc3 2 ♕h8+ ♗xh8 3 ♖xh8+ ♔g7 4 ♖1h7#.

However, fianchettoed king positions of this kind (with the defensive bishop, the knight on f6, and a pawn on e7) offer a great deal of resistance. Consequently, in spite of the thunder on the h-file, Black can answer 1 ♕h4 with **1...♘h5! 2 ♗xg7 bxa3! 3 ♕g5** (if 3 gxh5, then 3...♔xg7, while if 3 ♗d4, then 3...axb2+ 4 ♔b1 ♕a5) **3...axb2+ 4 ♔b1 ♔xg7[1]**, and now if 5 ♖xh5, then 5...♗a2+ 6 ♔xa2 b1♕+, while if 5 gxh5, then 5...♕xc3 is in Black's favour.

Because of this I have had to amend my original analysis of the diagrammed position and apply more drastic measures to eliminate the fianchettoed bishop.

---

1 In this line 4...♕xc3! is immediately decisive, since 5 ♗xc3 ♗a2+ leads to mate.

1 ♕h6!!

Clearly, 1...♘h5 will not do now because of 2 ♕xg7+, while if Black tries to parry the threat of 2 ♕h8+ by 1...♔f8 2 ♕h8+ ♘g8, White mates by 3 ♕xg8+ and 4 ♖h8+.

1...♗xh6+ 2 ♖xh6 g5 3 ♗d3!! *(D)*

After 3 ♖h8+ ♔g7 4 ♖1h7+ ♔g6 White only has perpetual check, while if 3 ♖xf6, Black can reply 3...♗c4 4 ♖h8+ ♔g7! 5 ♖fh6+ e5.

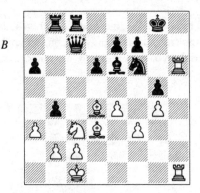

3...♗xg4

Black is also mated after other continuations, e.g.:

1) 3...♗c4 4 ♖h8+ ♔g7 5 ♖1h7+ ♔g6 6 e5+ ♗xd3 7 ♖h6+ ♔g7 8 exf6+ exf6 9 ♗xf6#.

2) 3...d5 4 ♖h8+ ♔g7 5 ♖1h7+ ♔g6 6 exd5+ ♘e4 7 ♖g7#.

3) 3...♘h7 4 ♖xh7 f6 5 ♖h8+ ♔f7 6 ♖1h7+ ♔g6 7 e5+ f5 8 gxf5+ ♗xf5 9 ♖h6+ ♔f7 10 e6+ ♗xe6 11 ♖6h7#.

4 ♖h8+ ♔g7 5 ♖1h7+ ♔g6 6 e5+ ♘e4 7 ♖h6+! ♔f5 8 ♗xe4+ ♔f4 9 ♘e2#

The attack on the queenside castled position

Before discussing the attack on the queenside castled position, one should first of all examine the differences between this type of castling and kingside castling. Some writers in the past have supposed that the difference is considerable and that castling long 'is much weaker than castling short'; this is a great exaggeration. The castled position after long or queenside castling differs from the short castled position only in this respect, that the positions of the king and rook are both a square nearer the centre of the board. This can be useful for the rook, but it usually presents difficulties to the king, which is safer on g1 than c1. Reckoning in terms of tempi, the following picture sums up the differences: the position on the queenside which would correspond symmetrically to the one given by short castling (king on g1 and rook on f1) is king on b1 and rook on c1, and to reach such a position after castling long would require two tempi. But let us now apply a different method of calculation: the player has castled on the kingside and then spends one tempo on the move ♖e1. The corresponding position to this on the queenside would be king on b1 and rook on d1, and for this only one move is needed after castling long. The conclusion to be drawn from this is simple – whenever the rook is well placed on the d-file, castling long is fundamentally as good as castling short; if the rook is in fact needed on the c-file it is weaker by two tempi, while if the rook is needed on a third square it is weaker by only one tempo.

In practice castling queenside usually occurs when the rook is well placed on the d-file, and indeed the need for it to be placed there is often the prime reason for adopting long castling. When reckoned in these terms, the practical difference between long and short castling disappears or becomes insignificant. There is yet another difference between the two forms of castling, but it is secondary and concerns the activity of the queen. However, here too the advantages and disadvantages tend to cancel each other out. Thus one can say that castling on the queenside is almost equal in status to castling on the kingside in general terms of tempo and security. If there are still players who doubt the security of castling on the queenside, it might be suggested that their reasons for this are probably of a subjective, rather than an objective, nature. That is to say, many players remember some bad experiences which they have had with castling long and are not aware of a very common mistake, one which is repeated over and over again: they accept the tempo gained on the d-file by castling long as a gift, without wanting to pay the price for it; they neglect the consolidating move ♔b1, and then, when their opponent suddenly sweeps down, it is already too late and there is no time left. The results, of course, are blamed on queenside castling.

In master chess castling on the kingside predominates, but this is not the result of some fundamental weakness of castling long; the reasons are of another, structural, kind. Castling on the queenside requires the development of three pieces, while in the case of castling short only two need be moved to clear the back rank. Another important point is that in order to castle on the queenside the queen has to be moved first, and the best moment for doing this in many openings occurs rather later, as moving the queen at an early stage of the game can turn out to be a loss of a tempo. This is an important reason for the comparative rarity of castling on the queenside, and the trend is given further impetus by the structure of modern openings, the majority of which are directed towards a struggle over the central squares. In this the c-pawn plays an important part both in covering the d-pawn and in effecting a lateral attack; this delays the queen's development on the one hand, and also slightly weakens the queenside on the other, consequently reducing the circumstances which favour castling long.

There are quite a few situations in the openings when castling on the queenside can be usefully applied, and in some cases one can say that it in fact represents the best solution to the basic problem of building up the position. We shall now list the main factors which would usually endorse the choice of long castling in a game:

1) The pawn position on the kingside has already been weakened, while that on the queenside is sound; this may incline the player towards castling long. (If castling on the kingside is quite impossible or is obstructed, then naturally there is no choice at all.)

2) The opponent's forces (pieces or pawns, or both) are favourably placed for an attack on the short castled position, but unfavourably for one on the long castled position.

3) The kingside is not sufficiently developed, while on the queenside the back rank is already clear. If this is the case when the situation demands castling as soon as possible, then castling takes place on the queenside.

4) One's opponent has castled on the kingside, and the weaknesses in his castled position can only be properly exploited by means of an assault by one or more pawns. If in such a case castling on the queenside is readily available and there are no other factors militating against it, one castles long rather than short. An assault by the h-pawn with the aim of opening up the h-file for the rook is often the answer to a fianchettoed king position, and in this case too castling on the queenside is indicated.

5) A rapid deployment of the rook on the d-file gains an important tempo or some other advantage, and in such a case castling long can afford an excellent solution.

The factors listed here are only intended as general hints for the player, and the particular characteristics of the actual position should be surveyed each time one makes a choice between castling moves. Black, particularly, should be careful if he intends to castle on the queenside, since experience has shown that the necessary conditions for long castling more often arise for White than for Black. When Black's long castling coincides with short castling by White one gets a case of opposite-side castled positions; this leads to an intensification of the game, which naturally favours the better developed side, and this in the majority of cases is White.

However, caution over deciding to castle on the queenside should not be over-done, since many cases arise where castling long is indicated but where the player does not do so because a prejudice about its risk deters him. Here is an ex-ample of unprejudiced castling on the queenside from the game Keres-Reshev-sky, World Championship Tournament, The Hague/Moscow 1948:

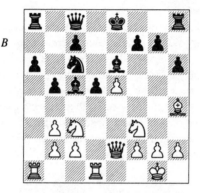

Black is to move; his position is apparently inferior, since he is threatened not only by ♘xd5 but also ♘xb5. Besides this, he has not yet castled, so that he is faced with a double task: to discover a reply to White's threats and also make the time to castle. Here is how Reshevsky solved the problem:

1...g5 2 ♗g3 ♕b7!

Black has already shown by 1...g5 that he does not intend to castle on the kingside, and now he gives up his pawn on d5 in order to use castling long to ob-tain an important tempo and gain control over the central squares d4 and d5 (2...♘e7 would be weak because of 3 ♘xb5).

3 ♘xd5 0-0-0!

Black's castling on the queenside in the Open Variation of the Ruy Lopez (which was how this game began) qualifies as a curiosity, and many masters shook their heads when they saw what Reshevsky had done. In this case it was correct to overcome the prejudice about the unsuitability of castling long in the Ruy Lopez, for here this very move provides a happy solution to the problem: it gives Black the time he needs and consolidates his king position better than short castling would. It should also be noticed that the weaknesses at a6 and b5 are not particularly marked, since White does not possess the move a4 which would properly probe them. Another point is that castling long has lent power to Black's g-pawn; its advance to g4 is important in the struggle for the square d4.

4 ♘f6

The knight here is 'attacking empty squares,' but 4 ♘c3 would have been no better. The most important point is that White cannot play 4 c4 to support the knight on d5, since it would be answered by 4...g4 5 ♘h4 (or 5 ♘e1 ♘d4 6 ♕d3 ♗f5) 5...♘d4 6 ♕d3, after which either 6...c6 or 6...♗xd5 is in Black's favour.

4...g4 5 ♘e1 ♘d4 6 ♕f1

If 6 ♕e4, then 6...♕a7!, threatening 7...♗f5.

6...h5

The rest of the game is not of interest to us here; Black's active piece play serves as sufficient compensation for the pawn, there is no question of his castled position being in danger, and it is really White who is in difficulties. In the end White did in fact lose the game after making some rather weak moves.

Our further consideration of the attack on the long castled position will be confined to those features which are specific to queenside castling. This means, in the main, that we need only consider positions where the king is still on c1, since if it has already retired to b1 a position has arisen which corresponds symmetrically to that after castling kingside.

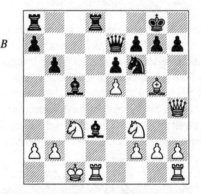

This position is taken from the game Rabinovich-Romanovsky, Moscow 1925. Black, to move, has no way of preventing exf6 and in desperation plays for a counterattack on the enemy king based on the pattern of Boden's Mate (see p.76).

1...♗a3! 2 exf6?

White, who has in fact the better of the game, here takes the wrong path and spends a tempo on 'burying the corpse on f6' instead of using it to consolidate his threatened king position, e.g. 2 ♖xd3! ♖xd3 3 ♔b1! and if 3...♕c5, then 4 ♘a4 and finally 5 exf6, etc.

2...♕c5 3 ♗d2?

After this second mistake Black has a winning position. White should have played 3 ♖xd3 ♖xd3 4 ♔b1! and if 4...♗xb2, then 5 ♘a4, or if 4...♖xc3, then 5 bxc3!, when Black can probably draw but cannot achieve more.

3...♗g6! *(D)*

The precious bishop retires and thus stops White playing ♘e1 followed by ♘c2 with gain of tempo.

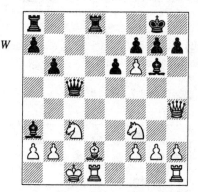

4 ♕a4

While this does not give his opponent much trouble, White's other moves are also of little use. The situation is now typical of attacks on the queenside castling position and a similar arrangement of pieces often arises in practice. So let us look at the whole repertoire of combinations at Black's disposal which lead to mate.

First, it is clear that White could not play 4 bxa3, because of 4...♕xa3#, with the typical pattern of Boden's Mate. Next, it can be seen that if 4 ♕f4, Black has 4...♖ac8, threatening 5...♕xc3+ and mate, thanks to the formidable effect of Black's bishops. It is true that White could meet 4...♖ac8 with 5 ♕e5, but then 5...♕b4 would be decisive. There still remain some other defences, which are worth setting out:

1) 4 ♖de1 ♖xd2! (if 4...♖ac8, White would reply 5 ♔d1[1]) 5 ♔xd2 (5 ♘xd2 is also inadequate, e.g. 5...♕xc3+ 6 ♔d1 ♕c2+[2] 7 ♔e2 ♕d3+ 8 ♔d1 ♖c8 9 ♖e4 ♗b4 10 ♖xb4 ♖c1+ 11 ♔xc1 ♕c2#) 5...♖d8+ 6 ♔e2 ♗d3+ 7 ♔d1 ♗e4+! 8 ♔e2 (or 8 ♘d2 ♖xd2+ 9 ♔xd2 ♕d4+ and mates) 8...♕c4+ 9 ♔e3 ♖d3+ and Black mates.

---

1   4...♖ac8 also wins as after 5 ♔d1 ♗xb2 White is defenceless.

2   Black can mate in two by 6...♗c2+.

2) 4 ♖he1 ♖ac8 5 ♖e3 ♕b5! (yet another threat arising from the position of the rook at c8!) 6 bxa3 ♕b1#.

3) 4 ♘e1 ♖d4 5 ♕g5 ♕b4 and mates.

4) 4 ♗e1! (relatively the best method of defence) 4...♖xd1+ (if 4...♕f5 5 ♖xd8+ ♖xd8, White has the reply 6 ♕e4!) 5 ♔xd1 ♖d8+ 6 ♗d2 (if 6 ♔c1, 6...♖d3 is decisive) 6...♗xb2 7 fxg7 ♖c8 and White must either give back the piece or consent to 8 ♘a4 ♕c2+ 9 ♔e2 ♕d3+ 10 ♔e1 ♗c1! 11 ♕b4 a5 12 ♕f4 ♖c4, when Black wins.

4...b5 5 ♕xa3

5 ♕xb5[1] is defeated by 5...♖ab8! 6 ♕xc5 ♗xb2#. Still another of the numerous mating patterns in this kind of position!

5...♕f5 0-1

For if 6 ♕b3, then 6...♖ac8 and 7...♕b1#.

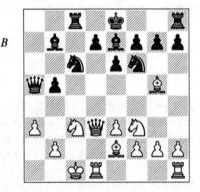

B

This position comes from Euwe-Colle, Amsterdam 1926. It is Black's move and he hits at White's castled position by means of a bishop sacrifice.

1...♗xa3! 2 ♗xf6 gxf6 3 ♔b1

If 3 bxa3, then 3...♘e5, while if 3 ♕xd7+ ♔f8, White is threatened by ...♕xc3+ and so has no time for ♕xb7.

3...♗xb2! 4 ♘a2

If 4 ♔xb2, then 4...♕b4+ 5 ♔c2 ♘e5 6 ♘xe5 ♗e4.

4...♘e5 5 ♘xe5 ♗d5 6 ♕xd5 exd5 7 ♘xd7 ♖a8 0-1

---

1   Vuković does not mention the far more resilient defence 5 ♕b3, when Black
     has to play very precisely to retain an advantage: 5...b4 6 ♗e3 ♕c7 7 ♖xd8+
     ♖xd8 8 ♘d4 ♖b8! 9 bxa3 bxc3 10 ♘b5 ♕c6 11 a4 a6 12 ♕c3 ♕xg2 13 ♖d1
     axb5 and White's king remains extremely exposed.

The following game serves as a demonstration both of how castling queenside forms part of a plan of development and of how an attack can be carried out against such a position.

Lasker – Marshall
St. Petersburg Final, 1914
Petroff Defence

1 e4 e5 2 ♘f3 ♘f6 3 ♘xe5 d6 4 ♘f3 ♘xe4 5 ♕e2

Morphy's old move; it is sound enough, though it gives White no more than a microscopic advantage.

5...♕e7 6 d3 ♘f6 7 ♗g5 ♗e6?!

Correct, of course, is 7...♕xe2+ 8 ♗xe2 ♗e7 or 7...♘bd7. Avoiding the exchange of queens favours White, whose position is the better developed. One might say that Lasker knew which opponents it paid to play drawing variations against!

8 ♘c3 ♘bd7 9 0-0-0

Castling on the queenside is completely justified in this position, where the bishop is hemmed in at f1. Moreover, on the d-file the rook supports the d-pawn in moving to d4 and then threatening to advance to d5.

9...h6 10 ♗h4 g5 11 ♗g3 ♘h5 12 d4 ♘xg3 13 hxg3 g4 14 ♘h4!?

A risky and adventurous move, typical of Lasker's play in the middlegame. The knight clearly has no good way of getting away from the h4-square, a circumstance which could have helped Black to equalize. Better would have been 14 ♘d2.

14...d5?

A decisive mistake. Black should have played 14...♘b6! and if 15 d5 then 15...♗d7. Against other attempts by White, the reply ...♕g5 plays an important part. However, moves like 14...♘b6! were not to Marshall's taste. What he really enjoyed was setting a trap for his opponent!

15 ♕b5! 0-0-0 *(D)*

Castling is forced, since 15...♕b4 comes to grief after 16 ♘xd5 ♕xb5 17 ♘xc7+. It was probably because of this trap that Marshall played 14...d5?, but Lasker naturally refuses to be diverted by the d-pawn and calmly plays for an attack on the castled position with 16 ♕a5[1].

---

1   Vuković doesn't actually say what the trap is – the point is that after 15...0-0-0, 16 ♘xd5 fails to 16...♗xd5 17 ♕xd5 ♕g5+ 18 ♕xg5 hxg5 and the knight is lost.

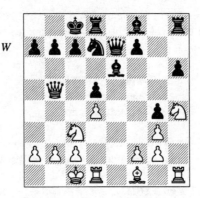

Perhaps Lasker even played 14 ♘h4!? exactly because he knew Marshall would be tempted to set a trap and thereby get himself ensnared in the attack on the castled king which now follows.

16 ♕a5 a6

Clearly, 16...♔b8 fails against 17 ♘b5.

17 ♗xa6!

A correct bishop sacrifice.

17...bxa6 18 ♕xa6+ ♔b8 19 ♘b5 ♘b6 *(D)*

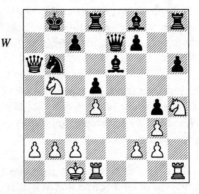

Now that the black king has moved from c8 to b8, the distinctive character of the queenside castling position no longer exists and the situation is merely a replica of a type of attack used against the short castled position.

An important advantage for the attacker in this position is his ability to bring a rook into action quickly (♖d3-b3), since without this Black could defend himself by ...♘c8 and then ...♗d7.

20 ♖d3 ♕g5+

This move simplifies White's task somewhat. However, Black could not have saved himself even by 20...♘c4 which contains the transparent trap 21 ♖b3? ♕g5+ 22 ♔b1 ♘d2+. At the time Lasker had reckoned on defeating 20...♘c4 in the following manner (and this has found its way into the commentaries): 21 ♖e1? (in order to be able to meet 21...♕g5+ with 22 ♖e3) 21...♖d6 22 ♘xd6 ♕xd6 23 ♖b3+ ♘b6 24 a4 ♗c8 25 ♖e8 ♕d7 26 ♕b5 ♕xb5 27 ♖xb5 ♔b7? 28 a5 ♗d7 29 ♖xf8 ♖xf8 30 ♖b4 and White goes on to capture the knight, after which he is a pawn up in the ending. Let us disregard any doubts about this ending, for Black has a stronger continuation than 27...♔b7, namely 27...♗g7 28 ♖xh8 ♗xh8; then White must play 29 a5 (otherwise the knight remains alive on b6) whereupon the main line runs 29...♗xd4 30 axb6 c6 31 ♖b3 ♗xf2 32 b7 (if White allows ...♔b7, then the position is still more favourable for Black) 32...♗e6 33 ♔d2 c5! 34 ♔e2 c4 35 ♖a3 ♗d4, and it is clearly White rather than Black who has to struggle for a draw. It is interesting to see how the original characteristic of the position (the inability of the knight on h4 to move) again emerges as the decisive factor as soon as the attack on the castled position peters out. Not even the best players are immune from such misfortunes!

This game, which was the decisive one in Lasker's victory at St. Petersburg, cannot be left to go on sleeping in the archives of chess history with an inaccurate commentary. Good games should not be allowed to go to their rest without good annotations as their lullabies! Therefore, we must show how in fact White does win after 20...♘c4 *(D)*.

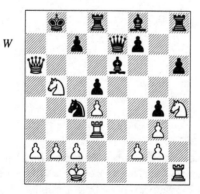

So that there will be no doubt about it, we shall supply two winning moves, both of them instructive as far as carrying out an attack in this kind of position is concerned.

1) 21 a4! c6 (if 21...♖d6 22 ♘xd6 ♕xd6 23 ♖b3+ ♘b6, White wins easily by 24 a5) 22 ♖b3! (not 22 ♕xc6? because of 22...♕b7, forcing the exchange of queens and thus bringing the attack to a halt; nor does 22 ♘a7 work, e.g. 22...♕xa7 23 ♖b3+ ♘b6! 24 ♖xb6+ ♔a8, when White has to exchange queens, leaving Black once again with the better game; obviously the intermediate 23...♘b6! is the key element here) 22...♕g5+ 23 ♔b1 ♘d2+ 24 ♔a2. Now Black is unable to take the rook on b3 with check, so White wins easily, e.g. 24...♕e7 25 ♕b6+ ♕b7 26 ♕xd8+, etc[1].

2) 21 ♘a7![2] ♖d6 22 ♖b3+ ♘b6 (forced, since 22...♖b6 is defeated by 23 ♘c6#) 23 a4 ♗g7 (or 23...♕d7 24 ♘b5! ♖c6 25 ♕a7+ ♔c8 26 a5) 24 ♘b5! and White wins.

21 ♔b1 ♗d6 22 ♖b3 ♖he8 23 a4 ♗f5 24 ♘a7 ♗d7 25 a5 ♕d2 26 axb6 ♖e1+ 27 ♔a2 c6 28 ♘b5! cxb5 29 ♕a7+ 1-0

29...♔c8 30 ♕a8+ ♗b8 leads to the picturesque 31 ♕a6#. In this 'posthumous finale' of the game Black's king and rook are back once again in the original long castling position!

---

1   Black's best defence is 24...♖d7, when White must find 25 f4! ♕f6 (25...gxf3 26 ♘xf3 deflects the knight from the attack on b3) 26 ♖c3! to keep an advantage.

2   Recent analysis by Kasparov reveals a third possibility: 21 ♖b3 ♕g5+ 22 ♔b1 ♘d2+ 23 ♔a1 ♘xb3+ 24 cxb3 ♗d6 25 ♕a7+ ♔c8 26 ♘xd6+ ♖xd6 (26...cxd6 27 f4! gxf3 28 ♘xf3 and the rook reaches c1) 27 ♕a8+ ♔d7 28 ♕xh8 with two extra pawns.

10 Defending against the attack on the castled king

In presenting, up to here, the various aspects of the attack on the castled king we have looked at the operation from the attacker's point of view. However, it is also true that the defence against such an attack has its own principles and particular characteristics, and it is therefore fitting that we should also try to discuss this defence systematically.

Chess literature tends for the most part to talk of *active* and *passive* defence as being the two main types of defence. Steinitz also introduced the term 'self-defence', and H. Kmoch (in his work *The Art of Defence*) speaks of 'automatic defence'. Although it is now fairly well established, this division is not really the happiest one for teaching purposes; moreover, when it is a question of defence against an attack on the castled king, it is an imprecise one.

I think it better to talk of *direct* and *indirect* defence of the castled position, in which case the direct defence is predominantly 'passive' and the indirect always 'active'. The difference between these kinds of defence is usually clearly marked, since the former involves the defence of the actual castling area or the removal of one's opponent's aggressive pieces, while in the latter case it is a question of actions further away from the castled position, which the defender uses to keep the attacker so busy that he fails to pursue his attack to its conclusion.

In actual play direct defensive moves usually occur in conjunction with those of an indirect kind, and the main rule is that direct defence should be *economical* and that indirect should be executed at *the right moment*. Economy in direct defence consists of not making superfluous moves and not employing an unnecessarily large number of pieces in defence. The right moment for indirect defence is fairly difficult to gauge, since it is normally determined by two interacting factors; on the one hand, when direct defence has reached the limits that necessary economy allows, and on the other, when the attacker has really made a move which commits him fairly strongly, i.e. he has staked his money on the success of the attack.

First, we shall set out clearly the various elements which go to make up each type of defence.

A. Direct Defence

1) Protecting the squares of the castled position, including so-called over-protection.

2) Transforming the castled position by moving the pawns in front of the king, a particular case being the setting-up of a blocked position.

3) Altering the castled position by moving the king. Here it should be kept in mind that each move by the king changes the situation, changes the conditions necessary for an attack and, above all, changes the possible focal-points. King moves fall into the following graded categories:

a) The consolidating move (e.g. ♔b1 in the case of queenside castling and ♔h1 in the case of kingside castling);

b) A more radical alteration of the situation as a result of moving the king (e.g. to f2, thus producing a so-called 'semi-castled' position);

c) A king's flight, i.e. when it goes out in front of the castled position. Steinitz called this the king's self-defence, an older and more correct term than that of 'automatic defence' applied by Kmoch.

4) Defence by means of repulsing one's opponent's pieces, through their capture, exchange, or ejection from powerful positions.

B. Indirect Defence

Before considering the ways of using the indirect method we must first of all examine three aspects of such a defence. The first is purely spatial, i.e. whether the defender carries out his own counterattack in the centre or on the wings; the second is concerned with the degree of the threat; and the third with the question of whether the indirect action turns at some point into the direct method of defence. In the following review we shall combine these three aspects:

1) The defender carries out a counterattack on the opposite side, where the attacker has castled. In such a case his action is usually itself an attack on the castled king, the position being one where the players have castled on opposite sides.

2) An action on the opposite side first of all prepares the ground (files, ranks, etc.), and then turns into an outflanking manoeuvre against the attacker's castled position, i.e. while the attacker is attacking along the files, the defender gains control of the attacker's first or second rank.

In this case, as in '1', the critical question is naturally either who will be the first to force mate or which of the two attacks will be brought to a halt through the diversion of pieces to provide a direct defence.

3) An action on any part of the board with the aim of gaining material.

Such an action obviously only has a point when a forced mate is not part of the attacker's plan. The critical continuation then is that which costs the defender the least. For instance, if he can 'pacify the attacker's wrath' at the price of a knight, then a counterattack which brings him a rook is worthwhile.

In practice the most important case is where the attacker sacrifices; the defender's repertoire is then greatly increased, since he is given various ways in which to return material in order to counter the attacker's plan. This method of returning material is extremely important; the extent to which it is possible affects the type of sacrifice which can be made, and the sacrifice is also a signal to the defender to counter with a sacrifice which would previously have been out of the question.

4) The counterattack results in material equality, but the question of position still remains open. Mate cannot be forced, both attacks are brought to a halt, and eventual simplification leads towards an ending. The resulting position, which is often extremely difficult to assess beforehand, is then decisive.

5) The defender's counterattack does not lead to a mating attack, nor to material or positional advantages, but instead consists of an eventual transition to the direct method.

As a rule, this takes the form of either attacking the enemy pieces 'from the rear' or of gaining control of a file or diagonal so as to cover a certain square in one's king position (e.g. when the white queen has captured the square c7 and from there covers the focal-point h2).

6) A special case of the kind of counterattack mentioned in '3' is provided by the advance of a queenside pawn majority. Its aim is to promote a pawn to a queen, and such an advantage justifies the most generous surrender of material in order to curb the attacker's forces.

7) Retaliation in the centre can have the features of sections '3' to '5' either separately or combined. The following possibilities are particularly worth noting here:

a) A central thrust demolishes or weakens the attacker's formation there and prepares the ground for further operations by the defender, or it enables him to transpose to direct defence 'via a turning manoeuvre';

b) The destruction of the pawn centre eliminates its auxiliary function with regard to an attack on the castled king. For example, the disappearance of a pawn on e5 can also mean the end of an attack on the castled king, if the pawn is vital to a certain continuation;

c) Because of the danger of a central thrust, many attackers at a suitable moment deliberately create a blocked position in the centre. As a rule such a central formation cannot be rapidly activated except by the sacrifice of a piece. If the attacker has already used a sacrifice in attack, the defender is presented with an opportunity of making a return sacrifice in the centre. For example, the defender's knight on c6 is sacrificed for White's pawns on e5 and d4, thereby creating the necessary conditions for various kinds of defence without loss of material;

d) The destruction of the attacker's centre usually gives the defender the prospect of better conditions for positional play, as mentioned in section '4'. For it is not only that the opponent's centre pawns disappear, but the actual central *squares* also come under the defender's control; consequently, if the attack is held, the considerable positional advantage enjoyed by the defender persists, even when the material is equally balanced, until well into the endgame.

This outline of defensive methods brings out above all else the richness of their variety and the flexible way in which they can be combined. Because of this, defence as a whole is harder than attack, and its finesses are as a rule more concealed than those of the attacker, a point already noticed long ago by Lasker. The importance of the centre must be particularly emphasized as the critical area where the decisive step is often made. The great variety of possibilities afforded by a defence based on an action against the centre gives such an operation first place in the defender's repertoire, and so every attacker must be able to calculate accurately what is likely to happen in the centre during an attack on the castled king.

Defence by over-protection

Passing now to some examples of direct defence, let us examine the following position, which can arise in the Closed Defence to the Ruy Lopez.

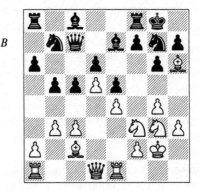

It is Black's move; he has to think how to supplement the direct defence of his king position, especially in view of White's threat of 1 ♘h2 followed by 2 f4 and 3 f5. Black plays:

1...♘d8 2 ♘h2 f6

Now 3 f4 can be met by 3...♘f7. Moreover, he can also answer most other moves by 3...♘f7, setting up a distinctive position with a 'double knight fianchetto'.

This position offers very strong resistance against all kinds of attack, and the reason for this lies in the over-protection of the squares f5, g5, and h5, at which points White might have been able to execute a breakthrough. These squares are now covered both by Black's pawns and his knights, an example of 'prophylactic over-protection', to use Nimzowitsch's phrase.

The over-protection which Black achieves by transferring his knight to f7 is in this case neither a passive nor an uneconomical means of defence. It is not difficult to establish that Black's knight on b7 has no better position anywhere than on f7 (if ...c4, for example, White plays b4 and does not allow ...♘c5); it is better to use the knight for defence, freeing Black's other pieces for later queenside activity. In some cases over-protection can mean economical direct defence; on the other hand, depending on the position, it may be superfluous.

Defence by blockade

A blocked pawn formation means a general reduction in the number of actions possible in any position, and as a result blockade is often the weapon employed by the weaker side. A means of defence which stands out as particularly important is the blockade of the pawns in front of the king.

W

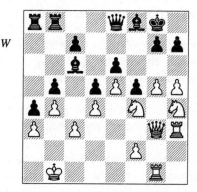

The continuation from the above position shows us first of all a typical case of defence by blockade, and then the way to overcome this method of defence.

Although White has the superior position with all his pieces directed against Black's kingside, he still can not achieve anything by 'normal' methods. If 1 g6, Black plays 1...h6, while if 1 h6, then 1...g6; in both cases blocking the pawns brings the attack to a halt. Attempts to break through by sacrificing a knight can simply be ignored by Black. Thus after 1 g6 h6 2 ♘f3 ♗d7 3 ♘g5 Black does not take the knight but waits; while if 1 h6 g6 2 ♘h5, Black again does not need to take, for by playing 2...♔h8 3 ♘f6 ♕f7 he can hold the draw.

White's only chance in this position is:

1 ♘hg6 ♗d7

Clearly, the knight cannot be taken. 1...♔f7 is met by 2 h6 and a breakthrough, since if 2...hxg6, then 3 h7 ♗e7 4 ♕h4 followed by 5 ♘xg6.

2 ♖gh1!

White must play with great precision and thoroughly prepare for the breakthrough by h6 and hxg7. If he tries 2 h6 immediately, then Black replies 2...hxg6; then 3 hxg7 ♗xg7 is not dangerous[1], while after 3 h7+ ♔h8 4 ♖h6 gxh6 5 gxh6 White's attack will probably not succeed.

2...c6 3 ♕h2 ♖b7 4 h6 hxg6 5 hxg7 ♗xg7 6 ♖h8+ and White wins.

Defence by elimination

Many examples could be given of defence based on the diversion or elimination of important attacking pieces, since such operations are often undertaken; however, they are limited on the whole to one or two moves and do not normally provide a complete system of defence but only force the attacker to remodel or reorganize his attack. Thus, for example, in the quite normal case where the attacker's knight has to retreat from g5 when faced with ...h6, the problem of defence has not as a rule been fundamentally solved, but rather the attacker has been obliged to redirect his attack, either by transferring his target from h7 to h6 or g7 or else by strengthening the pressure on h7 along the diagonal b1-h7. Special examples and analysis are not necessary in the case of such straightforward diversion of opposing pieces. We are interested here in those special cases when the diversion or elimination of the attacker's pieces represents the essence of the defence and is in fact fundamental in driving back the attacking force. The

---

[1]   Although after 4 ♕h4 followed by ♕h7+ White wins the g6-pawn, when the resulting position appears very unpleasant for Black. However, it is true that White risks nothing by building his position up further before playing h6.

simplest example of this is the exchange of queens, which is usually to the advantage of the defender and in many cases altogether eliminates the danger of attack. The queen is generally an essential piece in a mating attack and it is therefore useful to the defender if it is removed. However, other pieces too can be essential to an attack and can be the target of a defensive plan based on elimination. One of the most typical instances involves the attacker's bishop which is covering a network of weak squares. Such a visitor should, as soon as circumstances permit, be dismissed from the castling area or be eliminated by exchange. The following diagram shows a case of a bishop commanding a network of squares, and we give two possible continuations: the one actually taken, where Black misses the opportunity to defend himself by tackling the bishop; and an alternative one, which indicates the correct method of defence.

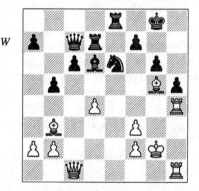

This position[1] comes from the game Blackburne-Schwarz, Berlin 1881, and it is White's move. He is a pawn down and, in addition, he has the inferior pawn structure. On the other hand, he enjoys far greater activity for his pieces and has prospects of controlling the network of weak dark squares around the enemy king. It is exactly with this in mind that he plays:

1 ♗f6 ♘f4+?

Black throws away the chance of defending himself by eliminating the bishop on f6 (with 1...♗e7!) and falls into a trap.

2 ♕xf4! ♗xf4 3 ♖xh5 gxh5 4 ♖xh5 and there is no remedy against mate on h8.

---

1 In the original edition, this diagram was incorrectly given without the black pawn on b5. Vuković's comments have been modified to take account of this correction.

The essential attacking piece here is the bishop on f6 and it should have been eliminated. Therefore the only correct course is 1...♗e7! *(D)*.

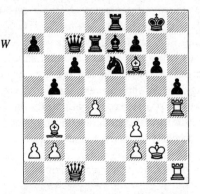

After 2 ♗e5 (or 2 ♗xe6 fxe6 3 ♕g5 ♗xf6 4 ♕xf6 ♕d8! and Black is the better placed) 2...♗d6 White has nothing better than 3 ♗f6 and a repetition of moves; on any other move the elimination of White's dark-squared bishop affords Black a complete defence and the prospect of victory on the basis of his other advantages. Thus after 3 f4 ♗xe5 4 dxe5 ♘g7 White has nothing, while he is too weak for 3 ♖xh5? because of 3...gxh5 4 ♖xh5 ♗xe5 5 dxe5 ♖d4, whereupon the threat of ...♘f4+ destroys all his hopes.

Before we leave the theme of defence by elimination, the reader must be warned of the mistakes which are often made in applying this method. Many players defend themselves by endeavouring to exchange all the attacker's aggressive pieces. Such a formula can easily lead to defeat. As a rule, one should aim to exchange those pieces which are essential to the execution of the attacker's mating threats, while on the other hand one should preserve those of one's own pieces which are carrying out an important defensive function. We have already seen how important it is to preserve the fianchettoed bishop, and much the same can be said for a knight at f6 covering the important square h7.

The king's self-defence

There is a graded scale which can be applied to the king's self-defence starting from the so-called consolidating move and ending with the full flight of the king to the other side of the board. Examples have already been given of the former type, so we shall begin with cases where the king is already definitely on the move, even though it may only be along the edge of the castling area. The next diagram is a typical example of self-defence by classically simple means: faced with White's pressure on h7, Black defends his pawn by advancing it and is not concerned about the square h7 itself; Black's king reduces the value of the square by moving, for it no longer comes into consideration as a focal-point.

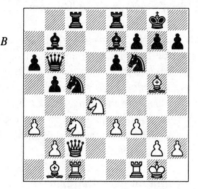

This position is from Bogoljubow-Réti, Carlsbad 1923. Black played:
1...h6! 2 ♗xf6 ♗xf6 3 ♕h7+ ♔f8

The Black king defends itself by flight; if now 4 ♕h8+ ♔e7, White's position would only be made worse by his loss of a tempo. In the actual game White's initiative dissolved after **4 ♖cd1 ♖ed8 5 ♔h1 ♔e7 6 ♘ce2 ♖h8 7 ♕c2 a5**, and, thanks to the good self-defence effected by his king, Black soon obtained rather the better game.

Another example of self-defence can be provided by my analysis of one of the critical positions in the game Reshevsky-Botvinnik, World Championship Tournament, The Hague/Moscow 1948.

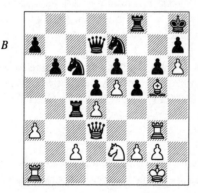

Botvinnik (Black) played here 1...♘g8?, which is an absolutely passive method of defence. It means that Black's king is left in the corner, and White is offered the chance to prepare the opening of the e-file by a pawn sacrifice based on ♗f6+. After the moves 2 ♖e1 ♕f7 3 c3 ♘a5 4 ♘f4 ♖c6 White made the mistake of playing 5 ♗f6+ too early, without the preparatory 5 ♖ge3!, and thus did not make correct use of Black's error; we will therefore not concern ourselves with the game's actual course.

Correct would have been 1...♔g8!, followed perhaps by ...♔f7, in which case the black king is only apparently 'courting danger'; in fact, it avoids all the difficulties associated with being in the corner and itself provides assistance in covering the important light squares e6 and g6; moreover, with the dark-square network alone White can clearly achieve nothing. Black is also left with an initiative on the queenside, where he is positionally set to win. If the reader tests the different variations after 1...♔g8, he will convince himself of the strength of the black king's self-defence in this position.

Capablanca – Ragozin
Moscow, 1935
Nimzo-Indian Defence

1 d4 ♘f6 2 c4 e6 3 ♘c3 ♗b4 4 a3 ♗xc3+ 5 bxc3 d6

5...c5 and 5...0-0 are more common nowadays.

6 ♕c2

Capablanca is happy to avoid 'auxiliary pawn moves', and here he prepares e4 with the aid of the queen and not by f3.

6...0-0 7 e4 e5 8 ♗d3 c5 9 ♘e2 ♘c6 10 d5 ♘e7?

White should have answered 8...c5 with an immediate d5, whereas now Black ought to have played 10...♘a5 followed by ...b6 and ...♗a6, according to the well-known plan for attacking c4. He moved the knight to e7 in order to prepare ...f5, but in this position Black is too weak for that.

11 f3 ♘d7

However one looks at it, Black is getting into a cramped and difficult position. He cannot make ...f5 work, as is shown by the following variation: 11...♘e8 12 g4 g6 13 ♗h6 ♘g7 14 0-0-0 f5? 15 gxf5 gxf5 16 ♖dg1 ♖f7 17 exf5 ♗xf5 18 ♗xg7 when White wins.

12 h4 ♘b6 13 g4 *(D)*

13...f6?

The beginning of a faulty plan. Black intends to move his king away from the endangered kingside. He does in fact succeed in conveying it without difficulty

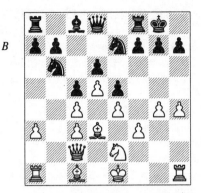

as far as a8, but in doing so he condemns himself to a passive game with no prospect of activity. Counterplay is possible only on the queenside, based on ...b5. That is where Black's chances lie, and consequently his king does not belong on the queen's wing but should stay where it is; the pawns in front of the king should not be touched, in order that he may retain as much chance as possible of defending himself by blocking the position. Correct therefore was 13...♗d7 planning ...♘a4 followed by ...a6 and ...b5. If White plays 14 a4 then 14...♕e8 15 a5 ♘bc8 followed by ...♖b8 and ...b5, etc.

14 ♘g3 ♔f7 15 g5 ♘g8 16 f4 ♔e8 17 f5 ♕e7 18 ♕g2!

Capablanca handles the game supremely calmly. His strategy results in his knight being established on the advanced post g7.

18...♔d8 19 ♘h5 ♔c7 20 gxf6 gxf6 21 ♘g7 ♗d7 22 h5 ♖ac8 23 h6 ♔b8 *(D)*

Now Black has a 'short castled position on the queenside'. White has everything else.

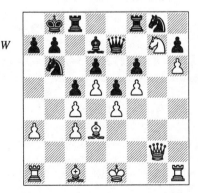

24 Rg1 Rf7 25 Rb1 Wf8 26 Ae2 Ka8 27 Ah5 Re7 28 Wa2 Wd8 29 Ad2 Na4 30 Wb3 Nb6 31 a4!

It is an irony of fate that Black's wandering king can be reached by an attack on the queenside too! If he now plays 31...Axa4, there follows 32 Wa2 Ad7 (or 32...Wd7 33 Rxb6 axb6 34 Ad1) 33 Ne6 Axe6 34 dxe6, and Black has no reply to Af7 and Axg8.

31...Rb8 32 a5 Nc8 33 Wa2 Wf8 34 Ae3 b6 35 a6

Black, who has been 'breathing through his gills' for a long time already, is now left with only his queen to move.

35...Wd8 36 Kd2 Wf8 37 Rb2 Wd8 38 Wb1 b5

At last he has had enough! Any further passive play would have permitted White to organize a winning breakthrough on the g-file.

39 cxb5 Nb6 40 Wa2 c4 41 Wa3 Wc7 42 Kc1 Rf8 43 Rbg2 Wb8 44 Wb4 Rd8 45 Rg3 Rf8 46 Ne6 Axe6

Or 46...Rc8 47 Axb6 axb6 48 a7! and Black loses his knight or is mated.

47 dxe6 Rc7

Otherwise Af7 is decisive.

48 Wxd6 Ne7 49 Rd1 1-0

49...Nbc8 could be answered by 50 Wb4 Nb6 51 Rg7 Nbc8 52 Rd7, etc.

Pawn majority on the wing

Passing now to the theme of indirect defence, we first of all examine a counterattack by means of a pawn majority on the queenside. An analysis of a classic masterpiece will be helpful here.

Pillsbury – Tarrasch
Hastings, 1895
Queen's Gambit Declined, Orthodox Defence

1 d4 d5 2 c4 e6 3 Nc3 Nf6 4 Ag5 Ae7 5 Nf3 Nbd7 6 Rc1 0-0 7 e3 b6

These days it is considered more accurate to play ...b6 before committing the b8-knight to d7.

8 cxd5 exd5 9 Ad3 Ab7 10 0-0 c5 11 Re1?!

A move which does not belong to the system and only wastes time. At this point Pillsbury usually played 11 Ne5 and his opponents allowed him to strengthen the position of his knight by f4. Marco later showed that after 11 Ne5 one should play 11...Nxe5 12 dxe5 Ne8 13 Af4 g6 14 Ah6 Ng7 15 f4 d4! answering 16 f5 with 16...Ag5.

Today 11 ♕e2 is considered strongest.

11...c4?

Thus Black creates a pawn majority on the wing but surrenders his influence in the centre. It is now known that *the situation in the centre is the more important; moreover, against an attack on the castled king it is easier to build up a counterattack using the centre* rather than by means of a slow advance of the wing pawns.

Instead of 11...c4? Black could have played, for example, 11...a6, which is in keeping with the system and does not immediately forsake the centre in the process. The modern answer would be 11...♘e4, with the aim of clarifying the situation.

12 ♗b1 a6 13 ♘e5 *(D)*

Because of Black's mistake this move is now extremely strong, since White is able to consolidate the knight on e5 and use it as the basis for a later attack on the king. 13...♘xe5 will not do now, since 14 dxe5 is extremely awkward for Black.

13...b5 14 f4

This formation with a knight on e5 and pawns on d4 and f4 is called the 'Pillsbury attack', and it was in this game that the attack originated. Pillsbury was still experimenting with his idea here, hence his unsystematic move 11 ♖e1?!.

14...♖e8

Black prepares to defend his king position by ...♘f8.

15 ♕f3 ♘f8 16 ♘e2 ♘e4 17 ♗xe7 ♖xe7

More precise, in fact, is 17...♕xe7 as will be seen from the note to Black's nineteenth move.

18 ♗xe4

Pillsbury's contemporaries were a little surprised by this exchange, which he used to make regularly in this system. In fact, the move is absolutely logical from the positional point of view. White cannot worry Black any more as regards his control of e4, and it is better that the square should be occupied by a blocked pawn than an active knight. In view of Black's complete hold on e4, White's bishop on b1 cannot be better employed than in dispatching Black's knight. This is an example of the logic, consistency, and lack of prejudice which runs through Pillsbury's style.

18...dxe4 19 ♕g3! f6

This move has been censured by earlier commentators because 'White's knight retreats with gain of tempo', but closer investigation shows that the move is not a bad one, or rather that Black has nothing better. 19...f5 would be dangerous (because of White's eventual assault with g4), but otherwise it is difficult to find a natural way of parrying White's threat of 20 f5 followed by ♘f4 or f6. It is important to note that 19...♕d6 20 f5 f6 fails because of 21 ♘g6! ♖d7 22 ♘gf4, when White has realized his aim of posting a knight on f4 without having to exchange queens. On the other hand, 19...♕c7 contains some dangers on account of 20 b3. If Black had recaptured with his queen on the seventeenth move, 19...♕d6 would now work, for 20 f5 f6 would force the exchange of queens. A small and instructive detail!

20 ♘g4 ♔h8 21 f5! ♕d7 22 ♖f1 ♖d8

Black is planning ...♕d6, but he should have noted that White will be unable to play the fundamentally important move ♘f4 for some time (because of ...♕xf5). He could therefore have devoted the tempo to preparing ...b4, e.g. by 22...♖c8.

23 ♖f4 *(D)*

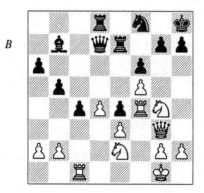

Here we shall stop a moment to describe the course of the game so far and to point out the characteristic features of the position.

Black released his pressure on the centre early on and thereby allowed White considerable freedom in arranging his pieces for an attack on the king. Against this attack Black built up a typical, direct defensive position which offers considerable, but not absolute, resistance. His principal weapon in the event of a further concentration of White's pieces is, however, an indirect defence in the shape of the advance of the pawn majority on the queenside. Against a whole series of attacking plans Black has successful replies in the form of retaliation on the flank; a particular point is that White cannot force the move ♘f4. It was because of this that Pillsbury decided on 23 ♖f4, i.e. he now abandons his preparations for ♘f4 and regroups with the apparent intention of attacking e4.

23...♕d6 24 ♕h4 ♖de8 25 ♘c3?

A weak move, for Black could now have played 25...b4 26 ♘a4 ♗d5 27 ♘c5 ♘d7 28 ♘xd7 ♖xd7, after which there is nothing left of White's attack, while on the queenside Black has moved closer to his goal. 25 ♘f2 was better, to prepare g4. Admittedly, if 25...♔g8!, then 26 g4 does not work (because of 26...g5 27 fxg6 ♘xg6 28 ♕xf6 ♘xf4! 29 ♕xd6 ♘xe2+ and 30...♘xc1, with a whole fistful of pieces for the queen); however, White can play 26 ♕h3, to be followed by ♖h4, g4, and ♘f4, etc.

25...♗d5? *(D)*

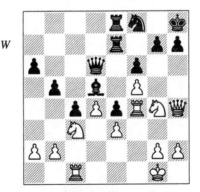

Not only does this throw away the chance of playing ...b4, it also allows White the following opportunity to simplify the position: 26 a4 b4 27 ♘xd5 ♕xd5 28 ♘xf6 gxf6 29 ♕xf6+ ♖g7 30 ♖g4 ♕f7 31 ♕xg7+ ♕xg7 32 ♖xg7 ♔xg7 33 ♖xc4, when the ending favours White.

26 ♘f2

White also retains the better prospects this way, though best would in fact have been 26 a4 as given above.

26...♛c6

Black could well have played 26...b4 and if 27 ♘e2 then 27...a5. 27 ♘cxe4? would fail against 27...♛c6 followed, after a knight retreat, by 28...♖xe3. However, the text move is also correct.

27 ♖f1?

A tactical mistake, since the rook is not well placed here.

27...b4 28 ♘e2 ♛a4?

This loses important tempi. Correct was 28...c3! 29 b3! (if 29 bxc3 then 29...♗c4 followed by ...♗xe2 and ...bxc3, after which Black's position is preferable) 29...a5 when Black proceeds along similar lines to those in the actual game (i.e. by ...♖a8 and ...a4, etc.) but much more quickly.

29 ♘g4 ♘d7 30 ♖4f2 *(D)*

The move is not a bad one, although it would not inspire commentators nowadays to pour on it the praise with which it was once honoured. The point is that by 30 ♘c1 c3 31 b3 White obtains a position analogous to that actually reached, and the only difference is that 30 ♖4f2 sets a trap for 30...♛xa2. However, even that trap is not so terrible, for after 31 ♘f4 ♗f7 32 ♘g6+ ♚g8! (Réti only analyses the inferior 32...♗xg6?) 33 ♘xe7+ ♖xe7 34 ♛g3 ♚f8 35 h3 (otherwise ...h5 wins the knight) 35...♛a5 Black still retains good prospects of counterplay, and it is not certain whether White can use his small material advantage to any real effect.

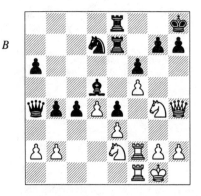

30...♚g8 31 ♘c1 c3 32 b3 ♛c6 33 h3
Preparing for ♘h2 and then g4-g5.
33...a5 34 ♘h2 a4 35 g4?

A mistake which luckily is not properly exploited. It was not yet time for a bayonet attack by g4. White should have played 35 bxa4 or else brought his queen back to the defence via g4 and d1.

35...axb3 36 axb3 ♖a8 37 g5

Since he lacks a satisfactory defence against ...♖a3 and ...♖xb3, White has no choice but to try to force home his attack on the enemy king.

37...♖a3 38 ♘g4 ♗xb3?

A decisive mistake, entirely altering the situation. Black should at this point have thought a little about defence himself, leaving the tit-bit on b3, which could not run away, until later. Correct was 38...fxg5! 39 ♕xg5 ♘f6 when both 40 ♘e5 ♕d6 and 40 ♖g2 ♔f8 leave Black the better placed. The essence of Black's defence in this case is the correctly-timed blockade of White's f-pawn by ...♘f6, without which there would be no answer to a breakthrough by White on that critical square (f6).

39 ♖g2!

The move which decides the game, since it threatens both gxf6 and ♘xf6+.

39...♔h8

After 39...fxg5 40 ♕xg5, 40...♘f6 is no longer feasible, and accordingly the breakthrough by f6 wins in all variations.

40 gxf6 gxf6?!

This loses quickly. A better resistance and even some chances of a draw were offered by the continuation 40...♘xf6 41 ♘e5 ♕e8 42 ♘xb3 ♖xb3 43 ♘g6+ ♔g8 44 ♘xe7+ ♕xe7 45 ♕g3.

41 ♘xb3 ♖xb3 *(D)*

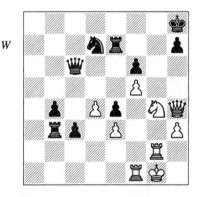

42 ♘h6! ♖g7 43 ♖xg7 ♔xg7 44 ♕g3+! ♔xh6 45 ♔h1 ♕d5
45...c2 would also be met by 46 ♖g1.

46 Rg1 Wxf5 47 Wh4+ Wh5 48 Wf4+ Wg5 49 Rxg5 fxg5 50 Wd6+ ⌾h5 51 Wxd7 c2

Black allows himself to be mated, but after 51...Rb1+ 52 ⌾g2 Rb2+ 53 ⌾g3 ⌾g6 Black must lose eventually.

52 Wxh7#

This famous game has its place in chess literature as a classic example of an attack on the castled king which is stronger than the counterattack on the queenside. But in the light of my annotations, which differ fundamentally from all annotations hitherto, from Tarrasch to Réti, this game takes on a new appearance. Black's numerous opportunities to strengthen his game at various stages point rather to the equal balance between the attack and the indirect defence, and it was only the decisive mistake on the thirty-eighth move which swung the balance in White's favour. This view of the game also qualifies it as a good example of the importance of indirect defence against an attack on the castled king, and of the part played by operations with wing pawns in particular.

Indirect defence by means of advancing a pawn majority on the queenside was at one time held in high esteem and was more often practised than nowadays; the real reason for this is that we have acquired a better understanding of the centre and the technique of centralization, thanks to the hypermodern school. It is clear that the player who has a majority on the wing, when the material is equally balanced, will usually not have the greater influence or pressure in the centre, nor will he have the necessary conditions for a central action. A majority on the wing is created at the expense of the centre and means giving up lateral pressure on the centre, and that is the sort of strategy which the masters of today are reluctant to adopt. The struggle for the centre is a characteristic feature of all present-day openings, and the centralization of the pieces is an important theme of modern positional play; as a result, a majority on the wing appears nowadays more as a by-product of a particular strategy than its primary aim (for example, in the Exchange Variation of the Grünfeld Defence).

Thus, concern for the centre is driving majority actions out of use, and it should be added that an indirect defence against an attack on the castled king is more effective and holds better prospects of success in the form of a central action than one using wing pawns. This is shown by the following general considerations.

1) Advancing pawns on the opposite wing is a slow process, since, as a rule, the whole pawn chain must move forward for a passed pawn to be created.

2) The attacker knows which pawn is going to be dangerous and so can arrange to contain it economically, either by preparing to block the pawn with a

piece or by planning ahead to sacrifice a piece for the passed pawn, which in fact means surrendering the piece in return for a considerable number of tempi.

3) Advancing pawns on the opposite wing is an action which is furthest in distance from the threatened castled position and which is the hardest to combine with, or transform into, direct defence.

These are the general deficiencies of indirect defence using the wing pawns, and they limit its use mainly to the following cases:

a) The attack on the castled king develops slowly, demanding a regrouping or perhaps a series of pawn moves; it does not lead to a forced mate, for a defence can be bought at the price of material;

b) Direct defence is on the whole sufficient but it may be usefully combined with something else; in other words, the defender has some tempi left over which he can devote to alternative actions, including those using the wing pawns.

These, then, are the general factors which speak for, or against, indirect defence by means of the wing pawns, but in this case too the reader must overcome any inclination to think merely in terms of formulae, since the essence of a formula often consists of 'exceptions which prove the rule'.

Defence by counterattack

Venturing further into the broad field of indirect defence, we next concern ourselves with a series of cases in which methods other than a pawn thrust in the centre are used. We shall examine five examples from the point of view of the following factors:

1) The area of the counterattack and the conditions underlying it.

2) The part played by the material situation in relation to positional considerations.

3) The interweaving of indirect defence with direct and the switching from one to the other.

4) The dependence of timing and the form of defence on the state of the attacker's commitments.

The following position is from the game K.Treybal-H.Wolf, Teplitz-Schönau 1922. Black, to move, has the task of organizing a defence against an attack on his king position. A single glance is enough to show that he has no move to make in the way of direct defence. The only move in keeping with that would be 1...♔h7, but that would simply make White's attack easier. For example, White will in any case play ♖f4-h4 and then (with the king on h7) the square g5 will be available for his queen, besides which there is a threat of ♗c1 followed by ♖xh6

with check. Therefore, indirect defence must be used to obstruct White's plan to gain control of h6. With that aim, only an action on the queenside can be considered, for Black cannot achieve anything in the centre.

1...a5 2 ♖f4 a4 3 ♖af1 axb3 4 axb3 ♖a2!

Very well played! Black first of all makes it difficult for White to redeploy his queen and bishop, a course which is necessary for an attack on h6; moreover, there is an eventual threat of ...♖xb2 followed by ...♘d3.

5 ♖h4 ♖b8

Suddenly Black threatens 6...♘xc4; he has worked up a definite counterattack, and White is still quite a long way from having any serious threats on the kingside.

6 ♕c3

Black has succeeded in persuading White's queen to leave the attacking diagonal. 6 ♖xh6 would not have worked because of 6...♖xb2 7 ♕g5 ♕g4 and White has nothing. An interesting possibility was 6 ♘f5, which probably leads to a draw; objectively, this would not have been at all bad, for Black could have gained some advantage after White's actual move. The analysis runs 6 ♘f5 gxf5 (6...♖xb2 fails against 7 ♘xh6+ ♗xh6 8 ♕xh6) 7 ♖xh6 ♖xb2 8 ♕g5+ ♘g6 9 ♖xg6+ fxg6 10 ♕xg6+ ♔h8 11 ♖f4 (this attempt does not give more than perpetual check, which White would also obtain by 11 ♕h5+) 11...♖b1+ 12 ♔f2 ♖b2+ 13 ♔e1 ♖b1+ (if 13...♕xe4+ 14 ♖xe4 fxe4, White wins by 15 f7!) 14 ♔d2 ♖b2+ 15 ♔c1 ♖b1+! 16 ♔xb1 ♖xb3+ 17 ♔a2 ♖b2+[1] 18 ♔a3 (or 18 ♔xb2 ♕e5+ and 19...♕xf4) 18...♖a2+, and White's king cannot escape from perpetual check.

6...♘xc4?

---

1   Black can play for a win by 17...♖h3! since after 18 gxh3 ♕xc4+ he can win the rook on f4 with a series of checks.

The wrong turning, since White now plays ♗c1 with gain of tempo, placing the bishop on the diagonal where it really belongs. The correct continuation of the defence consisted in giving, not taking, material, e.g. 6...♖xb2! 7 ♕xb2 ♘xc4 8 ♕c3 (or 8 ♕c1 ♘e5 9 ♖xh6 ♖xb3 after which both 10 ♕g5 ♕g4 and 10 ♖f5 ♘g4 are in Black's favour) 8...♘e5 9 ♖b1 c4 10 b4 ♕xf6 11 ♖h3 ♗g7 and Black has the better prospects. Wolf, of course, was not the master to decide on 'giving' when he could 'take'. His saying was: 'Why should I sacrifice when nobody sacrifices for me!?' But the consistent implementation of a plan with a sound positional basis often demands sacrificial conceptions, as in the analysis above, which is both typical and instructive. We can see here how an element of direct defence is also involved – the elimination of White's bishop, which plays an essential part in his mating plans. White's attack then flags, whereupon Black takes some pawns, centralizes his position, and brands White's rook on h4 as misplaced; the defence welds the various elements of the position into a single whole.

7 ♗c1 *(D)*

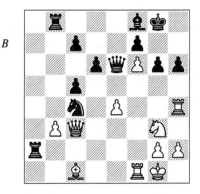

B

7...♘e5

In sharp positions like this everything should be considered, including moves like 7...g5. The latter represents a simultaneous combination of direct and indirect defence: Black drives back the rook, blocks the diagonal of the enemy bishop, and frees the square g6 for the knight – all direct elements – while the indirect appears in certain continuations where Black's g-pawn takes part in a counterattack. Let us look at some ways in which White can go astray after 7...g5. First of all, the 'natural' move 8 ♖h5? is unsatisfactory because of 8...♘e5 9 ♗xg5 (after 9 ♘f5 ♘g4! the attack on the e-pawn gains a tempo) 9...♖xb3 10 ♕c1 ♖xg3 11 hxg3 ♕g4.

Nor is 8 ♘f5? gxh4 9 ♕f3 ♘e5 10 ♕h5 good, e.g. 10...♖xb3 11 ♘xh6+ (or 11 ♗xh6 ♖bb2!) 11...♗xh6 12 ♕xh6 ♕g4 when the clearing of the g-file enables Black to cover the focal-point at g7. The g-pawn takes an active role in the continuation 8 ♖h3 g4 9 bxc4 gxh3 when the threat of ...♖xg2+ costs White a decisive tempo.

The correct response to 7...g5 is 8 ♖h3! g4 (if 8...♘e5 then 9 ♘f5 after which the b-pawn is protected) and now 9 ♖h5! (instead of 9 bxc4 as above) 9...♘e5 10 ♗xh6 ♗xh6 (if 10...♖xb3 then 11 ♕c1 wins) 11 ♖xh6 ♖xb3 12 ♕c1 ♘g6 13 ♖h8+ ♘xh8 14 ♕h6 and White wins. Here White's play against the focal-point g7 is unhindered, since g4 is blocked by Black's own pawn.

8 ♗xh6 ♗xh6?

At the very least, this is a tactical mistake; for, by 8...♖xb3 Black could have presented White with an exceptionally difficult problem and involved him in considerable risk if he persisted in playing for a win. The text move, however, gives White no difficulties and allows him to win easily.

Grünfeld and Becker, the authors of the tournament book – one of the best in the literature of the game – rightly censure Black's move, but their analysis of the continuation 8...♖xb3! is not correct. In the variation which they conclude with a drawn ending Black can eventually win, while in that which they consider won for Black the position can be resolved in White's favour. These lines together with my analysis will interest the reader as general studies of the middlegame. Here is a diagram after the alternative 8...♖xb3! *(D)*.

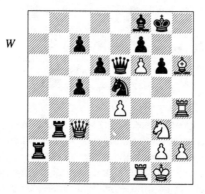

Grünfeld and Becker reach a draw as follows: 9 ♗xf8 g5! (otherwise ♗g7 and mate) 10 ♖h5 ♖xc3 11 ♗g7 ♘g6 12 ♘f5. In their opinion Black now has no defence against perpetual check by ♘h6+. In fact, Black still has something to say and can play 12...♖xg2+! 13 ♔h1 (if 13 ♔xg2 then 13...♕xe4+ and Black has no trouble picking up the rook on h5) 13...♖xh2+ 14 ♔xh2 (or 14 ♖xh2 ♕xe4+ followed by ...♘h4) 14...♕e5+ 15 ♔g1 ♖g3+ 16 ♔h2 (16 ♘xg3 ♕xg3+ 17 ♔h1 ♕g4 followed by ...♕xe4+, ...c4, etc.) 16...♖f3+ 17 ♔g1 (or 17 ♔g2 ♖xf5 18 exf5 ♕e2+ 19 ♖f2 ♘f4+) 17...♖xf1+ 18 ♔xf1 ♕f4+ and White loses either his rook or his knight.

The second line given by the same commentators aims to show that 8...♖xb3! cannot be answered by 9 ♕c1 because of 9...♘g4 10 ♗xf8 ♖bb2 11 ♗g7 ♖xg2+ 12 ♔h1 ♖xh2+ 13 ♖xh2 ♖xh2+ 14 ♔g1 ♕a2 and Black wins. But if White, instead of 11 ♗g7?, plays 11 ♕xb2! ♖xb2 12 ♗g7 then Black loses. Correct after 9 ♕c1 is at once 9...♖bb2 whereupon 10 ♗xf8 does not work because of 10...♖xg2+ 11 ♔h1 ♘g4!.

Now here is my analysis. First of all, let me explain why 9 ♗xf8? g5! 10 ♕c1, not mentioned by the commentators, does not work. Black replies 10...gxh4 and then 11 ♕h6 is useless on account of 11...♕g4 while 11 ♕g5+ fails against 11...♔xf8 12 ♘f5 ♖bb2! when White's attack is halted – he cannot get any further than ♕h6+ and ♘g7+ because of the threat of mate that faces him on g2 and h2. A third possibility is 11 ♘f5 ♖bb2! 12 ♘e7+ ♕xe7 13 ♕g5+ (if 13 ♕xb2 then 13...♕e6) 13...♔xf8 14 fxe7+ ♔e8 when it can be seen that White has achieved nothing. In return for his rooks Black will win the queen and the pawns on g2 and e7, thus obtaining an advantage in the ending.

The above diagram is a hard nut to crack, and the way to attempt it is as follows: 9 ♕c1! ♖bb2! 10 ♕xb2! ♖xb2 11 ♗xf8 g5 12 ♖h5 ♘g6 13 ♗g7. Now White has the same position as in the first line above but with a tempo less and a rook more. He wins in the following variations:

1) 13...c4 14 ♘f5 ♖xg2+ (otherwise ♘e7+ wins) 15 ♔xg2[1] ♕xe4+ 16 ♔g3 ♕e5+ 17 ♔h3 g4+ (if 17...♕c3+ the king escapes from the checks on g1) 18 ♔g2 ♕b2+ 19 ♔g1 ♕b6+ 20 ♖f2! ♕b1+ 21 ♔g2 ♕e4+ 22 ♔g3 ♕d3+ 23 ♔xg4 ♕d1+ (or 23...♘e5+ 24 ♔g5 ♘f3+ 25 ♔h6) 24 ♖f3! ♘e5+ 25 ♔g5 ♘xf3+ 26 ♔f4 ♕d2+ 27 ♘e3 ♕d4+ 28 ♔xf3 and White wins.

2) 13...♕g4 14 ♖h6 ♖b8 (parrying the threat of ♖xg6) 15 ♖e1 ♖e8 16 ♘f5 ♖xe4 (otherwise ♖xg6) 17 ♘e7+ ♖xe7 18 fxe7 ♘xe7 19 ♗f6 and White wins.

3) 13...♖b8 14 ♘f5 ♖e8 (if 14...♕xe4, then a round of checks by the knight – ♘h6+, ♘xf7+, ♘h6+, ♘f5+ – and finally f7+ leads to the win of the queen) 15 ♘h6+ ♔h7 16 ♘xf7+ ♔g8 17 ♘xg5 ♕e5 18 h4 ♖a8 (or 18...♖f8 19 f7+ ♔xg7 20 ♖h7#) 19 ♖h6 ♖a1 20 f7+ ♔xg7 21 ♖xg6+ ♔xg6 22 f8♕ and again White wins.

Of Black's other moves the most difficult to deal with is 13...♕c4, threatening 14...♕c2. White is then able to draw by 14 ♖a1 ♖a2 15 ♖b1 ♖b2[1] 16 ♖a1 etc., but can he also win? This may be left to the reader to examine; we shall return to the game, where Black played 8...♗xh6? *(D)*.

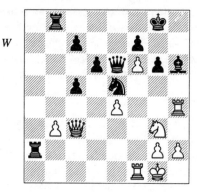

9 ♖xh6 ♕xb3

Black also loses after 9...♖xb3 10 ♕c1 ♘g4 11 ♕g5! ♖bb2 12 ♖xg6+.

10 ♕c1

Now the main defect in Black's eighth move can be seen: White is at once threatening 11 ♖h8+.

10...♘g4 11 ♘f5! ♖e8 12 ♖h4 ♖xe4 13 ♘e7+ ♖xe7 14 fxe7 ♖e2 15 ♖xg4 ♕e3+ 16 ♕xe3 ♖xe3 17 ♖xg6+! ♔h7 18 ♖gf6 1-0

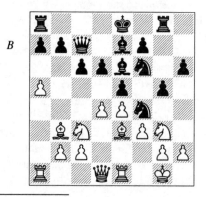

---

1   In this line 15...♕d4+ 16 ♔h1 ♖a1 wins for Black – indeed, White seems to be struggling after 13...♕c4.

This position, from the game Yates-Marco, The Hague 1921, arose after the moves **1 e4 e5 2 ᐁf3 d6 3 d4 ᐁd7 4 ♗c4 c6 5 ᐁc3 ♗e7 6 0-0 h6 7 ♗e3 ᐁgf6 8 ♗b3 ♛c7 9 ᐁd2 g5 10 a4 ᐁf8 11 a5 ᐁg6 12 ♖e1 ᐁf4 13 f3 ♖g8 14 ᐁf1 ♗e6 15 ᐁg3** *(D)*. Black has played his favourite Hanham Variation of the Philidor, obtaining the advantage and an attack on the white king; this is the natural result of White's extravagant treatment of the opening (unmotivated moves a5 and f3 at an earlier stage of the game). Marco (Black), to move, spoils his position by provoking d5 which he does in order to continue with a sacrifice in the old 'paprika style'.

15...♛d7?

Black had excellent prospects of carrying out an attack using his pawns (15...g4 or 15...h5) without any material risk, but he has seen the chance of a bishop sacrifice on h3 with play against the focal-point g2 and cannot resist it.

16 d5

White rightly falls in with Black's intentions and forces him to continue with ...♗h3.

16...♗h3 *(D)*

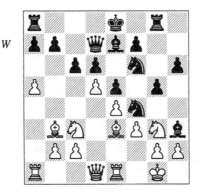

17 gxh3?

White decides to accept the sacrifice and to employ direct defence against the attack on his king. With good play he could certainly have come through by this method, but the right way to refute the offer is not by accepting it but by applying indirect defence in the shape of a counterattack on the queenside. After d5 there is also some point to the earlier advance a5, since an attack can now be made on Black's pawn chain at b7 and c6, as a result of which White obtains the better pawn structure and an advantage in space on the queenside and also frees the square d5 for a centralized piece. The analysis runs **17 a6!** ᐁxg2 (if 17...♗xg2 then 18 axb7 ♕xb7 19 ♗a4 when White wins the exchange and gains space, while if Black advances his b-pawn, then 18 dxc6 ♕c8 represents a strengthening of White's position, after which the conditions for accepting the sacrifice are extremely good) 18 axb7 ♕xb7 19 dxc6 (if 19 ♗a4 as mentioned by Tartakower in *The Hypermodern Game*, Black would reply 19...♘xe3 20 ♖xe3 ♗d7) 19...♕c8 20 ♘d5! (a typical example of play on the principle that the most important feature of the position, in this case White's pressure on the queenside, takes priority; it should be observed that in pursuing this policy White must also be prepared to lose the exchange) 20...♘xe1 (it might seem more consistent for Black not to make this capture but to press on with his assault; in fact, the chief attacking moves do not work, e.g. 20...h5 21 ♘xf6+ and 22 ♘xh5, 20...g4 21 ♘xe7 ♔xe7 22 ♘f5+ and White stands better and finally 20...♘xd5 21 ♗xd5 after which 21...♕c7, to prevent the advance of the c-pawn, is strongly answered by 22 b4) 21 ♕xe1 ♗e6 (Black must abandon his attack on the king and defend himself in the centre and on the queenside; the decisive factor is that 21...g4 is useless because of 22 f4) 22 ♕a5 ♗xd5 23 ♗xd5 ♘xd5 24 ♕xd5 ♕e6 (otherwise c7!) 25 b4! and White has an overwhelming game.

The chief feature of this line is the complete absence of direct defence. White gives up the pawn on g2 and the exchange, which effectively blunts Black's attack, while his excellently-founded action on the queenside gains in power with every move.

17...♕xh3 *(D)*

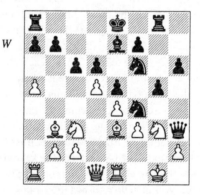

18 ♕d2?

After this excessively passive move Black has the better chances. In such positions it is often important to oppose the attacker's queen with one's own – in this case on f1. It was with this aim that Maroczy proposed 18 ♖e2! g4 19 ♕f1.

Naturally, White gladly offers the exchange in order to weaken the attack by giving back some material while at the same time still retaining some material advantage. Thus after 19...gxf3 20 ♛xf3 ♘xe2+ 21 ♘xe2 Black's only move to prevent White from consolidating completely is 21...♘g4, but then White immediately gets the chance to counterattack, i.e. 22 dxc6! ♛xh2+ 23 ♚f1 ♘xe3+ 24 ♛xe3. The further sharpening of the attack by 24...♗h4 would be dangerous because of 25 cxb7.

We shall examine two more variations arising out of 19...gxf3 20 ♛xf3 *(D)*:

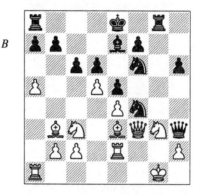

B

1) 20...♘6h5 21 ♗xf4! exf4 22 dxc6. Black cannot win a piece now, since 22...fxg3? permits the white queen to capture on f7, while 22...♘xg3 can be met by 23 ♖g2. Black must be modest and play 22...bxc6, allowing White to consolidate by 23 ♖g2. The risk involved in 22...0-0-0 is illustrated by the continuation 23 ♘d5! ♘xg3 (23...fxg3 24 ♛f5+ ♛xf5 25 ♘xe7+ ♚b8 26 exf5 favours White) 24 ♘xe7+ ♚b8 25 ♖g2 ♘e2+ 26 ♛xe2 f3 27 c7+ ♚xc7 28 ♘d5+ ♚b8 29 ♘f4!, with a characteristic switch from indirect to direct defence; after 29...♖xg2+ 30 ♛xg2 White captures the pawn on f3 and remains the better placed[1]!.

2) 20...♖g4 (covering the square f4, lessening the danger on f7, and preparing ...h5-h4) 21 a6! (logically switching to the positional motif on the queenside and thus exploiting the slower tempo of Black's attack betrayed by the move ...♖g4) 21...b6 (after 21...0-0-0? 22 axb7+ ♚b8 23 dxc6 Black would be in great difficulties) 22 dxc6 h5 23 ♚h1! (having made good his superiority on the queen's wing, White goes over to direct defence; he returns the extra piece in order to simplify into a favourable ending) 23...h4 (Black would recover less material by 23...♘xe2 24 ♘cxe2, since then 24...h4 is met by 25 ♛f1, when White clarifies the position

---

1   Actually this just wins for White.

at the further expense of his e-pawn[1]) 24 ♗xf4 exf4 (the alternative 24...♖xf4 25 ♕g2 is equally in White's favour) 25 ♕f1 ♖xg3 26 ♕xh3 ♖xh3 27 ♔g2 f3+ 28 ♔xh3 fxe2 29 ♖e1 with a clear advantage to White.

Now we return to the game after 18 ♕d2 *(D)*.

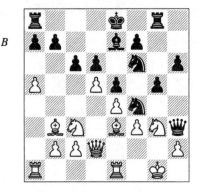

18...♘6h5?

Commentators have praised this move, which, however, could have allowed White to escape. Correct was 18...h5! which excludes the possibility of simplification and wins back the piece without giving up the attack[2].

19 ♕f2?

White misses the chance to liquidate the position which Maroczy pointed out: 19 ♘xh5! ♕xf3 20 ♗xf4 (forced) 20...gxf4+ 21 ♘g3 fxg3 22 h3! and Black's attack loses its power. He must be satisfied with winning the exchange by 22...♕f2+ 23 ♕xf2 gxf2+ 24 ♔xf2 ♗h4+ 25 ♔e2 ♗xe1 26 ♖xe1 with a probable draw.

19...g4 20 ♔h1

Interesting is 20 ♘xh5 ♘xh5 21 ♕g2 (or 21 f4 g3!) 21...gxf3! 22 ♕xg8+ ♔d7 when White's queen has not a single square on the g-file from which to defend g2.

20...gxf3 21 ♖g1 ♗h4 22 ♗xf4 exf4 23 ♘xh5 ♗xf2 24 ♖xg8+ ♔e7 25 ♘xf4 ♕h4 26 ♖g7

---

1   This is still not totally clear after 25...♖xg3 26 ♘xg3 ♕g4, but White can improve earlier by 25 ♘g1! ♖xg3 26 ♕xg3 with an instant win.

2   I do not see how this wins back the piece. White can play (amongst other promising ideas) 19 ♗c4 h4 20 ♗f1 ♕d7 21 dxc6 bxc6 22 ♘f5, and Black has nothing to show for his sacrifice.

Or 26 ♖xa8 ♗g3 27 h3 ♗xf4.

26...♔f8 27 ♖xf7+ ♔xf7 28 dxc6+ ♔g7 29 ♘e6+ ♔h8 30 ♘d5 bxc6 0-1

This game won the Second Brilliancy Prize.

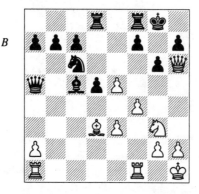

In this position Black is to move and must discover a defence against White's two threats of ♘h5 and ♘f5. It is fairly easy to reach the conclusion that there is not a large choice; only two moves are worth considering – 1...f5 and 1...♔h8. The first appears more natural than the second, but in fact only the second provides an adequate defence. If 1...f5?, White replies 2 ♗xf5!, after which 2...♖xf5 does not work because of 3 ♘xf5 gxf5 4 ♕g5+ ♔f7 5 ♕f6+ ♔e8 (or 5...♔g8 6 ♖f3) 6 e6, and Black loses; nor is 2...gxf5 satisfactory, e.g. 3 ♘h5 ♖d7 4 e6, when the rook is lost, since if 4...♖e7, then 5 ♖f3 is decisive; the one course remaining, therefore, is to decline the sacrifice by 2...♘e7, but then White plays 3 ♗d3, threatening f5 as well as ♘h5.

1...f5? is weak because it 'opens up the position', with the result that White's queen becomes even more effective and is always creating new threats. On the other hand, 1...♔h8, which is also primarily a form of direct defence, should enable Black, provided he can survive the immediate pressure, to make good his material advantage and territorial superiority on the queenside. Let us now examine this second move.

1...♔h8! 2 ♘f5

After 2 ♘h5 ♖g8 3 ♘f6 (otherwise 3...♗f8!) 3...♖g7 4 ♖f3 Black can just defend himself in time by 4...♕c3 5 ♖d1 ♗e7 and if 6 ♖h3, then 6...♗xf6.

2...♖g8 3 ♖f3 gxf5

Forced, since even 3...♗f8 does not prevent White from sacrificing his queen on h7 and mating with the rook on the h-file.

4 ♖h3 ♖g7 5 ♗xf5 *(D)*

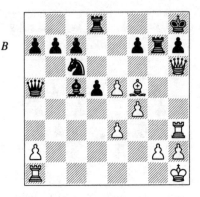

Now White threatens 6 ♗xh7 and 7 ♗g6+ followed by mate with the queen at h8, but Black is a knight up at this stage, so the possibility of defence by giving back material arises. As a result of this increase in his resources, Black's defence turns suddenly from direct to indirect, only in the end to return again, after the 'detour', to direct defence.

5...♕d2! 6 g3

If 6 ♖g3, then 6...♖dg8; anything else is answered by the same manoeuvre as now follows.

6...♗xe3 7 ♗xh7 ♗xf4! 8 ♕h5

Or 8 ♕xf4 ♕xf4 9 ♗f5+ ♔g8 10 gxf4 ♘d4 11 ♗d3 c5, when Black stands better.

8...♗h6 9 ♗f5 ♘xe5 10 ♕xh6+ ♕xh6 11 ♖xh6+ ♔g8 and Black has a winning advantage[1].

In this example too we observe how a successful defence is flexible and unites a diversity of elements. Direct and indirect defence alternate, the attacker's

---

1   Although Vuković is correct with his general principles, the above example is hardly a convincing demonstration; whatever Black plays, he cannot hope to defend the position with most of his pieces stuck far away on the queenside. After 1...♔h8 White can play 2 f5! ♘xe5 3 ♘h5 ♖g8 4 fxg6 fxg6 5 ♕g5! ♘d7 6 ♖f7 with a decisive attack, for example 6...♕c3 7 ♖d1 ♖df8 8 ♖xd7 ♕xd3 9 ♕e5+ and mates. Moreover, even one of Vuković's own lines favours White: after 2 ♘h5 ♖g8 3 ♘f6 ♖g7 4 ♖f3 ♕c3 5 ♖d1 ♗e7 White need not allow the capture on f6 but can simply play 6 ♕h4! threatening 7 ♖h3. Black has nothing better than 6...h5 7 ♕g5 ♗xf6 8 exf6 ♖h7 9 f5 ♕e5, but after 10 h4! he is clearly in serious trouble as his rook on h7 is totally out of play.

sacrifice provokes a counter-sacrifice from the defender, and in the end the basic soundness of Black's position proves itself.

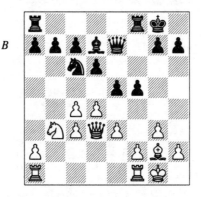

This position is from the game Rossolimo-Pachman, Hilversum 1947. It is Black's move; he has a promising game and ought really to continue along positional lines, e.g. 1...a5 2 a4 e4 3 ♕e2 b6, etc. Instead, he decides to 'invest his advantage in an attack on the king', though the conditions for this are not particularly suitable.

1...f4!? 2 exf4 exf4 3 c5!

Black opened his attack at the cost of his advantage in the centre. Now White, by ridding himself of his doubled pawns, eliminates the last element of Black's positional superiority, with the result that the latter has only his kingside attack left.

3...♕f7 4 ♗e4

As a general rule, the fianchettoed bishop protecting the castled position should not be touched, but here it is a question of gaining a tempo in order to play cxd6 before ♘d2. If at once 4 cxd6, Black replies 4...f3, attacking the bishop on g2.

4...♕h5

If 4...f3, White is not obliged to go in for the double-edged 5 ♗xh7+. He also has 5 cxd6 cxd6 6 ♘d2 ♗g4 7 ♕c4, forcing the exchange of queens.

5 cxd6 cxd6

Black's position is not strong enough for the uncompromising 5...f3 6 ♘d2 ♗g4. White would continue 7 ♖ab1, not allowing his opponent to escape from his material commitments; at the same time, he has a direct defence at hand in the shape of an attack on Black's queen by ♖b5. After, for instance, 7...♖f6 8 ♖xb7 Black's obligations are too great in proportion to the force of his attack.

Consequently, if 8...♖h6, White can permit himself 9 h4, a weakening which does not entail danger, since 9...g5 can be countered by 10 ♖b5. If instead 8...♕h3, then 9 ♘xf3 ♗xf3 (otherwise ♘h4 and ♗g2) 10 ♗xf3 ♖h6 11 ♖e1 leads to a win for White.

6 ♘d2

Now ...f3 is no longer possible.

6...♖f6 7 ♗f3 ♗g4 *(D)*

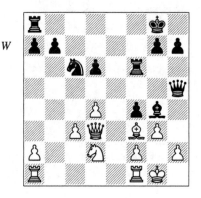

8 ♗xg4?

This exchange involves the loss of a tempo. White should have switched at once to a counterattack on the queenside, where he is the better placed, for example 8 ♖ab1! ♖h6 9 h4. Then, as we saw above, 9...g5 does not work, nor does 9...a6 because of 10 ♖xb7 g5 11 ♕c4+. Lastly, there is 9...d5 10 ♖xb7, and again 10...g5 is insufficient since after 11 ♗xd5+ ♔h8 12 ♗f7 ♗e2 13 ♕f5 White wins.

This is an example of how indirect defence, by clearing the ground on the queenside, makes it easier to revert to direct defence at the critical moment.

8...♕xg4 9 ♕f3 ♕h3 10 ♘e4?!

Here too 10 ♖ab1 would probably have been better.

10...♖h6 11 ♕g2 ♕h5 12 g4

After a period of timid play White aims to save himself by blocking the position.

12...♕h4 13 ♖ab1 ♖g6?!

This move and, in particular, the next, are not the best. Black should have played 13...♖e8 14 ♖fe1 (otherwise ...♖xe4) 14...♖e7, which would have enabled him to retain a slight advantage.

14 h3 h5?

Admittedly, this forces f3, which shuts the long diagonal to White's queen, but on the other hand, it undertakes an attacking obligation for which there is insufficient justification. The point is that Black is obliged to obtain some concrete advantage before his pawn at h5 becomes an anxiety and he is forced to strengthen White's position by exchanging it on g4. After this mistake White is the better placed and should in the end make his presence felt on the queenside.

15 f3 ♘a5 *(D)*

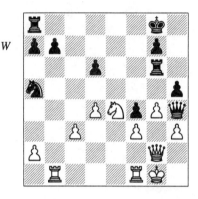

16 ♔h2

Though this does not mar White's position much, it would have been stronger to have played 16 ♖b5! ♘c4 17 ♕f2!, when Black's discomfort over the h-pawn is revealed in various ways. Thus, 17...♕xf2+ 18 ♖xf2 hxg4 19 fxg4 leaves two pawns *en prise*, one of which will obviously fall, while if 17...♕xh3, then 18 ♘g5 ♕g3+ (or 18...♖xg5 19 ♖xg5 hxg4 20 ♕h2 ♕xh2+ 21 ♔xh2 ♘e3[1] 22 ♖b1 gxf3 23 ♔g1 is good for White) 19 ♕xg3 fxg3 20 gxh5 a6 21 hxg6 axb5 22 ♖e1 and White is the better placed.

This line, wherein the union of direct and indirect defence is especially close, would have been a much better way of handling the position than the passive one actually chosen.

16...♘c4 17 ♖g1?

The decisive error. He should have played 17 ♕f2; then 17...♕e7 (17...♕xf2+ eventually loses a pawn) 18 gxh5 ♖h6 19 ♖g1 ♖xh5 20 ♖xb7! ♖xh3+ (or 20...♕xb7 21 ♘f6+) 21 ♔xh3 ♕xb7 22 ♕h4 leaves the advantage with White.

---

1   21...♘d2! leads to a rook and pawn ending which is winning for Black. White can improve earlier in this variation, but only to the extent of holding the balance. It is therefore doubtful if 16 ♖b5 was any stronger than the move played.

17...d5! 18 ♕e2

This loses material, but even the more stubborn 18 ♘c5 would not help much[1].

The deciding point here is that 18 ♕f2 does not work because of 18...♕xf2+ 19 ♘xf2 ♘d2!, and White loses the exchange.

18...hxg4 19 fxg4 ♖e6 20 ♕f2 ♕e7 21 ♖xb7 ♕xb7 22 ♘c5 ♕e7 23 ♘xe6 ♕xe6 24 ♕xf4 ♖f8 25 ♕g3 ♘d2 0-1

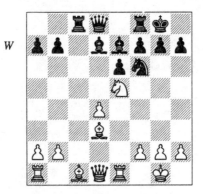

In this position White played:

1 ♖e3

He is clearly preparing to deploy the rook on g3 or h3 in order to attack the opposing king. Moves of this type belong on the whole to a rather more advanced stage of the game, when all the other pieces have been developed; they are also good in closed positions, where the opponent has no chance of counterattacking on an open file. However, even here this sortie on the part of the rook does not entail a very serious commitment for White, since the rook can turn back if it does not succeed in its mission.

1...♗c6 2 ♖g3 ♔h8

This parries the threat of 3 ♗h6 without weakening the castled position. 2...♗e4 3 ♗h6 ♗g6 is not so good because of 4 ♗xg6 hxg6 5 ♗e3, when White has attacking chances along the h-file.

3 ♗e3 ♗e4

Black is still applying prophylactic direct defence, since the conditions are not yet favourable for a counterattack; the exchange of light-squared bishops ought to lessen the force of the attack and at the same time clear the squares on the c-file for an eventual counterattack.

---

1   Actually White can resign after the reply 18...♘e3.

4 ♖h3?!

This threatens ♗xe4 followed by ♕h5, but it does not take sufficient account of temporal factors, with the result that the initiative now passes to Black. It would have been better to contest the c-file by 4 ♖c1.

4...♕d5 5 f3

The second logical step along a dangerous path: if the attack does not succeed, White will obviously suffer from the lack of communication between his rooks.

5...♗xd3 6 ♕xd3 *(D)*

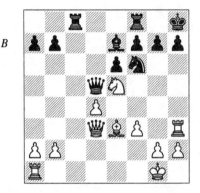

6...♗d6?

Up to here Black has correctly carried through a direct defence without weakening his pawn position, at the same time keeping his trumps in reserve (the c-file and control of the central post at d5). All this has been entirely appropriate to the fairly modest commitments taken on by White. Now he mistakenly supposes that the moment for a counterattack has arrived and makes a careless move, which White could have punished. The situation required direct defence to be continued for one more move, namely, by a renewed consolidation of the king's position by 6...♔g8. The reason is that Black may eventually be forced (by ♗g5) to play ...g6, after which ♗h6 would threaten the rook protecting f7. This point can be covered by the king after ...♔g8; consequently, Black may then use both his rooks on the c-file, while retaining a sufficient direct defence of the castled position by ...g6, if necessary. 6...h6 would be weaker on account of 7 g4, while 6...♖c7 is also incorrect, e.g. 7 ♗g5 h6 8 ♗f4 followed by g4.

7 ♗f4?

This throws away the chance of victory which was afforded by 7 ♘d7!. Owing to the threat of ♘xf6, Black loses the exchange. He is not helped by 7...♗xh2+ 8 ♖xh2! (not 8 ♔xh2? ♕xd7 9 ♗g5, since Black defends himself by 9...♕c7+ and

10...♛c2!) 8...♛xd7 9 ♗g5, when he either loses his knight or is mated. After the erroneous text move Black reasserts his advantage[1].

7...g6 8 g4

Black was threatening 8...♘h5; if 8 ♗h6, Black can of course reply 8...♗xe5.

8...♖c7 9 ♛e3 ♖fc8

Black's counterattack is growing rapidly in strength.

10 ♗g5 ♗xe5 11 dxe5 ♘g8

This is not a defensive move but a preparation for later action against the bishop by means of ...h6.

12 ♖g3

White concedes that his attack has been beaten off and tries to provide some resistance on the second rank. After 12 ♗f6+ ♘xf6 13 exf6 ♛c5 Black has the better ending.

12...♖c2 13 ♖g2 ♖xg2+ 14 ♔xg2 ♖c2+ 15 ♔g3 ♔g7! 16 ♗f4

The bishop is in danger! A sad fate for an unsuccessful attacker!

16...h6 17 h4 h5! 18 gxh5

Otherwise Black opens up White's king position by ...hxg4.

18...♘e7 19 ♛b3

19 h6+ ♔h7 would not help White either.

19...♘f5+ 20 ♔g4

He could have put up a better fight by 20 ♔h3, though even then Black's game is overwhelming.

20...♖c4 21 ♖e1

If 21 ♖d1, Black can play 21...♛xd1!.

21...♖xf4+ 22 ♔xf4 ♛d4+ 23 ♖e4 ♛f2! 24 ♔g5 ♛d2+ 25 ♖f4 ♛d8+ 26 ♔g4 ♛xh4#

If one leaves aside Black's unpunished mistake on the sixth move, then the whole course of the game is a good illustration of the relationship between the scale of the attacker's commitment and the method of defence employed. In the first phase White is not heavily committed by his rook's excursion and Black carries out a cautious direct defence without compromising his king position. He also maintains his hold on the c-file and the centre and eliminates one enemy unit – the light-squared bishop. With f3 and g4 White has already taken on greater obligations and so the time is ripe for indirect defence by means of an action along the c-file. As soon as another unit is eliminated (the knight on e5) it is all over with White's attack, whereas the counterattack grows from move to move, with

1   White has an even simpler win by 7 ♗g5!, after which Black must surrender a piece to avoid being mated on h7.

the lack of communication between the white rooks as the main cause of White's misfortune.

Defence by a central thrust

Attacks on the castled king in which the situation in the centre does not play a greater or lesser part are extremely rare, and as a rule it is precisely the soundness of the attacker's central formation which provides the basis for his attack. If this formation is not sound enough, the defender may use indirect defence against it in the first instance, aimed against the central formation's most vulnerable point.

Why is it that the centre is quite so important and sensitive in the particular case of an attack on the castled king? Because this kind of attack is one of the most complex and many-sided operations in chess, demanding the maximum collaboration of the pieces and a control over all possible consequences right up to the endgame. The centre is the most versatile area on the chessboard; it provides the best conditions for the full co-operation of the pieces – the basis on which positional play is founded and a prerequisite for a favourable endgame. Many-sidedness is the common property belonging to a sound attack on the castled king and to the centre, and this accounts for their mutual interdependence. Correct defence must also be many-sided – this we have seen in the last series of examples – and so each 'little crack in the centre' is more important to the defence than a variety of other weaknesses on the attacker's side.

In some of the examples so far we have seen the centre acting as the basis of an attack, while in others the defender has employed indirect defence based on destroying the attacker's centre by sacrificing a piece. We have noticed particularly the case where the defender strives to centralize his pieces – giving a position which as a rule makes possible a combination of direct defence and the indirect form on the other flank. It still remains for us to look at the case of defence by means of a pawn thrust against the attacker's central formation.

Before we pass on to examples, we must be clear that we are concerned here with a central thrust of a particular kind. For why should such a thrust be significant just at the critical phase of the attack? Why did the player not employ it earlier? The point is precisely that we are dealing here with cases where in fact the central thrust is *not useful before the crisis,* because the attacker has good replies to it. Only when he has increased his commitments and deployed his pieces for the attack does the moment for a thrust in the centre arise; and very often this occurs at a precise, given moment, not a move earlier or later.

The following famous game provides a good example of a defensive thrust in the centre.

Alekhine – Botvinnik
Nottingham, 1936
Sicilian Defence, Dragon Variation

1 e4 c5 2 ♘f3 d6 3 d4 cxd4 4 ♘xd4 ♘f6 5 ♘c3 g6 6 ♗e2 ♗g7 7 ♗e3 ♘c6 8 ♘b3 ♗e6 9 f4 0-0 10 g4 *(D)*

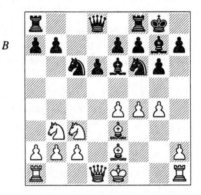

In choosing the pawn avalanche as a means of attacking the castled king at an early stage of the game, White has undertaken a considerable obligation to carry out his attack incisively to the end. For if Black has his say, his counterattack will find a mass of weak points, files, and diagonals in White's territory; if an endgame is reached, White's advanced pawns may easily become 'cannon-fodder'.

The moment of undertaking an obligation is also the moment of crisis, the moment for the thrust in the centre, which in the Sicilian as a whole, and in this position particularly, is unstable. Botvinnik perceived the correct moment and struck with 10...d5!.

10...d5!

Let us first see why ...d5 is correct at the precise moment when White plays g4. Let us suppose he has played 10 0-0 and examine the difference.

1) 10 0-0 d5? 11 e5 ♘e8 (11...d4 does not work, since White can simply take the pawn) 12 ♗f3 ♘c7 13 ♘c5, when Black must accept the weakening of his position by ♘xe6 fxe6, since 13...d4 is defeated by 14 ♗xc6.

2) 10 g4 d5! 11 e5 d4! (now this move is good) 12 ♘xd4 (or 12 exf6 ♗xf6, when Black wins the piece back with the better game) 12...♘xd4 13 ♗xd4 ♘xg4! 14 ♗xg4 ♗xg4, and Black preserves the material balance while gaining the advantage with regard to space, position, and time. There is undoubtedly a great difference between the first and second instances of ...d5.

Now the question arises why ...d5! is necessary in answer to 10 g4 and what happens if Black does not employ the defensive central thrust. This can be answered by citing the continuation of the game Foltys-Eliskases, Podebrad 1936, where in the same position Black met 10 g4 with 10...♘a5 aiming at the square c4. The continuation was 11 g5 ♘e8 12 ♗d4 (in the game Kan-Botvinnik, Moscow, 1936, 12 ♕d2 was played, but Foltys' move is better) 12...♖c8 13 h4 ♘c4 14 ♗xc4 ♖xc4 15 ♕d3 ♖c8 16 0-0-0 ♕d7 17 ♖d2 ♗g4 (to combat h5, but it surrenders d5 to the enemy knight) 18 ♘d5 b6 19 f5! (the avalanche begins to move; Black cannot take the pawn, since the eventual ♘xe7+ is decisive) 19...e6 20 ♗xg7 ♔xg7 21 f6+ ♔h8 22 ♘e7 ♖d8 23 ♘d4 ♕a4 24 ♔b1 ♘c7 25 h5 gxh5 26 ♖dh2 ♖d7 27 e5 (threatening 28 ♕xh7+ ♔xh7 29 ♖xh5+ mating) 27...♖xe7 28 ♖xh5 ♗xh5 29 ♖xh5 1-0

Now to return to the Nottingham game, in which Botvinnik did not allow himself to be smothered in this way.

11 f5

Clearly, this is the only alternative to 11 e5 which has already been analysed. If 11 exd5 ♘xd5 12 ♘xd5, Black would gladly exchange queens by 12...♕xd5, thus winning the b-pawn, to say nothing of the ending.

11...♗c8

Though the bishop has to withdraw, it is still aggressively placed as far as White's weak pawns at f5 and g4 are concerned.

12 exd5 ♘b4

There is to be no more talk of an attack on the king; the players are now concerned with a struggle for the centre pawn and the d5-square. If White holds out, he can expect success, but if Black overcomes the advancing pawn, the first player's prospects are poor.

13 d6? *(D)*

Whenever Alekhine made an unexpected move the world of commentators dutifully gave it one or two exclamation marks. This happened in the case of this move too, which abandons the struggle for the square d5 and, in fact, also risks losing the game.

A better line here is 13 ♗f3! gxf5 14 a3 fxg4 15 ♗g2. Suggested long ago by Dr Euwe, this was tried in the 2nd match game between Fischer and Reshevsky, New York 1961 when White secured an advantage after 15...♘a6 16 ♕d3 e6 17 0-0-0 ♘xd5 18 h3 g3 19 ♖hg1 ♕d6 20 ♗xd5 exd5 21 ♘xd5 ♔h8 22 ♗f4 ♕g6. Now Fischer played 23 ♕d2 but 23 ♕f3! seems to me to be even stronger.

13...♕xd6?

Alekhine's original assertion that 13...exd6! was impossible because of 14 a3 ♘c6 15 g5 ♘e8? 16 f6 etc., has remained unchallenged in chess literature. It is

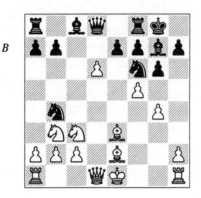

B

clear, however, that in this kind of situation it is worth looking to see whether the
sacrifice of a piece will work or not. Indeed, sound logic argues that it *must* work,
for the whole variation quoted by Alekhine so strengthens Black's position that
it is worth his giving up a knight for two pawns. Above all, White's position is
exposed as a result of his pawn advances: the thrust d6 leaves him without a
'backbone' in the centre; the reply ...exd6 opens up the e-file and the diagonal
d8-h4, while g5 relinquishes control of the c8-h3 diagonal to Black's c8-bishop.
The sacrifice can take a number of forms, but I shall give the one which seems
best to me. It runs 13...exd6! 14 a3 ♘c6 15 g5 ♖e8! with the following possibilities:

   1) 16 gxf6 ♖xe3 17 fxg7 (or 17 ♘d5 ♖e5 18 fxg7 ♕h4+ 19 ♔f1 ♗xf5! and
Black has a strong attack) 17...♕h4+ 18 ♔d2 (or 18 ♔f1 ♗xf5) 18...♕h6 19 ♔e1
and Black has excellent chances. He has no need to consent to a draw by
19...♕h4+ 20 ♔d2 ♕h6, but can play for a win with 19...♗xf5.

   2) 16 ♗d4 ♘xd4 17 ♘xd4 ♘g4 18 f6 ♗xf6 19 gxf6 ♕xf6 20 ♖f1 ♕h4+ 21
♔d2 ♘e3 22 ♘f3 ♕h6 and Black wins.

   3) 16 ♗f2 ♘e4 17 ♘xe4 (or 17 f6 ♘xc3 18 bxc3 ♗g4 19 ♘c1 ♕a5 20 ♗d4
♘xd4 21 ♕xd4 ♕xg5 22 fxg7 ♗xe2 23 ♘xe2 ♕g2 and Black wins) 17...♖xe4
18 f6 ♗g4 19 ♘c1 ♕a5+ 20 ♕d2 ♕e5 21 ♔f1 ♕xb2 22 ♗xg4 ♖xg4 23 ♖a2
♕b5+ 24 ♘e2 (alternatives are 24 ♘d3 ♕d5 and 24 ♕d3 ♕xg5) 24...♖e4 25
fxg7 ♖xe2 26 ♕xe2 ♕b1+ with advantage to Black.

   Botvinnik must certainly have prepared the move 10...d5! in his private analysis and so should have known all the important continuations. He had probably
not reckoned with 13 d6?, and when Alekhine confronted him with it, did not
venture on 13...exd6 but was bluffed into playing the drawing move 13...♕xd6?.
All great masters, from Homer onwards, have engaged in a little bluff at times.

   14 ♗c5 ♕f4!

14...♛xd1+ would have been weaker, e.g. 15 ♖xd1 ♞c6 (not 15...♞xc2+ 16 ♔d2!) and then White really can play 16 g5 ♞d7 17 f6.

15 ♖f1 ♛xh2

The breakthrough in the centre has allowed Black's queen to infiltrate into White's position, which was weakened by the move g4. Perpetual check is now already in sight.

16 ♗xb4 ♞xg4! 17 ♗xg4

An attempt to defend by 17 ♞e4 ♛h4+ 18 ♞f2? would result in unfortunate consequences, i.e. 18...♞e3 19 ♛d2 ♛xb4!, etc.

17...♛g3+ 18 ♖f2

Not 18 ♔d2 ♗h6+! nor 18 ♔e2 ♛xg4+ and 19...♛xb4.

18...♛g1+ 19 ♖f1 ♛g3+ 20 ♖f2 ♛g1+ ½-½

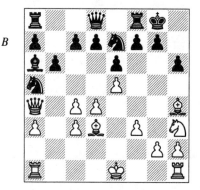

This position is from the game Kotov-Keres, Budapest Ct 1950. White's attack is extremely dangerous, his main threat being ♗b1 followed by ♛c2. It is Black's move, and the moment is clearly suitable for a thrust in the centre, where Black has not yet engaged his opponent. Keres decided on 1...d5?, but the correct choice was 1...d6!, as we shall see later. Let us first follow the course the game actually took.

1...d5? 2 ♗b1! (he surrenders both the pawn and the square c4 to Black and threatens ♛c2) **2...g5** (if 2...♗xc4, then 3 ♛c2 g6 4 ♛d2 ♔h7 5 ♗f6 ♞b3 6 ♞g5+ ♔g8 7 ♛f4 ♞xa1 8 ♛h4 h5 9 ♛xh5! followed by mate with the bishop on h7) **3 ♛c2 ♞g6 4 ♞f4! gxh4 5 ♞xg6 ♖e8 6 ♞h8! ♖e7 7 ♛h7+ ♔f8 8 f4 ♞xc4 9 f5 exf5 10 0-0 ♗c8 11 ♗xf5 ♗xf5 12 ♖xf5 ♔e8 13 ♖xf7 ♔d7 14 ♛f5+ ♔c6 15 ♛f6+ ♔d7 16 e6+ ♔c6** (or 16...♔d6 17 ♖xe7 ♛xe7 18 ♞f7+, winning the queen) **17 ♖xe7 ♛xh8 18 ♖xc7+ ♔b5** (or 18...♔xc7 19 ♛e7+ ♔b8 20 ♖f1) **19 ♛e7 a5 20 ♛d7+ ♔a6 21 ♖b1 1-0**

After 1...d5?, what is the outstanding feature of the play? Thanks to this move Black won the pawn on c4, but he neither obtained a proper counterattack nor did he harass White's 'captain in the centre', his pawn on e5. White's attack flowed on unchecked. So the move 1...d5? had only the form of a central thrust and, in essence, did not greatly alter the situation. *The true central thrust* here, which does in fact parry the attack, is 1...d6! – this has White's e-pawn as its target. Let us look at the variations that arise from this.

1...d6! *(D)*

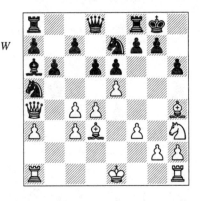

2 &b1

White could, admittedly, maintain his wedge in the centre by 2 f4, but Black would profit from this in two ways: f4 is closed to White's knight, while the continuation 2...&e8 3 &d1 &xc4 4 &b1 &f5 5 &c2 &c6 shows that Black also has a tempo more here, since the white queen has needed two moves to reach c2; the combination of these factors turns things in Black's favour.

2...dxe5 3 dxe5

Now 3 &c2 can of course be answered by 3...f5.

3...&e8 4 &c2 &g6 5 &f4

Or 5 0-0 &xc4 6 &e1 &b3 7 &a2 &d4! 8 cxd4 &xa2 9 &xa2 &xh4, when White is left with neither an attack nor any compensation for the exchange.

5...&xc4

The counterattack in the centre by ...d6 has attained its object: now White cannot sustain both his attack and his pawn on e5. He cannot achieve anything by 6 &h5 &cxe5 7 &f6 because of 7...&d3+ 8 &d1 &b5 9 a4 &xa4 10 &xa4 &xa4 and Black wins. If 6 &xg6 fxg6 7 &g3, Black plays 7...&d8, after which the threats of ...&d2 and ...&e3 guarantee him a material advantage. Should White take the g-pawn, then the exchange of queens leads to a won ending for Black.

The various continuations which result from the thrust 1...d6! provide good examples of the following themes:

1) the destruction of the centre when this centre is essential to the attack; in this case Black also gained space for a counterattack *via* the centre;

2) liquidating the position to bring about a favourable ending on the basis of the defender's strength in the centre.

Particular attention should be paid to those cases where the central thrust does not lead immediately to a decision but merely serves to maintain the tension in the centre. The next example illustrates the significance of this method of defence.

The diagram below is taken from the game Marshall-Burn, Paris 1900. The opening ran as follows: **1 d4 d5 2 c4 e6 3 ♘c3 ♘f6 4 ♗g5 ♗e7 5 e3 0-0 6 ♘f3 b6** (nowadays this is usually preceded by ...h6) **7 ♗d3 ♗b7 8 cxd5 exd5 9 ♗xf6** (the so-called Albin-Marshall Attack in the Queen's Gambit) **9...♗xf6 10 h4** (D)

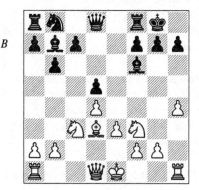

Here Burn timidly played **10...g6?**; this was followed by **11 h5 ♖e8 12 hxg6 hxg6 13 ♕c2 ♗g7?** (he should have played 13...♔g7 and if 14 0-0-0 then 14...♖h8) **14 ♗xg6 fxg6 15 ♕xg6 ♘d7 16 ♘g5 ♕f6 17 ♖h8+ ♔xh8 18 ♕h7#**.

In playing 10...g6? Burn probably wished to exclude the possibility of the classic bishop sacrifice; 10...h6? would not have been correct on account of 11 g4. But is the sacrifice really threatened? And has Black no better move to prevent it than one which weakens his king position? It is an interesting fact here that there is no threat of a sacrifice at all in the original position, yet, if Black plays 10...♖e8 or 10...♘d7, it is already, in practice anyway, rather dangerous, although it would still really be incorrect. Let us now play Black's most natural move, **10...c5!**, and see why the sacrifice is incorrect: 11 ♗xh7+ ♔xh7 12 ♘g5+

♔h6! (not 12...♔g6 because of 13 ♕d3+ nor 12...♔g8 on account of 13 ♕h5) 13
♘e2 (White's most incisive move) 13...g6 14 ♘f4 ♗xg5! (otherwise 15 h5 is
strong; 14...♔g7 fails against 15 ♘ge6+) 15 hxg5+ ♔g7 (if 15...♔xg5 then 16
♖h5+ affords good attacking prospects) 16 ♖h6 (had Black played ...♘d7 rather
than ...c5 on his tenth move, White would now have a chance with 16 ♕g4)
16...♖h8![1] (16...♕xg5 allows White to get some material back by 17 ♖xg6+) 17
♖xg6+ (or 17 ♕g4 ♖xh6 18 gxh6+ ♔h7) 17...fxg6 18 ♘e6+ ♔g8 19 ♘xd8
♖h1+ 20 ♔d2 ♖xd1+ 21 ♖xd1 ♗c8 22 dxc5 ♔f8! 23 c6 ♔e8 24 c7 ♘a6 with advantage to Black.

Accordingly, there was no threat of a sacrifice and Burn's 10...g6? simply
weakened the position without any necessity; this is always a much more dangerous thing than a forced weakening, as Tartakower so finely expressed in his
Hypermodern. (For compulsion creates antitheses and hence the possibility of
counterplay or compensation, while in the case of a voluntary weakening there is
only a naked weak spot without compensation!)

We shall now examine an example of play from the above diagram, where
Black correctly maintains the tension in the centre as a means of defence, while
avoiding as much as possible any weakening of his king position.

10...c5 11 g4

White sees that 11 ♕c2 g6 12 h5 can be answered by 12...♕e8 protecting g6
and threatening ...cxd4. If he then continues with 13 0-0-0 Black resolves the
central tension and starts an attack on the castled king (by 13...c4 14 ♗e2 b5,
etc.) which is stronger than White's. 11 ♕b1 meets a similar response – and
White can no longer castle queenside.

11...♖e8

Putting pressure on White's d-pawn; now 12 g5 fails against 12...♗xd4.

12 ♔f1

The pressure in the centre has made White resort to artificial castling.

12...g6 (D)

This weakening is necessary and well-founded here, and therefore not an error. Black perceives the prospects that his light-squared bishop has on the long
diagonal, and to open this up he needs to maintain the pressure against d4; to
achieve this his dark-squared bishop must also remain on its long diagonal, and
accordingly the square g7 must be vacated to provide against g5. Black is naturally not afraid of the 'hanging pawns' arising from dxc5; indeed he actually

---

1   16...♗c8 may be even stronger. By covering e6, Black eliminates the ♖xg6+
trick and can safely take on g5 next move.

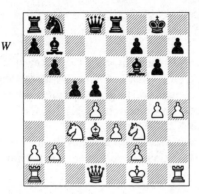

wants to induce them. In the presence of the two bishops such pawns are not usually considered a weakness in any case; here there is the additional matter of forcing open the light-squared diagonal.

The move 12...♞c6 is worth mentioning too; this also increases the pressure on the square d4, but it allows 13 g5 after which 13...cxd4 is insufficient on account of 14 gxf6 dxc3 15 ♗xh7+!. The classic bishop sacrifice, incorrect on the eleventh move and replaced by g4, has appeared in a correct form in an altered situation[1].

13 g5 ♗g7 14 h5 ♞c6 15 ♖h4

White holds his ground in the centre and at the same time prepares for an eventual doubling on the h-file.

15...♖c8

Not for the sake of the c-file, but to bring the rook to e7, where it will be equally well placed for attack and defence.

16 ♔g2 ♞b4

Black gives up the pressure on the centre temporarily in order to drive White's bishop back to b1, thus making it more difficult for the rook on a1 to go into action; this is important, since without both the rooks it is hard to carry out an attack on Black's 'artificially-fianchettoed' king position.

17 ♗b1

If 17 ♗b5 Black would be able to play 17...♖e4! aiming to eliminate the enemy rook, which is very annoying for him at h4. White could not accept the sacrifice, e.g. 18 ♞xe4 dxe4 19 ♞d2 cxd4!, etc.

17...♖c7 18 a3

---

1 Vuković offers no analysis to support his view that the sacrifice is correct in this position. It still looks unsound to me.

18 ♘b5 ♖ce7 19 ♘xa7? would be incorrect in view of 19...♗a6 20 a3 ♖xa7 21 axb4 ♗f1+.

18...♘c6 19 hxg6

White takes this pawn at a moment when 19...fxg6 would still be dangerous because of the possibility of 20 ♖xh7. If White waits any longer, hxg6 will lose its effect and the answer ...fxg6 will be good, opening up the f-file to Black's advantage. If 19 dxc5 Black has the powerful reply 19...♘e5!.

19...hxg6 20 ♘e2 ♖ce7 21 ♘f4 cxd4

The tension in the centre served Black well while he was defending. Now he turns to attack with the intention of conquering both the d-pawn and the square on which it stands.

22 exd4 *(D)*

If 22 ♘xd4, Black can either play 22...♘e5 or 22...♘xd4 23 exd4 ♖e1.

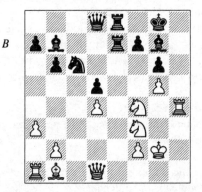

22...♖e4! 23 ♗xe4

If White does not accept the sacrifice, he loses his d-pawn.

23...dxe4 24 ♘h2

Or 24 ♘e5 ♘xd4 when Black is attacking the knight on e5 as well.

24...♘xd4 25 ♔g1 ♕xg5+ 26 ♖g4 ♕f5 27 ♕a4 ♗c6 28 ♕xa7 ♘f3+ and Black wins.

11 The phases of the attack on the castled king

The exposition up to this point may have appeared to some readers to have been a series of fragments, in which the various aspects of the attack on the castled king have been closely looked at but which still need to be combined into a whole. However, it was essential first to collect together as much knowledge as possible about the various elements of the attack on the castled king, then to get to know the main principles of defence against this attack, and only after that to begin to bring everything together in this chapter, which is devoted to the temporal aspect or phases of the attack on the castled king. The temporal aspect here is naturally a framework for the points we wish to make, which rest on the following basic theses, already fairly well elaborated in earlier chapters.

1) An attack on the castled king cannot be successfully carried out on the basis of the attacker's wishes or 'brilliance' alone, but the essential conditions for it must also be present.

2) These preconditions may be fulfilled to a greater or lesser degree, and the attacker's game must adapt itself accordingly.

3) The degree and type of these preconditions accurately determines the extent of the commitments which the attacker can undertake without harm; thus there is a logical and reciprocal relationship between preconditions and commitments, and by this the actual phase which the attack has reached can be recognized.

The proposition of these theses, which will be illustrated in later examples, leads us first of all to a brief discussion of preconditions and commitments.

Types of preconditions

Preconditions are naturally contained in the position itself, whether in the attacker's territory or his opponent's.

The attacker, for instance, may have his pieces strongly deployed in the vicinity of the enemy king position or aimed in that direction, and it may also be that the general mobility of his pieces or his advantage in space assists him in attacking.

At the same time, there must be some deficiencies in the *defender's* camp; the chief of these is the *vulnerability* of the king position, either through *weaknesses in the pawn structure* or because pieces are *misplaced* in relation to the castled position, being overburdened by obligations to cover squares on other parts of the board.

These and similar preconditions should generally be fulfilled at the *first or initial phase of the attack,* but it may also be that they can be *created* by force at this stage, e.g. by the provocation of weaknesses.

The second phase of an attack can follow a wide variety of courses. It may be a question of a quick attack leading to mate, usually by means of a sacrifice, and in this case it is naturally unimportant to talk of further preconditions. However, if the attack is slower or does not have an uncompromising character, the second phase is usually concerned with the creation of further conditions as guarantees of success. The following are among the most important operations at this stage: the provocation of further weaknesses; the exclusion of one's opponent's counterattack or its suppression; control of the centre; restraint against a central counter-thrust by one's opponent, and so on.

The third phase of an attack is of course characterized by the execution, either in the form of mate, of obtaining a decisive material advantage, or of being able to call off the actual attack on the king and obtain a positional advantage or favourable ending.

Types of commitment

To the above-mentioned types of preconditions necessary for an attack there also correspond various types of commitment which the attacker can, and indeed must, enter on, if he is going to attack.

The commitments which correspond to the *first phase* are, of course, minor ones, usually a question of tempi. A player, for instance, spends a tempo improving his prospects for an eventual attack, transferring a piece from one side of the board to the other or the like; admittedly, the degree of commitment involved is not great, but it can become significant if the attack on the king is never carried out. It is natural that contemporary masters, in an era of precise opening play, aim first of all at sound moves, which give nothing away to their opponents and constantly strengthen their general positional build-up; the result of play according to this recipe on both sides is that a drawn position is reached. It should also be said that Alekhine[1] knew how to instil a little aggressiveness into his moves even in the opening and create some conditions for attack with a minimum of commitments. This is precisely where his skill lay, and it is this which is lacking in many masters.

---

1   and Kasparov!

A somewhat greater degree of commitment is entailed in the *second phase*. It may be a question here of a sacrifice accompanied by considerable compensation, of the dislocation of a number of pieces, or, in particular, of the advance of the wing pawns, which as a rule represents a fairly far-reaching positional commitment. Still, in this phase too the sensible player aims to conduct his game with a minimum of commitments, unless he is undertaking an uncompromising mating attack that is certain to succeed. It is especially important that the attacker should avoid a pattern of thinking whereby an unclear attack is reckoned as part of his compensation. For instance, he may sacrifice a knight for two pawns and an 'attack'; when that 'attack' peters out, his reckoning naturally falls to the ground.

Assessment of preconditions and commitments

One of the attacker's most important tasks is assessing the extent to which the preconditions for an attack are present and the degree of commitment which may be incurred. The following positions provide examples of this task.

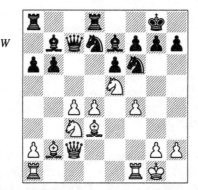

This position is from the game Botvinnik-Chekhover, Moscow 1935. It is White's move, and he has to decide on how to pursue what is already a promising initiative. He has the upper hand in the centre, a strong knight on e5, and well-placed bishops; all these factors together mean that he has some of the preconditions for an attack on the king, without yet having entered on any commitments. He can therefore be said to be on the threshold of the first phase and must consequently look for further moves which will prepare an attack, while committing himself as little as possible. Thus, it would clearly be out of the question to make a pawn advance with h3 and g4, since Black would then find it easy to parry the main threat, after which White would be left only with pawn weaknesses, to say nothing of the dangers which would arise on the diagonal a8-h1.

A slightly lesser degree of commitment would be entailed by White's manoeuvring his a1-rook to h3 via e1 and e3, but it can be shown that such a displacement of the rook would in fact be premature; Black could easily parry the threats involved and then himself prepare for the counter-thrust ...b5 (e.g. by ...♘f8 and ...♖ac8) thereby opening up the c-file, over which the white rook on h3 no longer has any influence. Because of this Botvinnik decided on a third plan, which involved the least degree of commitment; this consisted of transferring the c3-knight via d1 and f2 to h3 and thence on to g5. Admittedly, there is a definite commitment here too – in the shape of the number of tempi used; however, Black cannot really take advantage of this, and there is the additional point that the threat posed by the position of the knight on g5 is quite genuine and cannot be easily parried. Now here is the course that the game took:

1 ♕e2!

First White thoroughly eliminates the possibility of Black's playing ...b5.

1...♘f8 2 ♘d1 ♖a7

2...♘e8 would probably have been better.

3 ♘f2 ♕b8 4 ♘h3 h6

Now there is a weakness in the black king position as well. White still presses on.

5 ♘g5! hxg5 6 fxg5

This is of course already the second phase, since White is committed materially; at the same time, his attack breaks through. If now 6...♘6h7 7 ♗xf7 ♘xg5 (or 7...♗xg5 8 ♖xh7+ ♔xh7 9 ♕xe6[1]) 8 ♕h5 ♘gh7, then 9 d5 exd5 10 ♘h6+ ♔h8 11 ♕f7 ♘f6 12 ♕g8+ and 13 ♘f7#.

6...♘8d7 7 ♘xf7[2]

In fact, it would have been simpler and quicker to play 7 ♘xd7 ♖xd7 8 gxf6 ♗xf6 9 ♖xf6 gxf6 10 ♕g4+ ♔f8 11 ♗a3+ ♖d6 12 ♕f4 ♔e7 13 c5.

7...♔xf7 8 g6+ ♔g8 9 ♕xe6+ ♔h8 10 ♕h3+ ♔g8 11 ♗f5 ♘f8 12 ♗e6+ ♘xe6 13 ♕xe6+ ♔h8 14 ♕h3+ ♔g8 15 ♖xf6! ♗xf6 16 ♕h7+ ♔f8 17 ♖e1 ♗e5 18 ♕h8+ ♔e7 19 ♕xg7+ ♔d6 20 ♕xe5+ ♔d7 21 ♕f5+ ♔c6 22 d5+ ♔c5 23 ♗a3+ ♔xc4 24 ♕e4+ ♔c3 25 ♗b4+ ♔b2 26 ♕b1#

---

1   This allows 9...♗c8, when no win is apparent, so White should prefer 9 ♘xd8 ♕xd8 10 ♕xe6+ ♔h8 11 ♖ae1 with a large advantage.

2   Recent analysis has shown that this further sacrifice is quite wrong, in that Black could later play 8...♔f8! with fair defensive chances. Therefore White should have chosen 7 ♘xd7, as given by Vuković.

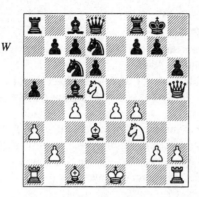

This position arose in the game Alekhine-Gilg, Semmering 1926. It is White's move, and he decided on an attack, although the preconditions were only partially fulfilled. Black's king position is weakened and some of White's pieces are well placed, but there is as yet no communication between his rooks. Meanwhile, it is of decisive importance that Black is able to launch a counterattack based on his control of d4 and the exposed position of the white king; the general instability in the centre is also to Black's advantage. We shall see how Alekhine's attack came to grief in this position.

1 g4?

Seeing that the preconditions for an attack have not been fulfilled, this additional commitment by White turns against him. The correct move, objectively speaking, was 1 ♗e3, which would have led to approximate equality but not to an attack on the king.

1...♘f6 2 ♘xf6+ ♕xf6 3 f5 ♘d4 4 g5 ♘xf3+ 5 ♕xf3 hxg5 6 h4 ♖e8! 7 ♔d1 *(D)*

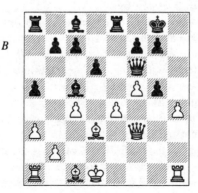

Black threatened 7...♕xf5.

7...gxh4 8 ♔c2 ♗d7

It is clear that White's attack has been repulsed and that he must now defend himself against an action by Black.

9 ♗d2 ♖a6! 10 ♕h5 ♗a4+ 11 ♔c1 ♖b6 12 ♖a2 ♗d4 13 b4 ♗e3 14 ♗xe3 ♕c3+ 15 ♗c2 ♕xe3+ 16 ♔b1 ♗xc2+ 17 ♖xc2 axb4 18 ♕xh4 bxa3+ 19 ♔a2 ♕h6!

Since the exchange of queens is now forced (if 20 ♕e1, then 20...♕f6 would be decisive) the danger on the h-file disappears and Black's superiority in the endgame is decisive. White lost the game in due course. The game is also, of course, a good example of indirect defence.

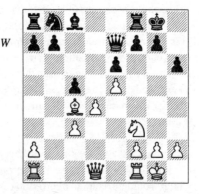

W

This position is from the game Gligorić-Kostić, Zagreb 1947. White was afraid that, if he allowed ...cxd4 cxd4, he would not be able to maintain his backward pawn at d4, so he played 1 d5 exd5 2 ♗xd5, intending to support the centralized bishop on d5, if necessary, by c4.

However, this is not a good plan, since it leaves White with an inflexible position as well as the danger of an inferior endgame. On the other hand, the backward d-pawn is not a great drawback, as long as White strives to obtain compensation in an attack on the king. The preconditions are in fact there, for Black's position has been weakened by ...h6, and White can rapidly post his queen and bishop on the b1-h7 diagonal and so force a further weakness in the shape of ...g6. It should also be noted that Black has no minor pieces on the kingside, while his knight and bishop on the queen's wing are obviously not suitably placed for defence. In the centre Black can only exchange pawns on d4, while a pawn advance on the queenside is too slow. The preconditions for an attack on the castled king are therefore fulfilled to a considerable measure; White can play for an attack – indeed *he must,* for otherwise he may well find himself in difficulty over the backward pawn.

1 ♕e2! ♘c6

If Black plays 1...♖d8 2 ♕e4 ♘d7 in order to have ...♘f8 in reserve, then the continuation 3 ♖fd1 cxd4 4 cxd4 ♘f8 5 ♗b3 leaves him at a loss to complete his development, whereas White can either play on the c-file or manoeuvre with ♘d2-c4-d6.

2 ♕e4 cxd4 3 cxd4 ♖d8

After 3...♘a5 4 ♗d3 g6, White first of all plays 5 ♖ac1, whereupon counter-play commencing with 5...♗d7 can be answered by 6 d5 exd5 7 ♕xd5. If 3...♘b4 4 a3, Black loses a tempo, since his knight cannot go to d5.

4 ♗d3 g6 5 ♖ac1 ♘b4 6 ♗b1 ♘d5 7 h4 h5

Otherwise 8 h5 is strong.

8 g4 hxg4 9 ♕xg4, and White has a promising kingside attack.

The creation of preconditions

The preconditions for a successful attack on the castled king can arise in a number of different ways. Some arise out of the normal process of building up a position; some are created by the player's own moves, which are specifically aimed at such an attack; some occur unnoticed, as it were, in the course of the game; and others are the result of risky or even faulty play by the opponent. Let us leave aside those cases where the preconditions are created 'unnoticed' or through faulty play and turn our attention to those whose origin is conscious and calculated. In this connection we are already acquainted with a rule which has few exceptions.

Of all the different preconditions for an attack on the king, one should create first those which entail the lesser degree of commitment, i.e. those which are of use not only in the event of an attack on the king, but also go to strengthen one's position in general.

Good posts for one's pieces, spatial advantage, strength in the centre, the security of one's own king – all these are factors of use in an attack on the castled king but which do not commit one to it. Commitment occurs gradually as weaknesses in the castled position are induced and as a flexible central formation is transformed into a fixed one (e.g. when, with pawns at e4 and d4, one plays e5). In other words, weaknesses in a castled position can be full of point if it comes to an attack, but otherwise they may be without significance or even useful to the side which has incurred them, e.g. ...h6 may provide a flight square for the king; or ...g6 may prepare the advance ...f5. Equally, a premature advance in the centre can entail a general positional commitment and so profit the opponent in various ways. More gradual commitments also arise from a regrouping of minor pieces outside the castling area but with the sole aim of attacking the castled king. It is already more difficult when it comes to transferring a rook to the third rank, since this rook will need some time to return and reopen communication with the other one, should the attack not succeed. The engagement of minor pieces in the vicinity of the castling area (e.g. as a result of moving a knight to g5) also involves a heavier commitment in terms of tempi. However, the heaviest commitments are those incurred in an attack carried out with the aid of pawns. Of these the heaviest is usually incurred by advancing the g-pawn, next comes the advance of the h-pawn, while advancing the f-pawn entails the least commitment. Now we have a small graduated scale for the degree of commitment incurred by the various operations which are necessary to create the preconditions for an attack on the castled king; it need not be emphasized, perhaps, that this scale has only a general and approximate validity. Let us now examine the following example from practical play.

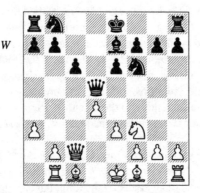

This position is from the opening stages of the game Alekhine-Weenink, Prague 1931. It is White to move.

1 ♗d3!

The textbooks gave ♗c4; Alekhine's move takes into account the fact that Black is about to castle kingside and threatens e4 and e5 followed by ♗xh7 (whether Black castles or not). As a result, Black has no better move than ...h6, which means that a weakness in his castled position has already been brought about, and without any special expenditure in time by White, since ♗d3 is a natural developing move in this position. Inducing weaknesses like this is naturally correct in any circumstances.

1...h6 2 e4 ♕d8 3 0-0 ♘bd7 4 b4

With his second move White occupied the centre, with his third he made his king secure, and now he safeguards his central position against the counter-thrust ...c5. Apart from this, b4 prepares the ground for piece regrouping on the queenside.

4...0-0 5 ♕e2

This contains the threat of 6 e5 followed by 7 ♕e4 but, at the same time, does not yet commit White in the centre.

It would be a mistake to play 5 e5 ♘d5 6 ♖b3 ♖e8 7 ♕e2 ♘f8, since Black would then have managed to centralize his knight at d5 and invalidate the attack based on ♕e4. The move e5 must clearly be reserved for a later moment when everything else is ready.

5...♖e8 6 ♖b3!

Primarily, this frees the square b1 for the bishop so that the queen may be placed in front of it on the diagonal b1-h7. It also makes it possible to transfer the rook to g3 or h3 as part of the attack later on, but it does not otherwise commit White to an attack on the castled king, since the rook can also be used for play, for instance, on the c-file.

6...♕c7 7 ♗b1 ♘h7 *(D)*

Black is too weak to fight back in the centre by 7...e5. After 8 dxe5 ♘xe5 9 ♘xe5 ♕xe5 10 ♗b2 White obtains a strong attacking position. If 7...♘f8 (in order to meet 8 e5 with 8...♘d5) then 8 ♘e5 followed by ♖g3, etc.

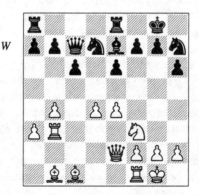

W

8 e5

This central pawn thrust commits White more than any other move hitherto. Clearly, he is now no longer thinking of the endgame but is intent on forcing home an attack on the castled king. It is of decisive importance that Black does not have ...♘d5 available; if he plays, for example, 8...♘b6, White's threats take effect even more quickly, e.g. 9 ♕e4 ♘f8 10 ♕g4 ♔h8 11 ♕h5, etc. So Black must resort to defence and not play for ...♘d5.

8...f5

To rid himself of some of the pressure. It also sets a trap, i.e. 9 ♕c4 ♘hf8 10 ♗xf5? ♘b6 11 ♗xe6+ ♔h8, when White loses his bishop.

9 exf6 ♗xf6 10 ♕e4 ♘hf8 11 ♕g4 ♔h8 12 ♕h5 ♘h7

Otherwise 13 ♗xh6 wins.

13 ♖e1 ♖ad8 14 g4!, and now we have reached the position which was dealt with on page 212. White's heaviest positional commitment in the game, the move g4, occurs exactly at the moment when the attack on the castled king has come to a head.

The reader should observe the *time sequence* of each operation in this game, particularly *with reference to the degree of commitment*. The mild commitment incurred by ♖b3!, the greater one by e5, and the heaviest one by g4, correspond exactly to the phases of the attack and to the strength of the threats which White has at his disposal.

After this example, in which we have seen the temporal relationship between the various operations designed to create the preconditions for an attack, let us turn to a separate examination of each of these operations.

First, the *inducement of weaknesses in the castled position*. This is an important operation, although it usually forms part of another operation and tends to be limited to one or two moves. It can take the form either of the unprovoked or faulty weakening of the castled position or of the correct advance of a pawn or pawns in front of the king which, because of faulty play later on, results in an appreciable weakness (e.g. when a flight square for the king, originally advantageous, becomes a weakness); then there is the case of the weakness which is enforced early on without any loss of tempo, while on the other hand, there are weak points which arise in the sacrificial whirlpool of the attack's final phase. All these cases show our theme in its wider sense. In the narrower sense, the inducement of weaknesses implies an operation on which the attacker spends one or more tempi with the sole aim of weakening his opponent's castled position in a definite way. An operation of this kind which entails an expenditure of several tempi represents a very real commitment, and so it usually belongs to a stage when most of the conditions necessary for an attack have already been fulfilled.

There have already been many examples of the inducement of weaknesses, so two will be sufficient here.

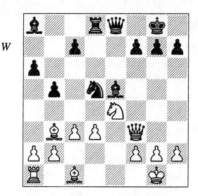

This position is from the game Lilienthal-Bondarevsky, USSR Absolute Championship, Leningrad/Moscow 1941. Black had come to grief through playing an incorrect version of the Marshall Attack in the Ruy Lopez; a pawn up, White does not have a hard task ahead.

1 &g5

Provoking Black to weaken his kingside by ...f6, which is difficult to avoid.

1...f6 2 &d2

White has devoted a tempo to inducing the weakness ...f6; we shall soon see that it is well worth it.

2...&h8 3 &e1 &f8 4 d4 &d6 5 &xd6 &xd6 6 &h5 g6

The threat of &e8+ provokes a new weakness.

7 &h4 &c6 8 f3 &g7 *(D)*

White threatened 9 &xd5 &xd5 10 &f4 &c6 11 &e7.

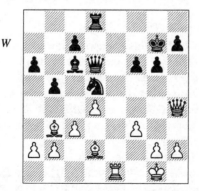

9 &h6+ &g8 10 &e4 g5

Black is lost anyway, with or without this; for example, he faced a threat of 11 ♗f4 ♕f8 12 ♗xc7.

11 ♕h5 ♕d7 12 ♗xg5! ♕f5

The main variation of the combination runs 12...fxg5 13 ♕xg5+ ♔f8 14 ♖f4+! ♘xf4 15 ♕g8+ ♔e7 16 ♕f7+ ♔d6 17 ♕xf4+ ♔e7 18 ♕f7+ ♔d6 19 ♕f6+ ♕e6 20 ♕xe6#.

13 ♕h6 ♔h8

White wins after both 13...♕xg5 14 ♖g4 and 13...fxg5 14 ♕xc6.

1-0

Black did not wait for the unanswerable 14 ♗xd5.

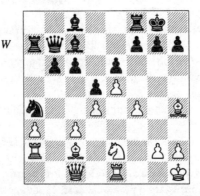

The continuation from this diagram shows the correct enforcing of a weakness on g6 followed up by consistent play against the focal-point g7; an alternative line illustrates how provocation can be exaggerated with the result that it turns against the attacker.

1 ♕d1

The queen, on its way to d3, gains a tempo by attacking the knight. The alternative 1 ♕b1 h6 2 ♕d1 b5 3 ♕d3 g6 is inferior. Here, besides the essential weakness at g6, White has also extracted a 'secondary' one at h6, but in fact this is not a weakness at all, since it simplifies Black's defence of the focal-point g7. For example, after 4 ♗f6 ♗d8 5 ♕h3 ♗xf6 6 exf6 ♔h7 7 ♖f1 ♖h8! 8 ♖f3 ♔g8 Black has defended himself against White's main threat of ♕xh6+, and consequently the situation is no longer clear.

1...b5 2 ♕d3 g6 3 ♗f6 ♗d8

Now 3...h6 proves too late, e.g. 4 ♕h3 ♔h7 5 ♖f1 ♗d8 6 ♖f3 ♗xf6 7 exf6 e5 (if 7...♖h8, then 8 ♕xh6+) 8 g4 exf4 9 ♕h5 ♖h8 10 ♘xf4 ♔g8 11 ♗xg6 fxg6 12 ♕xg6+ ♔f8 13 ♖e2, and White wins.

4 ♕h3 ♗xf6 5 exf6 h5 6 ♘g3 e5 7 ♕h4 ♗g4 8 ♘xh5! ♗xh5 9 ♕g5 ♔h7 10 ♕xh5+ followed by ♕h6 and ♕g7#.

The next three examples are concerned with cases where the creation of the preconditions for the attack on the king demands the removal of the opponent's pieces from defensive positions or their displacement in some way.

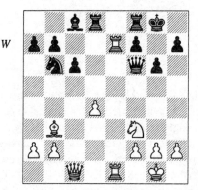

W

This position is taken from the game O'Kelly-Castaldi, Hilversum 1947. Here Black's king position has already been weakened, White's pieces are all well posted, and there is no danger of counterplay in the centre or, indeed, anywhere; the only real obstacle is Black's queen, which is defending the kingside well at the moment, e.g. if 1 ♕h6, then 1...♕g7. So the action White takes has the aim of inveigling Black's queen to as far away as b8!

1 ♕c5!

Threatening to win Black's a-pawn by 2 ♕a5.

1...♕d6

If 1...♖d7, then 2 ♖e8, after which both 2...♖d6 and 2...♕g7 are answered by 3 ♕a5.

2 ♕a5 ♕b8 3 ♕g5 ♘d5 4 ♕h6 1-0

There is no defence against ♘g5, e.g. 4...♕f4 5 ♘g5 ♘f6 6 ♗xf7+ ♔h8 7 ♗xg6.

Actions of this type might be called indirect attacks on the castled king.

In the following diagram, some of the preconditions for an attack on Black's king position are already present. White's pieces are fairly well placed, and the blocked centre makes it difficult for Black to counterattack. A breakthrough by ...b5-b4 would require rather lengthy preparation, while the other possibility –

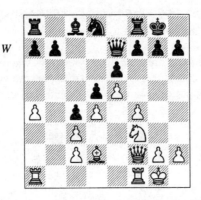

capturing White's a-pawn – would bring him too little in return for the tempi spent on it. On the other hand, there are Black's unweakened king position and White's weakness on the light squares. The latter makes itself felt if the position is opened up. But how is White to progress, if he is not to play f5, i.e. if he does not loosen up the situation on the light squares a little? Surely not by 1 ♘g5, which clearly involves a doubtful sacrifice. Nor by 1 g4 ♘c6 2 ♘h4, on which Black plays 2...f5; for while, logically, the blocked position should then be over-come by 3 exf6, in fact the reply 3...gxf6 opens up the prospect of counterplay for Black by ...e5.

There is no doubt about it: the position is not yet ripe for an attack on the king; it needs to be strengthened still further, or more exactly, the black pieces need to be driven further away. This can be done by playing the dark-squared bishop, with gain of tempo, on to the diagonal a3-f8, where it will settle.

1 ♗c1 ♖e8 2 ♗a3 ♕d7

The defence is even more difficult after 2...♕c7.

3 ♕h4 ♘c6

If 3...♕xa4?, then 4 ♗e7 ♕d7 5 ♗f6, when Black is without resource.

4 ♘g5 h6 5 ♘h3

Sacrificing the knight would be not only unclear but also superfluous. The more expendable pawns will now have their say and so bring about the weaken-ing of Black's king position.

5...♕d8 6 ♕h5 ♘e7 7 g4 ♘g6 8 g5 ♗d7 9 ♖f2!

The pawn on a4 does not count, but the one on c2 must be kept alive.

9...♗xa4 10 ♖g2 ♔h8

Otherwise White plays 11 gxh6 ♕h4 12 ♕xh4, followed by 13 ♖xg7+ and 14 ♘g5.

11 ♖f1 ♗d7 12 ♖g4 ♘f8 13 gxh6 g6 14 ♘g5 gxh5 15 ♘xf7+ ♔h7 16 ♖g7#

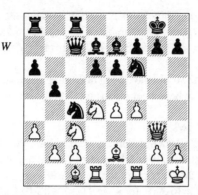

This position is from the game Yates-Takacs, Kecskemet 1927. The preconditions for an attack on Black's king position have been only partially fulfilled; White is hindered particularly by the possibility of a counterattack by Black in the centre or down the c-file. White's prospects would be better if he could succeed in driving away the f6-knight by e5 and then play ♘e4. To manage this he must first repulse the black knight from c4, which means sacrificing a pawn. That was just the sort of thing Yates was in the mood for.

1 b3! ♘xa3

Black falls in with White's plan and imperils his knight on a3. In taking on this commitment he enables White to acquire *additional preconditions for an attack on the king*. If Black had played 1...♘b6, which would have been better, White would have had to build up more slowly with 2 ♗b2.

2 e5! ♘e8?

Relatively the best solution for Black would have been to sacrifice a piece for three pawns by 2...♘xc2! 3 exf6 ♗xf6 4 ♘xc2 ♕xc3, although even then the advantage lies with White after 5 ♗d3.

2...dxe5 3 fxe5 ♕xc3 leads to interesting possibilities, for example 4 ♖d3! ♘e4 (or 4...♕c7 5 exf6 ♕xg3 6 ♖xg3, when Black's knight at a3 and his bishop at e7 are both hanging) 5 ♕f4 ♕b4 (alternatively, 5...♕c5 6 b4 ♕d5 7 ♗xa3, and White's threats are just too strong) 6 ♕xe4 ♘xc2 7 ♖h3 g6 8 ♕f4, and White wins.

3 ♘e4

Now the preconditions for an attack on the king are suddenly fulfilled. One black knight has been driven back to e8 and the other deflected to a3; while White's pawn on e5, supported by two good knights, provides a wedge in the centre. All this has cost only one pawn.

3...d5 4 ♘f6+!?

Although an interesting move, this is nevertheless not the strongest. Correct was 4 ♘g5 followed by ♗d3; for example, if 4...h6, then 5 ♘xf7 ♔xf7 6 ♗h5+ ♔g8 7 ♕g6 ♕d8 8 f5 exf5 9 e6 ♗c6 10 ♘xf5 wins for White.

4...♔h8

4...♗xf6 5 ♗xa3 ♗d8 would have been rather unpleasant for Black; however, White's attack would not have been so strong in that case on account of the defensive possibility ...f5.

5 ♕h4 ♘xf6 6 ♗d3 g6?

The decisive mistake. Black ought not to weaken his dark squares, particularly in view of the commitment of his dark-squared bishop to cover a3, as a result of which it is only half at the disposal of the defence. The right course to take was 6...h6! 7 ♗xa3 ♗xa3 8 exf6 ♗f8, for after 9 ♘f3 ♕d8 10 ♘e5 ♗e8 Black has a complete defence.

7 exf6 ♗f8 8 ♘f3 ♔g8 9 ♘g5 h6 10 ♗xa3

White captures the knight at precisely the most inconvenient moment for Black.

10...hxg5 (D)

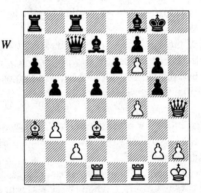

11 fxg5

White can also win simply by 11 ♕xg5 ♗xa3 12 ♗xg6 ♔f8 13 ♗xf7 ♔xf7 14 ♕g7+ ♔e8 15 f7+ ♔d8 16 ♕f6+ with a quick mate.

11...♗xa3 12 ♗xg6

If 12 ♖f3 e5, White must still play ♗xg6.

12...fxg6 13 ♖d3

Not 13 f7+, since 13...♔f8 14 ♕h8+ ♔e7 15 ♕f6+ sees Black's king wriggling out to d6.

13...♖f8

If Black meets the threat of 14 ♖h3 by 13...e5, his king would not have found refuge on d6. After the text move, Black hopes to meet 14 ♕h6 by 14...♔f7, heading for e8, but Yates now finds a new point at which to trouble him!

14 b4! ♗xb4 15 ♖h3! 1-0

If 15...♔f7, then 16 ♕xb4, and Black is either mated or loses his queen.

Of the cases where the opponent himself creates a precondition for an attack on the castled king the most important is that which involves the release of tension in the centre. The next diagram provides a good example.

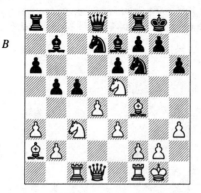

This position is from the game Euwe-Maroczy, Zandvoort 1936. It is Black's move.

1...c4?

This releases the tension in the centre and so creates the one precondition which White still lacked before he could embark on an attack against the enemy king. Maroczy, a great expert on defence, is playing here *under the influence of the thinking of the old school*, which paid insufficient attention to the problems of the centre. In the Orthodox Defence to the Queen's Gambit, resolving the central tension by ...c4 generally gives White a powerful attack on the king, for a counterattack based on a pawn majority on the wing is much slower than that which takes place in the centre.

The thematic move for Black here would be 1...♕b6, but that entails the danger of his knight being diverted from the defence of the square h7; e.g., 2 ♘xd7 ♘xd7 3 dxc5 ♘xc5 4 ♗b1, threatening ♕c2. Sounder, therefore, is 1...♖c8.

2 ♗b1 ♖e8

After 2...♘d5 3 ♘xd5 exd5 4 ♕c2 ♘f6 5 ♘g4 ♖e8 6 ♗e5 Black's position would be most uncomfortable.

3 ♕e2 ♘xe5?

Black's position is too weak for this method of defence; it allows White to get his rooks into active play via d1 and d4. He should have preferred 3...♘f8, although even then White would have retained the advantage.

4 dxe5 ♘h7 5 ♕h5 ♘f8 6 ♖cd1 ♕c7 7 ♗xh6!

Since Black abandoned the centre, the preconditions for a successful attack on his king have increased with every move. Now the situation is even ripe for a sacrifice.

7...gxh6 8 ♖d4 f5 9 exf6 ♗xf6 10 ♖g4+ ♗g7 11 ♕xh6 ♖ad8 *(D)*

White would have faced a harder task after 11...♖e7 12 ♘e2 e5, since he could not then have played 13 ♘g3 because of 13...♕c6, forcing the exchange of queens. White would have had to play 13 ♗f5 ♕c6 14 ♕g5.

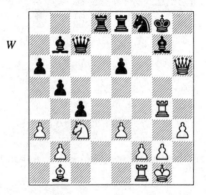

12 ♘e2 e5

If 12...♖d7, then the manoeuvre ♘g3-h5-f6+ is decisive.

13 ♘g3 ♖e6 14 ♕h4 ♖d3

14...♕e7 would not have worked because of 15 ♖xg7+!, but 14...e4 would have offered a little more resistance.

15 ♘f5 ♘g6 16 ♕h5 ♕f7 17 h4! ♗f8 18 ♘h6+ ♗xh6 19 ♕xh6 ♕h7 20 ♕g5 ♔f7 21 ♗xd3 cxd3 22 ♕f5+ 1-0

Old and modern styles in building up an attack on the king

The following three games reflect the differences of two periods and three individual styles in preparing and conducting attacks on the king. The first is a sample of old-time brilliance, showing the unfolding of an overwhelming attack resulting from feeble opening play by the opponent. In the second Black makes a risky experiment, and one of his pawns, wandering lonely among the white pieces on the kingside, remains as a consolation and the germ of the subsequent attack. In the third game the underlying conception of the attack is quite different, its main feature being Capablanca's rational and cautious method of ensuring that every possible means of counterplay on the part of his opponent is first suppressed.

Pillsbury – H. Wolf
Monte Carlo, 1903
Queen's Gambit Declined, Orthodox Defence

1 d4 d5 2 c4 e6 3 ♘c3 ♘f6 4 ♗g5 ♘bd7 5 ♘f3 ♗e7 6 e3 0-0 7 ♖c1 b6 8 cxd5 exd5 9 ♘e5

This is not the best. The normal way of building up the formation known as the Pillsbury Attack is 9 ♗d3 followed by 0-0 and ♘e5. However, even in this improved version, Pillsbury's entrenched knight is by no means as great an asset for White as it seemed to Pillsbury's contemporaries (see also the notes to the Pillsbury-Tarrasch game, p.258).

9...♗b7 10 f4 a6? *(D)*

The right procedure was 10...♘e8 11 ♗xe7 ♕xe7 12 ♕f3 ♘xe5 13 fxe5 ♖d8 14 ♗d3 f6, which shows up White's attack to be premature.

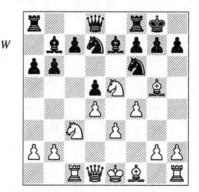

11 ♗d3 c5 12 0-0 c4?

We have censured this move in similar positions in the games Pillsbury-Tarrasch and Euwe-Maroczy. It was an error of judgement of a bygone period to abandon the important central tension for the sake of the dim chance of a slowly-advancing queenside pawn majority. It may be said here that modern knowledge of the importance of tension in the centre is the main deterrent against kingside attacks nowadays.

13 ♗f5 b5 14 ♖f3

A rook manoeuvre characteristic of the Pillsbury Attack. Its first aim is to provoke a weakening of the enemy king position in the shape of either ...g6 or ...h6.

14...♖e8

The feebleness of Black's defensive resources – a consequence of his earlier failure to play 12...♖e8 instead of 12...c4? – is shown in the alternative line 14...b4 15 ♘a4 h6 16 ♗xh6 gxh6 17 ♖g3+ ♔h8 18 ♘xd7 ♘xd7 19 ♕h5 and White wins. Therefore, Black cannot appease his opponent with the somewhat lesser evil of ...h6 but will be forced to play ...g6.

15 ♖h3 g6

If 15...h6 then 16 ♗xh6 gxh6 17 ♖g3+ ♔f8 18 ♗xd7 ♘xd7 19 ♕h5 and mates, while 15...♘f8 is answered by 16 ♗xf6 ♗xf6 17 ♗xh7+ ♘xh7 18 ♕h5.

16 ♗b1 ♘xe5

From bad to worse; 16...♘f8 offered a better chance of resistance.

17 fxe5 ♘d7 18 ♗xe7 ♖xe7 19 ♕f3 ♘f8 20 ♖f1 ♕d7 21 ♕f6 b4 (D)

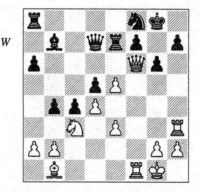

22 ♘a4

White has a won game anyway, but this is not the best move. Correct was 22 ♘e2 followed by either ♘f4-h5 or ♘g3-f5. Sacrificing the knight is the typical way to exploit positions of this kind; one of the critical variations runs 22 ♘e2 ♕c7 (or 22...♕d8 23 ♕h4 ♖c7 24 ♖f6) 23 ♘f4 ♖d8 24 ♘h5! gxh5 (or 24...♘e6 25 ♕h4 gxh5 26 ♕f6! and wins) 25 ♗xh7+ ♘xh7 26 ♖g3+ ♔f8 27 ♕h8#.

22...♕c7 23 ♘c5 ♗c8 24 ♖h6 a5

Unaware of the approaching trap, Black proceeds on his slow way. The immediate 24...♖b8 was more resourceful, for then 25 ♖f4 (25 ♘xa6 ♗xa6 26 ♕xa6 c3 yields good chances for Black) 25...♖b6 26 e6 ♖bxe6! (not 26...♗xe6? 27 ♗xg6!) 27 ♘xe6 ♖xe6 28 ♕g5 allows Black the chance to fight back by 28...c3 29 bxc3 ♕xc3. The best move for White after 24...♖b8 is 25 e4!.

25 ♖f4 ♖b8? *(D)*

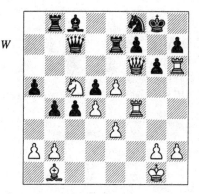

The final blunder; 25...♗e6 was the only move.

26 ♗xg6!

The *coup de grâce*. If now 26...♘xg6, then 27 ♖xg6+ hxg6 28 ♖h4.

26...♖b6 27 ♕xb6 ♘xg6

Or 27...♕xb6 28 ♗xf7+ and 29 ♖xb6.

28 ♕f6 ♖e8 29 ♖f1 ♗e6 30 ♕g5 ♔h8 31 ♕h5 ♘f8 32 ♘xe6 ♖xe6 33 ♖xe6 1-0

Rauzer – Botvinnik
Leningrad, 1933
Sicilian Defence, Dragon Variation

1 e4 c5 2 ♘f3 ♘c6 3 d4 cxd4 4 ♘xd4 ♘f6 5 ♘c3 d6 6 ♗e2 g6 7 ♗e3 ♗g7 8 ♘b3 ♗e6 9 f4 0-0 10 0-0 a5 11 ♘xa5

Nowadays this whole line is reckoned to be harmless for Black.

11...♕xa5 12 ♗f3 ♗c4 13 ♖e1 ♖fd8 14 ♕d2 ♕c7

Black withdraws his queen in order not to have constantly to reckon with ♘d5, which is admittedly not threatened at the moment but which may become a nuisance later.

15 ♖ac1?

The beginning of a faulty plan. White is preparing for b3 followed by c4, but he does not have the time to carry it out. Correct was 15 ♕f2 whereupon Black has nothing better than 15...♕a5.

15...e5 16 b3? *(D)*

White keeps to his faulty plan. A sounder line was 16 fxe5 dxe5 17 ♕f2 though Black would still have somewhat the superior game.

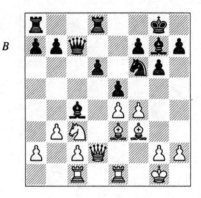

16...d5!?

A reckless conception, which has a flaw. The right way to continue was 16...♗a6 17 ♘d5 ♘xd5 18 ♕xd5 (if 18 exd5 then 18...e4 followed by ...♗c3) 18...exf4 19 ♗xf4 ♗c3! 20 ♖ed1 ♗b2 21 ♖b1 ♗e5 22 g3 ♕c3! with advantage to Black.

17 exd5!

After 17 bxc4 dxe4 Black would win back the piece with the better game; 17 ♘xd5 ♗xd5 18 exd5 e4 and 17 fxe5 ♘xe4 18 ♗xe4 dxe4 19 ♕f2 ♕xe5! are also favourable for Black.

17...e4 18 bxc4

After 18 ♘xe4 ♘xd5 Black retains the initiative without giving up any material, thanks to the threat of ...♘xe3 followed by ...♗d4.

18...exf3 19 c5!

19 gxf3? ♕xc4 20 ♖ed1 ♖ac8 21 ♗d4 is unsatisfactory on account of 21...♘xd5 22 ♗xg7 ♘xc3 23 ♕xc3 ♖xd1+, after which Black exchanges queens and reaches a won ending. Thus the pawn on f3 is left alive for the time being.

19...♕a5 20 ♖ed1?

White failed to find an answer to Black's double threat (...♘xd5 and ...♘g4) and instead of discovering the flaw in his opponent's bold plan, he gets himself into a difficult position.

Ragozin pointed out the continuation 20 ♕d3! ♘g4 21 ♘e4 f5 22 ♘g5 f2+ 23 ♗xf2 ♘xf2 24 ♔xf2 (if 24 ♕c4 then 24...♕c3 while if 24 ♕b3, Black plays 24...♗d4 25 d6+ ♔h8, and White has no more than a draw) 24...♕xc5+ 25 ♔g3. If Black were then to take the d-pawn, the material balance would be restored but at the cost of allowing White to assume the initiative. For example, after 25...♖xd5 (not 25...♕xd5 because of 26 ♖e8+) 26 ♕b3 Black is suddenly in difficulties owing to the threat of ♖cd1 which is decisive even against ...♔h8; consequently, he is forced to play 26...♕b5 27 ♖cd1 ♕xb3 28 cxb3 ♖xd1 29 ♖xd1 and go into an unfavourable ending with the white rook on the seventh rank. It is interesting that H. Müller, in his book on Botvinnik, ends the analysis at White's twenty-sixth move, stating that he will have to fight for a draw[1]!

20...♘g4 21 ♗d4 *(D)*

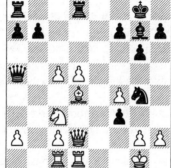

21...f2+!

The pawn virus begins to take effect. 22 ♗xf2 does not work on account of 22...♗xc3, while 22 ♔h1 is defeated by 22...♖xd5! 23 ♘xd5 f1♕+, and White loses his queen.

22 ♔f1 ♕a6+

Now the black queen hastens across to h4 via f6; out of the one small pawn there has grown a real kingside attack, which requires the assistance of the queen.

23 ♕e2

If 23 ♘e2 then 23...♗xd4 24 ♕xd4 ♖xd5 while 23 ♕d3 is met by 23...♗xd4 24 ♕xa6 ♘e3+ 25 ♔e2 f1♕+ 26 ♖xf1 bxa6.

Many years later Botvinnik published some new analysis of this game, in which he claimed that after 20 ♕d3, 20...b6! gives Black a satisfactory position.

23...♗xd4 24 ♖xd4 ♕f6 25 ♖cd1

25 ♕d3 would have posed Black a more difficult, though still soluble, task. 25...♕h4? is not good because of 26 ♕g3 ♘xh2+ 27 ♔xf2 when Black can only obtain perpetual check with his knight. Instead, Black would have to play 25...♖e8 26 d6 ♕h4 (not 26...♖e3? on account of 27 ♘d5) 27 ♖e4 ♘xh2+ 28 ♔e2 f5 29 ♕c4+ ♔f8 30 ♖e7 ♖xe7+ 31 dxe7+ ♕xe7+ 32 ♔xf2 ♘g4+ picking up the rook.

25...♕h4 26 ♕d3 ♖e8 27 ♖e4 f5 28 ♖e6 ♘xh2+ 29 ♔e2 ♕xf4 0-1

If 30 ♖f1, then 30...♖ad8 31 ♖xf2 ♖xe6+ 32 dxe6 ♕g4+ wins.

Capablanca – Kan
Moscow, 1935
Queen's Gambit Declined, Orthodox Defence

1 d4 ♘f6 2 c4 e6 3 ♘c3 d5 4 ♘f3 ♘bd7 5 ♗g5 ♗e7 6 e3 0-0 7 ♖c1 c6 8 ♗d3 dxc4 9 ♗xc4 ♘d5 10 ♗xe7 ♕xe7 11 0-0 ♘5b6?

The main line of this variation is 11...♘xc3 12 ♖xc3 e5. Moving the knight to b6 is not good, since it neglects to give proper consideration to the central squares; the result is that White's knights can now become very active there.

12 ♗b3 e5 13 ♘e4!

A strong move, which poses Black a difficult task. After 13...exd4 14 ♕xd4 he would find himself hard pressed for a satisfactory continuation.

13...h6? (D)

Creating an unnecessary weakness. Worth considering was the immediate 13...♔h8, preparing ...f5. White could then employ the following simplifying manoeuvre, probably his most promising course in this position: 14 dxe5 ♘xe5 15 ♘xe5 ♕xe5 16 ♕d6 ♘d7 17 ♕xe5 ♘xe5 18 ♘d6.

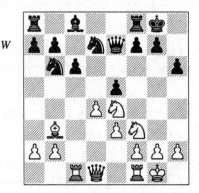

14 ♕d3 ♔h8 15 ♘g3 exd4 16 ♗c2!

An intermediate move, the purpose of which is to provoke the weakening ...g6.

16...♘f6 17 e4! g6

Owing to the threat of 18 e5, Black cannot avoid this weakness; if 17...♘bd7 then 18 ♘f5 is strong.

18 ♕xd4 ♗e6 19 h4?

Up to here White has built up a series of preconditions for an attack on the enemy king without making any moves which commit him to it. Now, without any real need, he goes in for such a move. Black's position is not yet ready to be taken by storm, so h4 is still premature. According to the scheme which we have worked out, now would be the time to complete the preconditions for the attack without incurring any positional commitments. White's queen is not yet secure in its possession of the long dark diagonal in view of the possibility of ...♖ad8 followed later by ...♘a4, and accordingly, priority should have been given to restraining such counterplay, e.g. by 19 b3 ♖ad8 20 ♕c3. Then after 20...♖ac8, intending ...c5, Black's plan would be frustrated by 21 ♕a5.

Moreover, h4 is unsuitable in that it makes it more difficult to carry out the thematic move f4 (because of the hole left on g4). However, White's position is strong enough to stand even h4 though it entails the expenditure of greater effort than otherwise would have been necessary.

19...♖ad8 20 ♕c3 ♔h7?

After this White's pawn on h4 acquires a function. A better plan would have been either to double rooks on the d-file by 20...♖d7 or to contest control of d4 by 20...c5.

21 ♖fe1 ♘bd7 22 ♗b1 ♖fe8 *(D)*

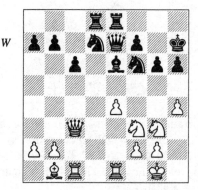

23 a3

Starting with 21 ♖fe1, this is already White's third consolidating move. Before storming the castled position White first of all excludes every prospect of counterplay by Black; a3 is intended particularly to deprive Black's queen of the square b4. *This type of preparation for an attack on the king* characterizes many of Capablanca's games. Alekhine preferred a different way of restraining counterplay, namely indirectly by means of dynamic blows. Hence the impression of Alekhine's excessive eagerness and Capablanca's exaggerated caution as the characteristics of their styles. In fact everything depends on the specific position; in some cases Alekhine's method is correct, in others Capablanca's.

23...♗g4

This makes it easier for White to go over to the attack. 23...♘f8 would not have worked because of 24 ♘f5 but 23...♕f8 deserved consideration.

24 ♘h2 h5 25 f3 ♗e6 26 f4 ♗g4 27 ♕e3

The queen comes within striking distance of the weakened network of dark squares around the enemy king. There is no need to worry about 27...♘g8, as then 28 ♘xg4 fxg4 29 ♔f2 is very strong.

27...a6 28 ♕f2 ♔g7 29 e5

This thrust in the centre signifies a critical phase of the attack; it is the prelude to the shattering of Black's pawn structure.

29...♘d5 30 ♘xg4 hxg4 31 h5 ♖h8 32 hxg6 fxg6 33 e6! ♘f8 34 ♗xg6! *(D)*

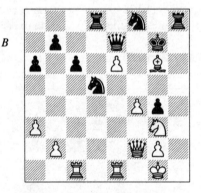

After thorough preparation White's attack is ripe for a sacrificial finish. In view of the threat of ♘f5+, Black has nothing better than to accept the offer.

34...♔xg6 35 ♕c2+ ♔f6 36 ♕f5+ ♔g7 37 ♕xg4+ ♔h7 38 ♔f2

This allows Black to prolong the game a little. White could have won at once by 38 ♖e5 ♘f6 39 ♕h4+ ♔g7 40 ♘f5+.

38...♛g7 39 ♛xg7+

Not, however, 39 ♛h4+ and 40 ♛xd8 on account of 40...♛d4+.

39...♚xg7 40 e7 ♖e8 41 exf8♛+ ♖exf8 42 f5 ♖h4 43 ♖cd1 ♖f4+ 44 ♚g1 ♖g4 45 ♖d3 ♚f7 46 ♚f2 ♖h8 47 ♖b3 b5 48 ♘e4 ♖h6 49 g3 ♖g8 50 ♚f3 a5 51 ♖d3 a4 52 ♖d2 1-0 (Black exceeded the time limit).

Fluctuations in the phases of attack

To conclude the chapter some observations should be added, with examples, to dissuade the reader from accepting the principles and maxims expounded as a rigid pattern. The game of chess is too complex and rich for it to be possible to reveal its finer points fully on the basis of a few formulae.

The practical player comes up against exceptions at every turn. Consequently, Lasker is right when he recommends in his book *Common Sense in Chess* that players should follow the principles of chess with a dash of humour...

So if we have already seen how the preconditions for an attack on the castled king are created and how the attacker's commitments grow in proportion to the force and form of his attack, it still remains to point out some cases where things develop rather differently: cases where the attack appears to slacken off and, instead of a vigorous assault, suddenly requires quiet moves; where the player only toys with his attack and is in fact aiming at other goals; or where great masters grope in the dark and fail to see something right in front of their noses.

Quiet moves that kindle the attack

So-called quiet moves are often only apparently quiet, and may in fact spark off a fire just as violent ones do. Moves of this type usually occur in positions where the attack appears to be flagging but has in fact reached a point at which a belated addition has to be made to the preconditions in the form of a quiet move, if the attacker is to get any further. Here are a few examples of this kind of quiet move, illustrating the fluctuations that occur in the phases of attack.

The following position is from the game Teichmann-Schlechter, Carlsbad 1911. It is White's move, and he begins with a sacrifice on f7.

1 ♗xf7+ ♚xf7 2 ♘g5+ ♚g8 3 ♛h5 ♘xf5 4 ♛xh7+ ♚f8 5 ♛xf5+ ♚g8

After 5...♚e7 6 ♛e6+ ♚d8 7 ♘f7+ Black would lose his queen.

6 ♛g6!

After a series of checks we suddenly get this quiet move, which does not provide any additional threat but merely blocks the g-pawn. This is precisely to the

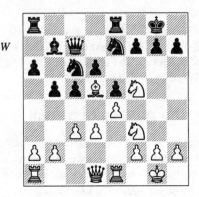

point in this position, since if, for example, 6 ♖e3, Black plays 6...g6 7 ♕xg6+ ♕g7, when White is still a long way from his goal. The fact that it is both possible and good to devote a whole tempo to blocking the g-pawn is a result of Black's inability to organize an effective defence. He cannot move his queen or rook to e7 on account of ♕h7+ and ♕h8#, while 6...♘e7 is answered by 7 ♕f7+ followed by 8 ♖e3.

The game ended **6...♕d7 7 ♖e3 1-0**, Black having no reply to 8 ♖f3 and 9 ♕h7#.

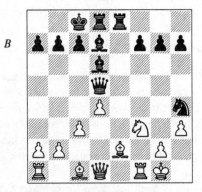

This position is from the game Steinitz–Lasker, London 1899. Black began with a double sacrifice.

1...♘xg2! 2 ♔xg2 ♗xh3+ 3 ♔f2

White cannot accept the second sacrifice; if 3 ♔xh3, then 3...♕h5+ 4 ♔g2 ♕g4+ 5 ♔h1 ♕h3+ 6 ♔g1 ♕g3+ 7 ♔h1 ♖e4 8 ♗g5 ♖de8!, etc.

3...f6!

A quiet move after the sacrifice. Black first deprives White's pieces of the squares e5 and g5 and at the same time prepares the advance of his g-pawn – a sound and positionally well-founded plan.

4 ♖g1 g5 5 ♗xg5

White's other moves all lose as well.

5...fxg5 6 ♖xg5 ♕e6 7 ♕d3 ♗f4 8 ♖h1

Black wins easily after both 8 ♖g7 ♗f5 and 8 ♖a5 ♖g8.

8...♗xg5 9 ♘xg5 ♕f6+ 10 ♗f3 ♗f5

If 11 ♕d2, then 11...h6 is decisive.

11 ♘xh7 ♕g6 12 ♕b5 c6 13 ♕a5 ♖e7 14 ♖h5 ♗g4 15 ♖g5 ♕c2+ 16 ♔g3 ♗xf3 0-1

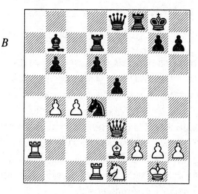

This position is from the game Ståhlberg-Alekhine, Hamburg 1930. It is Black's move, and he starts by provoking f3.

1...♖df7 2 f3 ♖f4

Opening the way for the queen.

3 ♗d3 ♕h5 4 ♗f1

Black threatened 4...e4.

4...♕g5 5 ♖f2 h6!

This apparently insignificant move is necessary in order to protect the queen in readiness for a combination starting with ...♖xf3. There is in fact an immediate threat of 6...♖xf3 7 ♕xg5 ♖xf2 followed, when White has parried the threat of mate on f1, by 8...hxg5, winning material.

6 ♔h1 ♖xf3 0-1

White did not notice the threat when he moved his king, so he resigned at this point. 6 ♕d2 would have offered more resistance, though even then Alekhine pointed out an easy win for Black by 6...♗xf3 7 ♘xf3 ♘xf3+ 8 ♖xf3 ♖xf3 9

♕xg5 ♖xf1+ 10 ♖xf1 ♖xf1+ 11 ♔xf1 hxg5, and White loses the king and pawn ending.

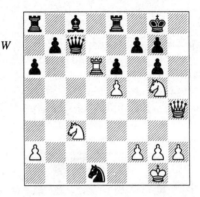

W

This position comes from an analysis of a critical variation in the game Marshall-Mieses, Cambridge Springs 1904. White has sacrificed a rook, and it is now his move. It would appear that the game must end in a rapid mating attack after 1 ♘ce4!?. However, this 'powerful move' is in fact weak, since Black plays 1...♘c3!, after which 2 ♘f6+ gxf6 3 exf6 does not work on account of 3...♘e2+ followed by 4...♕c1+, 5...♕b2+ and 6...♕xf6. If White tries 2 ♖d7, then Black cannot take the rook (e.g. 2...♕xd7 3 ♘d6![1] or 2...♗xd7 3 ♘f6+) but he can play 2...♘e2+ 3 ♔f1 ♕c1+ 4 ♔xe2 ♕xg5! 5 ♘xg5 ♗xd7, defending himself excellently and preserving the balance of material[2].

Another possibility is 1 ♖xd1, the intention being to safeguard the back rank. Black loses now if he plays 1...♕xc3, e.g. 2 ♕h7+ ♔f8 3 ♕h8+ ♔e7 4 ♕xg7, and if 4...♖f8, then 5 ♕f6+ and 6 ♖d8#. 1...♕xe5 is also bad after 2 ♘ce4 followed by f4. However, he still has the reply 1...♖d8!, which eliminates the danger on the d-file[3].

The correct procedure is to begin by checking, and only when Black's rook is engaged to go over to securing the position's foundations.

---

1   This move doesn't even have a serious threat, so Black can defend easily, for example by 3...♘b5. Instead, White should force a draw by 3 ♘f6+ gxf6 4 ♕h7+, etc.

2   Here 6 ♕h7+ ♔f8 7 ♕h8+ ♔e7 8 ♕xg7 appears very good for White, e.g. 8...♗b5+ 9 ♔e3 ♖f8 10 ♕f6+ ♔e8 11 ♘h7 ♖g8 12 ♕h4.

3   After 1...♖d8, 2 ♕h7+ ♔f8 3 ♕h8+ ♔e7 4 ♕xg7 ♖xd1+ 5 ♘xd1 wins the f7-pawn with check; the g-pawn then falls too, when White is clearly better.

1 ♕h7+ ♔f8 2 ♕h8+ ♔e7 3 ♕xg7 ♖f8 4 ♖xd1!

Just as soon as the attacking formation is completely developed, this precautionary waiting move follows with full force. Black is now powerless against the threat of ♕f6+ followed by ♘e4-d6+. If 4...♔e8, then 5 ♘h7 ♕e7 6 ♘xf8 ♕xf8 7 ♖d8+; while if 4...♗d7, then 5 ♕f6+ ♔e8 6 ♘ce4.

The solution is simple when it is demonstrated, but for psychological reasons it is difficult to find; first, because we would rather believe in 'finessing and strengthening the position by indirect moves' than in a banal pursuit of the king; and secondly, because the move ♖xd1 needs to be inserted at exactly the right moment.

Toying with an attack

An attack on the king as an alternative which never materializes but which acts solely as a subsidiary threat in the context of play with other objectives is a phenomenon which is abundantly represented in the games of the masters. The player merely toys with the plan of an attack on the king while, in fact, he is preparing and carrying out some other operation – a procedure which has a point if the threat to attack brings the player some advantage in tempi or helps the deployment of his pieces for the other operation. The advantage may take the form of the opponent's withdrawing a piece to the defence, as a result of which its effectiveness elsewhere is lost or diminished. Or it may be that the move by which the player has built up the threat of an attack at the same time gains a tempo for the other operation. These are the simple ingredients of an objective 'toying' with the attack on the castled king. The subjective or psychological exploitation of the threat to the castled position can also involve various other motives. The threat can, for example, produce a feeling of insecurity in the opponent, oblige him to spend too much time in thinking, or even induce him to make some precautionary move merely to relieve his anxiety by the easiest means available. This last case can often be seen in the games of weaker players, when they play ...h6 'for safety's sake', but in a subtler and less perceptible way it also happens that masters weaken their king positions in order to parry imaginary threats. We need only recall Burn's move ...g6 (page 289) as a defence against an incorrect classic bishop sacrifice! Questions like this fall outside the range of an objective treatment of the theme; the various forms of camouflage, the use of imaginary threats, speculation on an opponent's shortcomings, all these are features of practical play which have resulted from the dictates of that 'cruel, heavy-handed tournament machine' – the clock. We are interested here only in the objective (i.e. correct) threat and the objective (i.e. properly justified) reaction to it.

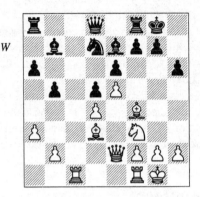

W

White is the better placed; he owes his superiority to the advanced position of his e-pawn, which secures him an advantage in space and cramps Black. The active placing of his pieces, the blocked centre, and the weakened enemy king position are all preconditions for an attack on the castled king. However, White has yet another advantage, namely, his rooks are united and he is a tempo ahead as regards control of the c-file; this would incline him towards a positional treatment of the game rather than an attack.

One asks oneself whether the best plan is to attack or play on the c-file? The answer is that one should threaten an attack and continue to promote the preconditions for it; then, if Black defends correctly, the prospects of successful play on the c-file will be enhanced.

Two moves which threaten the enemy king position are worth considering, i.e. 1 ♗b1, threatening ♕c2, and 1 ♕e3, which threatens a sacrificial assault on h6. If 1 ♗b1, Black plays 1...♖e8 and parries 2 ♕c2 with 2...♘f8. It would appear that the time is then ripe for play on the c-file, but after the continuation 3 ♕c7 ♕xc7 4 ♖xc7 ♖ab8 5 ♖fc1 it is clear that this particular bolt has been shot; Black plays 5...♗d8 followed by ...♗b6, and White has nothing left on the c-file. The other method is better.

1 ♕e3! ♖e8

This is forced; Black cannot defend himself without ...♘f8, as the following variations show:

1) 1...♖c8 2 ♗xh6 gxh6 3 ♕xh6 f5 4 exf6 ♖xf6 (or 4...♘xf6 5 ♕g6+ ♔h8 6 ♘g5, when Black has no defence against ♕h6+ followed by ♗h7+, ♗f5+ and ♗xe6+) 5 ♕h7+ ♔f8 6 ♕h8+ ♔f7 7 ♘g5#.

2) 1...♕b6 2 ♗xh6 gxh6 3 ♕xh6 f5 4 exf6 ♘xf6 (for 4...♖xf6 see above) 5 ♕g6+ ♔h8 6 ♘g5 ♗c8 7 ♖c3 e5 8 ♕h6+ ♔g8 9 ♗h7+ ♔h8 10 ♗f5+ ♔g8 11 ♕g6+ followed by mate.

3) 1...♘b6 2 ♗b1![1], and now, besides ♗xh6, there is also a threat of ♕d3, etc.
2 ♖c3 ♘f8

Black has to withdraw his knight to the defence, since there is once again a threat of ♗xh6. If, for example, 2...♕b6 (2...b4 3 axb4 ♗xb4 4 ♖b3 allows White to gain an important tempo for his attack) then 3 ♗xh6 gxh6 4 ♕xh6 ♘f8 5 ♘g5 ♗xg5 6 ♕xg5+ ♔h8 7 ♗b1.

3 ♖fc1 *(D)*

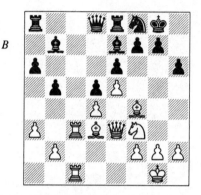

One might well consider strengthening the attack even further by 3 h4. However, that is a commitment, and its consequences are not clear. With 3 ♖fc1 White goes for play on the c-file, for which the conditions now are fundamentally better than in the position with which we started. On the one hand, White has gained the time to double rooks, and on the other, he has driven Black's knight back to f8, where it is now one tempo further away from the critical square c4, on which it clearly belongs. White owes his advantage here to his 'toying' with an attack on the castled king. The rest of the game is a matter of positional technique, and it could run as follows: **3...♖c8** (if Black allows ♖c7, then the threat of a sacrifice on h6 is renewed!) **4 ♖xc8 ♗xc8 5 ♕e1 ♗b7 6 ♗d2!** (if a good ending is White's objective, the dark-squared bishops should be exchanged as soon as possible) **6...♕d7 7 ♗b4 ♖c8** (or 7...♗d8 8 ♗a5, when 8...♗e7 fails against 9 ♖c7) **8 ♗xe7 ♖xc1 9 ♕xc1 ♕xe7 10 ♕c3 ♕d7** (if 10...♘d7, then 11 ♕c7 is decisive) **11 ♘d2**, and White has a considerable advantage by virtue of his better bishop and more active knight. Black cannot avoid exchanging queens, after which an exchange of knights or of the white bishop for the black knight would eventually leave White with a very favourable ending.

---

1   In this line White can still play 2 ♗xh6.

'Not seeing in front of one's nose'

It is a good thing to co-ordinate one's moves in an 'integrated action', but one should always try to see what is 'in front of one's nose'; that is, if one can mate at once, one should do so and not philosophize about pawns. This somehow happened once to Dr Vidmar, who (as White) reached the following position against Yates at London, 1922.

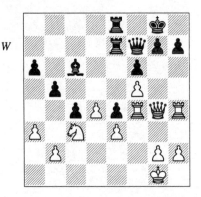

This position is one in which White can win easily, but in a misguided moment he hit on the idea of 'combining everything into an integral whole', i.e. he wanted both to attack and, at the same time, to 'cash in' on Black's e-pawn. As a result of this faulty desire to achieve two ends a drawn position was reached, which Black, however, proceeded to spoil and eventually to lose.

Let us look first at the course the game took.

1 d5?! ♗a8 2 ♕h3 h6 3 ♖fg4 ♔h7 4 ♘xe4? ♕f8 5 ♘xf6+

In his book *A Half-Century at the Chessboard* the great Yugoslav master records that he spent three-quarters of an hour thinking at this point and then decided on the sacrifice. After his incorrect capture of the e-pawn there was no other choice left.

5...♕xf6 6 ♖g6 ♕f8?

This is a mistake; Black now lost after **7 ♕g4! ♕f7 8 ♕g5 ♔h8** (otherwise ♕xh6+ wins) **9 f6 ♕xd5 10 ♖hxh6+ 1-0**.

Black could have drawn by playing the natural move 6...♕xb2, e.g. 7 ♖hxh6+ ♔g8 8 ♖h8+ ♔f7, and if 9 ♖xg7+, then 9...♕xg7 10 ♖h7 ♗xd5, when White has nothing better than perpetual check.

In the book mentioned above Dr Vidmar emphasizes how in this game the attack on the black king and the pressure on his e-pawn 'combined together to form a greater whole'. But it is precisely this false union of ideas which was the reason for White's failure to discover the correct path to victory as, after 4...♕f8, he listened to Big Ben chime quarter after quarter while his knight remained suspended in mid-air at e4. It is true that in the diagrammed position there are two factors making up White's advantage: a powerful kingside attack and a favourable knight versus bishop ending (once all the heavy pieces are exchanged). These two elements could only be combined if the attack led to the exchange of the queens and rooks, but the attack can break through without exchanges, and consequently it is beside the point how good the ending is. In fact, taking the pawn on e4 promotes neither White's attack nor his endgame prospects, but simply gives Black an opportunity of counterattacking along the e-file. Victory for White is an altogether easy matter, as long as he concerns himself entirely with the attack and forgets the pawn on e4:

1 ♕h3 h6 2 ♖fg4 ♔h7

This is all forced.

3 ♘e2! (D)

White simply transfers the knight to h5 and carefully avoids the poisonous pawn on e4!

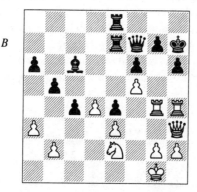

B

3...a5

White also wins after both 3...♖h8 4 ♘f4 ♗d7 5 ♖g6 ♔g8 6 ♘h5[1] and 3...♕f8 (or 3...♗d5 4 ♘f4) 4 ♘f4 followed by ♖g6 and ♘h5.

4 ♖g6 ♕f8 5 ♘f4 b4 6 ♘h5 ♖f7

Otherwise White wins even more quickly by ♘xf6+.

1　　Unfortunately this runs into 6...♕xg6, but White could have won earlier by 5 ♘h5 ♗xf5 6 ♖xg7+ ♕xg7 7 ♕xf5+ ♕g6 8 ♘xf6+ ♔g7 9 ♖g4.

7 ♘xg7 ♖xg7 8 ♖hxh6+ ♔g8 9 ♕h5!

The quickest and most precise.

9...♖xg6 10 ♖h8+ ♔f7 11 ♖h7+ ♕g7 12 ♕xg6+ with a quick mate.

This shows how play should have proceeded from the original position, but things would have gone much the same way if, instead of 4 ♘xe4?, White had played 4 ♘e2!, a point of which the reader can easily convince himself. 1 d5?! was only the first step along the wrong path, but 4 ♘xe4? was a mistake which could have cost half a point.

So it turned out that Dr Vidmar failed to see something 'in front of his nose' in London in 1922, nor did he see it thirty years later when he was writing his book. In this there is without doubt a touch of humour, the humour which Lasker recommended as an addition to every sizeable dose of chess principles.

From attack to endgame

A host of examples could be given to illustrate the transition from an attack on the king into the endgame. It may be a question of heading for a drawn position as a lesser evil to the failure which would result from continuing the attack; it may also be that one variation of the attacker's combination leads to an ending. However, cases such as these do not really belong here. We are only interested at this point in cases where the attacker deliberately calls off the attack because his success is better assured by a favourable endgame.

The classic exponent of the liquidation of an attack and the transition into the endgame was Pillsbury, so we shall open a series of examples with one of his games.

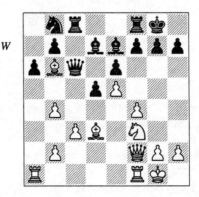

This position is from Pillsbury-Maroczy, Paris 1900. Although the situation is still far removed from the endgame, White is thinking about it all the same.

1 ♖a5

He prepares for the exchange of the dark-squared bishops by means of ♗c5, after which there is both an eventual threat of a bishop sacrifice on h7 and the prospect of an ending with White having a good knight against a bad bishop.

1...f5 2 ♔h1 ♖ce8

Avoiding the possibility of 3 ♗c5 ♗xc5 4 ♖xc5 ♕b6? 5 ♖xc8.

3 ♗c5 ♕c7 4 ♗xe7 ♖xe7 5 g4

The positional obligation entailed by such a move is balanced by the fact that in this position White has no need to fear the endgame. If his opponent's dark-squared bishop were still there, the move would be risky.

5...♘c6 6 ♖aa1 fxg4 7 ♕h4 g6 8 ♕xg4 ♖g7 9 h4 ♘e7?!

Black defends himself against an attack which is not dangerous and neglects something much more important, namely, the central point d4, which is of decisive significance in many types of ending. Precisely the opposite course was correct, that is, to increase his influence over d4 and at the same time, by 9...♕b6, to question White with regard to what his plans were for the dark-square network. In view of the threat of 10...♕e3 White would have to play 10 ♖ae1, after which 10...♔h8 11 ♖e2 d4, opening up the long light-square diagonal, already makes things easier for the defender.

10 ♘d4 ♘f5? *(D)*

And now 10...♘c6 was correct.

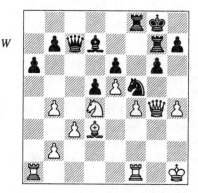

W

11 ♗xf5

A step closer to the ending with knight versus bad bishop. Pillsbury was a specialist in such exchanges.

11...gxf5 12 ♕h5 ♕d8

If 12...♗e8 13 ♕h6 ♖g6, White plays 14 ♖g1 and is one step further towards an endgame.

13 ♖g1 ♖ff7 14 ♕h6 ♕e7 15 ♘f3

White decides, after all, on an attack instead of simple liquidation by 15 ♖xg7+ and 16 ♖g1. While attacking, he is always guaranteed a good ending when he wants it.

15...♔h8 16 ♔h2 ♖f8 17 h5

Pillsbury intends to establish his knight on the outpost at g5 and so gives up the line of play leading to an ending which he has followed up to here.

The end of the game, which is no longer germane to our theme, runs as follows: **17...♖g4 18 ♘g5 ♖xf4 19 ♘f7+ ♕xf7 20 ♕xf4 ♕xh5+ 21 ♔g3 ♕e2 22 ♔h4 ♖c8 23 ♖ae1 ♕xb2 24 ♔h3 ♖xc3+ 25 ♖g3 ♖c2 26 ♖h1 ♖c8 27 ♕h6 1-0**[1]

If 27...♕xe5, then 28 ♕xh7+ and 29 ♔g2#.

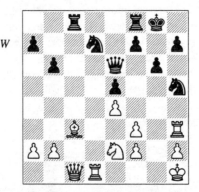

In this position from Bogoljubow-Przepiorka, Pistyan 1922 the liquidation leading to an ending comes as the direct consequence of White's combination.

1 ♖xh5 gxh5 2 ♖xd7 ♖xc3

Necessary, since 2...♕xd7 allows 3 ♕g5+ followed by 4 ♕f6+ and 5 ♗xe5.

3 ♘xc3 ♕xd7 4 ♕g5+ ♔h8 5 ♕f6+ ♔g8 6 ♘d5 ♖e8

If 6...h6, then 7 ♘e7+? ♔h7 8 ♘f5? would be incorrect on account of 8...♕d1+ and 9...♖g8+; however, White can play 7 ♕xh6 f5 8 ♕g6+ ♔h8 (or 8...♕g7 9 ♘e7+ ♔h8 10 ♕xh5+ ♕h7 11 ♘g6+, when White wins easily) 9 ♘f6 ♖xf6 10 ♕xf6+, and the ending is won for White.

---

1   This last section of the game certainly contains some ups and downs, but readers will have to look elsewhere for the details!

7 ♕g5+ ♔h8 8 ♘f6 ♕d8 9 ♕h6 ♕d1+ 10 ♔g2 ♖g8+ 11 ♘xg8 ♔xg8 12 ♕g5+, and White continued with ♕xe5 and won the ending.

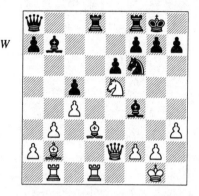

This position is from the game Botvinnik-Rabinovich, Leningrad 1934. At first White's attack follows a regular pattern.

1 ♘g4 ♘xg4 2 ♕xg4 ♗h6 3 ♗f6 ♖d7

Black could not play 3...♖xd3 4 ♖xd3 ♗e4 5 ♖g3 ♗g6 because of 6 ♕h4!, when White remains the exchange ahead. However, 3...♖c8 would have been better than the text move.

4 ♗f1

4 ♗xh7+ would also have been sufficient.

4...♕c8[1] 5 ♖xd7 ♕xd7 6 ♖d1 ♕c7 7 ♗g5!

White breaks off his attack and steers the game towards an ending in which there are two factors which ensure him a clear advantage: control of the d-file and play against Black's weak c-pawn.

7...♗xg5 8 ♕xg5 h6

White now continued with the thematic **9 ♕d2** allowing the reply **9...♗e4**; the result was that after **10 ♕d7 ♖c8 11 f3 ♗c2 12 ♖d2 ♗b1** Black's bishop got in among the small fry on the queenside, and it needed further incorrect play by Rabinovich before he eventually lost. Instead of 9 ♕d2, White should have played 9 ♕e3, which indirectly maintains his control of the d-file and also prepares for ♖d3 and ♕d2.

The next example will serve as an excellent conclusion to our discussion of the transition to the endgame. White's attack has got to the point where it exerts

---

1   Vuković incorrectly gave 4...♕e8 as the move played.

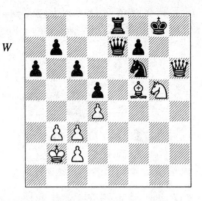

strong pressure on the focal-point h7, and it seems that the end must come quickly. However, appearances are deceptive, for there is no mate and Black can escape into an ending in which he can continue to resist.

Thus, after 1 ♗h7+ ♔h8 2 ♗g6+ ♔g8 3 ♗xf7+ ♕xf7 4 ♘xf7 ♔xf7, White runs out of checks and is unable to prevent Black from posting his rook on d7, after which it is not at all clear how White can win.

Another possibility is 1 ♘h7, and this leads to even greater material gains; Black is obliged to play 1...♘e4!, but after 2 ♗xe4 dxe4 3 ♘f6+ ♕xf6 4 ♕xf6 e3 the black pawn forces White's queen to retire, e.g. 5 ♕f1 (or 5 ♕g5+ ♔f8) 5...e2 6 ♕e1 ♔f8, and White can hardly count on victory.

Here we have, as a start, two ways in which the position resolves itself into an ending; the further analysis of the position should soon convince the reader that at every move there is a variety of possible simplifying lines, most of which lead to different types of endings.

The winning process for White is based on the *gradual preparation of the pawn structure* on the queenside in readiness for *the transition into an ending*. In this two factors are decisive: the first is that, besides his knight on f6, Black's queen is also immobilized since it cannot move from e7 because of the need to cover the squares f7 and f6; the second is that Black's pawns are also condemned to stay where they are. Any move on their part leads to Black's losing in the endgame after the manoeuvre ♗h7+, ♗g6+ and ♗xf7+. Accordingly, Black may only move his rook up and down, and even then he is denied the use of the square f8 because of ♘h7. Now for the analysis:

1 c4! ♖d8

Forced; White threatened 2 cxd5 cxd5 3 ♗h7+ ♔h8 4 ♗e4+ ♔g8 5 ♗xd5 ♖f8 6 ♕g6+ ♔h8 7 ♗xf7. If 1...dxc4, then 2 ♗h7+ followed by 3 ♗d3+ and 4 ♗xc4 wins in the same way.

2 c5!

A step further towards a favourable ending. If 2 cxd5, then Black's best reply is 2...♖xd5!. Also possible here is 2 ♗h7+ ♔h8 3 ♗g6+ ♔g8 4 ♗xf7+ ♕xf7 5 ♕h8+ ♔xh8 6 ♘xf7+ ♔g8 7 ♘xd8, but after 7...dxc4 8 bxc4 b5, Black's prospects of a draw are more than good.

2...♖a8

Now 2...♖e8 does not work because of 3 ♘h7 ♘e4 4 ♔c1!, when Black is left without the possibility of ...♕d6 (which would have been an effective answer prior to c5) and at the same time there is a threat of 5 ♗xe4, etc., now that the white king can hold the enemy e-pawn. If 4...f6, then 5 ♗xe4 dxe4 6 ♕g6+ ♔h8 7 ♘xf6 and White wins.

3 ♔a3 ♖b8

It is easy to see that after 3...a5 White will win an ending with queen versus rook and knight because the pawn on a5 must fall. If 3...b5, White similarly simplifies into an ending, and this time Black loses the pawns on a6 and c6, e.g. 4 ♗h7+ ♔h8 5 ♘xf7+ ♕xf7 6 ♗g6+ ♔g8 7 ♗xf7+ ♔xf7 8 ♕f4 ♖c8 9 ♔b4 ♔e7 10 ♕d6+ ♔f7 11 ♔a5 ♔g6 12 ♔xa6 followed by 13 ♔b7, etc.

4 ♔a4 ♖a8

If 4...b5+, then 5 cxb6 ♖xb6 6 ♗h7+ followed by capturing the queen at f7 and winning the ending of queen versus rook and knight, much as above.

5 c4! ♖b8 6 cxd5 cxd5 7 ♔a3!

White threatens 8 ♗h7+ followed by 9 ♗e4+ and 10 ♗xd5, which would not have worked at once on account of 10...♕d7+. Black's rook must now go to d8.

7...♖d8 8 ♗h7+ ♔h8 9 ♗g6+ ♔g8 10 ♗xf7+ ♕xf7 11 ♕h8+ ♔xh8 12 ♘xf7+ ♔g8 13 ♘xd8 and White has at last attained a won ending.

The reader may care to investigate this rather studied example further, all the secrets of which lie in the moves made by the pawns on the queenside; the final outcome of the ending rests with them, for without them White is unable to win.

12 The attack on the king as an integral part of the game

We have examined the various aspects of the attack on the castled king and have covered each topic on the basis of present-day knowledge of the art of chess. This material has been presented with all the difficulties and deficiencies of a pioneer, but with the joy of a discoverer who has seen in new knowledge a confirmation of his faith in the values of chess and his own general theory of the game. The attentive reader who has battled his way with the writer from chapter to chapter will have observed the steady widening of the problem of the attack on the king; we began with the basic techniques of combination and have progressed to the kind of understanding which characterizes mastery of the game. The logical path we have taken has justified its call for a high degree of effort in return for new knowledge; its purpose is to show us the significance of the attack on the castled king in the full context of a game of chess. From our examination of the defence against a kingside attack and of the phases of such an attack, it has become clear that a correct attack is conditioned by the situation on all parts of the board and also by all that has happened in the earlier course of the game. An attack on the king is not some strange, exceptional, and daring operation like a grand slam in bridge. It is an action which is both logical and necessary; an action on which a player decides at a certain stage of the game; sometimes, indeed, he *must* decide on it, if his opponent is not to obtain an advantage or if the position is not to fizzle out into a draw.

Lasker observed long ago that every action is essentially a diversion, a transition from equality to some spatial or temporal commitment. An attack on the king demands a very large diversion both in terms of the number of pieces involved and of the degree of commitment arising out of any pawn moves it entails. A considerable diversion of this kind also logically needs a considerable number of preconditions, as well as a knowledge of how these conditions are interrelated. It follows, therefore, that the attack on the castled king is an extremely difficult operation, which is based on a perfect mastery of all the forms of chess technique. Even in the early stages of the opening the first seeds of the preconditions for an attack on the king are already being sown, and the tense struggle for the central squares is tightly bound up with the successful outcome of the attack or defence. The characteristic features of a position, the weaknesses on both sides, and the elements that affect the endgame – all these accumulate and become intertwined in such a way that at a certain moment they impel the player to decide on the final objective of his play. This is the moment of crisis in the drama of the games of great masters, when it has to be decided whether it is best to continue promoting the preconditions for an attack on the king or to seek a favourable ending. The decision is not easy, for both courses demand not only technique but the ability to weld all the elements involved into a whole; moreover, we are still in the dark about many of the laws governing this process. Chess skill at the present time comprises a mastery of combinative techniques and the possession of mature positional judgement, while the science of the game has cleared up the problem of the centre in the majority of openings. However, we are still a long, long way from a thorough knowledge of the laws governing the methods of integrating all the elements into a strategic whole. And where there is insufficient knowledge one proceeds 'by feel', or in other words, one takes risks. The endgame and the attack on the king are two areas about which our knowledge is incomplete, but they are also two directions in which chess can be further explored and through which the ancient game can be raised to a still higher level.

We have said that there still exist areas in the art of chess where our knowledge is incomplete, and many of our readers may ask whether there are not at least some signposts pointing to where new knowledge might be found. The very attentive reader may also recall that mention was made in the Introduction of Alekhine's and Capablanca's understanding of the attack on the king and that a discussion on this subject was promised at the end of the book. Indeed, this is the right place for such a discussion, since the most difficult and arcane matters should be dealt with at the end, after everything else has been elucidated.

The discoveries of Alekhine and Capablanca

It is a slightly strange thesis that one should go back to the period before the Second World War and look for the culmination of the art of the attack on the king in the play of Alekhine and Capablanca. For have not Botvinnik and Smyslov, Keres and Bronstein, Reshevsky and Gligorić in their rich creativity in the field of chess discovered all that Alekhine and Capablanca knew and also gone on to add something else? It is indeed true that they have proceeded further in many respects, and perhaps even in their knowledge about the attack on the king they are the equals of the great masters of the past; in their actual games, however, they have not so far put it into practice to the full. If we delve into the whole of chess literature looking for games which serve to illuminate the logical integration of the attack on the castled king and the game in its entirety, then those of Alekhine and Capablanca remain the unsurpassed models; side by side with them may be placed a few of the games of Rubinstein, Keres, and Bronstein, though we shall find scarcely any new discoveries in them; the whole period from Alekhine's death to the present day has not been particularly fruitful in the sphere of the attack on the king. So one is justified in going back to Alekhine and Capablanca as the first to discover knowledge which to this day has been neither refuted nor superseded.

As far as these actual discoveries by Alekhine and Capablanca are concerned, it can be said that they did not take the form of some new principle but rather depended on a new way of thinking, which proceeded subjectively and therefore in a manner which cannot be expressed or comprehended on a theoretical basis; by these methods they discovered moves which fulfil the chief principle of the attack on the castled king, namely, *obtaining the maximum preconditions for an attack with the minimum of commitment.*

This principle in itself is a simple one and can be easily remembered, but playing in accordance with it is extremely difficult. Here two grades of values must be clearly distinguished: the one based on the value of the individual preconditions and the other on that of the successive commitments undertaken. This must then be resolved into a precisely ordered series of moves, while one must also be ready at any moment to convert the attack into some other thematic course of action – all of which requires considerable mastery.

From a close study of the games of Alekhine and Capablanca one can conclude that they did indeed use a perfected method of thinking in the sense mentioned above; only, in the case of Alekhine this thinking was more analytical and logical, while with Capablanca it was more artistically intuitive. However, the results of this thinking, that is, the actual moves, do not appear to differ greatly to the outside observer. However, Alekhine's discoveries can be somewhat more precisely defined than Capablanca's; Alekhine's output was more abundant, he 'lived chess' more deeply, and he was a more passionate analyser of his own games. A particular characteristic of his commentaries is the frequent use of the idea of commitment (just as with Lasker we get the idea of compensation, with Steinitz that of the balance of the position, and with Nimzowitsch that of centralization). One could say that of all masters Alekhine had the most refined sense of the degree of commitment, even though his temperament sometimes led him to be too eager.

When Alekhine, with apparent nonchalance, played, for instance, h4 against the French Defence, this appeared to his contemporaries to be 'the pretentiousness of genius', but a closer analysis today reveals that behind such moves there lay a great deal of mental calculation and hard logic, and that this move h4 belongs exactly when it was played; a move earlier it would have been weak and on the next it would be too late!

Further illustration of all these points will be better obtained by the reader from the actual games which follow.

Alekhine – Asztalos
Kecskemet, 1927
Queen's Gambit Declined

1 ♘f3 ♘f6 2 c4 e6 3 d4 d5 4 ♗g5 h6

A little experiment in the opening – and a dangerous one when Alekhine is on the other side of the board. The spatial advantage now obtained by White is worth more than Black's two bishops.

5 ♗xf6 ♕xf6 6 ♘c3 c6 7 ♕b3 ♘d7

Having started experimenting, Black ought to have gone on in like manner, e.g. 7...♕f5 8 e3 ♘d7 9 ♖d1 ♕g6, by which he would have put more difficulties in the way of White's plan to gain space in the centre.

8 e4 dxe4 9 ♘xe4 ♕f4 10 ♗d3 ♗e7 11 0-0 0-0 12 ♖fe1 ♖d8 13 ♖ad1 ♕c7

Black cannot complete his development as long as his queen remains on f4, for example 13...♘f6 14 ♘e5! ♖xd4 15 ♘xf6+ ♗xf6 16 g3 ♕g5 17 ♘f3 ♕c5 18 ♘xd4 ♗xd4 19 ♗h7+ followed by ♕d3+ and ♕xd4.

14 ♘g3 ♘f8 15 ♕c3 *(D)*

A useful move, which is intended, among other things, as a preparation for an eventual ♘h5, thereby provoking, by virtue of the threat of d5, a weakness in Black's king position. Black parries this with ...a5 and further moves on the queenside. We shall see at what cost!

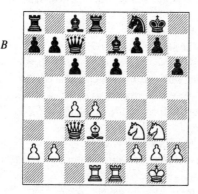

15...a5 16 a3 a4

Now 17 ♘h5 can be met by 17...♕a5. However, as a result of Black's advance of the a-pawn, his pawn structure on the queenside has lost its flexibility, which in its turn makes it easier for White to favourably resolve the tension in the centre.

17 ♘e5 ♕a5 18 ♕c1 ♗d7 19 c5!

This threatens ♘c4-b6 and thus induces Black to play ...b5, which leads to a blocked position on the queenside and restricts his counterplay in the event of White's launching an attack on the kingside.

19...b5 20 ♗e4 *(D)*

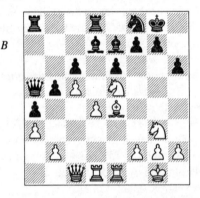

A series of preconditions for an attack on the king has been created: the weakness represented by the black pawn at h6; the aggressive placing of White's pieces; his control of the centre; and Black's limited resources on the queenside. White, however, is not in a hurry to attack, for he sees that he can use his pressure on c6 to improve the deployment of his own pieces and, at the same time, to constrict his opponent's.

20...♕c7 21 ♕c3 ♗e8 22 ♘e2!

White is thinking of the square b4.

22...♖a6 23 ♘c1 ♘d7

Against the threatening line-up of white knight at b4 and queen at f3 Black has only two expedients, namely, the direct weakening of his king position by ...f6 or an indirect weakening in the form of the exchange of his knight, which defends the square h7. Black decided on the latter course.

24 ♘xd7 ♖xd7 25 ♘d3 ♖d8 26 ♘e5 ♗f8

Black is sure that the enduring pressure on the diagonal against h7 will oblige him to play ...g6. Logically, therefore, he decides upon a delayed fianchetto as the best means of putting up some resistance.

27 h4!

The first move which really commits the attacker; the situation is also ready for it. It is directed against the future weakness on g6.

27...♖aa8 28 ♗b1 h5

He does not like the idea of 29 ♕c2 g6 30 h5.

29 ♕f3 g6 30 g4 hxg4 31 ♕xg4 ♗g7 32 ♗a2!

Before proceeding any further, White prevents ...f5, which Black cannot prepare by 32...♕e7 on account of 33 ♘xg6 and 34 ♖xe6.

32...b4 33 ♗c4!

White prefers to avoid 33 axb4 a3 which would allow Black to obtain counterplay.

33...bxa3 34 bxa3 ♕a5 35 ♕e4 ♕c7 36 ♕f4 ♖ab8 37 h5

This must come sooner or later.

37...gxh5 38 ♔h1 ♖b7 39 ♖g1 ♕e7 40 ♖xg7+!

White cannot count on success without this sacrifice to eliminate the fianchettoed bishop, Black's main line of defence.

40...♔xg7 41 ♖g1+ ♔h7 42 ♘xf7!? *(D)*

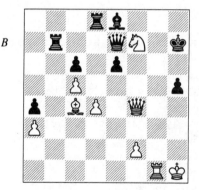

1-0

Having played so excellently and – as regards the method of preparing the attack on the king – so instructively, Alekhine concludes the game with a sacrifice that is not fully correct! I say 'concludes', because Asztalos took fright and resigned when he could well have played on. The continuation which Alekhine had in mind and which he expounded in the tournament book contained a loophole giving a draw, and even against White's best play Black would have had drawing chances. Let us first look at Alekhine's line.

42...♕xf7 43 ♗d3+ ♕g6 44 ♗xg6+

If 44 ♕g3, Black replies 44...♖g7, while 44 ♕f3 can be met by 44...♖d5. Thirdly, 44 ♕g5 ♕xd3 45 ♕g8+ ♔h6 46 ♕h8+ ♔h7 47 ♕f8+ ♕g7! 48 ♖xg7 ♖xg7 49 ♕f6+ ♗g6 50 ♕xd8 ♗e4+ probably results in a draw.

44...♗xg6 45 ♖xg6?

So far this is Alekhine's analysis. However, 45 ♕f6! ♖g8 46 ♕xe6 is stronger and does indeed win, though White still has a hard task ahead[1].

45...♔xg6 46 ♕e4+ ♔g7 47 ♕e5+

Here Alekhine concludes his analysis with the remark that Black 'after a few further checks, would inevitably lose one of his rooks.' In fact, he loses after all moves except 47...♔g6 followed by keeping the king on g6 or g7. After 48 ♕xe6+ ♔g7 49 ♕xc6 ♖b1+! 50 ♔g2 ♖xd4 51 ♕c7+ ♔g6 the checks cease, whereupon Black's rooks begin to deploy themselves for play against the king or the c-pawn. One cannot see how White can win; the position is very likely drawn. Alekhine unintentionally bluffed the unfortunate Asztalos and the jury, who on the basis of his analysis awarded him the Brilliancy Prize.

We must now point out what is objectively the strongest move and the continuation by which White wins. Thus (instead of 42 ♘xf7!?) he should have proceeded as follows:

42 ♕g3 ♕f8 (D)

Forced; if 42...f5, then 43 ♕g8+ followed by ♕h8+ and ♕f6+ is decisive, while if 42...♕f6, then 43 ♗d3+ wins.

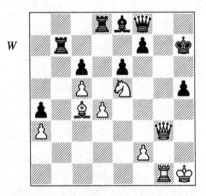

W

---

1   A distinct exaggeration. White has queen and pawn against rook and bishop, Black's remaining pawns are all weak and White has a passed f-pawn – I wouldn't expect many technical problems here!

43 ♕h4! f6

Both 43...♖d5 44 ♘g4 and 43...♖db8 44 ♕f6 ♖b3 45 ♗xe6 also win for White.

44 ♗d3+ ♔h8 45 ♗g6! ♖h7

Or 45...fxe5 46 ♕xh5+ ♔g7 47 ♗xe8+ and 48 ♕g5#.

46 ♗xh7 ♔xh7

After 46...fxe5 47 ♕xd8 ♕f3+ 48 ♖g2 Black has one more check before White mates him.

47 ♘g4 ♗g6

Or 47...♔h8 48 ♘xf6 ♗f7 49 ♘xh5 and White wins.

48 ♘xf6+ ♔g7 49 ♘xh5+

and Black loses his bishop with check.

Capablanca – Schroeder
New York, 1916
Queen's Gambit Declined, Orthodox Defence

1 d4 d5 2 ♘f3 e6 3 c4 ♘f6 4 ♘c3 ♘bd7 5 ♗g5 ♗e7 6 e3 0-0 7 ♖c1 a6 8 ♕c2

This is better than either 8 c5 or 8 a3, which Capablanca played in a number of games of his 1928 match against Alekhine, but best of all is 8 cxd5.

8...♖e8 9 ♗d3 dxc4 10 ♗xc4 b5 11 ♗d3 ♗b7?

At this point Black cannot spare the time to continue preparing ...c5; he should have played it at once.

12 a4! *(D)*

In order to entice the b-pawn to b4, which is useful for further play against the square c5.

12...b4 13 ♗xf6

This exchange is advantageous in two respects; first, for its 'clearance' of the square c5 and secondly, because it eliminates the possibility of a defence later on by ...♘f8.

13...♘xf6 14 ♘e4 ♘xe4 15 ♗xe4 ♗xe4 16 ♕xe4 c5

Sink or swim, Black must play this, for otherwise ♕c6 follows, fixing the backward c-pawn.

17 dxc5 ♕a5 18 b3 ♗xc5 19 ♘g5! *(D)*

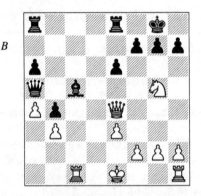

Can it be that White is justified in switching to an attack on the king after preparations which were clearly directed at the c-file? How does this fit in with our thesis on the need to fulfil a series of preconditions before opening an attack on the king? In fact, there is no contradiction; the preconditions are present, but they have arisen in a different way from those in the Alekhine-Asztalos game.

It is true that the preconditions for the attack on the castled king in this game have come about suddenly and somewhat incidentally; at the same time, this has occurred quite legitimately. The main point is that White's play, starting with 12 a4, serves two purposes: it maintains the pressure on the c-file and simultaneously improves the preconditions for an attack on the king. As a result of 12 a4 b4 and 18 b3 the position on the queenside became blocked, and this has reduced Black's prospects of counterplay, while 17 dxc5 resolved the tension in the centre.

Furthermore, 13 ♗xf6, 15 ♗xe4, and 16 ♕xe4 represent, in effect, a far-reaching elimination of Black's defending pieces; in the same way, the struggle revolving around the pawns on the c-file has forced Black (in 17...♕a5 and 18...♗xc5) to displace two pieces which are important for the defence of his king position. This is without doubt a full set of preconditions, built up with true

Capablanca virtuosity and elan. Now White's knight, a sort of *'equus ex machina'*, stirs up a whirlwind attack on the king, against which there is hardly an adequate defence.

19...h6?

Although Black has no really sound reply at his disposal, 19...f5 was the lesser evil. Then White does not gain much by 20 ♕e5 ♗b6 while if 20 ♕b7, Black plays 20...♕b6, and after 21 ♕f7+ ♔h8 22 ♕h5 h6 White's attack stops, for example, 23 h4? ♗xe3! 24 ♕g6 is not sound, since after 24...hxg5 25 hxg5+ ♔g8 White cannot give perpetual check, while 26 ♖h7 is weak on account of 26...♕d4. The best line is 20 ♕c4 ♖ac8! 21 ♘xe6 ♗b6 22 ♕xc8 ♖xc8 23 ♖xc8+ ♔f7 24 ♘g5+ ♔g6 25 ♘f3 ♕d5 26 0-0 ♗d8 followed by ...♗f6 with some chances of a draw[1]. This continuation would have been relatively the best way out for Black.

Better than the text move but worse perhaps than 19...f5 is 19...g6. An analysis of this move, which, though it may emanate from Capablanca, needs to be corrected, runs as follows: 19...g6 20 ♕f3 ♖f8 (everything else is weaker; 20...♖a7 in particular, does not work on account of 21 ♕c6) 21 ♕h3 h5 22 ♘xe6? fxe6 23 ♕xe6+ ♔h7 24 ♕d7+ ♔h8 25 ♕c6; now the analysis continues with 25...♖ac8?, missing the fact that Black can win by 25...♗xe3! 26 fxe3 ♕f5[2] 27 ♕f3 (forced) 27...♕d3 28 ♕e2 ♕xb3, obtaining an attack and, before long, a material advantage as well. This analysis can be improved by playing, instead of 21 ♕h3, 21 ♕f6 (threatening either 22 ♖c4 and 23 ♘xh7 or at once 22 ♘xh7) 21...♖ae8 (if 21...h6 then 22 ♘xe6 wins, while 21...♖ac8 is not good because of 22 ♖c4[3]) 22 ♕e5 ♗b6 23 ♕xa5 ♗xa5 24 ♔e2 ♖c8 25 ♘e4, when White has much the better ending, for example if 25...♖fd8, then 26 ♘c5 ♖c6 27 ♘b7 ♖xc1 28 ♖xc1 ♖d5 29 e4.

20 ♕h7+ ♔f8 21 ♕h8+ ♔e7 22 ♕xg7 hxg5 23 ♕xg5+ ♔d6 24 ♔e2 (D)

Two pawns, the exposed position of the black king, Black's commitments at c5, and White's rooks on the c- and d-files – all this is obviously more than sufficient compensation for the sacrificed knight. Capablanca also particularly

---

1   After 27 ♖c6+ ♗f6 28 ♘d4 I see no real chances for a draw; White has two rooks and a pawn for the queen, and Black's king is exposed. One line is 28...♔h5 29 ♖c4 ♗xd4 30 ♖d1, followed by ♖dxd4.

2   This allows a defence by 27 ♕c2, but Black can improve by 26...♕g5!, which does indeed win for Black.

3   After 21...♖ac8 22 ♖c4 Black can defend by 22...♖c7!, for example 23 ♘xh7 ♗e7 or 23 ♖h4 ♗e7. Thus it is hard to demonstrate an advantage for White after 19...g6.

B

stresses Black's inability to stop the advance of the h-pawn while White is tying him down on the queenside.

24...♖ac8 25 ♖c4 ♔c6 26 ♖hc1 ♔b6 27 h4 f5

Capablanca had reckoned on the following transition into a won ending: 27...♖c7 28 h5 ♖ec8 29 h6 ♗d6 30 ♕xa5+ ♔xa5 31 ♖xc7 ♖xc7 32 ♖xc7 ♗xc7 33 f4 ♗d8 34 g4 ♗f6 35 g5 ♗h8 36 e4 ♔b6 37 f5 followed by g6-g7.

28 ♕g7 ♖e7 29 ♕e5 ♖c6

This loses at once, but 29...♖ec7 has no future either in view of 30 h5.

30 ♖xc5 1-0

For, if 30...♖xc5 then 31 ♕d6+ is decisive.

Capablanca's virtuosity in integrating all the features of the position into a coherent whole is worthy of close attention.

Alekhine – Kmoch
San Remo, 1930
Nimzo-Indian Defence

1 d4 ♘f6 2 c4 e6 3 ♘c3 ♗b4 4 ♗d2

One of the most harmless continuations.

4...0-0 5 e3 d5 6 ♘f3 c5 7 a3 ♗xc3 8 ♗xc3 ♘e4 9 ♖c1 ♘xc3 10 ♖xc3 cxd4 11 exd4 ♘c6 12 ♗e2

If 12 c5 then Black can immediately play 12...e5.

12...dxc4 13 ♗xc4 ♕f6

White has not achieved very much in the opening. In view of the reduction in material his spatial advantage offers no more than approximate compensation for the isolated pawn.

14 0-0 ♖d8 15 ♖d3 ♗d7 16 ♖e1

By 16 ♕d2 White could have prepared to obtain clear equality by d5. However, he does not like the idea of a draw.

16...♗e8 17 ♕d2 ♘e7 18 ♘g5

As this threatens 19 ♘xe6 fxe6 20 ♖xe6, Black does not have time for 18...♗c6 or 18...♘f5.

18...♘d5 19 ♖f3 ♕e7 20 ♖g3 h6 *(D)*

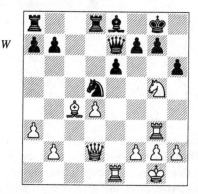

White has proceeded cautiously and prepared the ground for ♕d3, with the aim of provoking a weakening of the enemy king position in the shape of ...g6. For this reason Kmoch prefers to go in for ...h6, which weakens him less. White can only obtain results by attacking the king, for Black is the better placed for the endgame.

21 ♘f3

If 21 ♘e4 Black can reply 21...♕h4.

21...♕f6 22 ♖e4 ♘e7

Parrying the threat of ♖eg4.

23 ♘e5 ♘f5 24 ♖d3

White has managed to weaken the enemy king position, but he still lacks the preconditions for a real attack. A little regrouping is therefore needed, and above all the square d4 must be safeguarded. If 24 ♖f3 then 24...♗c6 25 ♘xc6 bxc6 is quite good for Black. Of the minor pieces the knights are more valuable than the bishops, from the point of view of both the attacker and his opponent.

24...♖ac8 25 h3 ♘d6?

Up to this point the author of *The Art of Defence* has defended correctly and preserved equality. Now, however, he goes astray in playing to exchange off his important knight, which is the main defender of his king position. Correct was 25...♗c6.

26 ♖f4 ♘xc4 27 ♘xc4 ♕g5 28 ♖g3 ♕d5 29 ♘e3 ♕c6 30 ♔h2 ♕c1 31 ♕b4 ♕c7 32 d5! *(D)*

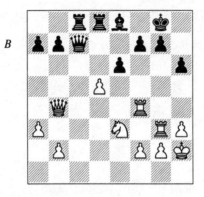

Apparently, Black has manoeuvred himself into a new defensive position, one which also affords the possibility of his inconveniencing White's queen further by ...a5. The only weak side of his manoeuvre is that it does not give sufficient attention to centralization. As a result, the alleged pawn weakling on d4 is transformed – ironically – into an aggressor, punishing Black for his neglect of the central squares.

32...a5

After 32...exd5 33 ♕d4 g6 (or 33...g5) 34 ♘f5 Black would quickly come to grief; equally bad is 32...e5 33 ♖fg4 g6 34 ♘f5.

33 ♕e4 ♖d6 34 ♕e5 g6 35 ♕h5!

If 35 ♖c4? Black could bring the attack to a halt by 35...♖c6!.

35...♖xd5

Or 35...♔h7 36 ♘g4! gxh5 37 ♘f6+ and mates.

36 ♘xd5 exd5 37 ♕xh6 ♕e5 38 ♖h4 ♕g7 1-0

Colle – Capablanca
Carlsbad, 1929
Colle System

1 d4 ♘f6 2 ♘f3 b6 3 e3 ♗b7 4 ♘bd2 e6 5 ♗d3 c5 6 0-0 ♘c6 7 c3

The formation with pawns on c3, d4, and e3, bishop on d3, and knights on d2 and f3 characterizes the Colle System. White's plan is to force through e3-e4 and then exchange his d2-knight for Black's f6-knight on this same square; he thereby creates some of the preconditions for an attack on the king without entailing any commitments. The Colle System, however, lacks positional depth and, consequently, Black does not have any great anxiety as regards the centre.

7...♗e7 8 e4 cxd4

Capablanca's treatment of the opening, adopting a Queen's Indian set-up, is both sound and also suitable for avoiding lines which equalize out to a draw. White's strong point in the centre is now eliminated, for he must recapture the pawn with his knight, otherwise 9 cxd4 ♘b4 10 ♗b1 ♗a6 leaves Black with the better game.

9 ♘xd4 0-0 10 ♕e2

First 10 ♘xc6 would have been sounder.

10...♘e5 11 ♗c2 ♕c8 12 f4

Preparation for an attack on the king, but also a weakening of the g1-a7 diagonal.

12...♗a6 13 ♕d1 ♘c6

Obviously not 13...♗xf1? on account of 14 fxe5. Moving the bishop to a6 had other points: on the one hand, to drive the white queen back and, on the other, to induce White to play ♖f3, whereby he undertakes *a commitment to attack* before the preconditions for a successful attack have matured.

14 ♖f3

Against 14 e5 Black has 14...♘d5 after which 15 ♗xh7+ does not work (because of 15...♔xh7 16 ♕h5+ ♔g8 17 ♖f3 f5 18 ♖h3 ♘xf4) while, given a free move, Black can consolidate his defences by playing 15...f5.

In the event of other, slower methods of attack Black has a sound defensive plan based on the effective use of the diagonals for his bishops and a centralized knight on d5. This will be seen in the further course of the game.

14...g6!

In view of the restricted range of activity of White's dark-squared bishop, this weakness is negligible. It is important for Black to exclude short-term dangers on the kingside, since he needs time to increase his pressure on the central squares.

15 ♘2b3 ♘xd4 16 ♘xd4 ♗b7 17 ♕e2 ♗c5 18 ♖h3 ♕c6!

Black forces e5 in order to gain the d5-square for his knight and open up the diagonal.

19 e5 ♘d5 (D)

20 ♕f2?!

Up to this point Colle's play has been a little pretentious but not really incorrect, for his commitments have not been decisive ones. Still, he should now have admitted that it was pointless to continue playing for an attack and striven, by paying careful attention to the central squares, to keep the game within the well-known 'margin of a draw'; for example, 20 ♗e3 ♗xd4 21 cxd4 ♖ac8 22 ♗b3!

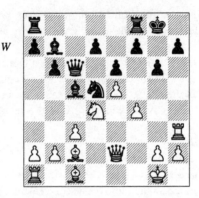

W

when Black, after 22...♘xe3 23 ♖xe3 clearly has nothing either in the centre or on the c-file; nor does 22...b5 or the like offer anything very much. (In Golombek's book *Capablanca's Hundred Best Games of Chess*, instead of 22 ♗b3!, the erroneous 22 ♖c1? is given; then Black does indeed get the upper hand by 22...♘xe3 23 ♖xe3 ♕c4.)

20...♗xd4?!

Satisfied with the centralization he has achieved, Black too now becomes rather presumptuous and opens up the c-file prematurely. 20...f5 followed by a quiet positional plan based on ...b5-b4 was probably best. In that event simplification by 21 ♘xc6 ♗xf2+ 22 ♔xf2 ♗xc6 would give Black the better ending, while if 21 ♗e3, then 21...♗xd4 22 cxd4 ♘b4 would be perfectly agreeable.

The move suggested, 20...f5, signifies that Black is satisfied with a small advantage, whereas Capablanca's idea aspires to dynamic play on the c- and f-files. However, the preconditions for this are insufficient, for *counterattacks too demand preconditions and entail commitments* just as attacks on the king do. The laws which determine the connection between the two types of action dictate the form, timing, and tempo of the counterattack in accordance with the state of the attack. Thus, the degree to which the attacking units have been diverted conditions the extent and force of the counterattack. In this case, therefore, direct defence by 20...f5 would have been better than 20...♗xd4.

21 cxd4 ♖ac8

The immediate 21...f6 did not work on account of 22 ♕h4 ♖f7 23 ♗xg6.

22 ♗d1!

Other moves by the bishop are defeated by 22...♕xc1+. 22 ♕h4 is also inadequate; for example, 22...♘f6! 23 ♖g3 ♕xc2 24 ♗e3 (to prevent ...♕d1+) 24...♘e4 25 ♖h3 h5 and Black wins.

22...f6! *(D)*

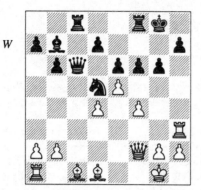

This much-praised move of Capablanca's is very economical in that it both attacks and defends in equal measure; it is probably Black's best, now that he has embarked on 20...♗xd4. It is also true that an attack generally collapses when the pawns in front of the king begin to 'bite', but in this case the question is no longer one of attack but of the overall state of the position. Black has in fact awoken possibilities for White on the c-file, and in the event of the game being opened up White's two bishops could come into their own.

23 ♕h4?

This gains a tempo for ♗f3 but neglects the development of his c1-bishop and a1-rook. The correct move was 23 ♗d2!. Capablanca's intention in that case was 23...♘xf4!? 24 ♗xf4 fxe5 25 ♗f3 e4 but the combination has a flaw: White does not play 26 ♗e2? (when 26...e3! wins) but 26 ♕h4!, and Black finds himself in difficulties. Moreover, 23 ♗d2! cannot be met by 23...fxe5, e.g. 24 ♖c1 ♕b5 (24...♕xc1 would not succeed against correct play by White) 25 ♖xc8 ♗xc8 26 ♕h4, whereupon 26...♖f7 27 ♕d8+ leads to a draw, 26...h5 is not good due to 27 ♕g5, while the complications following 26...♘f6 27 fxe5 ♗a6 28 ♖f3 seem full of uncertainty. Against 23 ♗d2! Black would probably have to play 23...d6 24 ♖c1 ♕d7, when 25 ♖xc8 ♗xc8 26 ♖f3 results in a complex struggle in which White's dark-squared bishop derives pleasure from every exchange on e5. This represents an analytical proof of the assertions made in the note to the twentieth move.

23...♖f7 24 ♗f3 ♕c4

Since 25 ♕f2 does not work (because of 25...♕xc1+) White is now lost.

25 ♗e3 ♘xe3 26 ♗xb7 ♘f5 27 ♕e1 ♖c7 28 ♗e4 ♕xd4+ 29 ♔h1 fxe5 30 ♗xf5 exf5 31 fxe5 ♖e7 32 ♖e3 ♕xb2 33 e6 dxe6 34 ♖xe6 ♔f7 0-1

This game is very instructive for the purpose of studying the complex connection between attack and indirect defence; the decisive points illustrating this were shown in their correct light only by a thorough revision of the commentary.

Index of Players

Numbers refer to pages
A number in bold indicates that the first-named player had White, e.g. Alekhine
was White against Asgeirsson but Black against Rubinstein

Index of Openings